LLM Engineer's H

Master the art of engineering large language models from concept to production

Paul Iusztin

Maxime Labonne

LLM Engineer's Handbook

Senior Publishing Product Manager: Gebin George

Acquisition Editor – Peer Reviews: Swaroop Singh

Project Editor: Amisha Vathare

Content Development Editor: Tanya D'cruz

Copy Editor: Safis Editing

Technical Editor: Karan Sonawane

Proofreader: Safis Editing

Indexer: Manju Arasan

Presentation Designer: Rajesh Shirsath

Developer Relations Marketing Executive: Anamika Singh

First published: October 2024

Production reference: 2171024

Published by Packt Publishing Ltd.
Grosvenor House
11 St Paul's Square
Birmingham
B3 1RB, UK.

ISBN 978-1-83620-007-9

www.packt.com

Forewords

As my co-founder at Hugging Face, Clement Delangue, and I often say, AI is becoming the default way of building technology.

Over the past 3 years, LLMs have already had a profound impact on technology, and they are bound to have an even greater impact in the coming 5 years. They will be embedded in more and more products and, I believe, at the center of any human activity based on knowledge or creativity.

For instance, coders are already leveraging LLMs and changing the way they work, focusing on higher-order thinking and tasks while collaborating with machines. Studio musicians rely on AI-powered tools to explore the musical creativity space faster. Lawyers are increasing their impact through **retrieval-augmented generation (RAG)** and large databases of case law.

At Hugging Face, we've always advocated for a future where not just one company or a small number of scientists control the AI models used by the rest of the population, but instead for a future where as many people as possible—from as many different backgrounds as possible—are capable of diving into how cutting-edge machine learning models actually work.

Maxime Labonne and Paul Iusztin have been instrumental in this movement to democratize LLMs by writing this book and making sure that as many people as possible can not only use them but also adapt them, fine-tune them, quantize them, and make them efficient enough to actually deploy in the real world.

Their work is essential, and I'm glad they are making this resource available to the community. This expands the convex hull of human knowledge.

Julien Chaumond

Co-founder and CTO, Hugging Face

As someone deeply immersed in the world of machine learning operations, I'm thrilled to endorse *The LLM Engineer's Handbook*. This comprehensive guide arrives at a crucial time when the demand for LLM expertise is skyrocketing across industries.

What sets this book apart is its practical, end-to-end approach. By walking readers through the creation of an LLM Twin, it bridges the often daunting gap between theory and real-world application. From data engineering and model fine-tuning to advanced topics like RAG pipelines and inference optimization, the authors leave no stone unturned.

I'm particularly impressed by the emphasis on MLOps and LLMOps principles. As organizations increasingly rely on LLMs, understanding how to build scalable, reproducible, and robust systems is paramount. The inclusion of orchestration strategies and cloud integration showcases the authors' commitment to equipping readers with truly production-ready skills.

Whether you're a seasoned ML practitioner looking to specialize in LLMs or a software engineer aiming to break into this exciting field, this handbook provides the perfect blend of foundational knowledge and cutting-edge techniques. The clear explanations, practical examples, and focus on best practices make it an invaluable resource for anyone serious about mastering LLM engineering.

In an era where AI is reshaping industries at breakneck speed, *The LLM Engineer's Handbook* stands out as an essential guide for navigating the complexities of large language models. It's not just a book; it's a roadmap to becoming a proficient LLM engineer in today's AI-driven landscape.

Hamza Tahir

Co-founder and CTO, ZenML

Contributors

About the authors

Paul Iusztin is a senior ML and MLOps engineer with over seven years of experience building GenAI, Computer Vision and MLOps solutions. His latest contribution was at Metaphysic, where he served as one of their core engineers in taking large neural networks to production. He previously worked at CoreAI, Everseen, and Continental. He is the Founder of Decoding ML, an educational channel on production-grade ML that provides posts, articles, and open-source courses to help others build real-world ML systems.

Maxime Labonne is the Head of Post-Training at Liquid AI. He holds a PhD. in ML from the Polytechnic Institute of Paris and is recognized as a Google Developer Expert in AI/ML. As an active blogger, he has made significant contributions to the open-source community, including the LLM Course on GitHub, tools such as LLM AutoEval, and several state-of-the-art models like NeuralDaredevil. He is the author of the best-selling book *Hands-On Graph Neural Networks Using Python*, published by Packt.

I want to thank my family and partner. Your unwavering support and patience made this book possible.

About the reviewer

Rany ElHousieny is an AI solutions architect and AI engineering manager with over two decades of experience in AI, NLP, and ML. Throughout his career, he has focused on the development and deployment of AI models, authoring multiple articles on AI systems architecture and ethical AI deployment. He has led groundbreaking projects at companies like Microsoft, where he spearheaded advancements in NLP and the Language Understanding Intelligent Service (LUIS). Currently, he plays a pivotal role at Clearwater Analytics, driving innovation in GenAI and AI-driven financial and investment management solutions.

I would like to thank Clearwater Analytics for providing a supportive and learning environment that fosters growth and innovation. The vision of our leaders, always staying ahead with the latest technologies, has been a constant source of inspiration. Their commitment to AI advancements made my experience of reviewing this book insightful and enriching. Special thanks to my family for their ongoing encouragement throughout this journey.

Join our book's Discord space

Join our community's Discord space for discussions with the authors and other readers:

https://packt.link/llmeng

Table of Contents

Chapter 8: Inference Optimization   289

Chapter 9: RAG Inference Pipeline   317

Preface

The field of **LLM** engineering has rapidly emerged as a critical area in artificial intelligence and machine learning. As LLMs continue to revolutionize natural language processing and generation, the demand for professionals who can effectively implement, optimize, and deploy these models in real-world scenarios has grown exponentially. LLM engineering encompasses a wide range of disciplines, from data preparation and model fine-tuning to inference optimization and production deployment, requiring a unique blend of software engineering, machine learning expertise, and domain knowledge.

Machine Learning Operations (MLOps) plays a crucial role in the successful implementation of LLMs in production environments. MLOps extends the principles of DevOps to machine learning projects, focusing on automating and streamlining the entire ML lifecycle. For LLMs, MLOps is particularly important due to the complexity and scale of these models. It addresses challenges such as managing large datasets, handling model versioning, ensuring reproducibility, and maintaining model performance over time. By incorporating MLOps practices, LLM projects can achieve greater efficiency, reliability, and scalability, ultimately leading to more successful and impactful deployments.

The LLM Engineer's Handbook is a comprehensive guide to applying best practices to the new field of LLM engineering. Throughout the chapters, readers will find simplified key concepts, practical techniques, and experts tips for every stage of the LLM lifecycle. The book covers topics such as data engineering, supervised fine-tuning, model evaluation, inference optimization, and **Retrieval-Augmented Generation (RAG)** pipeline development.

To illustrate these concepts in action, an end-to-end project called the LLM Twin will be developed throughout the book., with the goal of imitating someone's writing style and personality. This use case will demonstrate how to build a minimum viable product to solve a specific problem, using various aspects of LLM engineering and MLOps.

Readers can expect to gain a deeper understanding of how to collect and prepare data for LLMs, fine-tune models for specific tasks, optimize inference performance, and implement RAG pipelines. They will learn how to evaluate LLM performance, align models with human preferences, and deploy LLM-based applications. The book also covers essential MLOps principles and practices, enabling readers to build scalable, reproducible, and robust LLM applications.

Who this book is for

This book is intended for a wide range of technology professionals and enthusiasts interested in the practical applications of LLMs. It's ideal for software engineers aiming to transition into AI projects. While some familiarity with software development is beneficial, the book explains many concepts from the ground up, making it accessible even to those who are new to AI and machine learning.

For those already working with machine learning , this book will enhance your skills in implementing and deploying LLM-based systems. We provide a deep dive into the fundamentals of MLOps, guiding you through the process of creating a minimum viable product using an open-source LLM to solve real-world problems.

What this book covers

Chapter 1, Understanding the LLM Twin Concept and Architecture, introduces the LLM Twin project, which is used throughout the book as an end-to-end example of a production-level LLM application, and defines the FTI architecture for building scalable ML systems and applies it to the LLM Twin use case.

Chapter 2, Tooling and Installation, presents Python, MLOps, and cloud tools used to build real-world LLM applications, such as an orchestrator, experiment tracker, prompt monitoring and LLM evaluation tool. It shows how to use and install them locally for testing and development.

Chapter 3, Data Engineering, shows the implementation of a data collection pipeline that scrapes multiple sites, such as Medium, GitHub and Substack and stores the raw data in a data warehouse. It emphasizes collecting raw data from dynamic sources over static datasets for real-world ML applications.

Chapter 4, RAG Feature Pipeline, introduces RAG fundamental concepts, such as embeddings, the vanilla RAG framework, vector databases, and how to optimize RAG applications. It applies the RAG theory by architecting and implementing LLM Twin's RAG feature pipeline using software best practices.

Chapter 5, Supervised Fine-Tuning, explores the process of refining pre-trained language models for specific tasks using instruction-answer pairs. It covers creating high-quality datasets, implementing fine-tuning techniques like full fine-tuning, LoRA, and QLoRA, and provides a practical demonstration of fine-tuning a Llama 3.1 8B model on a custom dataset.

Chapter 6, Fine-Tuning with Preference Alignment, introduces techniques for aligning language models with human preferences, focusing on **Direct Preference Optimization (DPO)**. It covers creating custom preference datasets, implementing DPO, and provides a practical demonstration of aligning the TwinLlama-3.1-8B model using the Unsloth library.

Chapter 7, Evaluating LLMs, details various methods for assessing the performance of language models and LLM systems. It introduces general-purpose and domain-specific evaluations and discusses popular benchmarks. The chapter includes a practical evaluation of the TwinLlama-3.1-8B model using multiple criteria.

Chapter 8, Inference Optimization, covers key optimization strategies such as speculative decoding, model parallelism, and weight quantization. It discusses how to improve inference speed, reduce latency, and minimize memory usage, introducing popular inference engines and comparing their features.

Chapter 9, RAG Inference Pipeline, explores advanced RAG techniques by implementing methods such as self-query, reranking, and filtered vector search from scratch. It covers designing and implementing the LLM Twin's RAG inference pipeline and a custom retrieval module similar to what you see in popular frameworks such as LangChain.

Chapter 10, Inference Pipeline Deployment, introduces ML deployment strategies, such as online, asynchronous and batch inference, which will help in architecting and deploying the LLM Twin fine-tuned model to AWS SageMaker and building a FastAPI microservice to expose the RAG inference pipeline as a RESTful API.

Chapter 11, MLOps and LLMOps, presents what LLMOps is, starting with its roots in DevOps and MLOps. This chapter explains how to deploy the LLM Twin project to the cloud, such as the ML pipelines to AWS and shows how to containerize the code using Docker and build a CI/CD/CT pipeline. It also adds a prompt monitoring layer on top of LLM Twin's inference pipeline.

Appendix, MLOps Principles, covers the six MLOps principles used to build scalable, reproducible, and robust ML applications.

To get the most out of this book

To maximize your learning experience, you are expected to have, at the very least, a foundational understanding of software development principles and practices. Familiarity with Python programming is particularly beneficial, as the book's examples and code snippets are predominantly in Python. While prior experience with machine learning concepts is advantageous, it is not strictly necessary, as the book provides explanations for many fundamental AI and ML concepts. However, you should be comfortable with basic data structures, algorithms, and have some experience working with APIs and cloud services.

Familiarity with version control systems like Git is assumed, as this book has a GitHub repository for code examples. While this book is designed to be accessible to those who are new to AI and LLMs, if you have some background in these areas, you will find it easier to grasp the more advanced concepts and techniques we present.

Download the example code files

The code bundle for the book is hosted on GitHub at `https://github.com/PacktPublishing/LLM-Engineers-Handbook`. We also have other code bundles from our rich catalog of books and videos available at `https://github.com/PacktPublishing/`. Check them out!

Download the color images

We also provide a PDF file that has color images of the screenshots/diagrams used in this book. You can download it here: `https://packt.link/gbp/9781836200079`.

Conventions used

There are a number of text conventions used throughout this book.

`CodeInText`: Indicates code words in text, database table names, folder names, filenames, file extensions, pathnames, dummy URLs, user input, and Twitter handles. For example: "In the `format_samples` function, we apply the Alpaca chat template to each individual message."

A block of code is set as follows:

```
def format_samples(example):
    example["prompt"] = alpaca_template.format(example["prompt"])
    example["chosen"] = example['chosen'] + EOS_TOKEN
    example["rejected"] = example['rejected'] + EOS_TOKEN
    return {"prompt": example["prompt"], "chosen": example["chosen"],
"rejected": example["rejected"]}
```

When we wish to draw your attention to a particular part of a code block, the relevant lines or items are set in bold:

```python
def format_samples(example):
    example["prompt"] = alpaca_template.format(example["prompt"])
    example["chosen"] = example['chosen'] + EOS_TOKEN
    example["rejected"] = example['rejected'] + EOS_TOKEN
    return {"prompt": example["prompt"], "chosen": example["chosen"],
"rejected": example["rejected"]}
```

Any command-line input or output is written as follows:

```
poetry install --without aws
```

Bold: Indicates a new term, an important word, or words that you see on the screen. For instance, words in menus or dialog boxes appear in the text like this. For example: "To do so, go to the **Settings** tab at the top of the forked repository in GitHub. In the left panel, in the **Security** section, click on the **Secrets and Variables** toggle and, finally, click on **Actions**."

 Warnings or important notes appear like this.

 Tips and tricks appear like this.

Get in touch

Feedback from our readers is always welcome.

General feedback: Email feedback@packtpub.com and mention the book's title in the subject of your message. If you have questions about any aspect of this book, please email us at questions@packtpub.com.

Errata: Although we have taken every care to ensure the accuracy of our content, mistakes do happen. If you have found a mistake in this book, we would be grateful if you reported this to us. Please visit http://www.packtpub.com/submit-errata, click **Submit Errata**, and fill in the form.

Piracy: If you come across any illegal copies of our works in any form on the internet, we would be grateful if you would provide us with the location address or website name. Please contact us at copyright@packtpub.com with a link to the material.

If you are interested in becoming an author: If there is a topic that you have expertise in and you are interested in either writing or contributing to a book, please visit http://authors.packtpub.com.

Share your thoughts

Once you've read *LLM Engineer's Handbook, First Edition*, we'd love to hear your thoughts! Scan the QR code below to go straight to the Amazon review page for this book and share your feedback.

https://packt.link/r/1836200072

Your review is important to us and the tech community and will help us make sure we're delivering excellent quality content.

Download a free PDF copy of this book

Thanks for purchasing this book!

Do you like to read on the go but are unable to carry your print books everywhere?

Is your eBook purchase not compatible with the device of your choice?

Don't worry, now with every Packt book you get a DRM-free PDF version of that book at no cost.

Read anywhere, any place, on any device. Search, copy, and paste code from your favorite technical books directly into your application.

The perks don't stop there, you can get exclusive access to discounts, newsletters, and great free content in your inbox daily.

Follow these simple steps to get the benefits:

1. Scan the QR code or visit the link below:

https://packt.link/free-ebook/9781836200079

2. Submit your proof of purchase.
3. That's it! We'll send your free PDF and other benefits to your email directly.

1

Understanding the LLM Twin Concept and Architecture

By the end of this book, we will have walked you through the journey of building an end-to-end **large language model (LLM)** product. We firmly believe that the best way to learn about LLMs and production **machine learning (ML)** is to get your hands dirty and build systems. This book will show you how to build an LLM Twin, an AI character that learns to write like a particular person by incorporating its style, voice, and personality into an LLM. Using this example, we will walk you through the complete ML life cycle, from data gathering to deployment and monitoring. Most of the concepts learned while implementing your LLM Twin can be applied in other LLM-based or ML applications.

When starting to implement a new product, from an engineering point of view, there are three planning steps we must go through before we start building. First, it is critical to understand the problem we are trying to solve and what we want to build. In our case, what exactly is an LLM Twin, and why build it? This step is where we must dream and focus on the "Why." Secondly, to reflect a real-world scenario, we will design the first iteration of a product with minimum functionality. Here, we must clearly define the core features required to create a working and valuable product. The choices are made based on the timeline, resources, and team's knowledge. This is where we bridge the gap between dreaming and focusing on what is realistic and eventually answer the following question: "What are we going to build?".

Finally, we will go through a system design step, laying out the core architecture and design choices used to build the LLM system. Note that the first two components are primarily product-related, while the last one is technical and focuses on the "How."

These three steps are natural in building a real-world product. Even if the first two do not require much ML knowledge, it is critical to go through them to understand "how" to build the product with a clear vision. In a nutshell, this chapter covers the following topics:

- Understanding the LLM Twin concept
- Planning the MVP of the LLM Twin product
- Building ML systems with feature/training/inference pipelines
- Designing the system architecture of the LLM Twin

By the end of this chapter, you will have a clear picture of what you will learn to build throughout the book.

Understanding the LLM Twin concept

The first step is to have a clear vision of what we want to create and why it's valuable to build it. The concept of an LLM Twin is new. Thus, before diving into the technical details, it is essential to understand what it is, what we should expect from it, and how it should work. Having a solid intuition of your end goal makes it much easier to digest the theory, code, and infrastructure presented in this book.

What is an LLM Twin?

In a few words, an LLM Twin is an AI character that incorporates your writing style, voice, and personality into an LLM, which is a complex AI model. It is a digital version of yourself *projected* into an LLM. Instead of a generic LLM trained on the whole internet, an LLM Twin is fine-tuned on yourself. Naturally, as an ML model reflects the data it is trained on, this LLM will incorporate your writing style, voice, and personality. We intentionally used the word "projected." As with any other projection, you lose a lot of information along the way. Thus, this LLM will not *be you*; it will copy the side of you reflected in the data it was trained on.

It is essential to understand that an LLM reflects the data it was trained on. If you feed it Shakespeare, it will start writing like him. If you train it on Billie Eilish, it will start writing songs in her style. This is also known as style transfer. This concept is prevalent in generating images, too. For example, let's say you want to create a cat image using Van Gogh's style. We will leverage the style transfer strategy, but instead of choosing a personality, we will do it on our own persona.

To adjust the LLM to a given style and voice along with fine-tuning, we will also leverage various advanced **retrieval-augmented generation (RAG)** techniques to condition the autoregressive process with previous embeddings of ourselves.

We will explore the details in *Chapter 5* on fine-tuning and *Chapters 4* and *9* on RAG, but for now, let's look at a few examples to intuitively understand what we stated previously.

Here are some scenarios of what you can fine-tune an LLM on to become your twin:

- **LinkedIn posts and X threads**: Specialize the LLM in writing social media content.
- **Messages with your friends and family**: Adapt the LLM to an unfiltered version of yourself.
- **Academic papers and articles**: Calibrate the LLM in writing formal and educative content.
- **Code**: Specialize the LLM in implementing code as you would.

All the preceding scenarios can be reduced to one core strategy: collecting your digital data (or some parts of it) and feeding it to an LLM using different algorithms. Ultimately, the LLM reflects the voice and style of the collected data. Easy, right?

Unfortunately, this raises many technical and moral issues. First, on the technical side, how can we access this data? Do we have enough digital data to project ourselves into an LLM? What kind of data would be valuable? Secondly, on the moral side, is it OK to do this in the first place? Do we want to create a copycat of ourselves? Will it write using our voice and personality, or just try to replicate it?

Remember that the role of this section is not to bother with the "What" and "How" but with the "Why." Let's understand why it makes sense to have your LLM Twin, why it can be valuable, and why it is morally correct if we frame the problem correctly.

Why building an LLM Twin matters

As an engineer (or any other professional career), building a personal brand is more valuable than a standard CV. The biggest issue with creating a personal brand is that writing content on platforms such as LinkedIn, X, or Medium takes a lot of time. Even if you enjoy writing and creating content, you will eventually run out of inspiration or time and feel like you need assistance. We don't want to transform this section into a pitch, but we have to understand the scope of this product/project clearly.

We want to build an LLM Twin to write personalized content on LinkedIn, X, Instagram, Substack, and Medium (or other blogs) using our style and voice. It will not be used in any immoral scenarios, but it will act as your writing co-pilot. Based on what we will teach you in this book, you can get creative and adapt it to various use cases, but we will focus on the niche of generating social media content and articles. Thus, instead of writing the content from scratch, we can feed the skeleton of our main idea to the LLM Twin and let it do the grunt work.

Ultimately, we will have to check whether everything is correct and format it to our liking (more on the concrete features in the *Planning the MVP of the LLM Twin product* section). Hence, we project ourselves into a content-writing LLM Twin that will help us automate our writing process. It will likely fail if we try to use this particular LLM in a different scenario, as this is where we will specialize the LLM through fine-tuning, prompt engineering, and RAG.

So, why does building an LLM Twin matter? It helps you do the following:

- Create your brand
- Automate the writing process
- Brainstorm new creative ideas

What's the difference between a co-pilot and an LLM Twin?

A co-pilot and digital twin are two different concepts that work together and can be combined into a powerful solution:

- The co-pilot is an AI assistant or tool that augments human users in various programming, writing, or content creation tasks.
- The twin serves as a 1:1 digital representation of a real-world entity, often using AI to bridge the gap between the physical and digital worlds. For instance, an LLM Twin is an LLM that learns to mimic your voice, personality, and writing style.

With these definitions in mind, a writing and content creation AI assistant who writes like you is your LLM Twin co-pilot.

Also, it is critical to understand that building an LLM Twin is entirely moral. The LLM will be fine-tuned only on our personal digital data. We won't collect and use other people's data to try to impersonate anyone's identity. We have a clear goal in mind: creating our personalized writing copycat. Everyone will have their own LLM Twin with restricted access.

Of course, many security concerns are involved, but we won't go into that here as it could be a book in itself.

Why not use ChatGPT (or another similar chatbot)?

 This subsection will refer to using ChatGPT (or another similar chatbot) just in the context of generating personalized content.

We have already provided the answer. ChatGPT is not *personalized* to your writing style and voice. Instead, it is very generic, unarticulated, and wordy. Maintaining an original voice is critical for long-term success when building your brand. Thus, directly using ChatGPT or Gemini will not yield the most optimal results. Even if you are OK with sharing impersonalized content, mindlessly using ChatGPT can result in the following:

- **Misinformation due to hallucination**: Manually checking the results for hallucinations or using third-party tools to evaluate your results is a tedious and unproductive experience.
- **Tedious manual prompting**: You must manually craft your prompts and inject external information, which is a tiresome experience. Also, the generated answers will be hard to replicate between multiple sessions as you don't have complete control over your prompts and injected data. You can solve part of this problem using an API and a tool such as LangChain, but you need programming experience to do so.

From our experience, if you want high-quality content that provides real value, you will spend more time debugging the generated text than writing it yourself.

The key of the LLM Twin stands in the following:

- What data we collect
- How we preprocess the data
- How we feed the data into the LLM
- How we chain multiple prompts for the desired results
- How we evaluate the generated content

The LLM itself is important, but we want to highlight that using ChatGPT's web interface is exceptionally tedious in managing and injecting various data sources or evaluating the outputs. The solution is to build an LLM system that encapsulates and automates all the following steps (manually replicating them each time is not a long-term and feasible solution):

- Data collection
- Data preprocessing

- Data storage, versioning, and retrieval
- LLM fine-tuning
- RAG
- Content generation evaluation

Note that we never said not to use OpenAI's GPT API, just that the LLM framework we will present is LLM-agnostic. Thus, if it can be manipulated programmatically and exposes a fine-tuning interface, it can be integrated into the LLM Twin system we will learn to build. The key to most successful ML products is to be data-centric and make your architecture model-agnostic. Thus, you can quickly experiment with multiple models on your specific data.

Planning the MVP of the LLM Twin product

Now that we understand what an LLM Twin is and why we want to build it, we must clearly define the product's features. In this book, we will focus on the first iteration, often labeled the **minimum viable product (MVP)**, to follow the natural cycle of most products. Here, the main objective is to align our ideas with realistic and doable business objectives using the available resources to produce the product. Even as an engineer, as you grow up in responsibilities, you must go through these steps to bridge the gap between the business needs and what can be implemented.

What is an MVP?

An MVP is a version of a product that includes just enough features to draw in early users and test the viability of the product concept in the initial stages of development. Usually, the purpose of the MVP is to gather insights from the market with minimal effort.

An MVP is a powerful strategy because of the following reasons:

- **Accelerated time-to-market**: Launch a product quickly to gain early traction
- **Idea validation**: Test it with real users before investing in the full development of the product
- **Market research**: Gain insights into what resonates with the target audience
- **Risk minimization**: Reduces the time and resources needed for a product that might not achieve market success

Sticking to the *V* in MVP is essential, meaning the product must be *viable*. The product must provide an end-to-end user journey without half-implemented features, even if the product is minimal. It must be a working product with a good user experience that people will love and want to keep using to see how it evolves to its full potential.

Defining the LLM Twin MVP

As a thought experiment, let's assume that instead of building this project for this book, we want to make a real product. In that case, what are our resources? Well, unfortunately, not many:

- We are a team of three people with two ML engineers and one ML researcher
- Our laptops
- Personal funding for computing, such as training LLMs
- Our enthusiasm

As you can see, we don't have many resources. Even if this is just a thought experiment, it reflects the reality for most start-ups at the beginning of their journey. Thus, we must be very strategic in defining our LLM Twin MVP and what features we want to pick. Our goal is simple: we want to maximize the product's value relative to the effort and resources poured into it.

To keep it simple, we will build the features that can do the following for the LLM Twin:

- Collect data from your LinkedIn, Medium, Substack, and GitHub profiles
- Fine-tune an open-source LLM using the collected data
- Populate a vector database (DB) using our digital data for RAG
- Create LinkedIn posts leveraging the following:
    - User prompts
    - RAG to reuse and reference old content
    - New posts, articles, or papers as additional knowledge to the LLM
- Have a simple web interface to interact with the LLM Twin and be able to do the following:
    - Configure your social media links and trigger the collection step
    - Send prompts or links to external resources

That will be the LLM Twin MVP. Even if it doesn't sound like much, remember that we must make this system cost effective, scalable, and modular.

 Even if we focus only on the core features of the LLM Twin defined in this section, we will build the product with the latest LLM research and best software engineering and MLOps practices in mind. We aim to show you how to engineer a cost-effective and scalable LLM application.

Until now, we have examined the LLM Twin from the users' and businesses' perspectives. The last step is to examine it from an engineering perspective and define a development plan to understand how to solve it technically. From now on, the book's focus will be on the implementation of the LLM Twin.

Building ML systems with feature/training/inference pipelines

Before diving into the specifics of the LLM Twin architecture, we must understand an ML system pattern at the core of the architecture, known as the **feature/training/inference (FTI)** architecture. This section will present a general overview of the FTI pipeline design and how it can structure an ML application.

Let's see how we can apply the FTI pipelines to the LLM Twin architecture.

The problem with building ML systems

Building production-ready ML systems is much more than just training a model. From an engineering point of view, training the model is the most straightforward step in most use cases. However, training a model becomes complex when deciding on the correct architecture and hyperparameters. That's not an engineering problem but a research problem.

At this point, we want to focus on how to design a production-ready architecture. Training a model with high accuracy is extremely valuable, but just by training it on a static dataset, you are far from deploying it robustly. We have to consider how to do the following:

- Ingest, clean, and validate fresh data
- Training versus inference setups
- Compute and serve features in the right environment
- Serve the model in a cost-effective way
- Version, track, and share the datasets and models
- Monitor your infrastructure and models
- Deploy the model on a scalable infrastructure
- Automate the deployments and training

These are the types of problems an ML or MLOps engineer must consider, while the research or data science team is often responsible for training the model.

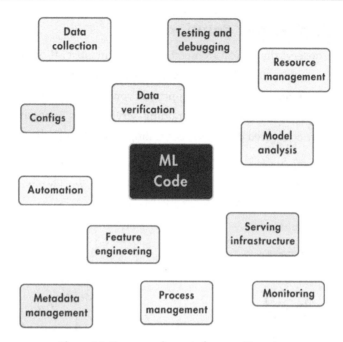

Figure 1.1: Common elements from an ML system

The preceding figure shows all the components the Google Cloud team suggests that a mature ML and MLOps system requires. Along with the ML code, there are many moving pieces. The rest of the system comprises configuration, automation, data collection, data verification, testing and debugging, resource management, model analysis, process and metadata management, serving infrastructure, and monitoring. The point is that there are many components we must consider when productionizing an ML model.

Thus, the critical question is this: How do we connect all these components into a single homogenous system? We must create a boilerplate for clearly designing ML systems to answer that question.

Similar solutions exist for classic software. For example, if you zoom out, most software applications can be split between a DB, business logic, and UI layer. Every layer can be as complex as needed, but at a high-level overview, the architecture of standard software can be boiled down to the previous three components.

Do we have something similar for ML applications? The first step is to examine previous solutions and why they are unsuitable for building scalable ML systems.

The issue with previous solutions

In *Figure 1.2*, you can observe the typical architecture present in most ML applications. It is based on a monolithic batch architecture that couples the feature creation, model training, and inference into the same component. By taking this approach, you quickly solve one critical problem in the ML world: the training-serving skew. The training-serving skew happens when the features passed to the model are computed differently at training and inference time.

In this architecture, the features are created using the same code. Hence, the training-serving skew issue is solved by default. This pattern works fine when working with small data. The pipeline runs on a schedule in batch mode, and the predictions are consumed by a third-party application such as a dashboard.

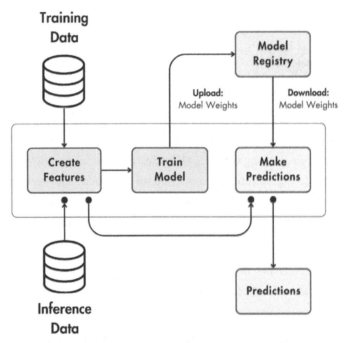

Figure 1.2: Monolithic batch pipeline architecture

Unfortunately, building a monolithic batch system raises many other issues, such as the following:

- Features are not reusable (by your system or others)
- If the data increases, you have to refactor the whole code to support PySpark or Ray
- It's hard to rewrite the prediction module in a more efficient language such as C++, Java, or Rust

- It's hard to share the work between multiple teams between the features, training, and prediction modules
- It's impossible to switch to streaming technology for real-time training

In *Figure 1.3*, we can see a similar scenario for a real-time system. This use case introduces another issue in addition to what we listed before. To make the predictions, we have to transfer the whole state through the client request so the features can be computed and passed to the model.

Consider the scenario of computing movie recommendations for a user. Instead of simply passing the user ID, we must transmit the entire user state, including their name, age, gender, movie history, and more. This approach is fraught with potential errors, as the client must understand how to access this state, and it's tightly coupled with the model service.

Another example would be when implementing an LLM with RAG support. The documents we add as context along the query represent our external state. If we didn't store the records in a vector DB, we would have to pass them with the user query. To do so, the client must know how to query and retrieve the documents, which is not feasible. It is an antipattern for the client application to know how to access or compute the features. If you don't understand how RAG works, we will explain it in detail in *Chapters 8* and *9*.

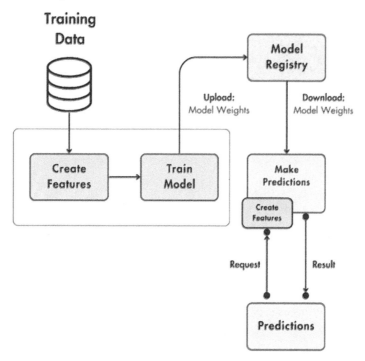

Figure 1.3: Stateless real-time architecture

In conclusion, our problem is accessing the features to make predictions without passing them at the client's request. For example, based on our first user movie recommendation example, how can we predict the recommendations solely based on the user's ID? Remember these questions, as we will answer them shortly.

Ultimately, on the other spectrum, Google Cloud provides a production-ready architecture, as shown in *Figure 1.4*. Unfortunately, even if it's a feasible solution, it's very complex and not intuitive. You will have difficulty understanding this if you are not highly experienced in deploying and keeping ML models in production. Also, it is not straightforward to understand how to start small and grow the system in time.

The following image is reproduced from work created and shared by Google and used according to terms described in the Creative Commons 4.0 Attribution License:

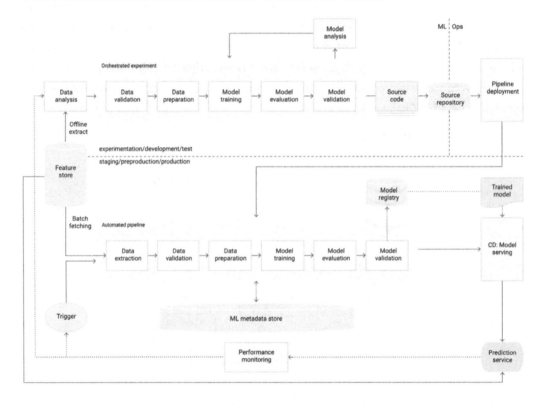

Figure 1.4: ML pipeline automation for CT (source: https://cloud.google.com/architecture/ mlops-continuous-delivery-and-automation-pipelines-in-machine-learning)

But here is where the FTI pipeline architectures kick in. The following section will show you how to solve these fundamental issues using an intuitive ML design.

The solution — ML pipelines for ML systems

The solution is based on creating a clear and straightforward mind map that any team or person can follow to compute the features, train the model, and make predictions. Based on these three critical steps that any ML system requires, the pattern is known as the FTI pipeline. So, how does this differ from what we presented before?

The pattern suggests that any ML system can be boiled down to these three pipelines: feature, training, and inference (similar to the DB, business logic, and UI layers from classic software). This is powerful, as we can clearly define the scope and interface of each pipeline. Also, it's easier to understand how the three components interact. Ultimately, we have just three instead of 20 moving pieces, as suggested in *Figure 1.4*, which is much easier to work with and define.

As shown in *Figure 1.5*, we have the feature, training, and inference pipelines. We will zoom in on each of them and understand their scope and interface.

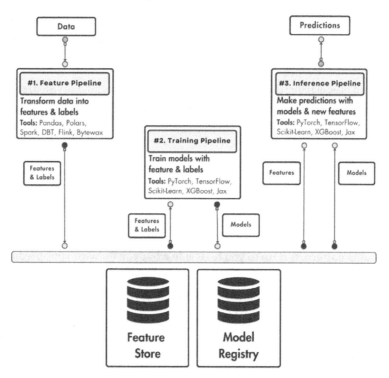

Figure 1.5: FTI pipelines architecture

Before going into the details, it is essential to understand that each pipeline is a different component that can run on a different process or hardware. Thus, each pipeline can be written using a different technology, by a different team, or scaled differently. The key idea is that the design is very flexible to the needs of your team. It acts as a mind map for structuring your architecture.

The feature pipeline

The feature pipeline takes raw data as input, processes it, and outputs the features and labels required by the model for training or inference. Instead of directly passing them to the model, the features and labels are stored inside a feature store. Its responsibility is to store, version, track, and share the features. By saving the features in a feature store, we always have a state of our features. Thus, we can easily send the features to the training and inference pipelines.

As the data is versioned, we can always ensure that the training and inference time features match. Thus, we avoid the training-serving skew problem.

The training pipeline

The training pipeline takes the features and labels from the features stored as input and outputs a train model or models. The models are stored in a model registry. Its role is similar to that of feature stores, but this time, the model is the first-class citizen. Thus, the model registry will store, version, track, and share the model with the inference pipeline.

Also, most modern model registries support a metadata store that allows you to specify essential aspects of how the model was trained. The most important are the features, labels, and their version used to train the model. Thus, we will always know what data the model was trained on.

The inference pipeline

The inference pipeline takes as input the features and labels from the feature store and the trained model from the model registry. With these two, predictions can be easily made in either batch or real-time mode.

As this is a versatile pattern, it is up to you to decide what you do with your predictions. If it's a batch system, they will probably be stored in a DB. If it's a real-time system, the predictions will be served to the client who requested them. Additionally, the features, labels, and models are versioned. We can easily upgrade or roll back the deployment of the model. For example, we will always know that model v1 uses features F1, F2, and F3, and model v2 uses F2, F3, and F4. Thus, we can quickly change the connections between the model and features.

Benefits of the FTI architecture

To conclude, the most important thing you must remember about the FTI pipelines is their interface:

- The feature pipeline takes in data and outputs the features and labels saved to the feature store.

- The training pipeline queries the features store for features and labels and outputs a model to the model registry.

- The inference pipeline uses the features from the feature store and the model from the model registry to make predictions.

It doesn't matter how complex your ML system gets, these interfaces will remain the same.

Now that we understand better how the pattern works, we want to highlight the main benefits of using this pattern:

- As you have just three components, it is intuitive to use and easy to understand.

- Each component can be written into its tech stack, so we can quickly adapt them to specific needs, such as big or streaming data. Also, it allows us to pick the best tools for the job.

- As there is a transparent interface between the three components, each one can be developed by a different team (if necessary), making the development more manageable and scalable.

- Every component can be deployed, scaled, and monitored independently.

The final thing you must understand about the FTI pattern is that the system doesn't have to contain only three pipelines. In most cases, it will include more. For example, the feature pipeline can be composed of a service that computes the features and one that validates the data. Also, the training pipeline can be composed of the training and evaluation components.

The FTI pipelines act as logical layers. Thus, it is perfectly fine for each to be complex and contain multiple services. However, what is essential is to stick to the same interface on how the FTI pipelines interact with each other through the feature store and model registries. By doing so, each FTI component can evolve differently, without knowing the details of each other and without breaking the system on new changes.

To learn more about the FTI pipeline pattern, consider reading *From MLOps to ML Systems with Feature/Training/Inference Pipelines* by Jim Dowling, CEO and co-founder of Hopsworks: https://www.hopsworks.ai/post/mlops-to-ml-systems-with-fti-pipelines. His article inspired this section.

Now that we understand the FTI pipeline architecture, the final step of this chapter is to see how it can be applied to the LLM Twin use case.

Designing the system architecture of the LLM Twin

In this section, we will list the concrete technical details of the LLM Twin application and understand how we can solve them by designing our LLM system using the FTI architecture. However, before diving into the pipelines, we want to highlight that we won't focus on the tooling or the tech stack at this step. We only want to define a high-level architecture of the system, which is language-, framework-, platform-, and infrastructure-agnostic at this point. We will focus on each component's scope, interface, and interconnectivity. In future chapters, we will cover the implementation details and tech stack.

Listing the technical details of the LLM Twin architecture

Until now, we defined what the LLM Twin should support from the user's point of view. Now, let's clarify the requirements of the ML system from a purely technical perspective:

- On the data side, we have to do the following:

    - Collect data from LinkedIn, Medium, Substack, and GitHub completely autonomously and on a schedule

    - Standardize the crawled data and store it in a data warehouse

    - Clean the raw data

    - Create instruct datasets for fine-tuning an LLM

    - Chunk and embed the cleaned data. Store the vectorized data into a vector DB for RAG.

- For training, we have to do the following:

    - Fine-tune LLMs of various sizes (7B, 14B, 30B, or 70B parameters)

    - Fine-tune on instruction datasets of multiple sizes

    - Switch between LLM types (for example, between Mistral, Llama, and GPT)

    - Track and compare experiments

- Test potential production LLM candidates before deploying them
- Automatically start the training when new instruction datasets are available.

- The inference code will have the following properties:

  - A REST API interface for clients to interact with the LLM Twin
  - Access to the vector DB in real time for RAG
  - Inference with LLMs of various sizes
  - Autoscaling based on user requests
  - Automatically deploy the LLMs that pass the evaluation step.

- The system will support the following LLMOps features:

  - Instruction dataset versioning, lineage, and reusability
  - Model versioning, lineage, and reusability
  - Experiment tracking
  - **Continuous training**, **continuous integration**, and **continuous delivery** (CT/CI/CD)
  - Prompt and system monitoring

 If any technical requirement doesn't make sense now, bear with us. To avoid repetition, we will examine the details in their specific chapter.

The preceding list is quite comprehensive. We could have detailed it even more, but at this point, we want to focus on the core functionality. When implementing each component, we will look into all the little details. But for now, the fundamental question we must ask ourselves is this: How can we apply the FTI pipeline design to implement the preceding list of requirements?

How to design the LLM Twin architecture using the FTI pipeline design

We will split the system into four core components. You will ask yourself this: "Four? Why not three, as the FTI pipeline design clearly states?" That is a great question. Fortunately, the answer is simple. We must also implement the data pipeline along the three feature/training/inference pipelines. According to best practices:

- The data engineering team owns the data pipeline
- The ML engineering team owns the FTI pipelines.

Given our goal of building an MVP with a small team, we must implement the entire application. This includes defining the data collection and FTI pipelines. Tackling a problem end to end is often encountered in start-ups that can't afford dedicated teams. Thus, engineers have to wear many hats, depending on the state of the product. Nevertheless, in any scenario, knowing how an end-to-end ML system works is valuable for better understanding other people's work.

Figure 1.6 shows the LLM system architecture. The best way to understand it is to review the four components individually and explain how they work.

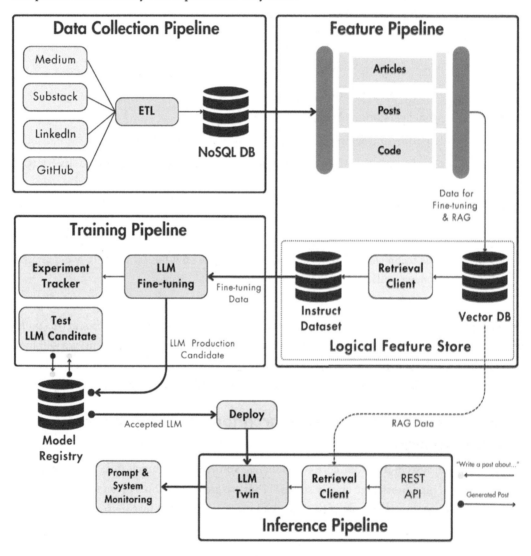

Figure 1.6: LLM Twin high-level architecture

Data collection pipeline

The data collection pipeline involves crawling your personal data from Medium, Substack, LinkedIn, and GitHub. As a data pipeline, we will use the **extract, load, transform** (**ETL**) pattern to extract data from social media platforms, standardize it, and load it into a data warehouse.

 It is critical to highlight that the data collection pipeline is designed to crawl data only from your social media platform. It will not have access to other people. As an example for this book, we agreed to make our collected data available for learning purposes. Otherwise, using other people's data without their consent is not moral.

The output of this component will be a NoSQL DB, which will act as our data warehouse. As we work with text data, which is naturally unstructured, a NoSQL DB fits like a glove.

Even though a NoSQL DB, such as MongoDB, is not labeled as a data warehouse, from our point of view, it will act as one. Why? Because it stores standardized raw data gathered by various ETL pipelines that are ready to be ingested into an ML system.

The collected digital data is binned into three categories:

- Articles (Medium, Substack)
- Posts (LinkedIn)
- Code (GitHub)

We want to abstract away the platform where the data was crawled. For example, when feeding an article to the LLM, knowing it came from Medium or Substack is not essential. We can keep the source URL as metadata to give references. However, from the processing, fine-tuning, and RAG points of view, it is vital to know what type of data we ingested, as each category must be processed differently. For example, the chunking strategy between a post, article, and piece of code will look different.

Also, by grouping the data by category, not the source, we can quickly plug data from other platforms, such as X into the posts or GitLab into the code collection. As a modular system, we must attach an additional ETL in the data collection pipeline, and everything else will work without further code modifications.

Feature pipeline

The feature pipeline's role is to take raw articles, posts, and code data points from the data warehouse, process them, and load them into the feature store.

The characteristics of the FTI pattern are already present.

Here are some custom properties of the LLM Twin's feature pipeline:

- It processes three types of data differently: articles, posts, and code
- It contains three main processing steps necessary for fine-tuning and RAG: cleaning, chunking, and embedding
- It creates two snapshots of the digital data, one after cleaning (used for fine-tuning) and one after embedding (used for RAG)
- It uses a logical feature store instead of a specialized feature store

Let's zoom in on the logical feature store part a bit. As with any RAG-based system, one of the central pieces of the infrastructure is a vector DB. Instead of integrating another DB, more concretely, a specialized feature store, we used the vector DB, plus some additional logic to check all the properties of a feature store our system needs.

The vector DB doesn't offer the concept of a training dataset, but it can be used as a NoSQL DB. This means we can access data points using their ID and collection name. Thus, we can easily query the vector DB for new data points without any vector search logic. Ultimately, we will wrap the retrieved data into a versioned, tracked, and shareable artifact—more on artifacts in *Chapter 2*. For now, you must know it is an MLOps concept used to wrap data and enrich it with the properties listed before.

How will the rest of the system access the logical feature store? The training pipeline will use the instruct datasets as artifacts, and the inference pipeline will query the vector DB for additional context using vector search techniques.

For our use case, this is more than enough because of the following reasons:

- The artifacts work great for offline use cases such as training
- The vector DB is built for online access, which we require for inference.

In future chapters, however, we will explain how the three data categories (articles, posts, and code) are cleaned, chunked, and embedded.

To conclude, we take in raw article, post, or code data points, process them, and store them in a feature store to make them accessible to the training and inference pipelines. Note that trimming all the complexity away and focusing only on the interface is a perfect match with the FTI pattern. Beautiful, right?

Training pipeline

The training pipeline consumes instruct datasets from the feature store, fine-tunes an LLM with it, and stores the tuned LLM weights in a model registry. More concretely, when a new instruct dataset is available in the logical feature store, we will trigger the training pipeline, consume the artifact, and fine-tune the LLM.

In the initial stages, the data science team owns this step. They run multiple experiments to find the best model and hyperparameters for the job, either through automatic hyperparameter tuning or manually. To compare and pick the best set of hyperparameters, we will use an experiment tracker to log everything of value and compare it between experiments. Ultimately, they will pick the best hyperparameters and fine-tuned LLM and propose it as the LLM production candidate. The proposed LLM is then stored in the model registry. After the experimentation phase is over, we store and reuse the best hyperparameters found to eliminate the manual restrictions of the process. Now, we can completely automate the training process, known as continuous training.

The testing pipeline is triggered for a more detailed analysis than during fine-tuning. Before pushing the new model to production, assessing it against a stricter set of tests is critical to see that the latest candidate is better than what is currently in production. If this step passes, the model is ultimately tagged as accepted and deployed to the production inference pipeline. Even in a fully automated ML system, it is recommended to have a manual step before accepting a new production model. It is like pushing the red button before a significant action with high consequences. Thus, at this stage, an expert looks at a report generated by the testing component. If everything looks good, it approves the model, and the automation can continue.

The particularities of this component will be on LLM aspects, such as the following:

- How do you implement an LLM agnostic pipeline?
- What fine-tuning techniques should you use?
- How do you scale the fine-tuning algorithm on LLMs and datasets of various sizes?
- How do you pick an LLM production candidate from multiple experiments?
- How do you test the LLM to decide whether to push it to production or not?

By the end of this book, you will know how to answer all these questions.

One last aspect we want to clarify is **CT**. Our modular design allows us to quickly leverage an ML orchestrator to schedule and trigger different system parts. For example, we can schedule the data collection pipeline to crawl data every week.

Then, we can trigger the feature pipeline when new data is available in the data warehouse and the training pipeline when new instruction datasets are available.

Inference pipeline

The inference pipeline is the last piece of the puzzle. It is connected to the model registry and logical feature store. It loads a fine-tuned LLM from the model registry, and from the logical feature store, it accesses the vector DB for RAG. It takes in client requests through a REST API as queries. It uses the fine-tuned LLM and access to the vector DB to carry out RAG and answer the queries.

All the client queries, enriched prompts using RAG, and generated answers are sent to a prompt monitoring system to analyze, debug, and better understand the system. Based on specific requirements, the monitoring system can trigger alarms to take action either manually or automatically.

At the interface level, this component follows exactly the FTI architecture, but when zooming in, we can observe unique characteristics of an LLM and RAG system, such as the following:

- A retrieval client used to do vector searches for RAG
- Prompt templates used to map user queries and external information to LLM inputs
- Special tools for prompt monitoring

Final thoughts on the FTI design and the LLM Twin architecture

We don't have to be highly rigid about the FTI pattern. It is a tool used to clarify how to design ML systems. For example, instead of using a dedicated features store just because that is how it is done, in our system, it is easier and cheaper to use a logical feature store based on a vector DB and artifacts. What was important to focus on were the required properties a feature store provides, such as a versioned and reusable training dataset.

Ultimately, we will explain the computing requirements of each component briefly. The data collection and feature pipeline are mostly CPU-based and do not require powerful machines. The training pipeline requires powerful GPU-based machines that could load an LLM and fine-tune it. The inference pipeline is somewhere in the middle. It still needs a powerful machine but is less compute-intensive than the training step. However, it must be tested carefully, as the inference pipeline directly interfaces with the user. Thus, we want the latency to be within the required parameters for a good user experience. However, using the FTI design is not an issue. We can pick the proper computing requirements for each component.

Also, each pipeline will be scaled differently. The data and feature pipelines will be scaled horizontally based on the CPU and RAM load. The training pipeline will be scaled vertically by adding more GPUs. The inference pipeline will be scaled horizontally based on the number of client requests.

To conclude, the presented LLM architecture checks all the technical requirements listed at the beginning of the section. It processes the data as requested, and the training is modular and can be quickly adapted to different LLMs, datasets, or fine-tuning techniques. The inference pipeline supports RAG and is exposed as a REST API. On the LLMOps side, the system supports dataset and model versioning, lineage, and reusability. The system has a monitoring service, and the whole ML architecture is designed with CT/CI/CD in mind.

This concludes the high-level overview of the LLM Twin architecture.

Summary

This first chapter was critical to understanding the book's goal. As a product-oriented book that will walk you through building an end-to-end ML system, it was essential to understand the concept of an LLM Twin initially. Afterward, we walked you through what an MVP is and how to plan our LLM Twin MVP based on our available resources. Following this, we translated our concept into a practical technical solution with specific requirements. In this context, we introduced the FTI design pattern and showcased its real-world application in designing systems that are both modular and scalable. Ultimately, we successfully applied the FTI pattern to design the architecture of the LLM Twin to fit all our technical requirements.

Having a clear vision of the big picture is essential when building systems. Understanding how a single component will be integrated into the rest of the application can be very valuable when working on it. We started with a more abstract presentation of the LLM Twin architecture, focusing on each component's scope, interface, and interconnectivity.

The following chapters will explore how to implement and deploy each component. On the MLOps side, we will walk you through using a computing platform, orchestrator, model registry, artifacts, and other tools and concepts to support all MLOps best practices.

References

- Dowling, J. (2024a, July 11). *From MLOps to ML Systems with Feature/Training/Inference Pipelines. Hopsworks.* `https://www.hopsworks.ai/post/mlops-to-ml-systems-with-fti-pipelines`

- Dowling, J. (2024b, August 5). *Modularity and Composability for AI Systems with AI Pipelines and Shared Storage. Hopsworks.* https://www.hopsworks.ai/post/modularity-and-composability-for-ai-systems-with-ai-pipelines-and-shared-storage

- Joseph, M. (2024, August 23). *The Taxonomy for Data Transformations in AI Systems. Hopsworks.* https://www.hopsworks.ai/post/a-taxonomy-for-data-transformations-in-ai-systems

- *MLOps: Continuous delivery and automation pipelines in machine learning.* (2024, August 28). Google Cloud. https://cloud.google.com/architecture/mlops-continuous-delivery-and-automation-pipelines-in-machine-learning

- Qwak. (2024a, June 2). *CI/CD for Machine Learning in 2024: Best Practices to build, test, and Deploy* | Infer. *Medium.* https://medium.com/infer-qwak/ci-cd-for-machine-learning-in-2024-best-practices-to-build-test-and-deploy-c4ad869824d2

- Qwak. (2024b, July 23). *5 Best Open Source Tools to build End-to-End MLOps Pipeline* in 2024. *Medium.* https://medium.com/infer-qwak/building-an-end-to-end-mlops-pipeline-with-open-source-tools-d8bacbf4184f

- Salama, K., Kazmierczak, J., & Schut, D. (2021). *Practitioners guide to MLOps: A framework for continuous delivery and automation of machine learning* (1st ed.) [PDF]. Google Cloud. https://services.google.com/fh/files/misc/practitioners_guide_to_mlops_whitepaper.pdf

Join our book's Discord space

Join our community's Discord space for discussions with the authors and other readers:

https://packt.link/llmeng

2

Tooling and Installation

This chapter presents all the essential tools that will be used throughout the book, especially in implementing and deploying the LLM Twin project. At this point in the book, we don't plan to present in-depth LLM, RAG, MLOps, or LLMOps concepts. We will quickly walk you through our tech stack and prerequisites to avoid repeating ourselves throughout the book on how to set up a particular tool and why we chose it. Starting with *Chapter 3*, we will begin exploring our LLM Twin use case by implementing a data collection ETL that crawls data from the internet.

In the first part of the chapter, we will present the tools within the Python ecosystem to manage multiple Python versions, create a virtual environment, and install the pinned dependencies required for our project to run. Alongside presenting these tools, we will also show how to install the LLM-Engineers-Handbook repository on your local machine (in case you want to try out the code yourself): https://github.com/PacktPublishing/LLM-Engineers-Handbook.

Next, we will explore all the MLOps and LLMOps tools we will use, starting with more generic tools, such as a model registry, and moving on to more LLM-oriented tools, such as LLM evaluation and prompt monitoring tools. We will also understand how to manage a project with multiple ML pipelines using ZenML, an orchestrator bridging the gap between ML and MLOps. Also, we will quickly explore what databases we will use for NoSQL and vector storage. We will show you how to run all these components on your local machine using Docker. Lastly, we will quickly review AWS and show you how to create an AWS user and access keys and install and configure the AWS CLI to manipulate your cloud resources programmatically. We will also explore SageMaker and why we use it to train and deploy our open-source LLMs.

If you are familiar with these tools, you can safely skip this chapter. We also explain how to install the project and set up all the necessary components in the repository's README. Thus, you also have the option to use that as more concise documentation if you plan to run the code while reading the book.

To sum all that up, in this chapter, we will explore the following topics:

- Python ecosystem and project installation
- MLOps and LLMOps tooling
- Databases for storing unstructured and vector data
- Preparing for AWS

By the end of this chapter, you will be aware of all the tools we will use across the book. Also, you will have learned how to install the LLM-Engineers-Handbook repository, set up the rest of the tools, and use them if you run the code while reading the book.

Python ecosystem and project installation

Any Python project needs three fundamental tools: the Python interpreter, dependency management, and a task execution tool. The Python interpreter executes your Python project as expected. All the code within the book is tested with Python 3.11.8. You can download the Python interpreter from here: https://www.python.org/downloads/. We recommend installing the exact Python version (Python 3.11.8) to run the LLM Twin project using pyenv, making the installation process straightforward.

Instead of installing multiple global Python versions, we recommend managing them using pyenv, a Python version management tool that lets you manage multiple Python versions between projects. You can install it using this link: https://github.com/pyenv/pyenv?tab=readme-ov-file#installation.

After you have installed pyenv, you can install the latest version of Python 3.11, using pyenv, as follows:

```
pyenv install 3.11.8
```

Now list all installed Python versions to see that it was installed correctly:

```
pyenv versions
```

You should see something like this:

```
# * system
```

```
#    3.11.8
```

To make Python 3.11.8 the default version across your entire system (whenever you open a new terminal), use the following command:

```
pyenv global 3.11.8
```

However, we aim to use Python 3.11.8 locally only in our repository. To achieve that, first, we have to clone the repository and navigate to it:

```
git clone https://github.com/PacktPublishing/LLM-Engineers-Handbook.git
cd LLM-Engineers-Handbook
```

Because we defined a .python-version file within the repository, pyenv will know to pick up the version from that file and use it locally whenever you are working within that folder. To double-check that, run the following command while you are in the repository:

```
python --version
```

It should output:

```
# Python 3.11.8
```

To create the .python-version file, you must run pyenv local 3.11.8 once. Then, pyenv will always know to use that Python version while working within a specific directory.

Now that we have installed the correct Python version using pyenv, let's move on to Poetry, which we will use as our dependency and virtual environment manager.

Poetry: dependency and virtual environment management

Poetry is one of the most popular dependency and virtual environment managers within the Python ecosystem. But let's start by clarifying what a dependency manager is. In Python, a dependency manager allows you to specify, install, update, and manage external libraries or packages (dependencies) that a project relies on. For example, this is a simple Poetry requirements file that uses Python 3.11 and the requests and numpy Python packages.

```
[tool.poetry.dependencies]
python = "^3.11"
requests = "^2.25.1"
numpy = "^1.19.5"


[build-system]
```

```
requires = ["poetry-core"]
build-backend = "poetry.core.masonry.api"
```

By using Poetry to pin your dependencies, you always ensure that you install the correct version of the dependencies that your projects work with. Poetry, by default, saves all its requirements in pyproject.toml files, which are stored at the root of your repository, as you can see in the cloned LLM-Engineers-Handbook repository.

Another massive advantage of using Poetry is that it creates a new Python virtual environment in which it installs the specified Python version and requirements. A virtual environment allows you to isolate your project's dependencies from your global Python dependencies and other projects. By doing so, you ensure there are no version clashes between projects. For example, let's assume that Project A needs numpy == 1.19.5, and Project B needs numpy == 1.26.0. If you keep both projects in the global Python environment, that will not work, as Project B will override Project A's numpy installation, which will corrupt Project A and stop it from working. Using Poetry, you can isolate each project in its own Python environment with its own Python dependencies, avoiding any dependency clashes.

You can install Poetry from here: https://python-poetry.org/docs/. We use Poetry 1.8.3 throughout the book. Once Poetry is installed, navigate to your cloned LLM-Engineers-Handbook repository and run the following command to install all the necessary Python dependencies:

```
poetry install --without aws
```

This command knows to pick up all the dependencies from your repository that are listed in the pyproject.toml and poetry.lock files. After the installation, you can activate your Poetry environment by running poetry shell in your terminal or by prefixing all your CLI commands as follows: poetry run <your command>.

One final note on Poetry is that it locks down the exact versions of the dependency tree in the poetry.lock file based on the definitions added to the project.toml file. While the pyproject.toml file may specify version ranges (e.g., requests = "^2.25.1"), the poetry.lock file records the exact version (e.g., requests = "2.25.1") that was installed. It also locks the versions of sub-dependencies (dependencies of your dependencies), which may not be explicitly listed in your pyproject.toml file. By locking all the dependencies and sub-dependencies to specific versions, the poetry.lock file ensures that all project installations use the same versions of each package. This consistency leads to predictable behavior, reducing the likelihood of encountering "works on my machine" issues.

Other tools similar to Poetry are Venv and Conda for creating virtual environments. Still, they lack the dependency management option. Thus, you must do it through Python's default requirements. txt files, which are less powerful than Poetry's lock files. Another option is Pipenv, which feature-wise is more like Poetry but slower, and uv, which is a replacement for Poetry built in Rust, making it blazing fast. uv has lots of potential to replace Poetry, making it worthwhile to test out: https://github.com/astral-sh/uv.

The final piece of the puzzle is to look at the task execution tool we used to manage all our CLI commands.

Poe the Poet: task execution tool

Poe the Poet is a plugin on top of Poetry that is used to manage and execute all the CLI commands required to interact with the project. It helps you define and run tasks within your Python project, simplifying automation and script execution. Other popular options are Makefile, Invoke, or shell scripts, but Poe the Poet eliminates the need to write separate shell scripts or Makefiles for managing project tasks, making it an elegant way to manage tasks using the same configuration file that Poetry already uses for dependencies.

When working with Poe the Poet, instead of having all your commands documented in a README file or other document, you can add them directly to your pyproject.toml file and execute them in the command line with an alias. For example, using Poe the Poet, we can define the following tasks in a pyproject.toml file:

```
[tool.poe.tasks]
test = "pytest"
format = "black ."
start = "python main.py"
```

You can then run these tasks using the poe command:

```
poetry poe test
poetry poe format
poetry poe start
```

You can install Poe the Poet as a Poetry plugin, as follows:

```
poetry self add 'poethepoet[poetry_plugin]'
```

To conclude, using a tool as a façade over all your CLI commands is necessary to run your application. It significantly simplifies the application's complexity and enhances collaboration as it acts as out-of-the-box documentation.

Assuming you have pyenv and Poetry installed, here are all the commands you need to run to clone the repository and install the dependencies and Poe the Poet as a Poetry plugin:

```
git clone https://github.com/PacktPublishing/LLM-Engineers-Handbook.gitcd
LLM-Engineers-Handbook
poetry install --without aws
poetry self add 'poethepoet[poetry_plugin]'
```

To make the project fully operational, there are still a few steps to follow, such as filling out a .env file with your credentials and getting tokens from OpenAI and Hugging Face. But this book isn't an installation guide, so we've moved all these details into the repository's README as they are useful only if you plan to run the repository: https://github.com/PacktPublishing/LLM-Engineers-Handbook.

Now that we have installed our Python project, let's present the MLOps tools we will use in the book. If you are already familiar with these tools, you can safely skip the following tooling section and move on to the *Databases for storing unstructured and vector data* section.

MLOps and LLMOps tooling

This section will quickly present all the MLOps and LLMOps tools we will use throughout the book and their role in building ML systems using MLOps best practices. At this point in the book, we don't aim to detail all the MLOps components we will use to implement the LLM Twin use case, such as model registries and orchestrators, but only provide a quick idea of what they are and how to use them. As we develop the LLM Twin project throughout the book, you will see hands-on examples of how we use all these tools. In *Chapter 11*, we will dive deeply into the theory of MLOps and LLMOps and connect all the dots. As the MLOps and LLMOps fields are highly practical, we will leave the theory of these aspects to the end, as it will be much easier to understand it after you go through the LLM Twin use case implementation.

Also, this section is not dedicated to showing you how to set up each tool. It focuses primarily on what each tool is used for and highlights the core features used throughout this book.

Still, using Docker, you can quickly run the whole infrastructure locally. If you want to run the steps within the book yourself, you can host the application locally with these three simple steps:

1. Have Docker 27.1.1 (or higher) installed.

2. Fill your .env file with all the necessary credentials as explained in the repository README.

3. Run poetry poe local-infrastructure-up to locally spin up ZenML (http://127.0.0.1:8237/) and the MongoDB and Qdrant databases.

You can read more details on how to run everything locally in the LLM-Engineers-Handbook repository README: https://github.com/PacktPublishing/LLM-Engineers-Handbook. Within the book, we will also show you how to deploy each component to the cloud.

Hugging Face: model registry

A model registry is a centralized repository that manages ML models throughout their lifecycle. It stores models along with their metadata, version history, and performance metrics, serving as a single source of truth. In MLOps, a model registry is crucial for tracking, sharing, and documenting model versions, facilitating team collaboration. Also, it is a fundamental element in the deployment process as it integrates with **continuous integration and continuous deployment (CI/CD)** pipelines.

We used Hugging Face as our model registry, as we can leverage its ecosystem to easily share our fine-tuned LLM Twin models with anyone who reads the book. Also, by following the Hugging Face model registry interface, we can easily integrate the model with all the frameworks around the LLMs ecosystem, such as Unsloth for fine-tuning and SageMaker for inference.

Our fine-tuned LLMs are available on Hugging Face at:

- **TwinLlama 3.1 8B** (after fine-tuning): https://huggingface.co/mlabonne/TwinLlama-3.1-8B

- **TwinLlama 3.1 8B DPO** (after preference alignment): https://huggingface.co/mlabonne/TwinLlama-3.1-8B-DPO

Figure 2.1: Hugging Face model registry example

For a quick demo, we have them available on Hugging Face Spaces:

- **TwinLlama 3.1 8B:** `https://huggingface.co/spaces/mlabonne/TwinLlama-3.1-8B`
- **TwinLlama 3.1 8B DPO:** `https://huggingface.co/spaces/mlabonne/TwinLlama-3.1-8B-DPO`

Most ML tools provide model registry features. For example, ZenML, Comet, and SageMaker, which we will present in future sections, also offer their own model registries. They are good options, but we picked Hugging Face solely because of its ecosystem, which provides easy shareability and integration throughout the open-source environment. Thus, you will usually select the model registry that integrates the most with your project's tooling and requirements.

ZenML: orchestrator, artifacts, and metadata

ZenML acts as the bridge between ML and MLOps. Thus, it offers multiple MLOps features that make your ML pipeline traceability, reproducibility, deployment, and maintainability easier. At its core, it is designed to create reproducible workflows in machine learning. It addresses the challenge of transitioning from exploratory research in Jupyter notebooks to a production-ready ML environment. It tackles production-based replication issues, such as versioning difficulties, reproducing experiments, organizing complex ML workflows, bridging the gap between training and deployment, and tracking metadata. Thus, ZenML's main features are orchestrating ML pipelines, storing and versioning ML pipelines as outputs, and attaching metadata to artifacts for better observability.

Instead of being another ML platform, ZenML introduced the concept of a *stack,* which allows you to run ZenML on multiple infrastructure options. A stack will enable you to connect ZenML to different cloud services, such as:

- An orchestrator and compute engine (for example, AWS SageMaker or Vertex AI)
- Remote storage (for instance, AWS S3 or Google Cloud Storage buckets)
- A container registry (for example, Docker Registry or AWS ECR)

Thus, ZenML acts as a glue that brings all your infrastructure and tools together in one place through its *stack* feature, allowing you to quickly iterate through your development processes and easily monitor your entire ML system. The beauty of this is that ZenML doesn't vendor-lock you into any cloud platform. It completely abstracts away the implementation of your Python code from the infrastructure it runs on. For example, in our LLM Twin use case, we used the AWS stack:

- SageMaker as our orchestrator and compute

- S3 as our remote storage used to store and track artifacts
- ECR as our container registry

However, the Python code contains no S3 or ECR particularities, as ZenML takes care of them. Thus, we can easily switch to other providers, such as Google Cloud Storage or Azure. For more details on ZenML *stacks*, you can start here: `https://docs.zenml.io/user-guide/production-guide/understand-stacks`.

 We will focus only on the ZenML features used throughout the book, such as orchestrating, artifacts, and metadata. For more details on ZenML, check out their starter guide: `https://docs.zenml.io/user-guide/starter-guide`.

The local version of the ZenML server comes installed as a Python package. Thus, when running `poetry install`, it installs a ZenML debugging server that you can use locally. In *Chapter 11*, we will show you how to use their cloud serverless option to deploy the ML pipelines to AWS.

Orchestrator

An orchestrator is a system that automates, schedules, and coordinates all your ML pipelines. It ensures that each pipeline—such as data ingestion, preprocessing, model training, and deployment—executes in the correct order and handles dependencies efficiently. By managing these processes, an orchestrator optimizes resource utilization, handles failures gracefully, and enhances scalability, making complex ML pipelines more reliable and easier to manage.

How does ZenML work as an orchestrator? It works with **pipelines** and **steps**. A pipeline is a high-level object that contains multiple steps. A function becomes a ZenML pipeline by being decorated with `@pipeline`, and a step when decorated with `@step`. This is a standard pattern when using orchestrators: you have a high-level function, often called a pipeline, that calls multiple units/steps/tasks.

Let's explore how we can implement a ZenML pipeline with one of the ML pipelines implemented for the LLM Twin project. In the code snippet below, we defined a ZenML pipeline that queries the database for a user based on its full name and crawls all the provided links under that user:

```
from zenml import pipeline
from steps.etl import crawl_links, get_or_create_user


@pipeline
```

```
def digital_data_etl(user_full_name: str, links: list[str]) -> None:
    user = get_or_create_user(user_full_name)
    crawl_links(user=user, links=links)
```

You can run the pipeline with the following CLI command: `poetry poe run-digital-data-etl`.
To visualize the pipeline run, you can go to your ZenML dashboard (at `http://127.0.0.1:8237/`)
and, on the left panel, click on the **Pipelines** tab and then on the **digital_data_etl** pipeline, as
illustrated in *Figure 2.2*:

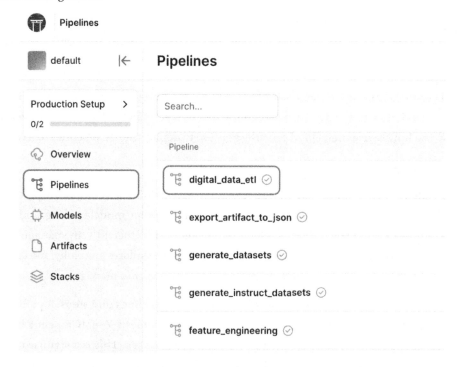

Figure 2.2: ZenML Pipelines dashboard

After clicking on the **digital_data_etl** pipeline, you can visualize all the previous and current
pipeline runs, as seen in *Figure 2.3*. You can see which one succeeded, failed, or is still running.
Also, you can see the stack used to run the pipeline, where the default stack is the one used to
run your ML pipelines locally.

Figure 2.3: ZenML digital_data_etl pipeline dashboard. Example of a specific pipeline

Now, after clicking on the latest **digital_data_etl** pipeline run (or any other run that succeeded or is still running), we can visualize the pipeline's steps, outputs, and insights, as illustrated in *Figure 2.4*. This structure is often called a **directed acyclic graph (DAG)**. More on DAGs in *Chapter 11*.

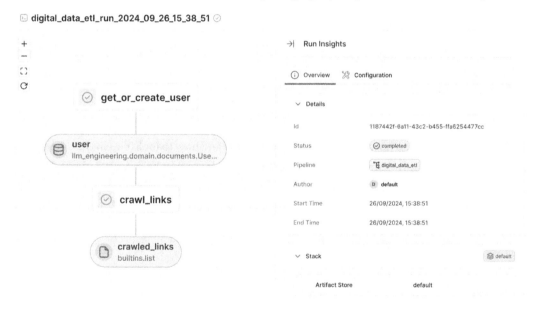

Figure 2.4: ZenML digital_data_etl pipeline run dashboard (example of a specific pipeline run)

By clicking on a specific step, you can get more insights into its code and configuration. It even aggregates the logs output by that specific step to avoid switching between tools, as shown in *Figure 2.5*.

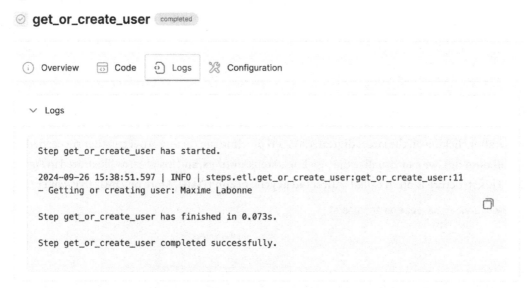

Figure 2.5: Example of insights from a specific step of the digital_data_etl pipeline run

Now that we understand how to define a ZenML pipeline and how to look it up in the dashboard, let's quickly look at how to define a ZenML step. In the code snippet below, we defined the get_ or_create_user() step, which works just like a normal Python function but is decorated with @step. We won't go into the details of the logic, as we will cover the ETL logic in *Chapter 3*. For now, we will focus only on the ZenML functionality.

```
from loguru import logger
from typing_extensions import Annotated
from zenml import get_step_context, step

from llm_engineering.application import utils
```

```python
from llm_engineering.domain.documents import UserDocument


@step
def get_or_create_user(user_full_name: str) -> Annotated[UserDocument,
"user"]:
    logger.info(f"Getting or creating user: {user_full_name}")

    first_name, last_name = utils.split_user_full_name(user_full_name)

    user = UserDocument.get_or_create(first_name=first_name, last_
name=last_name)


    return user
```

Within a ZenML step, you can define any Python logic your use case needs. In this simple example, we are just creating or retrieving a user, but we could replace that code with anything, starting from data collection to feature engineering and training. What is essential to notice is that to integrate ZenML with your code, you have to write modular code, where each function does just one thing. The modularity of your code makes it easy to decorate your functions with @step and then glue multiple steps together within a main function decorated with @pipeline. One design choice that will impact your application is deciding the granularity of each step, as each will run as a different unit on a different machine when deployed in the cloud.

To decouple our code from ZenML, we encapsulated all the application and domain logic into the llm_engineering Python module. We also defined the pipelines and steps folders, where we defined our ZenML logic. Within the steps module, we only used what we needed from the llm_engineering Python module (similar to how you use a Python package). In the pipelines module, we only aggregated ZenML steps to glue them into the final pipeline. Using this design, we can easily swap ZenML with another orchestrator or use our application logic in other use cases, such as a REST API. We only have to replace the ZenML code without touching the llm_engineering module where all our logic resides.

This folder structure is reflected at the root of the LLM-Engineers-Handbook repository, as illustrated in *Figure 2.6*:

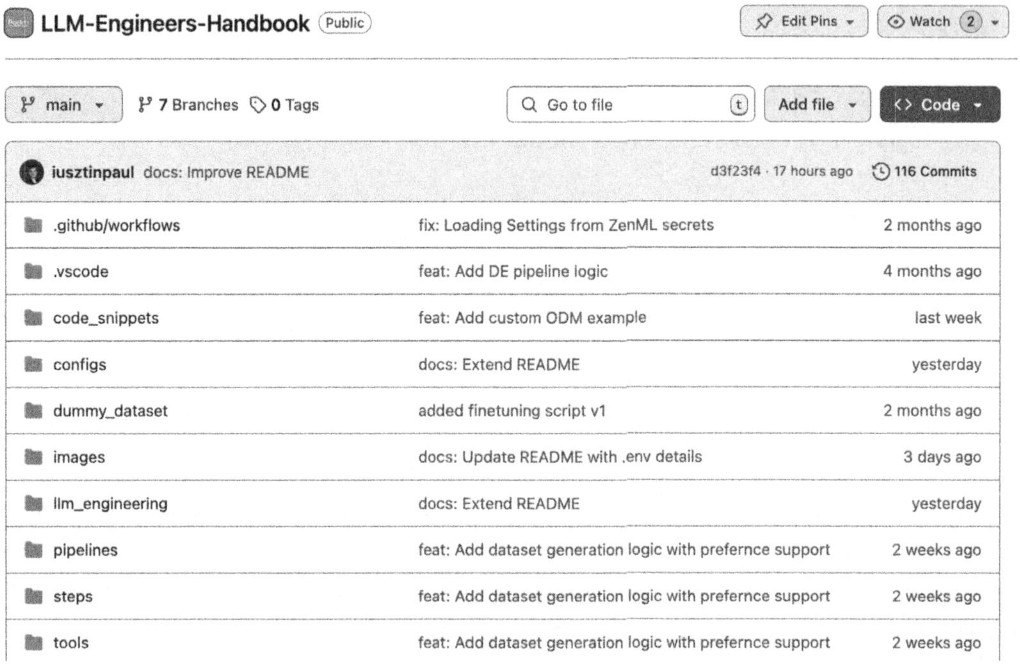

LLM-Engineers-Handbook (Public)		Edit Pins ▾ Watch 2 ▾
⌥ main ▾ ⌥ 7 Branches ⬠ 0 Tags	🔍 Go to file t Add file ▾	<> Code ▾
🧑 **iusztinpaul** docs: Improve README		d3f23f4 · 17 hours ago 🕐 116 Commits
📁 .github/workflows	fix: Loading Settings from ZenML secrets	2 months ago
📁 .vscode	feat: Add DE pipeline logic	4 months ago
📁 code_snippets	feat: Add custom ODM example	last week
📁 configs	docs: Extend README	yesterday
📁 dummy_dataset	added finetuning script v1	2 months ago
📁 images	docs: Update README with .env details	3 days ago
📁 llm_engineering	docs: Extend README	yesterday
📁 pipelines	feat: Add dataset generation logic with prefernce support	2 weeks ago
📁 steps	feat: Add dataset generation logic with prefernce support	2 weeks ago
📁 tools	feat: Add dataset generation logic with prefernce support	2 weeks ago

Figure 2.6: LLM-Engineers-Handbook repository folder structure

One last thing to consider when writing ZenML steps is that if you return a value, it should be serializable. ZenML can serialize most objects that can be reduced to primitive data types, but there are a few exceptions. For example, we used UUID types as IDs throughout the code, which aren't natively supported by ZenML. Thus, we had to extend ZenML's materializer to support UUIDs. We raised this issue to ZenML. Hence, in future ZenML versions, UUIDs will be supported, but it was an excellent example of the serialization aspect of transforming function outputs in artifacts.

Artifacts and metadata

As mentioned in the previous section, ZenML transforms any step output into an artifact. First, let's quickly understand what an artifact is. In MLOps, an **artifact** is any file(s) produced during the machine learning lifecycle, such as datasets, trained models, checkpoints, or logs. Artifacts are crucial for reproducing experiments and deploying models. We can transform anything into an artifact. For example, the model registry is a particular use case for an artifact. Thus, artifacts have these unique properties: they are versioned, sharable, and have metadata attached to them to understand what's inside quickly. For example, when wrapping your dataset with an artifact, you can add to its metadata the size of the dataset, the train-test split ratio, the size, types of labels, and anything else useful to understand what's inside the dataset without actually downloading it.

Let's circle back to our **digital_data_etl** pipeline example, where we had as a step output an artifact, the crawled links, which are an artifact, as seen in *Figure 2.7*

Figure 2.7: ZenML artifact example using the digital_data_etl pipeline as an example

By clicking on the `crawled_links` artifact and navigating to the **Metadata** tab, we can quickly see all the domains we crawled for a particular author, the number of links we crawled for each domain, and how many were successful, as illustrated in *Figure 2.8*:

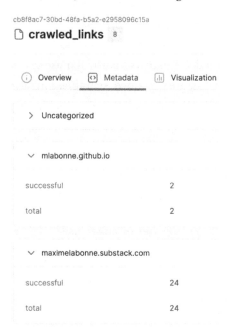

Figure 2.8: ZenML metadata example using the digital_data_etl pipeline as an example

A more interesting example of an artifact and its metadata is the generated dataset artifact. In *Figure 2.9*, we can visualize the metadata of the `instruct_datasets` artifact, which was automatically generated and will be used to fine-tune the LLM Twin model. More details on the `instruction datasets` are in *Chapter 5*. For now, we want to highlight that within the dataset's metadata, we have precomputed a lot of helpful information about it, such as how many data categories it contains, its storage size, and the number of samples per training and testing split.

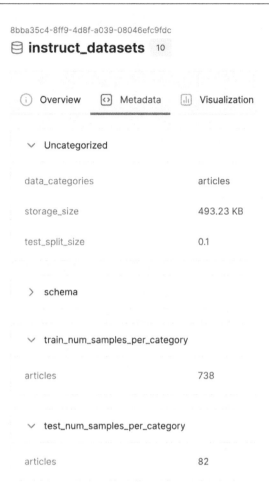

8bba35c4-8ff9-4d8f-a039-08046efc9fdc

🗄 **instruct_datasets** 10

ⓘ Overview 〈〉 Metadata 📊 Visualization

∨ Uncategorized

data_categories	articles
storage_size	493.23 KB
test_split_size	0.1

〉 schema

∨ train_num_samples_per_category

articles	738

∨ test_num_samples_per_category

articles	82

Figure 2.9: ZenML metadata example for the instruct_datasets artifact

The metadata is manually added to the artifact, as shown in the code snippet below. Thus, you can precompute and attach to the artifact's metadata anything you consider helpful for dataset discovery across your business and projects:

```
... # More imports
from zenml import ArtifactConfig, get_step_context, step


@step
def generate_intruction_dataset(
    prompts: Annotated[dict[DataCategory,
list[GenerateDatasetSamplesPrompt]], "prompts"]) -> Annotated[
```

```
    InstructTrainTestSplit,
    ArtifactConfig(
        name="instruct_datasets",
        tags=["dataset", "instruct", "cleaned"],
    ),
]:
    datasets = … # Generate datasets

    step_context = get_step_context()
    step_context.add_output_metadata(output_name="instruct_datasets",
metadata=_get_metadata_instruct_dataset(datasets))

    return datasets

def _get_metadata_instruct_dataset(datasets: InstructTrainTestSplit) ->
dict[str, Any]:
    instruct_dataset_categories = list(datasets.train.keys())
    train_num_samples = {
        category: instruct_dataset.num_samples for category, instruct_
dataset in datasets.train.items()
    }
    test_num_samples = {category: instruct_dataset.num_samples for
category, instruct_dataset in datasets.test.items()}

    return {
        "data_categories": instruct_dataset_categories,
        "test_split_size": datasets.test_split_size,
        "train_num_samples_per_category": train_num_samples,
        "test_num_samples_per_category": test_num_samples,
    }
```

Also, you can easily download and access a specific version of the dataset using its **Universally Unique Identifier (UUID)**, which you can find using the ZenML dashboard or CLI:

```
from zenml.client import Client

artifact = Client().get_artifact_version('8bba35c4-8ff9-4d8f-a039-
08046efc9fdc')
loaded_artifact = artifact.load()
```

The last step in exploring ZenML is understanding how to run and configure a ZenML pipeline.

How to run and configure a ZenML pipeline

All the ZenML pipelines can be called from the run.py file, accessed at tools/run.py in our GitHub repository. Within the run.py file, we implemented a simple CLI that allows you to specify what pipeline to run. For example, to call the digital_data_etl pipeline to crawl Maxime's content, you have to run:

```
python -m tools.run --run-etl --no-cache --etl-config-filename digital_
data_etl_maxime_labonne.yaml
```

Or, to crawl Paul's content, you can run:

```
python -m tools.run --run-etl --no-cache --etl-config-filename digital_
data_etl_paul_iusztin.yaml
```

As explained when introducing Poe the Poet, all our CLI commands used to interact with the project will be executed through Poe to simplify and standardize the project. Thus, we encapsulated these Python calls under the following poe CLI commands:

```
poetry poe run-digital-data-etl-maxime
poetry poe run-digital-data-etl-paul
```

We only change the ETL config file name when scraping content for different people. ZenML allows us to inject specific configuration files at runtime as follows:

```
config_path = root_dir / "configs" / etl_config_filename
assert config_path.exists(), f"Config file not found: { config_path }"
run_args_etl = {
    "config_path": config_path,
    "run_name": f"digital_data_etl_run_{dt.now().
strftime('%Y_%m_%d_%H_%M_%S')}"
}
  digital_data_etl.with_options()(**run_args_etl)
```

In the config file, we specify all the parameters that will input the pipeline as parameters. For example, the configs/digital_data_etl_maxime_labonne.yaml configuration file looks as follows:

```
parameters:
  user_full_name: Maxime Labonne # [First Name(s)] [Last Name]
  links:
    # Personal Blog
```

```
    - https://mlabonne.github.io/blog/posts/2024-07-29_Finetune_Llama31.
html
    - https://mlabonne.github.io/blog/posts/2024-07-15_The_Rise_of_
Agentic_Data_Generation.html
    # Substack
    - https://maximelabonne.substack.com/p/uncensor-any-llm-with-
abliteration-d30148b7d43e
    … # More Links
```

Where the `digital_data_etl` function signature looks like this:

```
@pipeline
def digital_data_etl(user_full_name: str, links: list[str]) -> str:
```

This approach allows us to configure each pipeline at runtime without modifying the code. We can also clearly track the inputs for all our pipelines, ensuring reproducibility. As seen in *Figure 2.10*, we have one or more configs for each pipeline.

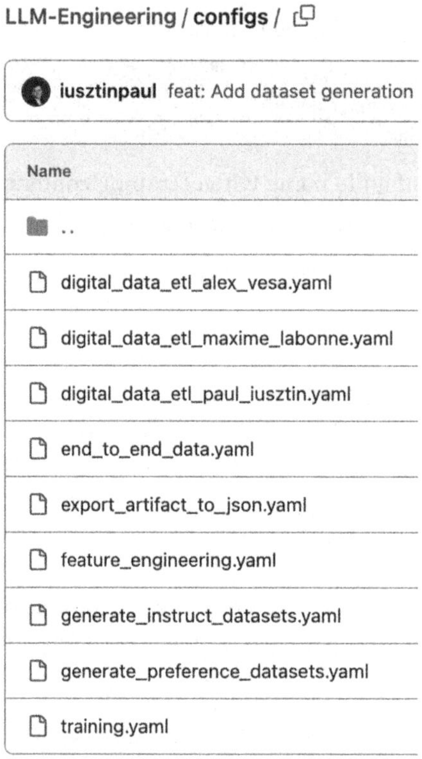

LLM-Engineering / configs /

iusztinpaul feat: Add dataset generation

Name
..
digital_data_etl_alex_vesa.yaml
digital_data_etl_maxime_labonne.yaml
digital_data_etl_paul_iusztin.yaml
end_to_end_data.yaml
export_artifact_to_json.yaml
feature_engineering.yaml
generate_instruct_datasets.yaml
generate_preference_datasets.yaml
training.yaml

Figure 2.10: ZenML pipeline configs

Other popular orchestrators similar to ZenML that we've personally tested and consider powerful are Airflow, Prefect, Metaflow, and Dagster. Also, if you are a heavy user of Kubernetes, you can opt for Agro Workflows or Kubeflow, the latter of which works only on top of Kubernetes. We still consider ZenML the best trade-off between ease of use, features, and costs. Also, none of these tools offer the stack feature that is offered by ZenML, which allows it to avoid vendor-locking you in to any cloud ecosystem.

In *Chapter 11*, we will explore in more depth how to leverage an orchestrator to implement MLOps best practices. But now that we understand ZenML, what it is helpful for, and how to use it, let's move on to the experiment tracker.

Comet ML: experiment tracker

Training ML models is an entirely iterative and experimental process. Unlike traditional software development, it involves running multiple parallel experiments, comparing them based on predefined metrics, and deciding which one should advance to production. An experiment tracking tool allows you to log all the necessary information, such as metrics and visual representations of your model predictions, to compare all your experiments and quickly select the best model. Our LLM project is no exception.

As illustrated in *Figure 2.11*, we used Comet to track metrics such as training and evaluation loss or the value of the gradient norm across all our experiments.

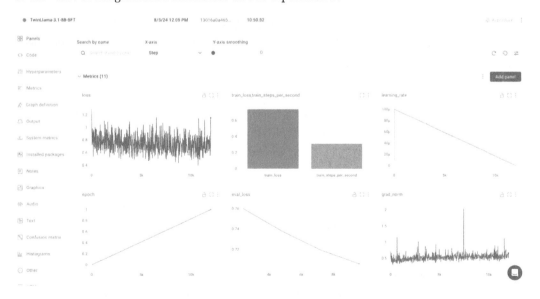

Figure 2.11: Comet ML training metrics example

Using an experiment tracker, you can go beyond training and evaluation metrics and log your training hyperparameters to track different configurations between experiments.

It also logs out-of-the-box system metrics such as GPU, CPU, or memory utilization to give you a clear picture of what resources you need during training and where potential bottlenecks slow down your training, as seen in *Figure 2.12*.

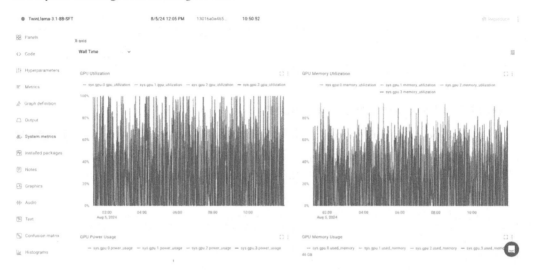

Figure 2.12: Comet ML system metrics example

You don't have to set up Comet locally. We will use their online version for free without any constraints throughout this book. Also, if you want to look more in-depth into the Comet ML experiment tracker, we made the training experiments tracked with Comet ML public while fine-tuning our LLM Twin models. You can access them here: `https://www.comet.com/mlabonne/llm-twin-training/view/new/panels`.

Other popular experiment trackers are W&B, MLflow, and Neptune. We've worked with all of them and can state that they all have mostly the same features, but Comet ML differentiates itself through its ease of use and intuitive interface. Let's move on to the final piece of the MLOps puzzle: Opik for prompt monitoring.

Opik: prompt monitoring

You cannot use standard tools and techniques when logging and monitoring prompts. The reason for this is complicated. We will dig into it in *Chapter 11*. However, to quickly give you some understanding, you cannot use standard logging tools as prompts are complex and unstructured chains.

When interacting with an LLM application, you chain multiple input prompts and the generated output into a trace, where one prompt depends on previous prompts.

Thus, instead of plain text logs, you need an intuitive way to group these traces into a specialized dashboard that makes debugging and monitoring traces of prompts easier.

We used Opik, an open-source tool made by Comet, as our prompt monitoring tool because it follows Comet's philosophy of simplicity and ease of use, which is currently relatively rare in the LLM landscape. Other options offering similar features are Langfuse (open source, `https://langfuse.com`), Galileo (not open source, `rungalileo.io`), and LangSmith (not open source, `https://www.langchain.com/langsmith`), but we found their solutions more cumbersome to use and implement. Opik, along with its serverless option, also provides a free open-source version that you have complete control over. You can read more on Opik at `https://github.com/comet-ml/opik`.

Databases for storing unstructured and vector data

We also want to present the NoSQL and vector databases we will use within our examples. When working locally, they are already integrated through Docker. Thus, when running `poetry poe local-infrastructure-up`, as instructed a few sections above, local images of Docker for both databases will be pulled and run on your machine. Also, when deploying the project, we will show you how to use their serverless option and integrate it with the rest of the LLM Twin project.

MongoDB: NoSQL database

MongoDB is one of today's most popular, robust, fast, and feature-rich NoSQL databases. It integrates well with most cloud ecosystems, such as AWS, Google Cloud, Azure, and Databricks. Thus, using MongoDB as our NoSQL database was a no-brainer.

When we wrote this book, MongoDB was used by big players such as Novo Nordisk, Delivery Hero, Okta, and Volvo. This widespread adoption suggests that MongoDB will remain a leading NoSQL database for a long time.

We use MongoDB as a NoSQL database to store the raw data we collect from the internet before processing it and pushing it into the vector database. As we work with unstructured text data, the flexibility of the NoSQL database fits like a charm.

Qdrant: vector database

Qdrant (`https://qdrant.tech/`) is one of the most popular, robust, and feature-rich vector databases. We could have used almost any vector database for our small MVP, but we wanted to pick something light and likely to be used in the industry for many years to come.

We will use Qdrant to store the data from MongoDB after it's processed and transformed for GenAI usability.

Qdrant is used by big players such as X (formerly Twitter), Disney, Microsoft, Discord, and Johnson & Johnson. Thus, it is highly probable that Qdrant will remain in the vector database game for a long time.

While writing the book, other popular options were Milvus, Redis, Weaviate, Pinecone, Chroma, and pgvector (a PostgreSQL plugin for vector indexes). We found that Qdrant offers the best trade-off between RPS, latency, and index time, making it a solid choice for many generative AI applications.

Comparing all the vector databases in detail could be a chapter in itself. We don't want to do that here. Still, if curious, you can check the *Vector DB Comparison* resource from Superlinked at `https://superlinked.com/vector-db-comparison`, which compares all the top vector databases in terms of everything you can think about, from the license and release year to database features, embedding models, and frameworks supported.

Preparing for AWS

This last part of the chapter will focus on setting up an AWS account (if you don't already have one), an AWS access key, and the CLI. Also, we will look into what SageMaker is and why we use it.

We picked AWS as our cloud provider because it's the most popular out there and the cloud in which we (the writers) have the most experience. The reality is that other big cloud providers, such as GCP or Azure, offer similar services. Thus, depending on your specific application, there is always a trade-off between development time (in which you have the most experience), features, and costs. But for our MVP, AWS, it's the perfect option as it provides robust features for everything we need, such as S3 (object storage), ECR (container registry), and SageMaker (compute for training and inference).

Setting up an AWS account, an access key, and the CLI

As AWS could change its UI/UX, the best way to instruct you on how to create an AWS account is by redirecting you to their official tutorial: `https://docs.aws.amazon.com/accounts/latest/reference/manage-acct-creating.html`.

After successfully creating an AWS account, you can access the AWS console at `http://console.aws.amazon.com`. Select **Sign in using root user email** (found under the **Sign in** button), then enter your account's email address and password.

Next, we must generate access keys to access AWS programmatically. The best option to do so is first to create an IAM user with administrative access as described in this AWS official tutorial: `https://docs.aws.amazon.com/streams/latest/dev/setting-up.html`

For production accounts, it is best practice to grant permissions with a policy of least privilege, giving each user only the permissions they require to perform their role. However, to simplify the setup of our test account, we will use the `AdministratorAccess` managed policy, which gives our user full access, as explained in the tutorial above and illustrated in *Figure 2.13*.

Figure 2.13: IAM user permission policies example

Next, you have to create an access key for the IAM user you just created using the following tutorial: `https://docs.aws.amazon.com/IAM/latest/UserGuide/id_credentials_access-keys.html`.

The access keys will look as follows:

```
aws_access_key_id = <your_access_key_id>
aws_secret_access_key = <your_secret_access_key>
```

Just be careful to store them somewhere safe, as you won't be able to access them after you create them. Also, be cautious with who you share them, as they could be used to access your AWS account and manipulate various AWS resources.

The last step is to install the AWS CLI and configure it with your newly created access keys. You can install the AWS CLI using the following link: `https://docs.aws.amazon.com/cli/latest/userguide/getting-started-install.html`.

After installing the AWS CLI, you can configure it by running aws `configure`. Here is an example of our AWS configuration:

```
[default]
aws_access_key_id = ************
aws_secret_access_key = ************
```

```
region = eu-central-1
output = json
```

For more details on how to configure the AWS CLI, check out the following tutorial: https://docs.aws.amazon.com/cli/v1/userguide/cli-configure-files.html.

Also, to configure the project with your AWS credentials, you must fill in the following variables within your .env file:

```
AWS_REGION="eu-central-1" # Change it with your AWS region. By default, we
use "eu-central-1".
AWS_ACCESS_KEY="<your_aws_access_key>"
AWS_SECRET_KEY="<your_aws_secret_key>"
```

An important note about costs associated with hands-on tasks in this book

All the cloud services used across the book stick to their freemium option, except AWS. Thus, if you use a personal AWS account, you will be responsible for AWS costs as you follow along in this book. While some services may fall under AWS Free Tier usage, others will not. Thus, you are responsible for checking your billing console regularly.

Most of the costs will come when testing SageMaker for training and inference. Based on our tests, the AWS costs can vary between $50 and $100 using the specifications provided in this book and repository.

See the AWS documentation on setting up billing alarms to monitor your costs at https://docs.aws.amazon.com/AmazonCloudWatch/latest/monitoring/monitor_estimated_charges_with_cloudwatch.html.

SageMaker: training and inference compute

The last topic of this chapter is understanding SageMaker and why we decided to use it. SageMaker is an ML platform used to train and deploy ML models. An official definition is as follows: AWS SageMaker is a fully managed machine learning service by AWS that enables developers and data scientists to build, train, and deploy machine learning models at scale. It simplifies the process by handling the underlying infrastructure, allowing users to focus on developing high-quality models efficiently.

We will use SageMaker to fine-tune and operationalize our training pipeline on clusters of GPUs and to deploy our custom LLM Twin model as a REST API that can be accessed in real time from anywhere in the world.

Why AWS SageMaker?

We must also discuss why we chose AWS SageMaker over simpler and more cost-effective options, such as AWS Bedrock. First, let's explain Bedrock and its benefits.

Amazon Bedrock is a serverless solution for deploying LLMs. Serverless means that there are no servers or infrastructure to manage. It provides pre-trained models, which you can access directly through API calls. When we wrote this book, they provided support only for Mistral, Flan, Llama 2, and Llama 3 (quite a limited list of options). You can send input data and receive predictions from the models without managing the underlying infrastructure or software. This approach significantly reduces the complexity and time required to integrate AI capabilities into applications, making it more accessible to developers with limited machine learning expertise. However, this ease of integration comes at the cost of limited customization options, as you're restricted to the pre-trained models and APIs provided by Amazon Bedrock. In terms of pricing, Bedrock uses a simple pricing model based on the number of API calls. This straightforward pricing structure makes it more efficient to estimate and control costs.

Meanwhile, SageMaker provides a comprehensive platform for building, training, and deploying machine learning models. It allows you to customize your ML processes entirely or even use the platform for research. That's why SageMaker is mainly used by data scientists and machine learning experts who know how to program, understand machine learning concepts, and are comfortable working with cloud platforms such as AWS. SageMaker is a double-edged sword regarding costs, following a pay-as-you-go pricing model similar to most AWS services. This means you have to pay for the usage of computing resources, storage, and any other services required to build your applications.

In contrast to Bedrock, even if the SageMaker endpoint is not used, you will still pay for the deployed resources on AWS, such as online EC2 instances. Thus, you have to design autoscaling systems that delete unused resources. To conclude, Bedrock offers an out-of-the-box solution that allows you to quickly deploy an API endpoint powered by one of the available foundation models. Meanwhile, SageMaker is a multi-functional platform enabling you to customize your ML logic fully.

So why did we choose SageMaker over Bedrock? Bedrock would have been an excellent solution for quickly prototyping something, but this is a book on LLM engineering, and our goal is to dig into all the engineering aspects that Bedrock tries to mask away. Thus, we chose SageMaker because of its high level of customizability, allowing us to show you all the engineering required to deploy a model.

In reality, even SageMaker isn't fully customizable. If you want complete control over your deployment, use EKS, AWS's Kubernetes self-managed service. In this case, you have direct access to the virtual machines, allowing you to fully customize how you build your ML pipelines, how they interact, and how you manage your resources. You could do the same thing with AWS ECS, AWS's version of Kubernetes. Using EKS or ECS, you could also reduce the costs, as these services cost considerably less.

To conclude, SageMaker strikes a balance between complete control and customization and a fully managed service that hides all the engineering complexity behind the scenes. This balance ensures that you have the control you need while also benefiting from the managed service's convenience.

Summary

In this chapter, we reviewed the core tools used across the book. First, we understood how to install the correct version of Python that supports our repository. Then, we looked over how to create a virtual environment and install all the dependencies using Poetry. Finally, we understood how to use a task execution tool like Poe the Poet to aggregate all the commands required to run the application.

The next step was to review all the tools used to ensure MLOps best practices, such as a model registry to share our models, an experiment tracker to manage our training experiments, an orchestrator to manage all our ML pipelines and artifacts, and metadata to manage all our files and datasets. We also understood what type of databases we need to implement the LLM Twin use case. Finally, we explored the process of setting up an AWS account, generating an access key, and configuring the AWS CLI for programmatic access to the AWS cloud. We also gained a deep understanding of AWS SageMaker and the reasons behind choosing it to build our LLM Twin application.

In the next chapter, we will explore the implementation of the LLM Twin project by starting with the data collection ETL that scrapes posts, articles, and repositories from the internet and stores them in a data warehouse.

References

- Acsany, P. (2024, February 19). *Dependency Management With Python Poetry*. `https://realpython.com/dependency-management-python-poetry/`

- Comet.ml. (n.d.). *comet-ml/opik: Open-source end-to-end LLM Development Platform*. GitHub. `https://github.com/comet-ml/opik`

- Czakon, J. (2024, September 25). *ML Experiment Tracking: What It Is, Why It Matters, and How to Implement It*. neptune.ai. `https://neptune.ai/blog/ml-experiment-tracking`

- Hopsworks. (n.d.). *ML Artifacts (ML Assets)?* Hopsworks. `https://www.hopsworks.ai/dictionary/ml-artifacts`

- *Introduction | Documentation | Poetry – Python dependency management and packaging made easy*. (n.d.). `https://python-poetry.org/docs`

- Jones, L. (2024, March 21). *Managing Multiple Python Versions With pyenv*. `https://realpython.com/intro-to-pyenv/`

- Kaewsanmua, K. (2024, January 3). *Best Machine Learning Workflow and Pipeline Orchestration Tools*. neptune.ai. `https://neptune.ai/blog/best-workflow-and-pipeline-orchestration-tools`

- MongoDB. (n.d.). *What is NoSQL?* NoSQL databases explained. `https://www.mongodb.com/resources/basics/databases/nosql-explained`

- Nat-N. (n.d.). *nat-n/poethepoet: A task runner that works well with poetry*. GitHub. `https://github.com/nat-n/poethepoet`

- Oladele, S. (2024, August 29). *ML Model Registry: The Ultimate Guide*. neptune.ai. `https://neptune.ai/blog/ml-model-registry`

- Schwaber-Cohen, R. (n.d.). *What is a Vector Database & How Does it Work? Use Cases + Examples*. Pinecone. `https://www.pinecone.io/learn/vector-database/`

- *Starter guide | ZenML Documentation*. (n.d.). `https://docs.zenml.io/user-guide/starter-guide`

- *Vector DB Comparison*. (n.d.). `https://superlinked.com/vector-db-comparison`

Join our book's Discord space

Join our community's Discord space for discussions with the authors and other readers:

`https://packt.link/llmeng`

3

Data Engineering

This chapter will begin exploring the LLM Twin project in more depth. We will learn how to design and implement the data collection pipeline to gather the raw data we will use in all our LLM use cases, such as fine-tuning or inference. As this is not a book on data engineering, we will keep this chapter short and focus only on what is strictly necessary to collect the required raw data. Starting with *Chapter 4*, we will concentrate on LLMs and GenAI, exploring its theory and concrete implementation details.

When working on toy projects or doing research, you usually have a static dataset with which you work. But in our LLM Twin use case, we want to mimic a real-world scenario where we must gather and curate the data ourselves. Thus, implementing our data pipeline will connect the dots regarding how an end-to-end ML project works. This chapter will explore how to design and implement an **Extract, Transform, Load** (**ETL**) pipeline that crawls multiple social platforms, such as Medium, Substack, or GitHub, and aggregates the gathered data into a MongoDB data warehouse. We will show you how to implement various crawling methods, standardize the data, and load it into a data warehouse.

We will begin by designing the LLM Twin's data collection pipeline and explaining the architecture of the ETL pipeline. Afterward, we will move directly to implementing the pipeline, starting with ZenML, which will orchestrate the entire process. We will investigate the crawler implementation and understand how to implement a dispatcher layer that instantiates the right crawler class based on the domain of the provided link while following software best practices. Next, we will learn how to implement each crawler individually. Also, we will show you how to implement a data layer on top of MongoDB to structure all our documents and interact with the database.

Finally, we will explore how to run the data collection pipeline using ZenML and query the collected data from MongoDB.

Thus, in this chapter, we will study the following topics:

- Designing the LLM Twin's data collection pipeline
- Implementing the LLM Twin's data collection pipeline
- Gathering raw data into the data warehouse

By the end of this chapter, you will know how to design and implement an ETL pipeline to extract, transform, and load raw data ready to be ingested into the ML application.

Designing the LLM Twin's data collection pipeline

Before digging into the implementation, we must understand the LLM Twin's data collection ETL architecture, illustrated in *Figure 3.1*. We must explore what platforms we will crawl to extract data from and how we will design our data structures and processes. However, the first step is understanding how our data collection pipeline maps to an ETL process.

An ETL pipeline involves three fundamental steps:

1. We **extract** data from various sources. We will crawl data from platforms like Medium, Substack, and GitHub to gather raw data.
2. We **transform** this data by cleaning and standardizing it into a consistent format suitable for storage and analysis.
3. We **load** the transformed data into a data warehouse or database.

For our project, we use MongoDB as our NoSQL data warehouse. Although this is not a standard approach, we will explain the reasoning behind this choice shortly.

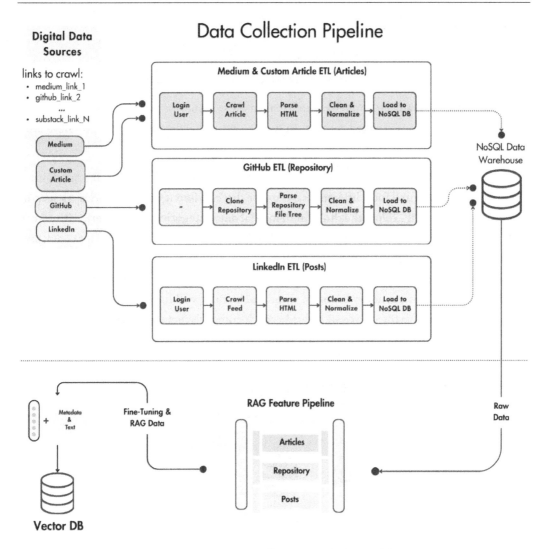

Figure 3.1: LLM Twin's data collection ETL pipeline architecture

We want to design an ETL pipeline that inputs a user and a list of links as input. Afterward, it crawls each link individually, standardizes the collected content, and saves it under that specific author in a MongoDB data warehouse.

Hence, the signature of the data collection pipeline will look as follows:

- **Input:** A list of links and their associated user (the author)
- **Output:** A list of raw documents stored in the NoSQL data warehouse

We will use user and author interchangeably, as in most scenarios across the ETL pipeline, a user is the author of the extracted content. However, within the data warehouse, we have only a user collection.

The ETL pipeline will detect the domain of each link, based on which it will call a specialized crawler. We implemented four different crawlers for three different data categories, as seen in *Figure 3.2*. First, we will explore the three fundamental data categories we will work with across the book. All our collected documents can be boiled down to an article, repository (or code), and post. It doesn't matter where the data comes from. We are primarily interested in the document's format. In most scenarios, we will have to process these data categories differently. Thus, we created a different domain entity for each, where each entity will have its class and collection in MongoDB. As we save the source URL within the document's metadata, we will still know its source and can reference it in our GenAI use cases.

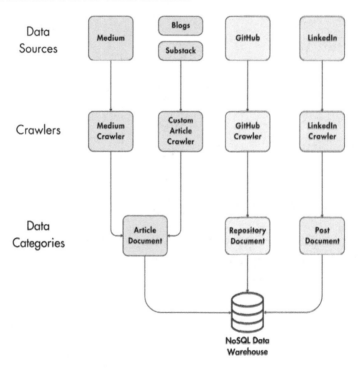

Figure 3.2: The relationship between the crawlers and the data categories

Our codebase supports four different crawlers:

- **Medium crawler:** Used to collect data from Medium. It outputs an article document. It logs in to Medium and crawls the HTML of the article's link. Then, it extracts, cleans, and normalizes the text from the HTML and loads the standardized text of the article into the NoSQL data warehouse.

- **Custom article crawler:** It performs similar steps to the Medium crawler but is a more generic implementation for collecting articles from various sites. Thus, as it doesn't implement any particularities of any platform, it doesn't perform the login step and blindly gathers all the HTML from a particular link. This is enough for articles freely available online, which you can find on Substack and people's blogs. We will use this crawler as a safety net when the link's domain isn't associated with the other supported crawlers. For example, when providing a Substack link, it will default to the custom article crawler, but when providing a Medium URL, it will use the Medium crawler.

- **GitHub crawler:** This collects data from GitHub. It outputs a repository document. It clones the repository, parses the repository file tree, cleans and normalizes the files, and loads them to the database.

- **LinkedIn crawler:** This is used to collect data from LinkedIn. It outputs multiple post documents. It logs in to LinkedIn, navigates to the user's feed, and crawls all the user's latest posts. For each post, it extracts its HTML, cleans and normalizes it, and loads it to MongoDB.

In the next section, we will examine each crawler's implementation in detail. For now, note that each crawler accesses a specific platform or site in a particular way and extracts HTML from it. Afterward, all the crawlers parse the HTML, extract the text from it, and clean and normalize it so it can be stored in the data warehouse under the same interface.

By reducing all the collected data to three data categories and not creating a new data category for every new data source, we can easily extend this architecture to multiple data sources with minimal effort. For example, if we want to start collecting data from X, we only have to implement a new crawler that outputs a post document, and that's it. The rest of the code will remain untouched. Otherwise, if we introduced the source dimension in the class and document structure, we would have to add code to all downstream layers to support any new data source. For example, we would have to implement a new document class for each new source and adapt the feature pipeline to support it.

For our proof of concept, crawling a few hundred documents is enough, but if we want to scale it to a real-world product, we would probably need more data sources to crawl from. LLMs are data-hungry. Thus, you need thousands of documents for ideal results instead of just a few hundred. But in many projects, it's an excellent strategy to implement an end-to-end project version that isn't the most accurate and iterate through it later. Thus, by using this architecture, you can easily add more data sources in future iterations to gather a larger dataset. More on LLM fine-tuning and dataset size will be covered in the next chapter.

How is the ETL process connected to the feature pipeline? The feature pipeline ingests the raw data from the MongoDB data warehouse, cleans it further, processes it into features, and stores it in the Qdrant vector DB to make it accessible for the LLM training and inference pipelines. *Chapter 4* provides more information on the feature pipeline. The ETL process is independent of the feature pipeline. The two pipelines communicate with each other strictly through the MongoDB data warehouse. Thus, the data collection pipeline can write data for MongoDB, and the feature pipeline can read from it independently and on different schedules.

Why did we use MongoDB as a data warehouse? Using a transactional database, such as MongoDB, as a data warehouse is uncommon. However, in our use case, we are working with small amounts of data, which MongoDB can handle. Even if we plan to compute statistics on top of our MongoDB collections, it will work fine at the scale of our LLM Twin's data (hundreds of documents). We picked MongoDB to store our raw data primarily because of the nature of our unstructured data: text crawled from the internet. By mainly working with unstructured text, selecting a NoSQL database that doesn't enforce a schema made our development easier and faster. Also, MongoDB is stable and easy to use. Their Python SDK is intuitive. They provide a Docker image that works out of the box locally and a cloud freemium tier that is perfect for proofs of concept, such as the LLM Twin. Thus, we can freely work with it locally and in the cloud. However, when working with big data (millions of documents or more), using a dedicated data warehouse such as Snowflake or BigQuery will be ideal.

Now that we've understood the architecture of the LLM Twin's data collection pipeline, let's move on to its implementation.

Implementing the LLM Twin's data collection pipeline

As we presented in *Chapter 2*, the entry point to each pipeline from our LLM Twin project is a ZenML pipeline, which can be configured at runtime through YAML files and run through the ZenML ecosystem. Thus, let's start by looking into the ZenML `digital_data_etl` pipeline. You'll notice that this is the same pipeline we used as an example in *Chapter 2* to illustrate ZenML. But this time, we will dig deeper into the implementation, explaining how the data collection works behind the scenes. After understanding how the pipeline works, we will explore the implementation of each crawler used to collect data from various sites and the MongoDB documents used to store and query data from the data warehouse.

ZenML pipeline and steps

In the code snippet below, we can see the implementation of the ZenML `digital_data_etl` pipeline, which inputs the user's full name and a list of links that will be crawled under that user (considered the author of the content extracted from those links). Within the function, we call two steps. In the first one, we look up the user in the database based on its full name. Then, we loop through all the links and crawl each independently. The pipeline's implementation is available in our repository at `pipelines/digital_data_etl.py`.

```python
from zenml import pipeline

from steps.etl import crawl_links, get_or_create_user


@pipeline
def digital_data_etl(user_full_name: str, links: list[str]) -> str:
    user = get_or_create_user(user_full_name)
    last_step = crawl_links(user=user, links=links)

    return last_step.invocation_id
```

Figure 3.3 shows a run of the digital_data_etl pipeline on the ZenML dashboard. The next phase is to explore the get_or_create_user and crawl_links ZenML steps individually. The step implementation is available in our repository at steps/etl.

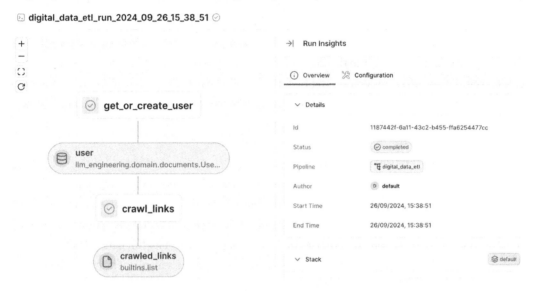

Figure 3.3: Example of a digital_data_etl pipeline run from ZenML's dashboard

We will start with the get_or_create_user ZenML step. We begin by importing the necessary modules and functions used throughout the script.

```
from loguru import logger
from typing_extensions import Annotated
from zenml import get_step_context, step


from llm_engineering.application import utils
from llm_engineering.domain.documents import UserDocument
```

Next, we define the function's signature, which takes a user's full name as input and retrieves an existing user or creates a new one in the MongoDB database if it doesn't exist:

```
@step
def get_or_create_user(user_full_name: str) -> Annotated[UserDocument,
    "user"]:
```

Using a utility function, we split the full name into first and last names. Then, we attempt to retrieve the user from the database or create a new one if it doesn't exist. We also retrieve the current step context and add metadata about the user to the output, which will be reflected in the metadata of the user ZenML output artifact:

```
logger.info(f"Getting or creating user: {user_full_name}")

first_name, last_name = utils.split_user_full_name(user_full_name)

user = UserDocument.get_or_create(first_name=first_name, last_
name=last_name)

step_context = get_step_context()
step_context.add_output_metadata(output_name="user", metadata=_get_
metadata(user_full_name, user))

return user
```

Additionally, we define a helper function called _get_metadata(), which builds a dictionary containing the query parameters and the retrieved user information, which will be added as metadata to the user artifact:

```
def _get_metadata(user_full_name: str, user: UserDocument) -> dict:
    return {
        "query": {
            "user_full_name": user_full_name,
        },
        "retrieved": {
            "user_id": str(user.id),
            "first_name": user.first_name,
            "last_name": user.last_name,
        },
    }
```

We will move on to the crawl_links ZenML step, which collects the data from the provided links. The code begins by importing essential modules and libraries for web crawling:

```
from urllib.parse import urlparse

from loguru import logger
```

```
from tqdm import tqdm
from typing_extensions import Annotated
from zenml import get_step_context, step

from llm_engineering.application.crawlers.dispatcher import
CrawlerDispatcher
from llm_engineering.domain.documents import UserDocument
```

Following the imports, the main function inputs a list of links written by a specific author. Within this function, a crawler dispatcher is initialized and configured to handle specific domains such as LinkedIn, Medium, and GitHub:

```
@step
def crawl_links(user: UserDocument, links: list[str]) ->
Annotated[list[str], "crawled_links"]:
    dispatcher = CrawlerDispatcher.build().register_linkedin().register_
medium().register_github()

    logger.info(f"Starting to crawl {len(links)} link(s).")
```

The function initializes variables to store the output metadata and count successful crawls. It then iterates over each link. It attempts to crawl and extract data for each link, updating the count of successful crawls and accumulating metadata about each URL:

```
    metadata = {}
    successfull_crawls = 0
    for link in tqdm(links):
        successfull_crawl, crawled_domain = _crawl_link(dispatcher, link,
user)
        successfull_crawls += successfull_crawl

        metadata = _add_to_metadata(metadata, crawled_domain, successfull_
crawl)
```

After processing all links, the function attaches the accumulated metadata to the output artifact:

```
    step_context = get_step_context()
    step_context.add_output_metadata(output_name="crawled_links",
metadata=metadata)

    logger.info(f"Successfully crawled {successfull_crawls} / {len(links)}
```

```
links.")

    return links
```

The code includes a helper function that attempts to extract information from each link using the appropriate crawler based on the link's domain. It handles any exceptions that may occur during extraction and returns a tuple indicating the crawl's success and the link's domain:

```python
def _crawl_link(dispatcher: CrawlerDispatcher, link: str, user:
UserDocument) -> tuple[bool, str]:
    crawler = dispatcher.get_crawler(link)
    crawler_domain = urlparse(link).netloc

    try:
        crawler.extract(link=link, user=user)

        return (True, crawler_domain)
    except Exception as e:
        logger.error(f"An error occurred while crawling: {e!s}")

        return (False, crawler_domain)
```

Another helper function is provided to update the metadata dictionary with the results of each crawl:

```python
def _add_to_metadata(metadata: dict, domain: str, successfull_crawl: bool)
-> dict:
    if domain not in metadata:
        metadata[domain] = {}
    metadata[domain]["successful"] = metadata.get(domain, {}).
get("successful", 0) + successfull_crawl
    metadata[domain]["total"] = metadata.get(domain, {}).get("total", 0) +
1

    return metadata
```

As seen in the abovementioned _crawl_link() function, the CrawlerDispatcher class knows what crawler to initialize based on each link's domain. The logic is then abstracted away under the crawler's extract() method. Let's zoom in on the CrawlerDispatcher class to understand how this works fully.

The dispatcher: How do you instantiate the right crawler?

The entry point to our crawling logic is the CrawlerDispatcher class. As illustrated in *Figure 3.4*, the dispatcher acts as the intermediate layer between the provided links and the crawlers. It knows what crawler to associate with each URL.

The CrawlerDispatcher class knows how to extract the domain of each link and initialize the proper crawler that collects the data from that site. For example, if it detects the https://medium.com domain when providing a link to an article, it will build an instance of the MediumCrawler used to crawl that particular platform. With that in mind, let's explore the implementation of the CrawlerDispatcher class.

 All the crawling logic is available in the GitHub repository at llm_engineering/application/crawlers.

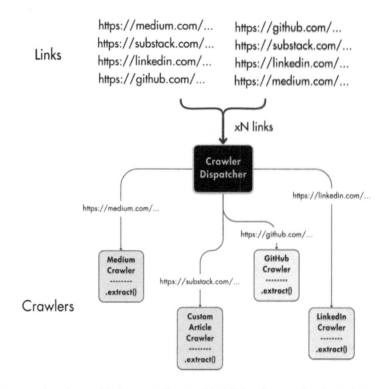

Figure 3.4: The relationship between the provided links, the CrawlerDispatcher, and the crawlers

We begin by importing the necessary Python modules for URL handling and regex, along with importing our crawler classes:

```python
import re
from urllib.parse import urlparse

from loguru import logger

from .base import BaseCrawler
from .custom_article import CustomArticleCrawler
from .github import GithubCrawler
from .linkedin import LinkedInCrawler
from .medium import MediumCrawler
```

The CrawlerDispatcher class is defined to manage and dispatch appropriate crawler instances based on given URLs and their domains. Its constructor initializes a registry to store the registered crawlers.

```python
class CrawlerDispatcher:
    def __init__(self) -> None:
        self._crawlers = {}
```

As we are using the builder creational pattern to instantiate and configure the dispatcher, we define a build() class method that returns an instance of the dispatcher:

```python
    @classmethod
    def build(cls) -> "CrawlerDispatcher":
        dispatcher = cls()

        return dispatcher
```

The dispatcher includes methods to register crawlers for specific platforms like Medium, LinkedIn, and GitHub. These methods use a generic register() method under the hood to add each crawler to the registry. By returning self, we follow the builder creational pattern (more on the builder pattern: https://refactoring.guru/design-patterns/builder). We can chain multiple register_*() methods when instantiating the dispatcher as follows: CrawlerDispatcher.build().register_linkedin().register_medium().

```python
    def register_medium(self) -> "CrawlerDispatcher":
        self.register("https://medium.com", MediumCrawler)
```

```
        return self

    def register_linkedin(self) -> "CrawlerDispatcher":
        self.register("https://linkedin.com", LinkedInCrawler)

        return self

    def register_github(self) -> "CrawlerDispatcher":
        self.register("https://github.com", GithubCrawler)

        return self
```

The generic register() method normalizes each domain to ensure its format is consistent before it's added as a key to the self._crawlers registry of the dispatcher. This is a critical step, as we will use the key of the dictionary as the domain pattern to match future links with a crawler:

```
    def register(self, domain: str, crawler: type[BaseCrawler]) -> None:
        parsed_domain = urlparse(domain)
        domain = parsed_domain.netloc

        self._crawlers[r"https://(www\.)?{}/*".format(re.escape(domain))]
 = crawler
```

Finally, the get_crawler() method determines the appropriate crawler for a given URL by matching it against the registered domains. If no match is found, it logs a warning and defaults to using the CustomArticleCrawler.

```
    def get_crawler(self, url: str) -> BaseCrawler:
        for pattern, crawler in self._crawlers.items():
            if re.match(pattern, url):
                return crawler()
        else:
            logger.warning(f"No crawler found for {url}. Defaulting to
 CustomArticleCrawler.")

            return CustomArticleCrawler()
```

The next step in understanding how the data collection pipeline works is analyzing each crawler individually.

The crawlers

Before exploring each crawler's implementation, we must present their base class, which defines a unified interface for all the crawlers. As shown in *Figure 3.4*, we can implement the dispatcher layer because each crawler follows the same signature. Each class implements the extract() method, allowing us to leverage OOP techniques such as polymorphism, where we can work with abstract objects without knowing their concrete subclass. For example, in the _crawl_link() function from the ZenML steps, we had the following code:

```
crawler = dispatcher.get_crawler(link)
crawler.extract(link=link, user=user)
```

Note how we called the extract() method without caring about what specific type of crawler we instantiated. To conclude, working with abstract interfaces ensures core reusability and ease of extension.

Base classes

Now, let's explore the BaseCrawler interface, which can be found in the repository at https://github.com/PacktPublishing/LLM-Engineers-Handbook/blob/main/llm_engineering/application/crawlers/base.py.

```
from abc import ABC, abstractmethod

class BaseCrawler(ABC):
    model: type[NoSQLBaseDocument]

    @abstractmethod
    def extract(self, link: str, **kwargs) -> None: ...
```

As mentioned above, the interface defines an extract() method that takes as input a link. Also, it defines a model attribute at the class level that represents the data category document type used to save the extracted data into the MongoDB data warehouse. Doing so allows us to customize each subclass with different data categories while preserving the same attributes at the class level. We will soon explore the NoSQLBaseDocument class when digging into the document entities.

We also extend the BaseCrawler class with a BaseSeleniumCrawler class, which implements reusable functionality that uses Selenium to crawl various sites, such as Medium or LinkedIn. **Selenium** is a tool for automating web browsers. It's used to interact with web pages programmatically (like logging into LinkedIn, navigating through profiles, etc.).

Selenium can programmatically control various browsers such as Chrome, Firefox, or Brave. For these specific platforms, we need Selenium to manipulate the browser programmatically to log in and scroll through the newsfeed or article before being able to extract the entire HTML. For other sites, where we don't have to go through the login step or can directly load the whole page, we can extract the HTML from a particular URL using more straightforward methods than Selenium.

 For the Selenium-based crawlers to work, you must install Chrome on your machine (or a Chromium-based browser such as Brave).

The code begins by setting up the necessary imports and configurations for web crawling using Selenium and the ChromeDriver initializer. The chromedriver_autoinstaller ensures that the appropriate version of ChromeDriver is installed and added to the system path, maintaining compatibility with the installed version of your Google Chrome browser (or other Chromium-based browser). Selenium will use the ChromeDriver to communicate with the browser and open a headless session, where we can programmatically manipulate the browser to access various URLs, click on specific elements, such as buttons, or scroll through the newsfeed. Using the chromedriver_autoinstaller, we ensure we always have the correct ChromeDriver version installed that matches our machine's Chrome browser version.

```python
import time
from tempfile import mkdtemp

import chromedriver_autoinstaller
from selenium import webdriver
from selenium.webdriver.chrome.options import Options

from llm_engineering.domain.documents import NoSQLBaseDocument

# Check if the current version of chromedriver exists
# and if it doesn't exist, download it automatically,
# then add chromedriver to path
chromedriver_autoinstaller.install()
```

Next, we define the BaseSeleniumCrawler class for use cases where we need Selenium to collect the data, such as collecting data from Medium or LinkedIn.

Its constructor initializes various Chrome options to optimize performance, enhance security, and ensure a headless browsing environment. These options disable unnecessary features like GPU rendering, extensions, and notifications, which can interfere with automated browsing. These are standard configurations when crawling in headless mode:

```python
class BaseSeleniumCrawler(BaseCrawler, ABC):
    def __init__(self, scroll_limit: int = 5) -> None:
        options = webdriver.ChromeOptions()

        options.add_argument("--no-sandbox")
        options.add_argument("--headless=new")
        options.add_argument("--disable-dev-shm-usage")
        options.add_argument("--log-level=3")
        options.add_argument("--disable-popup-blocking")
        options.add_argument("--disable-notifications")
        options.add_argument("--disable-extensions")
        options.add_argument("--disable-background-networking")
        options.add_argument("--ignore-certificate-errors")
        options.add_argument(f"--user-data-dir={mkdtemp()}")
        options.add_argument(f"--data-path={mkdtemp()}")
        options.add_argument(f"--disk-cache-dir={mkdtemp()}")
        options.add_argument("--remote-debugging-port=9226")
```

After configuring the Chrome options, the code allows subclasses to set any additional driver options by calling the set_extra_driver_options() method. It then initializes the scroll limit and creates a new instance of the Chrome driver with the specified options:

```python
        self.set_extra_driver_options(options)

        self.scroll_limit = scroll_limit
        self.driver = webdriver.Chrome(
            options=options,
        )
```

The BaseSeleniumCrawler class includes placeholder methods for set_extra_driver_options() and login(), which subclasses can override to provide specific functionality. This ensures modularity, as every platform has a different login page with a different HTML structure:

```python
    def set_extra_driver_options(self, options: Options) -> None:
```

```
        pass

    def login(self) -> None:
        pass
```

Finally, the `scroll_page()` method implements a scrolling mechanism to navigate through pages, such as LinkedIn, up to a specified scroll limit. It scrolls to the bottom of the page, waits for new content to load, and repeats the process until it reaches the end of the page or the scroll limit is exceeded. This method is essential for feeds where the content appears as the user scrolls:

```
    def scroll_page(self) -> None:
        """Scroll through the LinkedIn page based on the scroll limit."""
        current_scroll = 0
        last_height = self.driver.execute_script("return document.body.
scrollHeight")
        while True:
            self.driver.execute_script("window.scrollTo(0, document.body.
scrollHeight);")
            time.sleep(5)
            new_height = self.driver.execute_script("return document.body.
scrollHeight")
            if new_height == last_height or (self.scroll_limit and
current_scroll >= self.scroll_limit):
                break
            last_height = new_height
            current_scroll += 1
```

We've understood what the base classes of our crawlers look like. Next, we will look into the implementation of the following specific crawlers:

- `GitHubCrawler(BaseCrawler)`
- `CustomArticleCrawler(BaseCrawler)`
- `MediumCrawler(BaseSeleniumCrawler)`

 You can find the implementation of the above crawlers in the GitHub repository at https://github.com/PacktPublishing/LLM-Engineers-Handbook/tree/main/llm_engineering/application/crawlers.

GitHubCrawler class

The GithubCrawler class is designed to scrape GitHub repositories, extending the functionality of the BaseCrawler. We don't have to log in to GitHub through the browser, as we can leverage Git's clone functionality. Thus, we don't have to leverage any Selenium functionality. Upon initialization, it sets up a list of patterns to ignore standard files and directories found in GitHub repositories, such as .git, .toml, .lock, and .png, ensuring that unnecessary files are excluded from the scraping process:

```
class GithubCrawler(BaseCrawler):
    model = RepositoryDocument

    def __init__(self, ignore=(".git", ".toml", ".lock", ".png")) -> None:
        super().__init__()
        self._ignore = ignore
```

Next, we implement the extract() method, where the crawler first checks if the repository has already been processed and stored in the database. If it exists, it exits the method to prevent storing duplicates:

```
def extract(self, link: str, **kwargs) -> None:
    old_model = self.model.find(link=link)
    if old_model is not None:
        logger.info(f"Repository already exists in the database: {link}")

        return
```

If the repository is new, the crawler extracts the repository name from the link. Then, it creates a temporary directory to clone the repository to ensure that the cloned repository is cleaned up from the local disk after it's processed:

```
    logger.info(f"Starting scrapping GitHub repository: {link}")

    repo_name = link.rstrip("/").split("/")[-1]

    local_temp = tempfile.mkdtemp()
```

Within a try block, the crawler changes the current working directory to the temporary directory and executes the git clone command in a different process:

```
    try:
```

```
        os.chdir(local_temp)
        subprocess.run(["git", "clone", link])
```

After successfully cloning the repository, the crawler constructs the path to the cloned repository. It initializes an empty dictionary used to aggregate the content of the files in a standardized way. It walks through the directory tree, skipping over any directories or files that match the ignore patterns. For each relevant file, it reads the content, removes any spaces, and stores it in the dictionary with the file path as the key:

```
        repo_path = os.path.join(local_temp, os.listdir(local_temp)[0])  #
        tree = {}
        for root, _, files in os.walk(repo_path):
            dir = root.replace(repo_path, "").lstrip("/")
            if dir.startswith(self._ignore):
                continue

            for file in files:
                if file.endswith(self._ignore):
                    continue
                file_path = os.path.join(dir, file)
                with open(os.path.join(root, file), "r", errors="ignore")
    as f:
                    tree[file_path] = f.read().replace(" ", "")
```

It then creates a new instance of the `RepositoryDocument` model, populating it with the repository content, name, link, platform information, and author details. The instance is then saved to MongoDB:

```
        user = kwargs["user"]
        instance = self.model(
            content=tree,
            name=repo_name,
            link=link,
            platform="github",
            author_id=user.id,
            author_full_name=user.full_name,
        )
        instance.save()
```

Finally, whether the scraping succeeds or an exception occurs, the crawler ensures that the temporary directory is removed to clean up any resources used during the process:

```
except Exception:
    raise
finally:
    shutil.rmtree(local_temp)


logger.info(f"Finished scrapping GitHub repository: {link}")
```

CustomArticleCrawler class

The CustomArticleCrawler class takes a different approach to collecting data from the internet. It leverages the AsyncHtmlLoader class to read the entire HTML from a link and the Html2TextTransformer class to extract the text from that HTML. Both classes are made available by the langchain_community Python package, as seen below, where we import all the necessary Python modules:

```
from urllib.parse import urlparse

from langchain_community.document_loaders import AsyncHtmlLoader
from langchain_community.document_transformers.html2text import
Html2TextTransformer
from loguru import logger

from llm_engineering.domain.documents import ArticleDocument

from .base import BaseCrawler
```

Next, we define the CustomArticleCrawler class, which inherits from BaseCrawler. As before, we don't need to log in or use the scrolling functionality provided by Selenium. In the extract method, we first check if the article exists in the database to avoid duplicating content:

```
class CustomArticleCrawler(BaseCrawler):
    model = ArticleDocument

    def extract(self, link: str, **kwargs) -> None:
        old_model = self.model.find(link=link)
        if old_model is not None:
```

```
        logger.info(f"Article already exists in the database: {link}")

        return
```

If the article doesn't exist, we proceed to scrape it. We use the `AsyncHtmlLoader` class to load the HTML from the provided link. After, we transform it into plain text using the `Html2TextTransformer` class, which returns a list of documents. We are only interested in the first document. As we delegate the whole logic to these two classes, we don't control how the content is extracted and parsed. That's why we used this class as a fallback system for domains where we don't have anything custom implemented. These two classes follow the LangChain paradigm, which provides high-level functionality that works decently in most scenarios. It is fast to implement but hard to customize. That is one of the reasons why many developers avoid using LangChain in production use cases:

```
        logger.info(f"Starting scrapping article: {link}")

        loader = AsyncHtmlLoader([link])
        docs = loader.load()

        html2text = Html2TextTransformer()
        docs_transformed = html2text.transform_documents(docs)
        doc_transformed = docs_transformed[0]
```

We get the page content from the extracted document, plus relevant metadata such as the `title`, `subtitle`, `content`, and `language`:

```
        content = {
            "Title": doc_transformed.metadata.get("title"),
            "Subtitle": doc_transformed.metadata.get("description"),
            "Content": doc_transformed.page_content,
            "language": doc_transformed.metadata.get("language"),
        }
```

Next, we parse the URL to determine the platform (or domain) from which the article was scraped:

```
        parsed_url = urlparse(link)
        platform = parsed_url.netloc
```

We then create a new instance of the article model, populating it with the extracted content. Finally, we save this instance to the MongoDB data warehouse:

```
        user = kwargs["user"]
```

```
        instance = self.model(
            content=content,
            link=link,
            platform=platform,
            author_id=user.id,
            author_full_name=user.full_name,
        )
        instance.save()

        logger.info(f"Finished scrapping custom article: {link}")
```

So far, we have seen how to crawl GitHub repositories and random sites using LangChain utility functions. Lastly, we must explore a crawler using Selenium to manipulate the browser programmatically. Thus, we will continue with the MediumCrawler implementation.

MediumCrawler class

The code begins by importing essential libraries and defining the MediumCrawler class, which inherits from BaseSeleniumCrawler:

```
from bs4 import BeautifulSoup
from loguru import logger

from llm_engineering.domain.documents import ArticleDocument

from .base import BaseSeleniumCrawler


class MediumCrawler(BaseSeleniumCrawler):
    model = ArticleDocument
```

Within the MediumCrawler class, we leverage the set_extra_driver_options() method to extend the default driver options used by Selenium:

```
    def set_extra_driver_options(self, options) -> None:
        options.add_argument(r"--profile-directory=Profile 2")
```

The extract() method implements the core functionality, first checking whether the article exists in the database to prevent duplicate entries.

If the article is new, the method proceeds to navigate to the article's link and scroll through the page to ensure all content is loaded:

```python
def extract(self, link: str, **kwargs) -> None:
    old_model = self.model.find(link=link)
    if old_model is not None:
        logger.info(f"Article already exists in the database: {link}")

        return

    logger.info(f"Starting scrapping Medium article: {link}")

    self.driver.get(link)
    self.scroll_page()
```

After fully loading the page, the method uses BeautifulSoup to parse the HTML content and extract the article's title, subtitle, and full text. BeautifulSoup is a popular Python library for web scraping and parsing HTML or XML documents. Thus, we used it to extract all the HTML elements we needed from the HTML accessed with Selenium. Finally, we aggregate everything into a dictionary:

```python
soup = BeautifulSoup(self.driver.page_source, "html.parser")
title = soup.find_all("h1", class_="pw-post-title")
subtitle = soup.find_all("h2", class_="pw-subtitle-paragraph")

data = {
    "Title": title[0].string if title else None,
    "Subtitle": subtitle[0].string if subtitle else None,
    "Content": soup.get_text(),
}
```

Finally, the method closes the WebDriver to free up resources. It then creates a new ArticleDocument instance, populates it with the extracted content and user information provided via kwargs, and saves it to the database:

```python
self.driver.close()

user = kwargs["user"]
instance = self.model(
```

```
                platform="medium",
                content=data,
                link=link,
                author_id=user.id,
                author_full_name=user.full_name,
        )
        instance.save()

        logger.info(f"Successfully scraped and saved article: {link}")
```

With that, we conclude the `MediumCrawler` implementation. The LinkedIn crawler follows a similar pattern to the Medium one, where it uses Selenium to log in and access the feed of a user's latest posts. Then, it extracts the posts and scrolls through the feed to load the next page until a limit is hit. You can check the full implementation in our repository at `https://github.com/PacktPublishing/LLM-Engineers-Handbook/blob/main/llm_engineering/application/crawlers/linkedin.py`.

With the rise of LLMs, collecting data from the internet has become a critical step in many real-world AI applications. Hence, more high-level tools have appeared in the Python ecosystem, such as Scrapy (`https://github.com/scrapy/scrapy`), which crawls websites and extracts structured data from their pages, and Crawl4AI (`https://github.com/unclecode/crawl4ai`), which is highly specialized in crawling data for LLMs and AI applications.

In this section, we've looked at implementing three types of crawlers: one that leverages the `git` executable in a subprocess to clone GitHub repositories, one that uses LangChain utilities to extract the HTML of a single web page, and one that leverages Selenium for more complex scenarios where we have to navigate through the login page, scroll the article to load the entire HTML, and extract it into text format. The last step is understanding how the document classes we've used across the chapter, such as the `ArticleDocument`, work.

The NoSQL data warehouse documents

We had to implement three document classes to structure our data categories. These classes define the specific attributes we require for a document, such as the content, author, and source link. It is best practice to structure your data in classes instead of dictionaries, as the attributes we expect for each item are more verbose, reducing run errors. For example, when accessing a value from a Python dictionary, we can never be sure it is present or its type is current. By wrapping our data items with classes, we can ensure each attribute is as expected.

By leveraging Python packages such as Pydantic, we have out-of-the-box type validation, which ensures consistency in our datasets. Thus, we modeled the data categories as the following document classes, which we already used in the code up until point:

- `ArticleDocument` class
- `PostDocument` class
- `RepositoryDocument` class

These are not simple Python data classes or Pydantic models. They support read and write operations on top of the MongoDB data warehouse. To inject the read-and-write functionality into all the document classes without repeating any code, we used the **Object-Document Mapping (ODM)** software pattern, which is based on the **object-relational mapping (ORM)** pattern. Thus, let's first explore ORM, then move to ODM, and, finally, dig into our custom ODM implementation and document classes.

The ORM and ODM software patterns

Before we talk about software patterns, let's see what ORM is. It's a technique that lets you query and manipulate data from a database using an object-oriented paradigm. Instead of writing SQL or API-specific queries, you encapsulate all the complexity under an ORM class that knows how to handle all the database operations, most commonly CRUD operations. Thus, working with ORM removes the need to handle the database operations manually and reduces the need to write boilerplate code manually. An ORM interacts with a SQL database, such as PostgreSQL or MySQL.

Most modern Python applications use ORMs when interacting with the database. Even though SQL is still a popular choice in the data world, you rarely see raw SQL queries in Python backend components. The most popular Python ORM is SQLAlchemy (https://www.sqlalchemy.org/). Also, with the rise of FastAPI, SQLModel is (https://github.com/fastapi/sqlmodel) a common choice, which is a wrapper over SQLAlchemy that makes the integration easier with FastAPI.

For example, using SQLAlchemy, we defined a `User` ORM with the ID and name fields. The `User` ORM is mapped to the `users` table within the SQL database. Thus, when we create a new user and commit it to the database, it is automatically saved to the `users` table. The same applies to all the CRUD operations on top of the `User` class.

```
from sqlalchemy import Column, Integer, String, create_engine
from sqlalchemy.orm import declarative_base, sessionmaker

Base = declarative_base()
```

```
# Define a class that maps to the users table.
  class User(Base):
    __tablename__ = "users"

    id = Column(Integer, primary_key=True)
    name = Column(String)
```

Using the User ORM, we can quickly insert or query users directly from Python without writing a line of SQL. Note that an ORM usually supports all **CRUD** operations. Here is a code snippet that shows how to save an instance of the User ORM to a SQLite database:

```
engine = create_engine("sqlite:///:memory:")
Base.metadata.create_all(engine)

# Create a session used to interact with the database.
Session = sessionmaker(bind=engine)
session = Session()

# Add a new user.
new_user = User(name="Alice")
session.add(new_user)
session.commit()
```

Also, this is how we can query a user from the users SQLite table:

```
user = session.query(User).first()
if user:
print(f"User ID: {user.id}")
print(f"User name: {user.name}")
```

 Find the entire script and how to run it in the GitHub repository at code_snippets/03_ orm.py.

The ODM pattern is extremely similar to ORM, but instead of working with SQL databases and tables, it works with NoSQL databases (such as MongoDB) and unstructured collections. As we work with NoSQL databases, the data structure is centered on collections, which store JSON-like documents rather than rows in tables.

To conclude, ODM simplifies working with document-based NoSQL databases and maps object-oriented code to JSON-like documents. We will implement a light ODM module on top of MongoDB to fully understand how ODM works.

Implementing the ODM class

This section will explore how to implement an ODM class from scratch. This is an excellent exercise to learn how ODM works and sharpen our skills in writing modular and reusable Python classes. Hence, we will implement a base ODM class called NoSQLBaseDocument, from which all the other documents will inherit to interact with the MongoDB data warehouse.

 The class can be found in our repository at llm_engineering/domain/base/nosql. py.

The code starts by importing essential modules and setting up the database connection. Through the _database variable, we establish a connection to the database specified in the settings, which is by default called twin:

```
import uuid
from abc import ABC
from typing import Generic, Type, TypeVar

from loguru import logger
from pydantic import UUID4, BaseModel, Field
from pymongo import errors

from llm_engineering.domain.exceptions import ImproperlyConfigured
from llm_engineering.infrastructure.db.mongo import connection
from llm_engineering.settings import settings


_database = connection.get_database(settings.DATABASE_NAME)
```

Next, we define a type variable T bound to the NoSQLBaseDocument class. The variable leverages Python's generic module, allowing us to generalize the class's types. For example, when we implement the ArticleDocument class, which will inherit from the NoSQLBaseDocument class, all the instances where T was used will be replaced with the ArticleDocument type when analyzing the signature of functions (more on Python generics: https://realpython.com/python312-typing).

The NoSQLBaseDocument class is then declared as an abstract base class inheriting from Pydantic's BaseModel, Python's Generic (which provides the functionality described earlier), and ABC (making the class abstract) classes. This class serves as the foundational ODM class:

```python
T = TypeVar("T", bound="NoSQLBaseDocument")


class NoSQLBaseDocument(BaseModel, Generic[T], ABC):
```

Within the NoSQLBaseDocument class, an id field is defined as a UUID4, with a default factory generating a unique UUID. The class also implements the __eq__ and __hash__ methods to allow instances to be compared and used in hashed collections like sets or as dictionary keys based on their unique id attribute:

```python
id: UUID4 = Field(default_factory=uuid.uuid4)


def __eq__(self, value: object) -> bool:
    if not isinstance(value, self.__class__):
        return False

    return self.id == value.id


def __hash__(self) -> int:
    return hash(self.id)
```

The class provides methods for converting between MongoDB documents and class instances. The from_mongo() class method transforms a dictionary retrieved from MongoDB into an instance of the class. The to_mongo() instance method converts the model instance into a dictionary suitable for MongoDB insertion:

```python
@classmethod
def from_mongo(cls: Type[T], data: dict) -> T:
    if not data:
        raise ValueError("Data is empty.")

    id = data.pop("_id")

    return cls(**dict(data, id=id))


def to_mongo(self: T, **kwargs) -> dict:
```

```
        exclude_unset = kwargs.pop("exclude_unset", False)
        by_alias = kwargs.pop("by_alias", True)

        parsed = self.model_dump(exclude_unset=exclude_unset, by_alias=by_
    alias, **kwargs)

        if "_id" not in parsed and "id" in parsed:
            parsed["_id"] = str(parsed.pop("id"))

        for key, value in parsed.items():
            if isinstance(value, uuid.UUID):
                parsed[key] = str(value)

        return parsed
```

The save() method allows an instance of the model to be inserted into a MongoDB collection. It retrieves the appropriate collection, converts the instance into a MongoDB-compatible document leveraging the to_mongo() method described above, and attempts to insert it into the database, handling any write errors that may occur:

```
def save(self: T, **kwargs) -> T | None:
    collection = _database[self.get_collection_name()]
    try:
        collection.insert_one(self.to_mongo(**kwargs))

        return self
    except errors.WriteError:
        logger.exception("Failed to insert document.")

        return None
```

The get_or_create() class method attempts to find a document in the database matching the provided filter options. If a matching document is found, it is converted into an instance of the class. If not, a new instance is created with the filter options as its initial data and saved to the database:

```
@classmethod
def get_or_create(cls: Type[T], **filter_options) -> T:
    collection = _database[cls.get_collection_name()]
    try:
```

```
            instance = collection.find_one(filter_options)
            if instance:
                return cls.from_mongo(instance)

            new_instance = cls(**filter_options)
            new_instance = new_instance.save()

            return new_instance
        except errors.OperationFailure:
            logger.exception(f"Failed to retrieve document with filter
    options: {filter_options}")

            raise
```

The bulk_insert() class method allows multiple documents to be inserted into the database at once:

```
@classmethod
def bulk_insert(cls: Type[T], documents: list[T], **kwargs) -> bool:
    collection = _database[cls.get_collection_name()]
    try:
        collection.insert_many([doc.to_mongo(**kwargs) for doc in
documents])

        return True
    except (errors.WriteError, errors.BulkWriteError):
        logger.error(f"Failed to insert documents of type {cls.__name__}")

        return False
```

The find() class method searches for a single document in the database that matches the given filter options:

```
@classmethod
def find(cls: Type[T], **filter_options) -> T | None:
    collection = _database[cls.get_collection_name()]
    try:
        instance = collection.find_one(filter_options)
```

```
        if instance:
            return cls.from_mongo(instance)

        return None
    except errors.OperationFailure:
        logger.error("Failed to retrieve document.")


        return None
```

Similarly, the bulk_find() class method retrieves multiple documents matching the filter options.
It converts each retrieved MongoDB document into a model instance, collecting them into a list:

```
@classmethod
def bulk_find(cls: Type[T], **filter_options) -> list[T]:
    collection = _database[cls.get_collection_name()]
    try:
        instances = collection.find(filter_options)
        return [document for instance in instances if (document := cls.
from_mongo(instance)) is not None]
    except errors.OperationFailure:
        logger.error("Failed to retrieve document.")


        return []
```

Finally, the get_collection_name() class method determines the name of the MongoDB collection associated with the class. It expects the class to have a nested Settings class with a name attribute specifying the collection name. If this configuration is missing, an ImproperlyConfigured
exception will be raised specifying that the subclass should define a nested Settings class:

```
@classmethod
def get_collection_name(cls: Type[T]) -> str:
    if not hasattr(cls, "Settings") or not hasattr(cls.Settings, "name"):
        raise ImproperlyConfigured(
            "Document should define an Settings configuration class with
the name of the collection."
        )


    return cls.Settings.name
```

We can configure each subclass using the nested Settings class, such as defining the collection name, or anything else specific to that subclass. Within the Python ecosystem, there is an ODM implementation on top of MongoDB, called mongoengine, which you can find on GitHub. It follows a pattern similar to ours but more comprehensive. We implemented it by ourselves, as it was an excellent exercise to practice writing modular and generic code following best OOP principles, which are essential for implementing production-level code.

Data categories and user document classes

The last piece of the puzzle is to see the implementation of the subclasses that inherit from the NoSQLBaseDocument base class. These are the concrete classes that define our data categories. You've seen these classes used across the chapter when working with articles, repositories, and posts within the crawler classes.

We begin by importing the essential Python modules and the ODM base class:

```python
from abc import ABC
from typing import Optional

from pydantic import UUID4, Field

from .base import NoSQLBaseDocument
from .types import DataCategory
```

We define an enum class, where we centralize all our data category types. These variables will act as constants in configuring all our ODM classes throughout the book.

 The class can be found in the repository at llm_engineering/domain/types.py.

```python
from enum import StrEnum


class DataCategory(StrEnum):
    PROMPT = "prompt"
    QUERIES = "queries"

    INSTRUCT_DATASET_SAMPLES = "instruct_dataset_samples"
```

```
    INSTRUCT_DATASET = "instruct_dataset"
    PREFERENCE_DATASET_SAMPLES = "preference_dataset_samples"
    PREFERENCE_DATASET = "preference_dataset"


    POSTS = "posts"
    ARTICLES = "articles"
    REPOSITORIES = "repositories"
```

The Document class is introduced as an abstract base model for other documents on top of the NoSQLBaseDocument ODM class. It includes common attributes like content, platform, and author details, providing a standardized structure for documents that will inherit from it:

```
class Document(NoSQLBaseDocument, ABC):
    content: dict
    platform: str
    author_id: UUID4 = Field(alias="author_id")
    author_full_name: str = Field(alias="author_full_name")
```

Finally, specific document types are defined by extending the Document class. The RepositoryDocument, PostDocument, and ArticleDocument classes represent different categories of data, each with unique fields and settings that specify their respective collection names in the database:

```
class RepositoryDocument(Document):
    name: str
    link: str

    class Settings:
        name = DataCategory.REPOSITORIES


class PostDocument(Document):
    image: Optional[str] = None
    link: str | None = None

    class Settings:
        name = DataCategory.POSTS
```

```python
class ArticleDocument(Document):
    link: str

    class Settings:
        name = DataCategory.ARTICLES
```

Finally, we define the `UserDocument` class, which is used to store and query all the users from the LLM Twin project:

```python
class UserDocument(NoSQLBaseDocument):
    first_name: str
    last_name: str

    class Settings:
        name = "users"

    @property
    def full_name(self):
        return f"{self.first_name} {self.last_name}"
```

By implementing the `NoSQLBaseDocument` ODM class, we had to focus solely on the fields and specific functionality of each document or domain entity. All the CRUD functionality is delegated to the parent class. Also, by leveraging Pydantic to define the fields, we have out-of-the-box type validation. For example, when creating an instance of the `ArticleDocument` class, if the provided link is `None` or not a string, it will throw an error signaling that the data is invalid.

With that, we've finished implementing our data collection pipeline, starting with the ZenML components. Then, we looked into the implementation of the crawlers and, finally, wrapped it up with the ODM class and data category documents. The last step is to run the data collection pipeline and ingest raw data into the MongoDB data warehouse.

Gathering raw data into the data warehouse

ZenML orchestrates the data collection pipeline. Thus, leveraging ZenML, the data collection pipeline can be run manually, scheduled, or triggered by specific events. Here, we will show you how to run it manually, while we will discuss the other scenarios in *Chapter 11* when digging deeper into MLOps.

We configured a different pipeline run for each author. We provided a ZenML configuration file for Paul Iusztin's or Maxime Labonne's data. To call the data collection pipeline to collect Maxime's data, for example, you can run the following CLI command:

```
poetry poe run-digital-data-etl-maxime
```

That will call the pipeline with the following ZenML YAML configuration file:

```
parameters:
  user_full_name: Maxime Labonne # [First Name(s)] [Last Name]
  links:
    # Personal Blog
    - https://mlabonne.github.io/blog/posts/2024-07-29_Finetune_Llama31.
html
    - https://mlabonne.github.io/blog/posts/2024-07-15_The_Rise_of_
Agentic_Data_Generation.html
    # Substack
    - https://maximelabonne.substack.com/p/uncensor-any-llm-with-
abliteration-d30148b7d43e
    - https://maximelabonne.substack.com/p/create-mixtures-of-experts-
with-mergekit-11b318c99562
    - https://maximelabonne.substack.com/p/merge-large-language-models-
with-mergekit-2118fb392b54
    … # More Substack Links
```

In *Figure 3.3* earlier, we saw the pipeline's run DAG and details in ZenML's dashboard. Meanwhile, *Figure 3.5* shows the user output artifact generated by this data collection pipeline. You can inspect the query user_full_name and the retrieved user from the MongoDB database, for which we collected the links in this specific run.

Figure 3.5: Example of the user output artifact after running the data collection pipeline using Maxime's configuration file

Also, in *Figure 3.6*, you can observe the crawled_links output artifact, which lists all the domains from which we collected data, the total number of links crawled for each domain, and the number of successfully collected links.

We want to highlight again the power of these artifacts, as they trace each pipeline's results and metadata, making it extremely easy to monitor and debug each pipeline run individually.

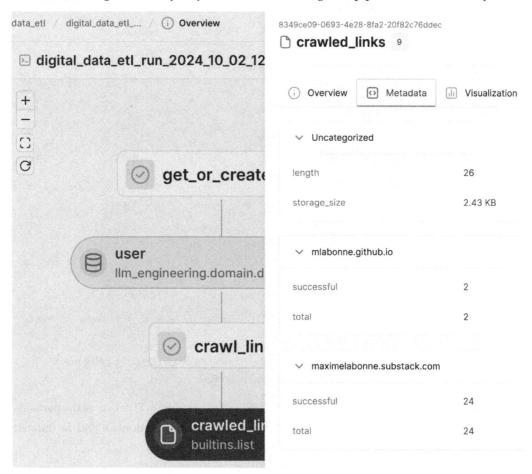

Figure 3.6: Example of the crawled_links output artifact after running the data collection pipeline using Maxime's configuration file

Now, we can download the `crawled_links` artifact anywhere in our code by running the following code, where the ID of the artifact can be found in ZenML and is unique for every artifact version:

```
from zenml.client import Client

artifact = Client().get_artifact_version('8349ce09-0693-4e28-8fa2-
20f82c76ddec')
loaded_artifact = artifact.load()
```

For example, we can easily run the same data collection pipeline but with Paul Iusztin's YAML configuration, listed below:

```
parameters:
  user_full_name: Paul Iusztin # [First Name(s)] [Last Name]
  links:
    # Medium
    - https://medium.com/decodingml/an-end-to-end-framework-for-
production-ready-llm-systems-by-building-your-llm-twin-2cc6bb01141f
    - https://medium.com/decodingml/a-real-time-retrieval-system-for-rag-
on-social-media-data-9cc01d50a2a0
    - https://medium.com/decodingml/sota-python-streaming-pipelines-for-
fine-tuning-llms-and-rag-in-real-time-82eb07795b87
    … # More Medium Links
    # Substack
    - https://decodingml.substack.com/p/real-time-feature-pipelines-
with?r=1ttoeh
    - https://decodingml.substack.com/p/building-ml-systems-the-right-
way?r=1ttoeh
    - https://decodingml.substack.com/p/reduce-your-pytorchs-code-
latency?r=1ttoeh
    … # More Substack Links
```

To run the pipeline using Paul's configuration, we call the following poe command:

```
poetry poe run-digital-data-etl-paul
```

That, under the hood, calls the following CLI command that references Paul's config file:

```
poetry run python -m tools.run --run-etl --no-cache --etl-config-filename
digital_data_etl_paul_iusztin.yaml
```

You can find all the configs in the repository in the `configs/` directory. Also, using poe, we configured a command that calls the data collection pipeline for all the supported authors:

```
poetry poe run-digital-data-etl
```

We can easily query the MongoDB data warehouse using our ODM classes. For example, let's query all the articles collected for Paul Iusztin:

```
from llm_engineering.domain.documents import ArticleDocument, UserDocument
```

```
user = UserDocument.get_or_create(first_name="Paul", last_name="Iusztin")
articles = ArticleDocument.bulk_find(author_id=str(user.id))

print(f"User ID: {user.id}")
print(f"User name: {user.first_name} {user.last_name}")
print(f"Number of articles: {len(articles)}")
print("First article link:", articles[0].link)
```

The output of the code from above is:

```
User ID: 900fec95-d621-4315-84c6-52e5229e0b96
User name: Paul Iusztin
Number of articles: 50
First article link: https://medium.com/decodingml/an-end-to-end-framework-
for-production-ready-llm-systems-by-building-your-llm-twin-2cc6bb01141f
```

With only two lines of code, we can query and filter our MongoDB data warehouse using any ODM defined within our project.

Also, to ensure that your data collection pipeline works as expected, you can search your MongoDB collections using your **IDE's MongoDB plugin,** which you must install separately. For example, you can use this plugin for VSCode: `https://www.mongodb.com/products/tools/vs-code`. For other IDEs, you can use similar plugins or external NoSQL visualization tools. After connecting to the MongoDB visualization tool, you can connect to our local database using the following URI: `mongodb://llm_engineering:llm_engineering@127.0.0.1:27017`. For a cloud MongoDB cluster, you must change the URI, which we will explore in *Chapter 11*.

And just like that, you've learned how to run the data collection pipeline with different ZenML configs and how to visualize the output artifacts of each run. We also looked at how to query the data warehouse for a particular data category and author. Thus, we've finalized our data engineering chapter and can move to the conclusion.

Troubleshooting

The raw data stored in the MongoDB database is central to all future steps. Thus, if you haven't successfully run the code from this chapter due to any issues with the crawlers, this section provides solutions for fixing potential issues to allow you to move forward.

Selenium issues

It is a well-known issue that running Selenium can cause problems due to issues with the browser driver, such as the ChromeDriver. Thus, if the crawlers that use Selenium, such as the MediumCrawler, fail due to problems with your ChromeDriver, you can easily bypass this by commenting out the Medium links added to the data collection YAML configs. To do so, go to the configs/ directory and find all the YAML files that start with digital_data_etl_*, such as digital_data_etl_maxime_labonne.yaml. Open them and comment on all the Medium-related URLs, as illustrated in *Figure 3.7*. You can leave out the Substack or personal blog URLs as these use the CustomArticleCrawler, which is not dependent on Selenium.

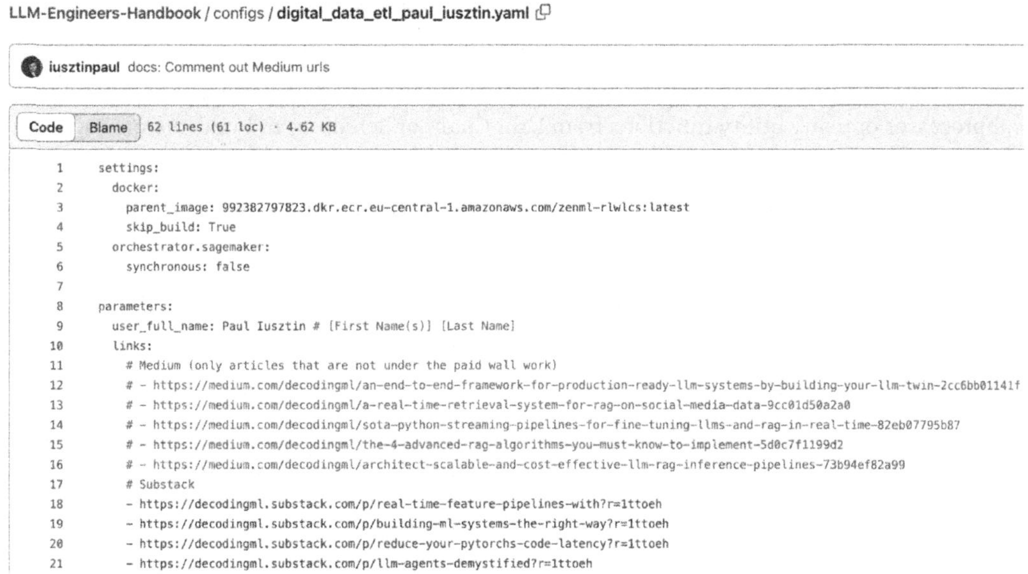

LLM-Engineers-Handbook / configs / **digital_data_etl_paul_iusztin.yaml**

iusztinpaul docs: Comment out Medium urls

| Code | Blame | 62 lines (61 loc) · 4.62 KB |

```
1    settings:
2      docker:
3        parent_image: 992382797823.dkr.ecr.eu-central-1.amazonaws.com/zenml-rlwlcs:latest
4        skip_build: True
5      orchestrator.sagemaker:
6        synchronous: false
7
8    parameters:
9      user_full_name: Paul Iusztin # [First Name(s)] [Last Name]
10     links:
11       # Medium (only articles that are not under the paid wall work)
12       # - https://medium.com/decodingml/an-end-to-end-framework-for-production-ready-llm-systems-by-building-your-llm-twin-2cc6bb01141f
13       # - https://medium.com/decodingml/a-real-time-retrieval-system-for-rag-on-social-media-data-9cc01d50a2a0
14       # - https://medium.com/decodingml/sota-python-streaming-pipelines-for-fine-tuning-llms-and-rag-in-real-time-82eb07795b87
15       # - https://medium.com/decodingml/the-4-advanced-rag-algorithms-you-must-know-to-implement-5d0c7f1199d2
16       # - https://medium.com/decodingml/architect-scalable-and-cost-effective-llm-rag-inference-pipelines-73b94ef82a99
17       # Substack
18       - https://decodingml.substack.com/p/real-time-feature-pipelines-with?r=1ttoeh
19       - https://decodingml.substack.com/p/building-ml-systems-the-right-way?r=1ttoeh
20       - https://decodingml.substack.com/p/reduce-your-pytorchs-code-latency?r=1ttoeh
21       - https://decodingml.substack.com/p/llm-agents-demystified?r=1ttoeh
```

Figure 3.7: Fix Selenium issues when crawling raw data

Import our backed-up data

If nothing works, there is the possibility of populating the MongoDB database with your backed-up data saved under the data/data_warehouse_raw_data directory. This will allow you to proceed to the fine-tuning and inference sections without running the data collection ETL code. To import all the data within this directory, run:

```
poetry poe run-import-data-warehouse-from-json
```

After running the CLI command from above, you will have a one-to-one replica of the dataset we used while developing the code. To ensure the import is completed successfully, you should have 88 articles and 3 users in your MongoDB database.

Summary

In this chapter, we've learned how to design and build the data collection pipeline for the LLM Twin use case. Instead of relying on static datasets, we collected our custom data to mimic re-al-world situations, preparing us for real-world challenges in building AI systems.

First, we examined the architecture of LLM Twin's data collection pipeline, which functions as an ETL process. Next, we started digging into the pipeline implementation. We began by understanding how we can orchestrate the pipeline using ZenML. Then, we looked into the crawler implementation. We learned how to crawl data in three ways: using CLI commands in subprocesses or using utility functions from LangChain or Selenium to build custom logic that programmatically manipulates the browser. Finally, we looked into how to build our own ODM class, which we used to define our document class hierarchy, which contains entities such as articles, posts, and repositories.

At the end of the chapter, we learned how to run ZenML pipelines with different YAML configuration files and explore the results in the dashboard. We also saw how to interact with the MongoDB data warehouse through the ODM classes.

In the next chapter, we will cover the key steps of the RAG feature pipeline, including chunking and embedding documents, ingesting these documents into a vector DB, and applying pre-re-trieval optimizations to improve performance. We will also set up the necessary infrastructure programmatically using Pulumi and conclude by deploying the RAG ingestion pipeline to AWS.

References

- Breuss, M. (2023, July 26). *Beautiful Soup: Build a Web Scraper With Python*. https://realpython.com/beautiful-soup-web-scraper-python/

- David, D. (2024, July 8). *Guide to Web Scraping with Selenium in 2024*. Bright Data. https://brightdata.com/blog/how-tos/using-selenium-for-web-scraping

- Hjelle, G. A. (2023, October 21). *Python 3.12 Preview: Static Typing Improvements*. https://realpython.com/python312-typing/

- *ORM Quick Start — SQLAlchemy 2.0 documentation*. (n.d.). https://docs.sqlalchemy.org/en/20/orm/quickstart.html

- Ramos, L. P. (2023, August 4). *Python and MongoDB: Connecting to NoSQL Databases.* `https://realpython.com/introduction-to-mongodb-and-python/`

- Refactoring.Guru. (2024, January 1). *Builder.* `https://refactoring.guru/design-patterns/builder`

- *What is ETL? A complete guide.* (n.d.). Qlik. `https://www.qlik.com/us/etl`

Join our book's Discord space

Join our community's Discord space for discussions with the authors and other readers:

`https://packt.link/llmeng`

4

RAG Feature Pipeline

Retrieval-augmented generation (RAG) is fundamental in most generative AI applications. RAG's core responsibility is to inject custom data into the **large language model (LLM)** to perform a given action (e.g., summarize, reformulate, and extract the injected data). You often want to use the LLM on data it wasn't trained on (e.g., private or new data). As fine-tuning an LLM is a highly costly operation, RAG is a compelling strategy that bypasses the need for constant fine-tuning to access that new data.

We will start this chapter with a theoretical part that focuses on the fundamentals of RAG and how it works. We will then walk you through all the components of a naïve RAG system: chunking, embedding, and vector DBs. Ultimately, we will present various optimizations used for an advanced RAG system. Then, we will continue exploring LLM Twin's RAG feature pipeline architecture. At this step, we will apply all the theoretical aspects we discussed at the beginning of the chapter. Finally, we will go through a practical example by implementing the LLM Twin's RAG feature pipeline based on the system design described throughout the book.

The main sections of this chapter are:

- Understanding RAG
- An overview of advanced RAG
- Exploring the LLM Twin's RAG feature pipeline architecture
- Implementing the LLM Twin's RAG feature pipeline

By the end of this chapter, you will have a clear and comprehensive understanding of what RAG is and how it is applied to our LLM Twin use case.

Understanding RAG

RAG enhances the accuracy and reliability of generative AI models with information fetched from external sources. It is a technique complementary to the internal knowledge of the LLMs. Before going into the details, let's understand what RAG stands for:

- **Retrieval**: Search for relevant data
- **Augmented**: Add the data as context to the prompt
- **Generation**: Use the augmented prompt with an LLM for generation

Any LLM is bound to understand the data it was trained on, sometimes called parameterized knowledge. Thus, even if the LLM can perfectly answer what happened in the past, it won't have access to the newest data or any other external sources on which it wasn't trained.

Let's take the most powerful model from OpenAI as an example, which, in the summer of 2024, is GPT-4o. The model is trained on data up to October 2023. Thus, if we ask what happened during the 2020 pandemic, it can be answered perfectly due to its parametrized knowledge. However, it will not know the answer if we ask about the 2024 European Football Championship results due to its bounded parametrized knowledge. Another scenario is that it will start confidently hallucinating and provide a faulty answer.

RAG overcomes these two limitations of LLMs. It provides access to external or latest data and prevents hallucinations, enhancing generative AI models' accuracy and reliability.

Why use RAG?

We briefly explained the importance of using RAG in generative AI applications earlier. Now, we will dig deeper into the "why," following which we will focus on what a naïve RAG framework looks like.

For now, to get an intuition about RAG, you have to know that when using RAG, we inject the necessary information into the prompt to answer the initial user question. After that, we pass the augmented prompt to the LLM for the final answer. Now, the LLM will use the additional context to answer the user question.

There are two fundamental problems that RAG solves:

- Hallucinations
- Old or private information

Hallucinations

If a chatbot without RAG is asked a question about something it wasn't trained on, there is a high chance that it will give you a confident answer about something that isn't true. Let's take the 2024 European Football Championship as an example. If the model is trained up to October 2023 and we ask it something about the tournament, it will most likely come up with a random answer that is hard to differentiate between reality and truth. Even if the LLM doesn't hallucinate all the time, it raises concerns about the trustworthiness of its answers. Thus, we must ask ourselves: "When can we trust the LLM's answers?" and "How can we evaluate if the answers are correct?".

By introducing RAG, we enforce the LLM to always answer solely based on the introduced context. The LLM will act as the reasoning engine, while the additional information added through RAG will act as the single source of truth for the generated answer. By doing so, we can quickly evaluate if the LLM's answer is based on the external data or not.

Old information

Any LLM is trained or fine-tuned on a subset of the total world knowledge dataset. This is due to three main issues:

- **Private data**: You cannot train your model on data you don't own or have the right to use.
- **New data**: New data is generated every second. Thus, you would have to constantly train your LLM to keep up.
- **Costs**: Training or fine-tuning an LLM is an extremely costly operation. Hence, it is not feasible to do it on an hourly or daily basis.

RAG solves these issues, as you no longer have to constantly fine-tune your LLM on new data (or even private data). Directly injecting the necessary data to respond to user questions into the prompts that are fed to the LLM is enough to generate correct and valuable answers.

To conclude, RAG is key for a robust and flexible generative AI system. But how do we inject the right data into the prompt based on the user's questions? We will dig into the technical aspects of RAG in the next sections.

The vanilla RAG framework

Every RAG system is similar at its roots. We will first focus on understanding RAG in its simplest form. Later, we will gradually introduce more advanced RAG techniques to improve the system's accuracy. Note that we will use vanilla and naive RAG interchangeably to avoid repetition.

A RAG system is composed of three main modules independent of each other:

- **Ingestion pipeline**: A batch or streaming pipeline used to populate the vector DB
- **Retrieval pipeline**: A module that queries the vector DB and retrieves relevant entries to the user's input
- **Generation pipeline**: The layer that uses the retrieved data to augment the prompt and an LLM to generate answers

As these three components are classes or services of their own, we will dig into each separately. But for now, let's try to answer the question "How are these three modules connected?". Here is a very simplistic overview:

1. On the backend side, the ingestion pipeline runs either on a schedule or constantly to populate the vector DB with external data.
2. On the client side, the user asks a question.
3. The question is passed to the retrieval module, which preprocesses the user's input and queries the vector DB.
4. The generation pipelines use a prompt template, user input, and retrieved context to create the prompt.
5. The prompt is passed to an LLM to generate the answer.
6. The answer is shown to the user.

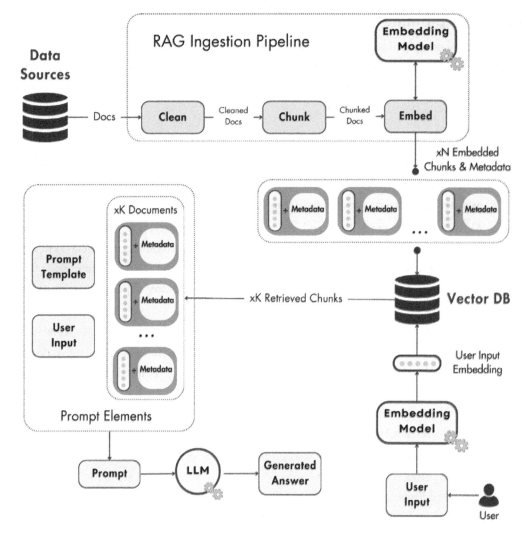

Figure 4.1: Vanilla RAG architecture

You must implement RAG in your generative AI application when you need access to any type of external information. For example, when implementing a financial assistant, you most likely need access to the latest news, reports, and prices before providing valuable answers. Or, if you build a traveling recommender, you must retrieve and parse a list of potential attractions, restaurants, and activities. At training time, LLMs don't have access to your specific data, so you will often have to implement a RAG strategy in your generative AI project. Now, let's dig into the ingestion, retrieval, and generation pipelines.

Ingestion pipeline

The RAG ingestion pipeline extracts raw documents from various data sources (e.g., data warehouse, data lake, web pages, etc.). Then, it cleans, chunks (splits into smaller sections), and embeds the documents. Ultimately, it loads the embedded chunks into a vector DB (or other similar vector storage).

Thus, the RAG ingestion pipeline is split into the following:

- The **data extraction module** gathers all the necessary data from various sources such as DBs, APIs, or web pages. This module is highly dependent on your data. It can be as easy as querying your data warehouse or something more complex such as crawling Wikipedia.
- A **cleaning layer** standardizes and removes unwanted characters from the extracted data. For example, you must remove all invalid characters from your input text, such as non-ASCII and bold and italic characters. Another popular cleaning strategy is to replace URLs with placeholders. However, your cleaning strategy will vary depending on your data source and embedding model.
- The **chunking module** splits the cleaned documents into smaller ones. As we want to pass the document's content to an embedding model, this is necessary to ensure it doesn't exceed the model's input maximum size. Also, chunking is required to separate specific regions that are semantically related. For example, when chunking a book's chapter, the most optimal way is to group similar paragraphs into the same section or chunk. By doing so, at the retrieval time, you will add only the essential data to the prompt.
- The **embedding component** uses an embedding model to take the chunk's content (text, images, audio, etc.) and project it into a dense vector packed with semantic value—more on embeddings in the *What are embeddings?* section below.
- The **loading module** takes the embedded chunks along with a metadata document. The metadata will contain essential information such as the embedded content, the URL to the source of the chunk, and when the content was published on the web. The embedding is used as an index to query similar chunks, while the metadata is used to access the information added to augment the prompt.

At this point, we have a RAG ingestion pipeline that takes raw documents as input, processes them, and populates a vector DB. The next step is to retrieve relevant data from the vector store correctly.

Retrieval pipeline

The retrieval components take the user's input (text, image, audio, etc.), embed it, and query the vector DB for similar vectors to the user's input.

The primary function of the retrieval step is to project the user's input into the same vector space as the embeddings used as an index in the vector DB. This allows us to find the top K's most similar entries by comparing the embeddings from the vector storage with the user's input vector. These entries then serve as content to augment the prompt that is passed to the LLM to generate the answer.

You must use a distance metric to compare two vectors, such as the Euclidean or Manhattan distance. But the most popular one is the cosine distance, which is equal to 1 minus the cosine of the angle between two vectors, as follows:

$$Cosine\ Distance\ =\ 1\ -\ \cos(\theta)\ =\ 1\ -\ \frac{A \cdot B}{||\ A\ ||\ \cdot\ ||\ B\ ||}$$

It ranges from -1 to 1, with a value of -1 when vectors **A** and **B** are in opposite directions, 0 if they are orthogonal, and 1 if they point in the same direction.

Most of the time, the cosine distance works well in non-linear complex vector spaces. However, it is essential to notice that choosing the proper distance between two vectors depends on your data and the embedding model you use.

One critical factor to highlight is that the user's input and embeddings must be in the same vector space. Otherwise, you cannot compute the distance between them. To do so, it is essential to preprocess the user input in the same way you processed the raw documents in the RAG ingestion pipeline. This means you must clean, chunk (if necessary), and embed the user's input using the same functions, models, and hyperparameters. This is similar to how you have to preprocess the data into features in the same way between training and inference; otherwise, the inference will yield inaccurate results—a phenomenon also known as the training-serving skew.

Generation pipeline

The last step of the RAG system is to take the user's input, retrieve data, pass it to an LLM, and generate a valuable answer.

The final prompt results from a system and prompt template populated with the user's query and retrieved context. You might have a single prompt template or multiple prompt templates, depending on your application. Usually, all the prompt engineering is done at the prompt template level.

Below, you can see a dummy example of what a generic system and prompt template look like and how they are used together with the retrieval logic and the LLM to generate the final answer:

```python
system_template = """
You are a helpful assistant who answers all the user's questions politely.
"""

prompt_template = """
Answer the user's question using only the provided context. If you cannot
answer using the context, respond with "I don't know."

Context: {context}
User question: {user_question}
"""

user_question = "<your_question>"
retrieved_context = retrieve(user_question)

prompt = f"{system_template}\n"
prompt += prompt_template.format(context=retrieved_context, user_
question=user_question)

answer  = llm(prompt)
```

As the prompt templates evolve, each change should be tracked and versioned using **machine learning operations (MLOps)** best practices. Thus, during training or inference time, you always know that a given answer was generated by a specific version of the LLM and prompt template(s). You can do this through Git, store the prompt templates in a DB, or use specific prompt management tools such as LangFuse.

As we've seen in the retrieval pipeline, some critical aspects that directly impact the accuracy of your RAG system are the embeddings of the external data, usually stored in vector DBs, the embedding of the user's query, and how we can find similarities between the two using functions such as the cosine distance. To better understand this part of the RAG algorithm, let's zoom in on what embeddings are and how they are computed.

What are embeddings?

Imagine you're trying to teach a computer to understand the world. Embeddings are like a particular translator that turns these things into a numerical code. This code isn't random, though, because similar words or items end up with codes that are close to each other. It's like a map where words with similar meanings are clustered together.

With that in mind, a more theoretical definition is that embeddings are dense numerical representations of objects encoded as vectors in a continuous vector space, such as words, images, or items in a recommendation system. This transformation helps capture the semantic meaning and relationships between the objects. For instance, in **natural language processing (NLP)**, embeddings translate words into vectors where semantically similar words are positioned closely together in the vector space.

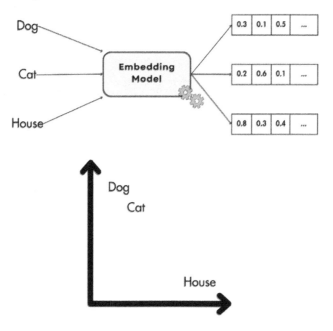

Figure 4.2: What are embeddings?

A popular method is visualizing the embeddings to understand and evaluate their geometrical relationship. As the embeddings often have more than 2 or 3 dimensions, usually between 64 and 2048, you must project them again to 2D or 3D.

For example, you can use UMAP (`https://umap-learn.readthedocs.io/en/latest/index.html`), a dimensionality reduction method well known for keeping the geometrical properties between the points when projecting the embeddings to 2D or 3D. Another popular algorithm for dimensionality reduction when visualizing vectors is t-SNE (`https://scikit-learn.org/stable/modules/generated/sklearn.manifold.TSNE.html`). However, compared to UMAP, it is more stochastic and doesn't preserve the topological relationships between the points.

A dimensionality reduction algorithm, such as PCA, UMAP, and t-SNE, is a mathematical technique used to reduce the number of input variables or features in a dataset while preserving the data's essential patterns, structure, and relationships. The goal is to transform high-dimensional data into a lower-dimensional form, making it easier to visualize, interpret, and process while minimizing the loss of important information. These methods help to address the "curse of dimensionality," improve computational efficiency, and often enhance the performance of ML algorithms.

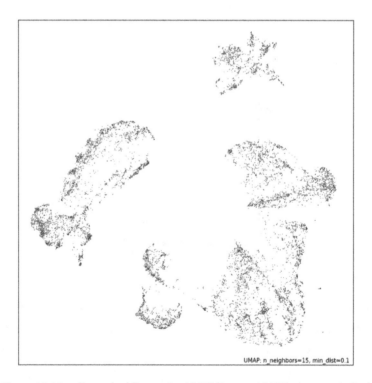

Figure 4.3: Visualize embeddings using UMAP (Source: UMAP's documentation)

Why embeddings are so powerful

Firstly, ML models work only with numerical values. This is not a problem when working with tabular data, as the data is often in numerical form or can easily be processed into numbers. Embeddings come in handy when we want to feed words, images, or audio data into models.

For instance, when working with transformer models, you tokenize all your text input, where each token has an embedding associated with it. The beauty of this process lies in its simplicity; the input to the transformer is a sequence of embeddings, which can be easily and confidently interpreted by the dense layers of the neural network.

Based on this example, you can use embeddings to encode any categorical variable and feed it to an ML model. But why not use other simple methods, such as **one-hot encoding?** When working with categorical variables with high cardinality, such as language vocabularies, you will suffer from the curse of dimensionality when using other classical methods. For example, if your vocabulary has 10,000 tokens, then only one token will have a length of 10,000 after applying one-hot encoding. If the input sequence has N tokens, that will become N * 10,000 input parameters. If N >= 100, often, when inputting text, the input is too large to be usable. Another issue with other classical methods that don't suffer from the curse of dimensionality, such as **hashing**, is that you lose the semantic relationships between the vectors.

One-hot encoding is a technique that converts categorical variables into a binary matrix representation. Each category is represented as a unique binary vector. For each categorical variable, a binary vector is created with a length equal to the number of unique categories, where all values are zero except for the index corresponding to the specific category, which is set to one. The method preserves all information about the categories. It is simple and interpretable. However, a significant disadvantage is that it can lead to a high-dimensional feature space if the categorical variable has many unique values, making the method impractical.

Feature hashing, also known as hashing encoding or the "hash trick," is a technique used to convert categorical variables into numerical features by applying a hash function to the category values. Compared to one-hot encoding, the method is not bound to the number of unique categories, but it reduces the dimensionality of the feature space by mapping categories into a fixed number of bins or buckets. Thus, it reduces the dimensionality of the feature space, which is particularly useful when dealing with high-cardinality categorical variables. This makes it efficient in terms of memory usage and computational time. However, there is a risk of collisions, where different categories might map to the same bin, leading to a loss of information. The mapping makes the method uninterpretable. Also, it is difficult to understand the relationship between the original categories and the hashed features.

Embeddings help us encode categorical variables while controlling the output vector's dimension. They also use ingenious ways to condense information into a lower dimension space than naive hashing tricks.

Secondly, embedding your input reduces the size of its dimension and condenses all of its semantic meaning into a dense vector. This is an extremely popular technique when working with images, where a CNN encoder module maps the high-dimensional meaning into an embedding, which is later processed by a CNN decoder that performs the classification or regression steps.

The following image shows a typical CNN layout. Imagine tiny squares within each layer. Those are the "receptive fields." Each square feeds information to a single neuron in the previous layer. As you move through the network, two key things are happening:

- **Shrinking the picture**: Special "subsampling" operations make the layers smaller, focusing on essential details.
- **Learning features**: "Convolution" operations, on the other hand, actually increase the layer size as the network learns more complex features from the image.

Finally, a fully connected layer at the end takes all this processed information and transforms it into the final vector embedding, a numerical image representation.

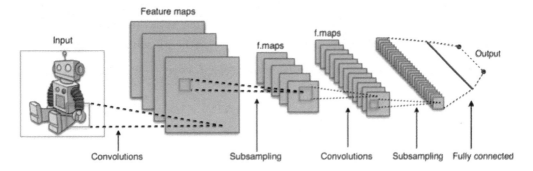

Figure 4.4: Creating embeddings from an image using a CNN (Image source)

 The preceding image is sourced from *Wikimedia Commons* (https://commons. wikimedia.org/wiki/File:Typical_cnn.png) and licensed under the Creative Commons Attribution-ShareAlike 4.0 International License (CC BY-SA 4.0: https:// creativecommons.org/licenses/by-sa/4.0/deed.en).

How are embeddings created?

Embeddings are created by deep learning models that understand the context and semantics of your input and project it into a continuous vector space.

Various deep learning models can be used to create embeddings, varying by the data input type. Thus, it is fundamental to understand your data and what you need from it before picking an embedding model.

For example, when working with text data, one of the early methods used to create embeddings for your vocabulary is Word2Vec and GloVe. These are still popular methods used today for simpler applications.

Another popular method is to use encoder-only transformers, such as BERT, or other methods from its family, such as RoBERTa. These models leverage the encoder of the transformer architecture to smartly project your input into a dense vector space that can later be used as embeddings.

To quickly compute the embeddings in Python, you can conveniently leverage the Sentence Transformers Python package (also available in Hugging Face's transformer package). This tool provides a user-friendly interface, making the embedding process straightforward and efficient.

In the code snippet below, you can see how we loaded a model from SentenceTransformer, computed the embeddings for three sentences, and, ultimately, computed the cosine similarity between them. The similarity between one sentence and itself is always 1. Also, the similarity between the first and second sentences is approximately 0, as the sentences have nothing in common. In contrast, the value between the first and third one is higher as there is some overlapping context:

```python
from sentence_transformers import SentenceTransformer

model = SentenceTransformer("all-MiniLM-L6-v2")

sentences = [
"The dog sits outside waiting for a treat.",
"I am going swimming.",
"The dog is swimming."
]

embeddings = model.encode(sentences)
print(embeddings.shape)
# Output: [3, 384]

similarities = model.similarity(embeddings, embeddings)
print(similarities)
# Output:
# tensor([[ 1.0000, -0.0389, 0.2692],
# [-0.0389, 1.0000, 0.3837],
# [ 0.2692, 0.3837, 1.0000]])
#
# similarities[0, 0] = The similarity between the first sentence and
itself.
# similarities[0, 1] = The similarity between the first and second
sentence.
# similarities[2, 1] = The similarity between the third and second
sentence.
```

The source code for the preceding snippet can be found at https://github.com/PacktPublishing/ LLM-Engineering/blob/main/code_snippets/08_text_embeddings.py.

The examples in the embeddings section can be run within the virtual environment used across the book, as it contains all the required dependencies.

The best-performing embedding model can change with time and your specific use case. You can find particular models on the **Massive Text Embedding Benchmark** (**MTEB**) on Hugging Face. Depending on your needs, you can consider the best-performing model, the one with the best accuracy, or the one with the smallest memory footprint. This decision is solely based on your requirements (e.g., accuracy and hardware). However, Hugging Face and SentenceTransformer make switching between different models straightforward. Thus, you can always experiment with various options.

When working with images, you can embed them using **convolutional neural networks** (**CNNs**). Popular CNN networks are based on the ResNet architecture. However, we can't directly use image embedding techniques for audio recordings. Instead, we can create a visual representation of the audio, such as a spectrogram, and then apply image embedding models to those visuals. This allows us to capture the essence of images and sounds in a way computers can understand.

By leveraging models like CLIP, you can practically embed a piece of text and an image in the same vector space. This allows you to find similar images using a sentence as input, or the other way around, demonstrating the practicality of CLIP.

In the following code snippet, we use CLIP to encode a crazy cat image and three sentences. Ultimately, we use cosine similarity to compute the resemblance between the picture and the sentences:

```
from io import BytesIO

import requests
from PIL import Image
from sentence_transformers import SentenceTransformer


response = requests.get(
"https://github.com/PacktPublishing/LLM-Engineering/blob/main/images/
crazy_cat.jpg?raw=true"
)
```

```
image = Image.open(BytesIO(response.content))

model = SentenceTransformer("clip-ViT-B-32")

img_emb = model.encode(image)
text_emb = model.encode(
["A crazy cat smiling.",
"A white and brown cat with a yellow bandana.",
"A man eating in the garden."]
)
print(text_emb.shape) # noqa
# Output: (3, 512)

similarity_scores = model.similarity(img_emb, text_emb)
print(similarity_scores) # noqa
# Output: tensor([[0.3068, 0.3300, 0.1719]])
```

The source code can be found at https://github.com/PacktPublishing/LLM-Engineering/blob/main/code_snippets/08_text_image_embeddings.py.

Here, we provided a small introduction to how embeddings can be computed. The realm of specific implementations is vast, but what is important to know is that embeddings can be computed for most digital data categories, such as words, sentences, documents, images, videos, and graphs.

It's crucial to grasp that you must use specialized models when you need to compute the distance between two different data categories, such as the distance between the vector of a sentence and of an image. These models are designed to project both data types into the same vector space, such as CLIP, ensuring accurate distance computation.

Applications of embeddings

Due to the generative AI revolution, which uses RAG, embeddings have become extremely popular in information retrieval tasks, such as semantic search for text, code, images, and audio, and long-term memory of agents. But before generative AI, embeddings were already heavily used in:

- Representing categorical variables (e.g., vocabulary tokens) that are fed to an ML model
- Recommender systems by encoding the users and items and finding their relationship
- Clustering and outlier detection
- Data visualization by using algorithms such as UMAP

- Classification by using the embeddings as features
- Zero-shot classification by comparing the embedding of each class and picking the most similar one

The last step to fully understanding how RAG works is to examine vector DBs and how they leverage embeddings to retrieve data.

More on vector DBs

Vector DBs are specialized DBs designed to efficiently store, index, and retrieve vector embeddings. Traditional scalar-based DBs struggle with the complexity of vector data, making vector DBs crucial for tasks like real-time semantic search.

While standalone vector indices like FAISS are effective for similarity search, they lack vector DBs' comprehensive data management capabilities. Vector DBs support CRUD operations, metadata filtering, scalability, real-time updates, backups, ecosystem integration, and robust data security, making them more suited for production environments than standalone indices.

How does a vector DB work?

Think of how you usually search a DB. You type in something specific, and the system spits out the exact match. That's how traditional DBs work. Vector DBs are different. Instead of perfect matches, we look for the closest neighbors of the query vector. Under the hood, a vector DB uses **approximate nearest neighbor (ANN)** algorithms to find these close neighbors.

While ANN algorithms don't return the top matches for a given search, standard nearest neighbor algorithms are too slow to work in practice. Also, it is shown empirically that using only approximations of the top matches for a given input query works well enough. Thus, the trade-off between accuracy and latency ultimately favors ANN algorithms.

This is a typical workflow of a vector DB:

1. **Indexing vectors**: Vectors are indexed using data structures optimized for high-dimensional data. Common indexing techniques include **hierarchical navigable small world (HNSW)**, random projection, **product quantization (PQ)**, and **locality-sensitive hashing (LSH)**.

2. **Querying for similarity**: During a search, the DB queries the indexed vectors to find those most similar to the input vector. This process involves comparing vectors based on similarity measures such as cosine similarity, Euclidean distance, or dot product. Each has unique advantages and is suitable for different use cases.

3. **Post-processing results**: After identifying potential matches, the results undergo post-processing to refine accuracy. This step ensures that the most relevant vectors are returned to the user.

Vector DBs can filter results based on metadata before or after the vector search. Both approaches have trade-offs in terms of performance and accuracy. The query also depends on the metadata (along with the vector index), so it contains a metadata index user for filtering operations.

Algorithms for creating the vector index

Vector DBs use various algorithms to create the vector index and manage searching data efficiently:

*   **Random projection**: Random projection reduces the dimensionality of vectors by projecting them into a lower-dimensional space using a random matrix. This technique preserves the relative distances between vectors, facilitating faster searches.

*   **PQ**: PQ compresses vectors by dividing them into smaller sub-vectors and then quantizing these sub-vectors into representative codes. This reduces memory usage and speeds up similarity searches.

*   **LSH**: LSH maps similar vectors into buckets. This method enables fast approximate nearest neighbor searches by focusing on a subset of the data, reducing the computational complexity.

*   **HNSW**: HNSW constructs a multi-layer graph where each node represents a set of vectors. Similar nodes are connected, allowing the algorithm to navigate the graph and find the nearest neighbors efficiently.

These algorithms enable vector DBs to efficiently handle complex and large-scale data, making them a perfect fit for a variety of AI and ML applications.

DB operations

Vector DBs also share common characteristics with standard DBs to ensure high performance, fault tolerance, and ease of management in production environments. Key operations include:

*   **Sharding and replication**: Data is partitioned (sharded) across multiple nodes to ensure scalability and high availability. Data replication across nodes helps maintain data integrity and availability in case of node failures.

- **Monitoring**: Continuous monitoring of DB performance, including query latency and resource usage (RAM, CPU, disk), helps maintain optimal operations and identify potential issues before they impact the system.

- **Access control**: Implementing robust access control mechanisms ensures that only authorized users can access and modify data. This includes role-based access controls and other security protocols to protect sensitive information.

- **Backups**: Regular DB backups are critical for disaster recovery. Automated backup processes ensure that data can be restored to a previous state in case of corruption or loss.

An overview of advanced RAG

The vanilla RAG framework we just presented doesn't address many fundamental aspects that impact the quality of the retrieval and answer generation, such as:

- Are the retrieved documents relevant to the user's question?

- Is the retrieved context enough to answer the user's question?

- Is there any redundant information that only adds noise to the augmented prompt?

- Does the latency of the retrieval step match our requirements?

- What do we do if we can't generate a valid answer using the retrieved information?

From the questions above, we can draw two conclusions. The first one is that we need a robust evaluation module for our RAG system that can quantify and measure the quality of the retrieved data and generate answers relative to the user's question. We will discuss this topic in more detail in *Chapter 9*. The second conclusion is that we must improve our RAG framework to address the retrieval limitations directly in the algorithm. These improvements are known as advanced RAG.

The vanilla RAG design can be optimized at three different stages:

- **Pre-retrieval**: This stage focuses on how to structure and preprocess your data for data indexing optimizations as well as query optimizations.

- **Retrieval**: This stage revolves around improving the embedding models and metadata filtering to improve the vector search step.

- **Post-retrieval**: This stage mainly targets different ways to filter out noise from the retrieved documents and compress the prompt before feeding it to an LLM for answer generation.

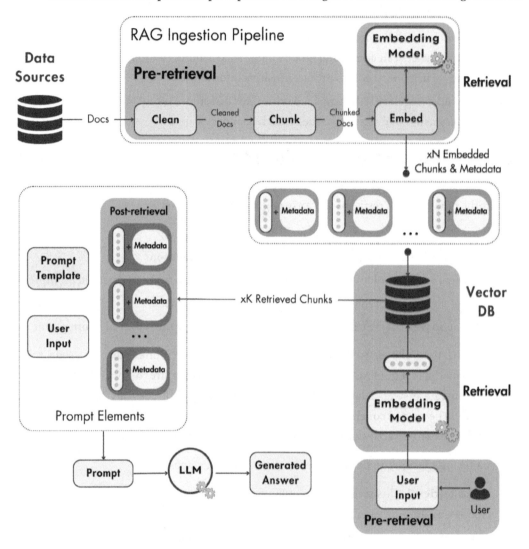

Figure 4.5: The three stages of advanced RAG

This section is not meant to be an exhaustive list of all the advanced RAG methods available. The goal is to build an intuition about what can be optimized. We will use only examples based on text data, but the principles of advanced RAG remain the same regardless of the data category. Now, let's zoom in on all three components.

Pre-retrieval

The pre-retrieval steps are performed in two different ways:

- **Data indexing**: It is part of the RAG ingestion pipeline. It is mainly implemented within the cleaning or chunking modules to preprocess the data for better indexing.

- **Query optimization**: The algorithm is performed directly on the user's query before embedding it and retrieving the chunks from the vector DB.

As we index our data using embeddings that semantically represent the content of a chunked document, most of the **data indexing** techniques focus on better preprocessing and structuring the data to improve retrieval efficiency, such as:

- **Sliding window**: The sliding window technique introduces overlap between text chunks, ensuring that important context near chunk boundaries is retained, which enhances retrieval accuracy. This is particularly beneficial in domains like legal documents, scientific papers, customer support logs, and medical records, where critical information often spans multiple sections. The embedding is computed on the chunk along with the overlapping portion. Hence, the sliding window improves the system's ability to retrieve relevant and coherent information by maintaining context across boundaries.

- **Enhancing data granularity**: This involves data cleaning techniques like removing irrelevant details, verifying factual accuracy, and updating outdated information. A clean and accurate dataset allows for sharper retrieval.

- **Metadata**: Adding metadata tags like dates, URLs, external IDs, or chapter markers helps filter results efficiently during retrieval.

- **Optimizing index structures**: It is based on different data index methods, such as various chunk sizes and multi-indexing strategies.

- **Small-to-big**: The algorithm decouples the chunks used for retrieval and the context used in the prompt for the final answer generation. The algorithm uses a small sequence of text to compute the embedding while preserving the sequence itself and a wider window around it in the metadata. Thus, using smaller chunks enhances the retrieval's accuracy, while the larger context adds more contextual information to the LLM.

The intuition behind this is that if we use the whole text for computing the embedding, we might introduce too much noise, or the text could contain multiple topics, which results in a poor overall semantic representation of the embedding.

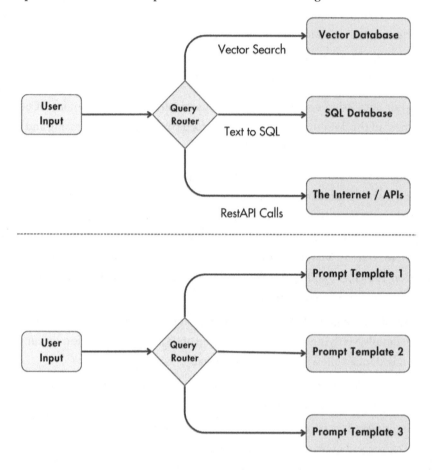

Figure 4.6: Query routing

On the **query optimization** side, we can leverage techniques such as query routing, query rewriting, and query expansion to refine the retrieved information for the LLM further:

- **Query routing**: Based on the user's input, we might have to interact with different categories of data and query each category differently. Query rooting is used to decide what action to take based on the user's input, similar to if/else statements. Still, the decisions are made solely using natural language instead of logical statements.

As illustrated in Figure 4.6, let's assume that, based on the user's input, to do RAG, we can retrieve additional context from a vector DB using vector search queries, a standard SQL DB by translating the user query to an SQL command, or the internet by leveraging REST API calls. The query router can also detect whether a context is required, helping us avoid making redundant calls to external data storage. Also, a query router can be used to pick the best prompt template for a given input. For example, in the LLM Twin use case, depending on whether the user wants an article paragraph, a post, or a code snippet, you need different prompt templates to optimize the creation process. The routing usually uses an LLM to decide what route to take or embeddings by picking the path with the most similar vectors. To summarize, query routing is identical to an if/else statement but much more versatile as it works directly with natural language.

- **Query rewriting**: Sometimes, the user's initial query might not perfectly align with the way your data is structured. Query rewriting tackles this by reformulating the question to match the indexed information better. This can involve techniques like:

    - **Paraphrasing**: Rephrasing the user's query while preserving its meaning (e.g., "What are the causes of climate change?" could be rewritten as "Factors contributing to global warming").

    - **Synonym substitution**: Replacing less common words with synonyms to broaden the search scope (e.g., " joyful" could be rewritten as "happy").

    - **Sub-queries**: For longer queries, we can break them down into multiple shorter and more focused sub-queries. This can help the retrieval stage identify relevant documents more precisely.

- **Hypothetical document embeddings** (HyDE): This technique involves having an LLM create a hypothetical response to the query. Then, both the original query and the LLM's response are fed into the retrieval stage.

- **Query expansion**: This approach aims to enrich the user's question by adding additional terms or concepts, resulting in different perspectives of the same initial question. For example, when searching for "disease," you can leverage synonyms and related terms associated with the original query words and also include "illnesses" or "ailments."

- **Self-query**: The core idea is to map unstructured queries into structured ones. An LLM identifies key entities, events, and relationships within the input text. These identities are used as filtering parameters to reduce the vector search space (e.g., identify cities within the query, for example, "Paris," and add it to your filter to reduce your vector search space).

Both data indexing and query optimization pre-retrieval optimization techniques depend highly on your data type, structure, and source. Thus, as with any data processing pipeline, no method always works, as every use case has its own particularities and gotchas. Optimizing your pre-retrieval RAG layer is experimental. Thus, what is essential is to try multiple methods (such as the ones enumerated in this section), reiterate, and observe what works best.

Retrieval

The retrieval step can be optimized in two fundamental ways:

- **Improving the embedding models** used in the RAG ingestion pipeline to encode the chunked documents and, at inference time, transform the user's input.
- **Leveraging the DB's filter and search features.** This step will be used solely at inference time when you have to retrieve the most similar chunks based on user input.

Both strategies are aligned with our ultimate goal: to enhance the vector search step by leveraging the semantic similarity between the query and the indexed data.

When improving the embedding models, you usually have to fine-tune the pre-trained embedding models to tailor them to specific jargon and nuances of your domain, especially for areas with evolving terminology or rare terms.

Instead of fine-tuning the embedding model, you can leverage instructor models (`https://huggingface.co/hkunlp/instructor-xl`) to guide the embedding generation process with an instruction/prompt aimed at your domain. Tailoring your embedding network to your data using such a model can be a good option, as fine-tuning a model consumes more computing and human resources.

In the code snippet below, you can see an example of an Instructor model that embeds article titles about AI:

```
from InstructorEmbedding import INSTRUCTOR


model = INSTRUCTOR("hkunlp/instructor-base")


sentence = "RAG Fundamentals First"


instruction = "Represent the title of an article about AI:"
```

```
embeddings = model.encode([[instruction, sentence]])
print(embeddings.shape) # noqa
# Output: (1, 768)
```

The source code can be found at https://github.com/PacktPublishing/LLM-Engineering/blob/main/code_snippets/08_instructor_embeddings.py.

 To run the instructor code, you have to create a different virtual environment and activate it:

```
python3 -m venv instructor_venv && source instructor_venv/bin/activate
```

 And install the required Python dependencies:

```
pip install sentence-transformers==2.2.2 InstructorEmbedding==1.0.1
```

On the other side of the spectrum, here is how you can improve your retrieval by leveraging classic filter and search DB features:

- **Hybrid search**: This is a vector and keyword-based search blend. Keyword-based search excels at identifying documents containing specific keywords. When your task demands pinpoint accuracy and the retrieved information must include exact keyword matches, hybrid search shines. Vector search, while powerful, can sometimes struggle with finding exact matches, but it excels at finding more general semantic similarities. You leverage both keyword matching and semantic similarities by combining the two methods. You have a parameter, usually called alpha, that controls the weight between the two methods. The algorithm has two independent searches, which are later normalized and unified.

- **Filtered vector search**: This type of search leverages the metadata index to filter for specific keywords within the metadata. It differs from a hybrid search in that you retrieve the data once using only the vector index and perform the filtering step before or after the vector search to reduce your search space.

In practice, on the retrieval side, you usually start with filtered vector search or hybrid search, as they are fairly quick to implement. This approach gives you the flexibility to adjust your strategy based on performance. If the results are not as expected, you can always fine-tune your embedding model.

Post-retrieval

The post-retrieval optimizations are solely performed on the retrieved data to ensure that the LLM's performance is not compromised by issues such as limited context windows or noisy data. This is because the retrieved context can sometimes be too large or contain irrelevant information, both of which can distract the LLM.

Two popular methods performed at the post-retrieval step are:

- **Prompt compression**: Eliminate unnecessary details while keeping the essence of the data.
- **Re-ranking**: Use a cross-encoder ML model to give a matching score between the user's input and every retrieved chunk. The retrieved items are sorted based on this score. Only the top N results are kept as the most relevant. As you can see in *Figure 4.7*, this works because the re-ranking model can find more complex relationships between the user input and some content than a simple similarity search. However, we can't apply this model at the initial retrieval step because it is costly. That is why a popular strategy is to retrieve the data using a similarity distance between the embeddings and refine the retrieved information using a re-raking model, as illustrated in Figure 4.8.

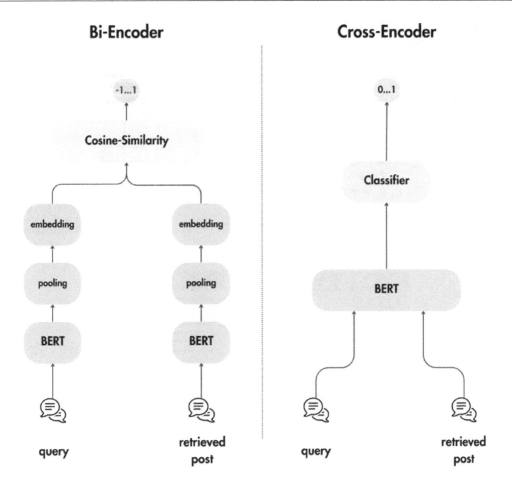

Figure 4.7: Bi-encoder (the standard embedding model) versus cross-encoder

The abovementioned techniques are far from an exhaustive list of all potential solutions. We used them as examples to get an intuition on what you can (and should) optimize at each step in your RAG workflow. The truth is that these techniques can vary tremendously by the type of data you work with.

For example, if you work with multi-modal data such as text and images, most of the techniques from earlier won't work as they are designed for text only.

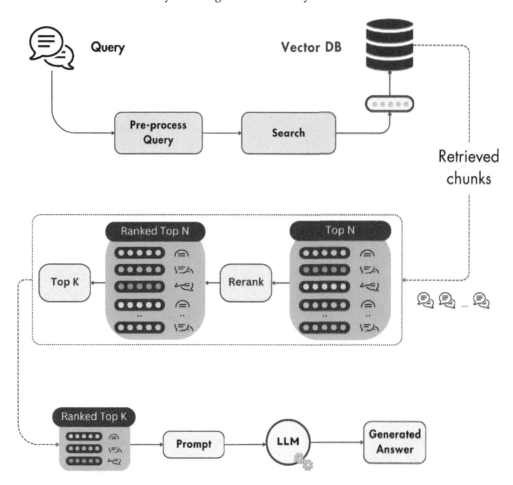

Figure 4.8: The re-ranking algorithm

To summarize, the primary goal of these optimizations is to enhance the RAG algorithm at three key stages: pre-retrieval, retrieval, and post-retrieval. This involves preprocessing data for improved vector indexing, adjusting user queries for more accurate searches, enhancing the embedding model, utilizing classic filtering DB operations, and removing noisy data. By keeping these goals in mind, you can effectively optimize your RAG workflow for data processing and retrieval

Exploring the LLM Twin's RAG feature pipeline architecture

Now that you have a strong intuition and understanding of RAG and its workings, we will continue exploring our particular LLM Twin use case. The goal is to provide a hands-on end-to-end example to solidify the theory presented in this chapter.

Any RAG system is split into two independent components:

- The **ingestion pipeline** takes in raw data, cleans, chunks, embeds, and loads it into a vector DB.
- The **inference pipeline** queries the vector DB for relevant context and ultimately generates an answer by levering an LLM.

In this chapter, we will focus on implementing the RAG ingestion pipeline, and in *Chapter 9*, we will continue developing the inference pipeline.

With that in mind, let's have a quick refresher on the problem we are trying to solve and where we get our raw data. Remember that we are building an end-to-end ML system. Thus, all the components talk to each other through an interface (or a contract), and each pipeline has a single responsibility. In our case, we ingest raw documents, preprocess them, and load them into a vector DB.

The problem we are solving

As presented in the previous chapter, this book aims to show you how to build a production-ready LLM Twin backed by an end-to-end ML system. In this chapter specifically, we want to design a RAG feature pipeline that takes raw social media data (e.g., articles, code repositories, and posts) from our MongoDB data warehouse. The text of the raw documents will be cleaned, chunked, embedded, and ultimately loaded to a feature store. As discussed in *Chapter 1*, we will implement a logical feature store using ZenML artifacts and a Qdrant vector DB.

As we want to build a fully automated feature pipeline, we want to sync the data warehouse and logical feature store. Remember that, at inference time, the context used to generate the answer is retrieved from the vector DB. Thus, the speed of synchronization between the data warehouse and the feature store will directly impact the accuracy of our RAG algorithm.

Another key consideration is how to automate the feature pipeline and integrate it with the rest of our ML system. Our goal is to minimize any desynchronization between the two data storages, as this could potentially compromise the integrity of our system.

To conclude, we must design a feature pipeline that constantly syncs the data warehouse and logical feature store while processing the data accordingly. Having the data in a feature store is critical for a production-ready ML system. The LLM Twin inference pipeline will query it for RAG, while the training pipeline will consume tracked and versioned fine-tuning datasets from it.

The feature store

The **feature store** will be the **central access point** for all the features used within the training and inference pipelines. The training pipeline will use the cleaned data from the feature store (stored as artifacts) to fine-tune LLMs. The inference pipeline will query the vector DB for chunked documents for RAG. That is why we are designing a feature pipeline and not only a RAG ingestion pipeline. In practice, the feature pipeline contains multiple subcomponents, one of which is the RAG logic.

Remember that the feature pipeline is mainly used as a mind map to navigate the complexity of ML systems. It clearly states that it takes raw data as input and then outputs features and optional labels, which are stored in the feature store. Thus, a good intuition is to consider that all the logic between the data warehouse and the feature store goes into the feature pipeline namespace, consisting of one or more sub-pipelines. For example, we will implement another pipeline that takes in cleaned data, processes it into instruct datasets, and stores it in artifacts; this also sits under the feature pipeline umbrella as the artifacts are part of the logical feature store. Another example would be implementing a data validation pipeline on top of the raw data or computed features.

Another important observation to make is that text data stored as strings are not considered features if you follow the standard conventions. A feature is something that is fed directly into the model. For example, we would have to tokenize the instruct datasets or chunked documents to be considered features. Why? Because the tokens are fed directly to the model and not the sentences as strings. Unfortunately, this makes the system more complex and unflexible. Thus, we will do the tokenization at runtime. But this observation is important to understand as it's a clear example that you don't have to be too rigid about the feature/training/inference (FTI) architecture. You have to take it and adapt it to your own use case.

Where does the raw data come from?

As a quick reminder, all the raw documents are stored in a MongoDB data warehouse. The data warehouse is populated by the data collection ETL pipeline presented in *Chapter 3*. The ETL pipeline crawls various platforms such as Medium and Substack, standardizes the data, and loads it into MongoDB. Check out *Chapter 3* for more details on this topic.

Designing the architecture of the RAG feature pipeline

The last step is to architect and go through the design of the RAG feature pipeline of the LLM Twin application. We will use a batch design scheduled to poll data from the MongoDB data warehouse, process it, and load it to a Qdrant vector DB. The first question to ask ourselves is, "Why a batch pipeline?"

But before answering that, let's quickly understand how a batch architecture works and behaves relative to a streaming design.

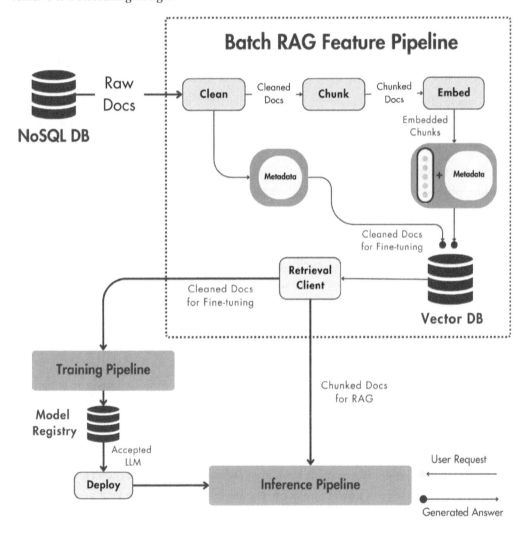

Figure 4.9: The architecture of the LLM Twin's RAG feature pipeline

Batch pipelines

A batch pipeline in data systems refers to a data processing method where data is collected, processed, and stored in predefined intervals and larger volumes, also known as "batches". This approach differs from real-time or streaming data processing, where data is processed continuously as it arrives. This is what happens in a batch pipeline:

1. **Data collection**: Data is collected from various sources and stored until sufficient amounts are accumulated for processing. This can include data from DBs, logs, files, and other sources.

2. **Scheduled processing**: Data processing is scheduled at regular intervals, for example, hourly or daily. During this time, the collected data is processed in bulk. This can involve data cleansing, transformation, aggregation, and other operations.

3. **Data loading**: After processing, the data is loaded into the target system, such as a DB, data warehouse, data lake, or feature store. This processed data is then available for analysis, querying, or further processing.

Batch pipelines are particularly useful when dealing with large volumes of data that do not require immediate processing. They offer several advantages, including:

*   **Efficiency**: Batch processing can handle large volumes of data more efficiently than real-time processing, allowing for optimized resource allocation and parallel processing.

*   **Complex processing**: Batch pipelines can perform complex data transformations and aggregations that might be too resource-intensive for real-time processing.

*   **Simplicity**: Batch processing systems' architectures are often simpler than those of real-time systems, making them easier to implement and maintain.

Batch versus streaming pipelines

When implementing feature pipelines, you have two main design choices: batch and streaming. Thus, it is worthwhile to see the difference between the two and understand why we chose a batch architecture over a streaming one for our LLM Twin use case.

You can effortlessly write a dedicated chapter on streaming pipelines, which suggests its complexity over a batch design. However, as streaming architectures become increasingly popular, one must have an intuition of how they work to choose the best option for your application.

The core elements of streaming applications are a distributed event streaming platform such as Apache Kafka or Redpanda to store events from multiple clients and a streaming engine such as Apache Flink or Bytewax to process the events. To simplify your architecture, you can swap your event streaming platform with queues, such as RabbitMQ, to store the events until processed. *Table 4.1* compares batch and streaming pipelines based on multiple criteria such as processing schedule and complexity:

Aspect	Batch pipeline	Streaming pipeline
Processing schedule	Processes data at regular intervals (e.g., every minute, hourly, daily).	Processes data continuously, with minimal latency.
Efficiency	Handles large volumes of data more efficiently, optimizing resource allocation and parallel processing.	Handles single data points, providing immediate insights and updates, allowing for rapid response to changes.
Processing complexity	Capable of performing complex data transformations and aggregations.	Designed to handle high-velocity data streams with low latency.
Use cases	Suitable for scenarios where immediate data processing is not critical. Commonly used in data warehousing, reporting, ETL processes, and feature pipelines.	Ideal for applications requiring real-time analytics, features, monitoring, and event-driven architectures.
System complexity	Compared to streaming pipelines, systems are generally simpler to implement and maintain.	More complex to implement and maintain due to the need for low-latency processing, fault tolerance, and scalability. The tooling is also more advanced and complicated.

Table 4.1: Batch versus streaming pipelines

For example, streaming pipelines are extremely powerful in social media recommender systems like TikTok. When using social media, user behavior changes frequently. A typical scenario is that you want to relax at a certain point in time and mostly look at videos of puppies. Still, after 15 minutes, you get bored and want something more serious, such as educative content or news. This means the recommender system has to capture these behavior changes without delay to keep you engaged. As the transition between interests is cyclical and not predictable, you can't use a batch pipeline that runs every 30 minutes or every hour to generate more content. You can run it every minute to create new content, but, at the same time, it will result in unnecessary costs, as most predictions will not be consumed. By implementing a streaming pipeline, you update the features of specific users in real time, which are then passed to a chain of models that predict the new recommendations.

Streaming architectures are also the backbone of real-time fraud detection algorithms, such as those used at Stripe or PayPal. In this context, it's critical to identify potentially fraudulent transactions as they occur, not after a few minutes or hours as a batch pipeline would process them. The same urgency applies to high-frequency trading platforms that make stock predictions based on the constant influx of market data, enabling traders to make decisions within milliseconds.

On the other hand, you can use a batch architecture for an offline recommender system. For example, when implementing one for an e-commerce or streaming platform, you don't need the system to be so reactive, as the user's behavior rarely changes. Thus, updating the recommendations periodically, such as every night, based on historical user behavior data using a batch pipeline is easier to implement and cheaper.

Another popular example of batch pipelines is the ETL design used to extract, transform, and load data for different use cases. The ETL design is widespread in data pipelines used to move data from one DB to another. Some practical use cases include aggregating data for analytics, where you have to extract data from multiple sources, aggregate it, and load it to a data warehouse connected to a dashboard. The analytics domains can be widespread, from e-commerce and marketing to finance and research.

The data collection pipeline used in the LLM Twin use case is another example of an ETL pipeline that extracts data from the internet, structures it, and loads it into a data warehouse for future processing.

Along with prediction or feature freshness, another disadvantage of batch pipelines over streaming ones is that you usually make redundant predictions. Let's take the example of a recommender system for a streaming platform like Netflix. Every night, you make the predictions for all users. There is a significant chance that a large chunk of users won't log in that day. Also, users usually don't browse all the recommendations but stick to the first ones. Thus, only a portion of predictions are used, wasting computing power on all the others.

That's why a popular strategy is to start with a batch architecture, as it's faster and easier to implement. After the product is in place, you gradually move to a streaming design to reduce costs and improve the user experience.

To conclude, we have used a batch architecture (and not a streaming one) to implement the LLM Twin's feature pipeline for the following reasons:

- **Does not require immediate data processing**: Even if syncing the data warehouse and feature store is critical for an accurate RAG system, a delay of a few minutes is acceptable. Thus, we can schedule the batch pipeline to run every minute, constantly syncing the two data storages. This technique works because the data volume is small. The whole data warehouse will have only thousands of records, not millions or billions. Hence, we can quickly iterate through them and sync the two DBs.

- **Simplicity**: As stated earlier, implementing a streaming pipeline is two times more complex. In the real world, you want to keep your system as simple as possible, making it easier to understand, debug, and maintain. Also, simplicity usually translates to lower infrastructure and development costs.

In *Figure 8.10*, we compare what tools you can use based on your architecture (streaming versus batch) and the quantity of data you have to process (small versus big data). In our use case, we are in the smaller data and batch quadrant, where we picked a combination of vanilla Python and generative AI tools such as LangChain, Sentence Transformers, and Unstructured.

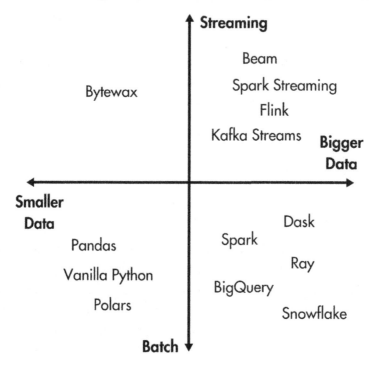

Figure 4.10: Tools on the streaming versus batch and smaller versus bigger data spectrum

In the *Change data capture: syncing the data warehouse and feature store* section later in this chapter, we will discuss when switching from a batch architecture to a streaming one makes sense.

Core steps

Most of the RAG feature pipelines are composed of five core steps. The one implemented in the LLM Twin architecture makes no exception. Thus, you can quickly adapt this pattern for other RAG applications, but here is what the LLM Twin's RAG feature pipeline looks like:

1. **Data extraction**: Extract the latest articles, code repositories, and posts from the MongoDB data warehouse. At the extraction step, you usually aggregate all the data you need for processing.

2. **Cleaning**: The data from the data warehouse is standardized and partially clean, but we have to ensure that the text contains only useful information, is not duplicated, and can be interpreted by the embedding model. For example, we must clean and normalize all non-ASCII characters before passing the text to the embedding model. Also, to keep the information semantically dense, we decided to replace all the URLs with placeholders and remove all emojis. The cleaning step is more art than **science**. Hence, after you have the first iteration with an evaluation mechanism in place, you will probably reiterate and improve it.

3. **Chunking**: You must adopt various chunking strategies based on each data category and embedding model. For example, when working with code repositories, you want the chunks broader, whereas when working with articles, you want them narrower or scoped at the paragraph level. Depending on your data, you must decide if you split your document based on the chapter, section, paragraph, sentence, or just a fixed window size. Also, you have to ensure that the chunk size doesn't exceed the maximum input size of the embedding model. That is why you usually chunk a document based on your data structure and the maximum input size of the model.

4. **Embedding**: You pass each chunk individually to an embedding model of your choice. Implementation-wise, this step is usually the simplest, as tools such as SentenceTransformer and Hugging Face provide high-level interfaces for most embedding models. As explained in the *What are embeddings?* section of this chapter, at this step, the most critical decisions are to decide what model to use and whether to fine-tune it or not. For example, we used an `"all-mpnet-base-v2"` embedding model from *SentenceTransformer*, which is relatively tiny and runs on most machines. However, we provide a configuration file where you can quickly configure the embedding model with something more powerful based on the state of the art when reading this book. You can quickly find other options on the MTEB on Hugging Face (`https://huggingface.co/spaces/mteb/leaderboard`).

5. **Data loading**: The final step combines the embedding of a chunked document and its metadata, such as the author and the document ID, content, URL, platform, and creation date. Ultimately, we wrap the vector and the metadata into a structure compatible with Qdrant and push it to the vector DB. As we want to use Qdrant as the single source of truth for the features, we also push the cleaned documents (before chunking) to Qdrant. We can push data without vectors, as the metadata index of Qdrant behaves like a NoSQL DB. Thus, pushing metadata without a vector attached to it is like using a standard NoSQL engine.

Change data capture: syncing the data warehouse and feature store

As highlighted a few times in this chapter, data is constantly changing, which can result in DBs, data lakes, data warehouses, and feature stores getting out of sync. **Change data capture (CDC)** is a strategy that allows you to optimally keep two or more data storage types in sync without computing and I/O overhead. It captures any CRUD operation done on the source DB and replicates it on a target DB. Optionally, you can add preprocessing steps in between the replication.

The syncing issues also apply when building a feature pipeline. One key design choice concerns how to sync the data warehouse with the feature store to have data fresh enough for your particular use case.

In our LLM Twin use case, we chose a naïve approach out of simplicity. We implemented a batch pipeline that is triggered periodically or manually. It reads all the raw data from the data warehouse, processes it in batches, and inserts new records or updates old ones from the Qdrant vector DB. This works fine when you are working with a small number of records, at the order of thousands or tens of thousands. But our naïve approach raises the following questions:

- What happens if the data suddenly grows to millions of records (or higher)?

- What happens if a record is deleted from the data warehouse? How is this reflected in the feature store?

- What if we want to process only the new or updated items from the data warehouse and not all of them?

Fortunately, the CDC pattern can solve all of these issues. When implementing CDC, you can take multiple approaches, but all of them use either a push or pull strategy:

- **Push:** The source DB is the primary driver in the push approach. It actively identifies and transmits data modifications to target systems for processing. This method ensures near-instantaneous updates at the target, but data loss can occur if target systems are inaccessible. To mitigate this, a messaging system is typically employed as a buffer.

- **Pull:** The pull method assigns a more passive role to the source DB, which only records data changes. Target systems periodically request these changes and handle updates accordingly. While this approach lightens the load on the source, it introduces a delay in data propagation. A messaging system is again essential to prevent data loss during periods of target system unavailability.

In summary, the push method is ideal for applications demanding immediate data access, whereas the pull method is better suited for large-scale data transfers where real-time updates aren't critical. With that in mind, there are different methods to detect changes in data. Thus, let's list the main CDC patterns that are used in the industry:

- **Timestamp-based**: The approach involves adding a modification time column to DB tables, usually called LAST_MODIFIED or LAST_UPDATED. Downstream systems can query this column to identify records that have been updated since their last check. While simple to implement, this method is limited to tracking changes, not deletions, and imposes performance overhead due to the need to scan entire tables.

- **Trigger-based**: The trigger-based approach utilizes DB triggers to automatically record data modifications in a separate table upon INSERT, UPDATE, or DELETE operations, often known as the event table. This method provides comprehensive change tracking but can impact the DB performance due to the additional write operations involved for each event.

- **Log-based**: DBs maintain transaction logs to record all data modifications, including timestamps. Primarily used for recovery, these logs can also be leveraged to propagate changes to target systems in real time. This approach minimizes the performance impact on the source DB. As a huge advantage, it avoids additional processing overhead on the source DB, captures all data changes, and requires no schema modification. But on the opposite side, it lacks standardized log formats, leading to vendor-specific implementations.

 For more details on CDC, I recommend *What is Change Data Capture?* from Confluent's blog: https://www.confluent.io/en-gb/learn/change-data-capture/.

With these CDC techniques in mind, we could quickly implement a pull timestamp-based strategy in our RAG feature pipeline to sync the data warehouse and feature store more optimally when the data grows. Our implementation is still pull-based but doesn't check any last updated field in the source DB; it just pulls everything from the data warehouse.

However, the most popular and optimal technique in the industry is the log-based one. It doesn't add any I/O overhead to the source DB, has low latency, and supports all CRUD operations. The biggest downside is its development complexity, which requires a queue to capture all the CRUD events and a streaming pipeline to process them.

As this is an LLM book and not a data engineering one, we wanted to keep things simple, but it's important to know that these techniques exist, and you can always upgrade your current implementation when it doesn't fit your application requirements anymore.

Why is the data stored in two snapshots?

We store two snapshots of our data in the logical feature store:

- **After the data is cleaned**: For fine-tuning LLMs
- **After the documents are chunked and embedded**: For RAG

Why did we design it this way? Remember that the features should be accessed solely from the feature store for training and inference. Thus, this adds consistency to our design and makes it cleaner.

Also, storing the data cleaned specifically for our fine-tuning and embedding use case in the MongoDB data warehouse would have been an antipattern. The data from the warehouse is shared all across the company. Thus, processing it for a specific use case is not good practice. Imagine another summarization use case where we must clean and preprocess the data differently. We must create a new "Cleaned Data" table prefixed with the use case name. We have to repeat that for every new use case. Therefore, to avoid having a spaghetti data warehouse, the data from the data warehouse is generic and is modeled to specific applications only in downstream components, which, in our case, is the feature store.

Ultimately, as we mentioned in the *Core steps* section, you can leverage the metadata index of a vector DB as a NoSQL DB. Based on these factors, we decided to keep the cleaned data in Qdrant, along with the chunked and embedded versions of the documents.

As a quick reminder, when operationalizing our LLM Twin system, the create instruct dataset pipeline, explained in *Chapter 5*, will read the cleaned documents from Qdrant, process them, and save them under a versioned ZenML artifact. The training pipeline requires a dataset and not plain documents. This is a reminder that our logical feature store comprises the Qdrant vector DB for online serving and ZenML artifacts for offline training.

Orchestration

ZenML will orchestrate the batch RAG feature pipeline. Using ZenML, we can schedule it to run on a schedule, for example, every hour, or quickly manually trigger it. Another option is to trigger it after the ETL data collection pipeline finishes.

By orchestrating the feature pipeline and integrating it into ZenML (or any other orchestration tool), we can operationalize the feature pipeline with the end goal of **continuous training (CT)**.

We will go into all the details of orchestration, scheduling, and CT in *Chapter 11*.

Implementing the LLM Twin's RAG feature pipeline

The last step is to review the LLM Twin's RAG feature pipeline code to see how we applied everything we discussed in this chapter. We will walk you through the following:

- ZenML code
- Pydantic domain objects
- A custom **object-vector mapping** (OVM) implementation
- The cleaning, chunking, and embedding logic for all our data categories

We will take a top-down approach. Thus, let's start with the Settings class and ZenML pipeline.

Settings

We use Pydantic Settings (https://docs.pydantic.dev/latest/concepts/pydantic_settings/) to define a global Settings class that loads sensitive or non-sensitive variables from a .env file. This approach also gives us all the benefits of Pydantic, such as type validation. For example, if we provide a string for the QDRANT_DATABASE_PORT variable instead of an integer, the program will crash. This behavior makes the whole application more deterministic and reliable.

Here is what the Settings class looks like with all the variables necessary to build the RAG feature pipeline:

```python
from pydantic import BaseSettings

class Settings(BaseSettings):
    class Config:
        env_file = ".env"
        env_file_encoding = "utf-8"

    ... # Some other settings...

    # RAG
    TEXT_EMBEDDING_MODEL_ID: str = "sentence-transformers/all-MiniLM-
L6-v2"
    RERANKING_CROSS_ENCODER_MODEL_ID: str = "cross-encoder/ms-marco-
MiniLM-L-4-v2"
    RAG_MODEL_DEVICE: str = "cpu"
```

```
    # QdrantDB Vector DB
    USE_QDRANT_CLOUD: bool = False
    QDRANT_DATABASE_HOST: str = "localhost"
    QDRANT_DATABASE_PORT: int = 6333
    QDRANT_CLOUD_URL: str = "str"
    QDRANT_APIKEY: str | None = None


    … # More settings…

settings = Settings()
```

As stated in the internal Config class, all the variables have default values or can be overridden by providing a .env file.

ZenML pipeline and steps

The ZenML pipeline is the entry point for the RAG feature engineering pipeline. It reflects the five core phases of RAG ingestion code: extracting raw documents, cleaning, chunking, embedding, and loading them to the logical feature store. The calls within the feature_engineering() function are ZenML steps, representing a single execution unit performing the five phases of RAG. The code is available in the GitHub repository at https://github.com/PacktPublishing/LLM-Engineers-Handbook/blob/main/pipelines/feature_engineering.py:

```
from zenml import pipeline

from llm_engineering.interfaces.orchestrator.steps import feature_
engineering as fe_steps

@pipeline
def feature_engineering(author_full_names: list[str]) -> None:
    raw_documents = fe_steps.query_data_warehouse(author_full_names)

    cleaned_documents = fe_steps.clean_documents(raw_documents)
     last_step_1 = fe_steps.load_to_vector_db(cleaned_documents)

    embedded_documents = fe_steps.chunk_and_embed(cleaned_documents)
    last_step_2 = fe_steps.load_to_vector_db(embedded_documents)

    return [last_step_1.invocation_id, last_step_2.invocation_id]
```

Figure 4.11 shows how multiple feature engineering pipeline runs look in ZenML's dashboard.

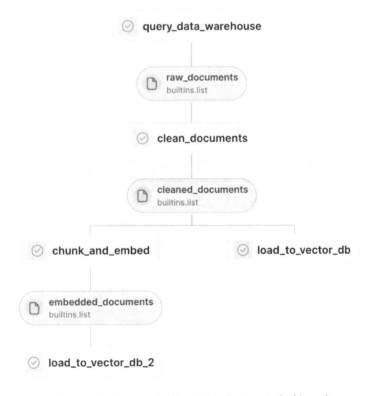

Figure 4.11: Feature pipeline runs in the ZenML dashboard

Figure 8.12 shows the DAG of the RAG feature pipeline, where you can follow all the pipeline steps and their output artifacts. Remember that whatever is returned from a ZenML step is automatically saved as an artifact, stored in ZenML's artifact registry, versioned, and shareable across the application.

Figure 4.12: Feature pipeline DAG in the ZenML dashboard

The final puzzle piece is understanding how to configure the RAG feature pipeline dynamically. All its available settings are exposed as function parameters. Here, we need only a list of author's names, as seen in the function's signature: `feature_engineering(author_full_names: list[str])`. We inject a YAML configuration file at runtime that contains all the necessary values based on different use cases. For example, the following configuration includes a list of all the authors of this book as we want to populate the feature store with data from all of us (available in the GitHub repository at `configs/feature_engineering.yaml`):

```
parameters:
  author_full_names:
    - Alex Vesa
    - Maxime Labonne
    - Paul Iusztin
```

The beauty of this approach is that you don't have to modify the code to configure the feature pipeline with different input values. You have to provide a different configuration file when running it, as follows:

```
feature_engineering.with_options(config_path=".../feature_engineering.yaml")
()
```

You can either hardcode the path to the config file or provide the `config_path` from the CLI, which allows you to modify the pipeline's configuration between different runs. Out of simplicity, we hard-coded the configuration file. Thus, we can call the feature engineering pipeline calling the `run.py` script as follows:

```
python -m tools.run --no-cache --run-feature-engineering
```

However, you can easily add another CLI argument to pass the `config_path` variable. Also, you can run the feature pipeline using the following poe command:

```
poetry poe run-feature-engineering-pipeline
```

Let's move forward to the ZenML steps and sequentially zoom in on all of them. The source code for all the feature engineering pipeline steps is available on GitHub at `"steps/feature_engineering"`. We will begin with the first step, which involves querying the data warehouse for new content to process into features.

Querying the data warehouse

The first thing to notice is that a step is a Python function decorated with @step, similar to how a ZenML pipeline works. The function below takes as input a list of authors' full names and performs the following core steps:

- It attempts to get or create a UserDocument instance using the first and last names, appending this instance to the authors list. If the user doesn't exist, it throws an error.
- It fetches all the raw data for the user from the data warehouse and extends the documents list to include these user documents.
- Ultimately, it computes a descriptive metadata dictionary logged and tracked in ZenML.

```
… # other imports
from zenml import get_step_context, step


@step
def query_data_warehouse(
    author_full_names: list[str],
) -> Annotated[list, "raw_documents"]:
    documents = []
    authors = []
    for author_full_name in author_full_names:
        logger.info(f"Querying data warehouse for user: {author_full_
name}")

        first_name, last_name = utils.split_user_full_name(author_full_
name)
        logger.info(f"First name: {first_name}, Last name: {last_name}")
        user = UserDocument.get_or_create(first_name=first_name, last_
name=last_name)
        authors.append(user)

        results = fetch_all_data(user)
        user_documents = [doc for query_result in results.values() for doc
in query_result]

        documents.extend(user_documents)

    step_context = get_step_context()
```

```
    step_context.add_output_metadata(output_name="raw_documents",
metadata=_get_metadata(documents))


    return documents
```

The fetch function leverages a thread pool that runs each query on a different thread. As we have multiple data categories, we have to make a different query for the articles, posts, and repositories, as they are stored in different collections. Each query calls the data warehouse, which is bounded by the network I/O and data warehouse latency, not by the machine's CPU. Thus, by moving each query to a different thread, we can parallelize them. Ultimately, instead of adding the latency of each query as the total timing, the time to run this fetch function will be the max between all the calls.

Using threads to parallelize I/O-bounded calls is good practice in Python, as they are not locked by the Python **Global Interpreter Lock (GIL)**. In contrast, adding each call to a different process would add too much overhead, as a process takes longer to spin off than a thread.

In Python, you want to parallelize things with processes only when the operations are CPU or memory-bound because the GIL affects them. Each process has a different GIL. Thus, parallelizing your computing logic, such as processing a batch of documents or images already loaded in memory, isn't affected by Python's GIL limitations.

```python
def fetch_all_data(user: UserDocument) -> dict[str,
list[NoSQLBaseDocument]]:
    user_id = str(user.id)
    with ThreadPoolExecutor() as executor:
        future_to_query = {
            executor.submit(__fetch_articles, user_id): "articles",
            executor.submit(__fetch_posts, user_id): "posts",
            executor.submit(__fetch_repositories, user_id):
"repositories",
        }

        results = {}
        for future in as_completed(future_to_query):
            query_name = future_to_query[future]
            try:
                results[query_name] = future.result()
            except Exception:
```

```
                    logger.exception(f"'{query_name}' request failed.")

                    results[query_name] = []

        return results
```

The _get_metadata() function takes the list of queried documents and authors and counts the number of them relative to each data category:

```python
def _get_metadata(documents: list[Document]) -> dict:
    metadata = {
        "num_documents": len(documents),
    }
    for document in documents:
        collection = document.get_collection_name()
        if collection not in metadata:
            metadata[collection] = {}
        if "authors" not in metadata[collection]:
            metadata[collection]["authors"] = list()

        metadata[collection]["num_documents"] = metadata[collection].
get("num_documents", 0) + 1
        metadata[collection]["authors"].append(document.author_full_name)

    for value in metadata.values():
        if isinstance(value, dict) and "authors" in value:
            value["authors"] = list(set(value["authors"]))

    return metadata
```

We will expose this metadata in the ZenML dashboard to quickly see some statistics on the loaded data. For example, in *Figure 4.13*, we accessed the metadata tab of the query_data_warehouse() step, where you can see that, within that particular run of the feature pipeline, we loaded 76 documents from three authors. This is extremely powerful for monitoring and debugging batch pipelines.

You can always extend it with anything that makes sense for your use case.

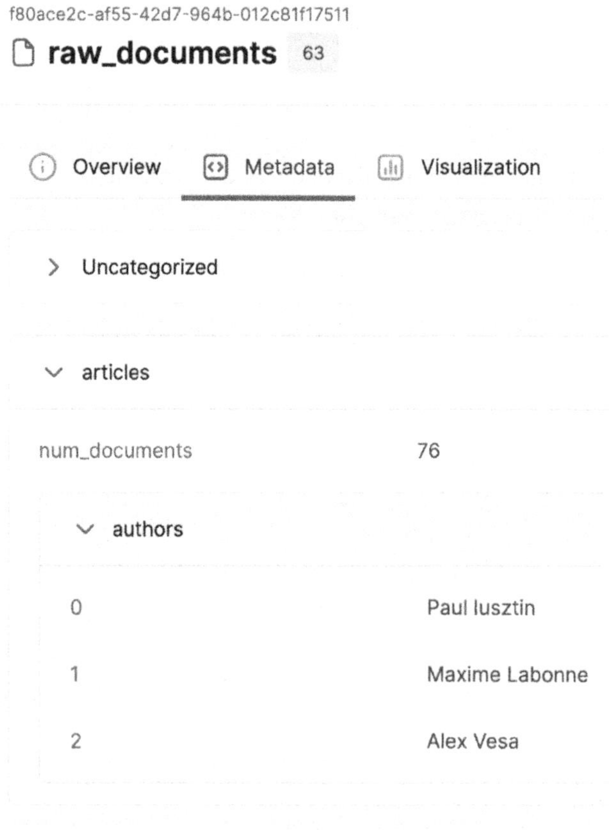

f80ace2c-af55-42d7-964b-012c81f17511

☐ **raw_documents**   63

| ⓘ Overview | ‹› Metadata | ⏿ Visualization |

> Uncategorized

∨ articles

num_documents   76

∨ authors

0   Paul Iusztin

1   Maxime Labonne

2   Alex Vesa

Figure 4.13: Metadata of the "query the data warehouse" ZenML step

Cleaning the documents

In the cleaning step, we iterate through all the documents and delegate all the logic to a CleaningDispatcher who knows what cleaning logic to apply based on the data category. Remember that we want to apply, or have the ability to apply in the future, different cleaning techniques on articles, posts, and code repositories.

```
@step
def clean_documents(
    documents: Annotated[list, "raw_documents"],
) -> Annotated[list, "cleaned_documents"]:
    cleaned_documents = []
    for document in documents:
```

```
            cleaned_document = CleaningDispatcher.dispatch(document)
            cleaned_documents.append(cleaned_document)

    step_context = get_step_context()
    step_context.add_output_metadata(output_name="cleaned_documents",
metadata=_get_metadata(cleaned_documents))

    return cleaned_documents
```

The computed metadata is similar to what we logged in the query_data_warehouse() step. Thus, let's move on to chunking and embedding.

Chunk and embed the cleaned documents

Similar to how we cleaned the documents, we delegate the chunking and embedding logic to a dispatcher who knows how to handle each data category. Note that the chunking dispatcher returns a list instead of a single object, which makes sense as the document is split into multiple chunks. We will dig into the dispatcher in the "The dispatcher layer" section of this chapter.

```
@step
def chunk_and_embed(
    cleaned_documents: Annotated[list, "cleaned_documents"],
) -> Annotated[list, "embedded_documents"]:
    metadata = {"chunking": {}, "embedding": {}, "num_documents":
len(cleaned_documents)}

    embedded_chunks = []
    for document in cleaned_documents:
        chunks = ChunkingDispatcher.dispatch(document)
        metadata["chunking"] = _add_chunks_metadata(chunks,
metadata["chunking"])

        for batched_chunks in utils.misc.batch(chunks, 10):
            batched_embedded_chunks = EmbeddingDispatcher.
dispatch(batched_chunks)
            embedded_chunks.extend(batched_embedded_chunks)

    metadata["embedding"] = _add_embeddings_metadata(embedded_chunks,
metadata["embedding"])
    metadata["num_chunks"] = len(embedded_chunks)
```

```
metadata["num_embedded_chunks"] = len(embedded_chunks)

step_context = get_step_context()
step_context.add_output_metadata(output_name="embedded_documents",
metadata=metadata)


return embedded_chunks
```

In *Figure 4.14*, you can see the metadata of the chunking and embedding ZenML step. For example, you can quickly understand that we transformed 76 documents into 2,373 chunks, or the properties we used for chunking articles, such as a chunk_size of 500 and a chunk_overlap of 50.

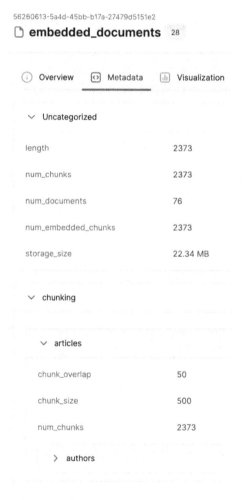

Figure 4.14: Metadata of the embedding and chunking ZenML step, detailing the uncategorized and chunking dropdowns

In Figure 4.15, the rest of the ZenML metadata from the embedding and chunking step details the embedding model and its properties used to compute the vectors.

56260613-5a4d-45bb-b17a-27479d5151e2

🗋 **embedded_documents** 28

ⓘ Overview   ⟨⟩ Metadata   📊 Visualization

> Uncategorized

> chunking

∨ embedding

   ∨ articles

   embedding_model_id   sentence-transformers/all-MiniLM-L6-v2

   embedding_size   384

   max_input_length   256

     ∨ authors

     0   Paul Iusztin

     1   Maxime Labonne

     2   Alex Vesa

Figure 4.15: Metadata of the embedding and chunking ZenML step, detailing the embedding dropdown

As ML systems can break at any time while in production due to drifts or untreated use cases, leveraging the metadata section to monitor the ingested data can be a powerful tool that will save debugging days, translating to tens of thousands of dollars or more for your business.

Loading the documents to the vector DB

As each article, post, or code repository sits in a different collection inside the vector DB, we have to group all the documents based on their data category. Then, we load each group in bulk in the Qdrant vector DB:

```python
@step
def load_to_vector_db(
    documents: Annotated[list, "documents"],
) -> None:
    logger.info(f"Loading {len(documents)} documents into the vector
database.")

    grouped_documents = VectorBaseDocument.group_by_class(documents)
    for document_class, documents in grouped_documents.items():
        logger.info(f"Loading documents into {document_class.get_
collection_name()}")
        for documents_batch in utils.misc.batch(documents, size=4):
            try:
                document_class.bulk_insert(documents_batch)
            except Exception:
                return False

    return True
```

Pydantic domain entities

Before investigating the dispatchers, we must understand the domain objects we work with. To some extent, in implementing the LLM Twin, we are following the **domain-driven design (DDD)** principles, which state that domain entities are the core of your application. Thus, before proceeding, it's important to understand the hierarchy of the domain classes we are working with.

 The code for the domain entities is available on GitHub at https://github.com/ PacktPublishing/LLM-Engineering/tree/main/llm_engineering/domain.

We used Pydantic to model all our domain entities. When we wrote the book, choosing Pydantic was a no-brainer, as it is the go-to Python package for writing data structures with out-of-the-box type validation. As Python is a dynamically typed language, using Pydantic for type validation at runtime makes your system order of times more robust, as you can be sure that you are always working with the right type of data.

The domain of our LLM Twin application is split into two dimensions:

- **The data category**: Post, article, and repository
- **The state of the data**: Cleaned, chunked, and embedded

We decided to create a base class for each state of the document, resulting in having the following base abstract classes:

- `class CleanedDocument(VectorBaseDocument, ABC)`
- `class Chunk(VectorBaseDocument, ABC)`
- `class EmbeddedChunk(VectorBaseDocument, ABC)`

Note that all of them inherit the `VectorBaseDocument` class, which is our custom **OVM** implementation, which we will explain in the next section of this chapter. Also, it inherits from ABC, which makes the class abstract. Thus, you cannot initialize an object out of these classes; you may only inherit from them. That is why base classes are always marked as abstract.

Each base abstract class from above (which models the state) will have a subclass that adds the data category dimension. For example, the `CleanedDocument` class will have the following subclasses:

- `class CleanedPostDocument(CleanedDocument)`
- `class CleanedArticleDocument(CleanedDocument)`
- `class CleanedRepositoryDocument(CleanedDocument)`

As we can see in *Figure 8.16*, we will repeat the same logic for the `Chunk` and `EmbeddedChunk` base abstract classes. We will implement a specific document class for each data category and state combination, resulting in nine types of domain entities. For example, when ingesting a raw document, the cleaning step will yield a `CleanedArticleDocument` instance, the chunking step will return a list of `ArticleChunk` objects, and the embedding operation will return `EmbeddedArticleChunk` instances that encapsulate the embedding and all the necessary metadata to ingest in the vector DB.

The same will happen for the posts and repositories.

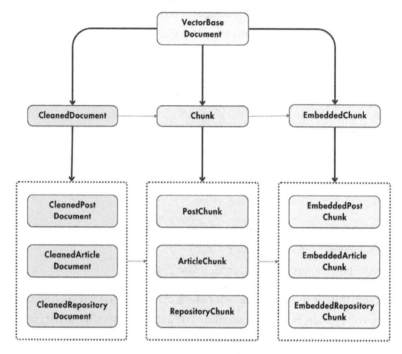

Figure 4.16: Domain entities class hierarchy and their interaction

We chose this design because the list of states will rarely change, and we want to extend the list of data categories. Thus, structuring the classes after the state allows us to plug another data category by inheriting these base abstract classes.

Let's see the complete code for the hierarchy of the cleaned document. All the attributes of a cleaned document will be saved within the metadata of the vector DB. For example, the metadata of a cleaned article document will always contain the content, platform, author ID, author full name, and link of the article.

Another fundamental aspect is the Config internal class, which defines the name of the collection within the vector DB, the data category of the entity, and whether to leverage the vector index when creating the collection:

```
class CleanedDocument(VectorBaseDocument, ABC):
    content: str
    platform: str
    author_id: UUID4
    author_full_name: str
```

```
class CleanedPostDocument(CleanedDocument):
    image: Optional[str] = None

    class Config:
        name = "cleaned_posts"
        category = DataCategory.POSTS
        use_vector_index = False

class CleanedArticleDocument(CleanedDocument):
    link: str

    class Config:
        name = "cleaned_articles"
        category = DataCategory.ARTICLES
        use_vector_index = False

class CleanedRepositoryDocument(CleanedDocument):
    name: str
    link: str

    class Config:
        name = "cleaned_repositories"
        category = DataCategory.REPOSITORIES
        use_vector_index = False
```

To conclude this section, let's also take a look at the base abstract class of the chunk and embedded chunk:

```
class Chunk(VectorBaseDocument, ABC):
    content: str
    platform: str
    document_id: UUID4
    author_id: UUID4
    author_full_name: str
    metadata: dict = Field(default_factory=dict)

… # PostChunk, ArticleChunk, RepositoryChunk
```

```
class EmbeddedChunk(VectorBaseDocument, ABC):
    content: str
    embedding: list[float] | None
    platform: str
    document_id: UUID4
    author_id: UUID4
    author_full_name: str
    metadata: dict = Field(default_factory=dict)


… # EmbeddedPostChunk, EmbeddedArticleChunk, EmbeddedRepositoryChunk
```

We also defined an enum that aggregates all our data categories in a single structure of constants:

```
class DataCategory(StrEnum):
    POSTS = "posts"
    ARTICLES = "articles"
    REPOSITORIES = "repositories"
```

The last step to fully understand how the domain objects work is to zoom into the VectorBaseDocument OVM class.

OVM

The term OVM is inspired by the **object-relational mapping (ORM)** pattern we discussed in *Chapter 3*. We called it OVM because we work with embedding and vector DBs instead of structured data and SQL tables. Otherwise, it follows the same principles as an ORM pattern.

Similar to what we did in *Chapter 3*, we will implement our own OVM version. Even if our custom example is simple, it's a powerful example of how to write modular and extendable classes by leveraging OOP best practices and principles.

 The full implementation of the VectorBaseDocument class is available on GitHub at https://github.com/PacktPublishing/LLM-Engineering/blob/main/llm_engineering/domain/base/vector.py.

Our OVM base class is called VectorBaseDocument. It will support CRUD operations on top of Qdrant. Based on our application's demands, we limited it only to create and read operations, but it can easily be extended to update and delete functions.

Let's take a look at the definition of the VectorBaseDocument class:

```python
from pydantic import UUID4, BaseModel
from typing import Generic

from llm_engineering.infrastructure.db.qdrant import connection

T = TypeVar("T", bound="VectorBaseDocument")

class VectorBaseDocument(BaseModel, Generic[T], ABC):
    id: UUID4 = Field(default_factory=uuid.uuid4)

    @classmethod
    def from_record(cls: Type[T], point: Record) -> T:
        _id = UUID(point.id, version=4)
        payload = point.payload or {}

        attributes = {
            "id": _id,
            **payload,
        }
        if cls._has_class_attribute("embedding"):
            payload["embedding"] = point.vector or None

        return cls(**attributes)

    def to_point(self: T, **kwargs) -> PointStruct:
        exclude_unset = kwargs.pop("exclude_unset", False)
        by_alias = kwargs.pop("by_alias", True)

        payload = self.dict(exclude_unset=exclude_unset, by_alias=by_
alias, **kwargs)

        _id = str(payload.pop("id"))
        vector = payload.pop("embedding", {})
        if vector and isinstance(vector, np.ndarray):
```

```
        vector = vector.tolist()

    return PointStruct(id=_id, vector=vector, payload=payload)
```

- The VectorBaseDocument class inherits from Pydantic's BaseModel and helps us structure a single record's attributes from the vector DB. Every OVM will be initialized by default with UUID4 as its unique identifier. Using generics—more precisely, by inheriting from Generic[T]—the signatures of all the subclasses of the VectorBaseDocument class will adapt to that given class. For example, the from_record() method of the Chunk() class, which inherits VectorBaseDocument, will return the Chunk type, which drastically helps the static analyzer and type checkers such as mypy (https://mypy.readthedocs.io/en/stable/).

The from_record() method adapts a data point from Qdrant's format to our internal structure based on Pydantic. On the other hand, the to_point() method takes the attributes of the current instance and adapts them to Qdrant's PointStruct() format. We will leverage these two methods for our create and read operations.

Ultimately, all operations made to Qdrant will be done through the connection instance, which is instantiated in the application's infrastructure layer.

The bulk_insert() method maps each document to a point. Then, it uses the Qdrant connection instance to load all the points to a given collection in Qdrant. If the insertion fails once, it tries to create the collection and do the insertion again. Often, it is good practice to split your logic into two functions. One private function contains the logic, in our case _bulk_insert(), and one public function handles all the errors and failure scenarios.

```python
class VectorBaseDocument(BaseModel, Generic[T], ABC):
    … # Rest of the class

    @classmethod
    def bulk_insert(cls: Type[T], documents: list["VectorBaseDocument"])
-> bool:
        try:
            cls._bulk_insert(documents)
        except exceptions.UnexpectedResponse:
            logger.info(
                f"Collection '{cls.get_collection_name()}' does not exist.
Trying to create the collection and reinsert the documents."
```

```
                )

            cls.create_collection()

            try:
                cls._bulk_insert(documents)
            except exceptions.UnexpectedResponse:
                logger.error(f"Failed to insert documents in '{cls.get_
collection_name()}'.")

                return False

        return True

    @classmethod
    def _bulk_insert(cls: Type[T], documents: list["VectorBaseDocument"])
-> None:
        points = [doc.to_point() for doc in documents]

        connection.upsert(collection_name=cls.get_collection_name(),
points=points)
```

The collection name is inferred from the Config class defined in the subclasses inheriting the OVM:

```
class VectorBaseDocument(BaseModel, Generic[T], ABC):
    … # Rest of the class



    @classmethod
    def get_collection_name(cls: Type[T]) -> str:
        if not hasattr(cls, "Config") or not hasattr(cls.Config, "name"):
            raise ImproperlyConfigured(
                "The class should define a Config class with" "the 'name'
property that reflects the collection's name."
            )

        return cls.Config.name
```

Now, we must define a method that lets us read all the records from the vector DB (without using vector similarity search logic). The bulk_find() method enables us to scroll (or list) all the records from a collection. The function below scrolls the Qdrant vector DB, which returns a list of data points, which are ultimately mapped to our internal structure using the from_record() method.

The limit parameters control how many items we return at once, and the offset signals the ID of the point from which Qdrant starts returning records.

```python
class VectorBaseDocument(BaseModel, Generic[T], ABC):
    … # Rest of the class

    @classmethod
    def bulk_find(cls: Type[T], limit: int = 10, **kwargs) ->
tuple[list[T], UUID | None]:
        try:
            documents, next_offset = cls._bulk_find(limit=limit, **kwargs)
        except exceptions.UnexpectedResponse:
            logger.error(f"Failed to search documents in '{cls.get_
collection_name()}'.")

            documents, next_offset = [], None

        return documents, next_offset

    @classmethod
    def _bulk_find(cls: Type[T], limit: int = 10, **kwargs) ->
tuple[list[T], UUID | None]:
        collection_name = cls.get_collection_name()

        offset = kwargs.pop("offset", None)
        offset = str(offset) if offset else None

        records, next_offset = connection.scroll(
            collection_name=collection_name,
            limit=limit,
            with_payload=kwargs.pop("with_payload", True),
            with_vectors=kwargs.pop("with_vectors", False),
            offset=offset,
```

```
            **kwargs,
        )
        documents = [cls.from_record(record) for record in records]
        if next_offset is not None:
            next_offset = UUID(next_offset, version=4)

        return documents, next_offset
```

The last piece of the puzzle is to define a method that performs a vector similarity search on a provided query embedding. Like before, we defined a public search() and private _search() method. The search is performed by Qdrant when calling the connection.search() function.

```
class VectorBaseDocument(BaseModel, Generic[T], ABC):
    … # Rest of the class

    @classmethod
    def search(cls: Type[T], query_vector: list, limit: int = 10,
**kwargs) -> list[T]:
        try:
            documents = cls._search(query_vector=query_vector,
limit=limit, **kwargs)
        except exceptions.UnexpectedResponse:
            logger.error(f"Failed to search documents in '{cls.get_
collection_name()}'.")

            documents = []

        return documents

    @classmethod
    def _search(cls: Type[T], query_vector: list, limit: int = 10,
**kwargs) -> list[T]:
        collection_name = cls.get_collection_name()
        records = connection.search(
            collection_name=collection_name,
            query_vector=query_vector,
            limit=limit,
            with_payload=kwargs.pop("with_payload", True),
            with_vectors=kwargs.pop("with_vectors", False),
```

```
        **kwargs,
    )
    documents = [cls.from_record(record) for record in records]

    return documents
```

Now that we understand what our domain entities look like and how the OVM works, let's move on to the dispatchers who clean, chunk, and embed the documents.

The dispatcher layer

A dispatcher inputs a document and applies dedicated handlers based on its data category (article, post, or repository). A handler can either clean, chunk, or embed a document.

Let's start by zooming in on the CleaningDispatcher. It mainly implements a dispatch() method that inputs a raw document. Based on its data category, it instantiates and calls a handler that applies the cleaning logic specific to that data point:

```
class CleaningDispatcher:
    cleaning_factory = CleaningHandlerFactory()

    @classmethod
    def dispatch(cls, data_model: NoSQLBaseDocument) ->
VectorBaseDocument:
        data_category = DataCategory(data_model.get_collection_name())
        handler = cls.cleaning_factory.create_handler(data_category)
        clean_model = handler.clean(data_model)

        logger.info(
            "Data cleaned successfully.",
            data_category=data_category,
            cleaned_content_len=len(clean_model.content),
        )

        return clean_model
```

The key in the dispatcher logic is the CleaningHandlerFactory(), which instantiates a different cleaning handler based on the document's data category:

```
class CleaningHandlerFactory:
    @staticmethod
```

```
    def create_handler(data_category: DataCategory) ->
CleaningDataHandler:
        if data_category == DataCategory.POSTS:
            return PostCleaningHandler()
        elif data_category == DataCategory.ARTICLES:
            return ArticleCleaningHandler()
        elif data_category == DataCategory.REPOSITORIES:
            return RepositoryCleaningHandler()
        else:
            raise ValueError("Unsupported data type")
```

The Dispatcher or Factory classes are nothing fancy, but they offer an intuitive and simple interface for applying various operations to your documents. When manipulating documents, instead of worrying about their data category and polluting your business logic with if-else statements, you have a class dedicated to handling that. You have a single class that cleans any document, which respects the DRY (don't repeat yourself) principles from software engineering. By respecting DRY, you have a single point of failure, and the code can easily be extended. For example, if we add an extra type, we must extend only the Factory class instead of multiple occurrences in the code.

The ChunkingDispatcher and EmbeddingDispatcher follow the same pattern. They use a ChunkingHandlerFactory and, respectively, an EmbeddingHandlerFactory that initializes the correct handler based on the data category of the input document. Afterward, they call the handler and return the result.

 The source code of all the dispatchers and factories can be found on GitHub at https://github.com/PacktPublishing/LLM-Engineers-Handbook/blob/main/llm_engineering/application/preprocessing/dispatchers.py

The Factory class leverages the abstract factory creational pattern (https://refactoring.guru/design-patterns/abstract-factory), which instantiates a family of classes implementing the same interface. In our case, these handlers implement the clean() method regardless of the handler type.

Also, the Handler class family leverages the strategy behavioral pattern (https://refactoring.guru/design-patterns/strategy) used to instantiate when you want to use different variants of an algorithm within an object and be able to switch from one algorithm to another during runtime.

Intuitively, in our dispatcher layer, the combination of the factory and strategy patterns works as follows:

1. Initially, we knew we wanted to clean the data, but as we knew the data category only at runtime, we couldn't decide on what strategy to apply.

2. We can write the whole code around the cleaning code and abstract away the logic under a Handler() interface, which will represent our strategy.

3. When we get a data point, we apply the abstract factory pattern and create the correct cleaning handler for its data type.

4. Ultimately, the dispatcher layer uses the handler and executes the right strategy.

By doing so, we:

- Isolate the logic for a given data category.

- Leverage polymorphism to avoid filling up the code with hundreds of if-else statements.

- Make the code modular and extendable. When a new data category arrives, we must implement a new handler and modify the Factory class without touching any other part of the code.

 Until now, we have just modeled our entities and how the data flows in our application. We haven't written a single piece of cleaning, chunking, or embedding code. That is one big difference between a quick demo and a production-ready application. In a demo, you don't care about software engineering best practices and structuring your code to make it future-proof. However, writing clean, modular, and scalable code is critical for its longevity when building a real-world application.

The last component of the RAG feature pipeline is the implementation of the cleaning, chunking, and embedding handlers.

The handlers

The handler has a one-on-one structure with our domain, meaning that every entity has its own handler, as shown in Figure 8.17. In total, we will have nine Handler classes that follow the next base interfaces:

- class CleaningDataHandler()
- class ChunkingDataHandler()
- class EmbeddingDataHandler()

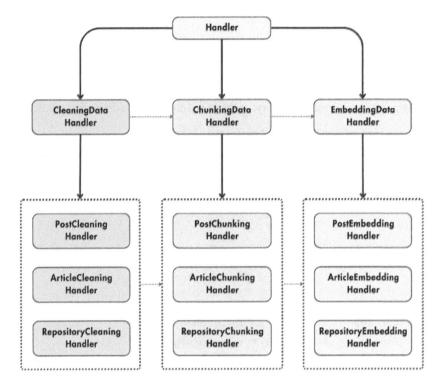

Figure 4.17: Handler class hierarchy and their interaction

 The code for all the handlers is available on GitHub at `https://github.com/`
`PacktPublishing/LLM-Engineering/tree/main/llm_engineering/`
`application/preprocessing`.

Let's examine each handler family and see how it is implemented.

The cleaning handlers

The `CleaningDataHandler()` strategy interface looks as follows:

```
… # Other imports.
from typing import Generic, TypeVar


DocumentT = TypeVar("DocumentT", bound=Document)
CleanedDocumentT = TypeVar("CleanedDocumentT", bound=CleanedDocument)


class CleaningDataHandler(ABC, Generic[DocumentT, CleanedDocumentT]):
```

```python
@abstractmethod
def clean(self, data_model: DocumentT) -> CleanedDocumentT:
    pass
```

Now, for every post, article and repository, we have to implement a different handler, as follows:

```python
class PostCleaningHandler(CleaningDataHandler):
    def clean(self, data_model: PostDocument) -> CleanedPostDocument:
        return CleanedPostDocument(
            id=data_model.id,
            content=clean_text(" #### ".join(data_model.content.
values())),
            … # Copy the rest of the parameters from the data_model
object.
        )


class ArticleCleaningHandler(CleaningDataHandler):
    def clean(self, data_model: ArticleDocument) ->
CleanedArticleDocument:
        valid_content = [content for content in data_model.content.
values() if content]

        return CleanedArticleDocument(
            id=data_model.id,
            content=clean_text(" #### ".join(valid_content)),
            platform=data_model.platform,
            link=data_model.link,
            author_id=data_model.author_id,
            author_full_name=data_model.author_full_name,
        )


class RepositoryCleaningHandler(CleaningDataHandler):
    def clean(self, data_model: RepositoryDocument) ->
CleanedRepositoryDocument:
        return CleanedRepositoryDocument(
            id=data_model.id,
```

```
                content=clean_text(" #### ".join(data_model.content.
    values())),
                … # Copy the rest of the parameters from the data_model
    object.
            )
```

The handlers input a raw document domain entity, clean the content, and return a cleaned document. All the handlers use the `clean_text()` function to clean the text. Out of simplicity, we used the same cleaning technique for all the data categories. Still, in a real-world setup, we would have to further optimize and create a different cleaning function for each data category. The strategy pattern makes this a breeze, as we swap the cleaning function in the handlers, and that's it.

The cleaning steps applied in the `clean_text()` function are the same ones discussed in *Chapter 5* in the *Creating an instruction dataset* section. We don't want to repeat ourselves. Thus, for a refresher, check out that chapter. At this point, we mostly care about automating and integrating the whole logic into the RAG feature pipeline. Thus, after operationalizing the ML system, all the cleaned data used for fine-tuning will be accessed from the logical feature store, making it the single source of truth for accessing data.

The chunking handlers

First, let's examine the `ChunkingDataHandler()` strategy handler. We exposed the `metadata` dictionary as a property to aggregate all the necessary properties required for chunking in a single structure. By structuring it like this, we can easily log everything to ZenML to track and debug our chunking logic. The handler takes cleaned documents as input and returns chunk entities. All the handlers can be found on GitHub at https://github.com/PacktPublishing/LLM-Engineering/tree/main/llm_engineering/application/preprocessing.

```
… # Other imports.
from typing import Generic, TypeVar


CleanedDocumentT = TypeVar("CleanedDocumentT", bound=CleanedDocument)
ChunkT = TypeVar("ChunkT", bound=Chunk)

 class ChunkingDataHandler(ABC, Generic[CleanedDocumentT, ChunkT]):

    @property
    def metadata(self) -> dict:
        return {
```

```
                "chunk_size": 500,
                "chunk_overlap": 50,
            }

        @abstractmethod
        def chunk(self, data_model: CleanedDocumentT) -> list[ChunkT]:
            pass
```

Let's understand how the `ArticleChunkingHandler()` class is implemented. The first step is to override the metadata property and customize the type of properties the chunking logic requires. For example, when working with articles, we are interested in the chunk's minimum and maximum length.

The handler's `chunk()` method inputs cleaned article documents and returns a list of article chunk entities. It uses the `chunk_text()` function to split the cleaned content into chunks. The chunking function is customized based on the `min_length` and `max_length` metadata fields. The chunk_id is computed as the MD5 hash of the chunk's content. Thus, if the two chunks have precisely the same content, they will have the same ID, and we can easily deduplicate them. Lastly, we create a list of chunk entities and return them.

```
class ArticleChunkingHandler(ChunkingDataHandler):
    @property
    def metadata(self) -> dict:
        return {
            "min_length": 1000,
            "max_length": 1000,
        }

    def chunk(self, data_model: CleanedArticleDocument) ->
list[ArticleChunk]:
        data_models_list = []

        cleaned_content = data_model.content
        chunks = chunk_article(
            cleaned_content, min_length=self.metadata["min_length"], max_
length=self.metadata["max_length"]
        )

        for chunk in chunks:
```

```
                    chunk_id = hashlib.md5(chunk.encode()).hexdigest()
                    model = ArticleChunk(
                        id=UUID(chunk_id, version=4),
                        content=chunk,
                        platform=data_model.platform,
                        link=data_model.link,
                        document_id=data_model.id,
                        author_id=data_model.author_id,
                        author_full_name=data_model.author_full_name,
                        metadata=self.metadata,
                    )
                    data_models_list.append(model)


        return data_models_list
```

The last step is to dig into the `chunk_article()` function, which mainly does two things:

- It uses a regex to find all the sentences within the given text by looking for periods, question marks, or exclamation points followed by a space. However, it avoids splitting into cases where the punctuation is part of an abbreviation or initialism (like "e.g." or "Dr.")

- It groups sentences into a single chunk until the `max_length` limit is reached. When the maximum size is reached, and the chunk size is bigger than the minimum allowed value, it is added to the final list the function returns.

```
def chunk_article(text: str, min_length: int, max_length: int) ->
list[str]:
    sentences = re.split(r"(?<!\w\.\w.)(?<![A-Z][a-z]\.)(?<=\.|\?|\!)\s",
text)

    extracts = []
    current_chunk = ""
    for sentence in sentences:
        sentence = sentence.strip()
        if not sentence:
            continue

        if len(current_chunk) + len(sentence) <= max_length:
            current_chunk += sentence + " "
        else:
```

```
        if len(current_chunk) >= min_length:
            extracts.append(current_chunk.strip())
        current_chunk = sentence + " "

    if len(current_chunk) >= min_length:
        extracts.append(current_chunk.strip())

    return extracts
```

The `PostChunkingHandler` and `RepositoryChunkingHandler`, available on GitHub at `llm_engineering/application/preprocessing/chunking_data_handlers.py`, have a similar structure to the ArticleChunkingHandler. However, they use a more generic chunking function called `chunk_text()`, worth looking into. The `chunk_text()` function is a two-step process that has the following logic:

1. It uses a `RecursiveCharacterTextSplitter()` from LangChain to split the text based on a given separator or chunk size. Using the separator, we first try to find paragraphs in the given text, but if there are no paragraphs or they are too long, we cut it at a given chunk size.

2. Notice that we want to ensure that the chunk doesn't exceed the maximum input length of the embedding model. Thus, we pass all the chunks created above into a `SenteceTrans formersTokenTextSplitter()`, which considers the maximum input length of the model. At this point, we also apply the `chunk_overlap` logic, as we want to do it only after we validate that the chunk is small enough.

```
… # Other imports.
from langchain.text_splitter import RecursiveCharacterTextSplitter,
SentenceTransformersTokenTextSplitter

from llm_engineering.application.networks import
EmbeddingModelSingleton

def chunk_text(text: str, chunk_size: int = 500, chunk_overlap: int
= 50) -> list[str]:
    character_splitter = RecursiveCharacterTextSplitter(separato
rs=["\n\n"], chunk_size=chunk_size, chunk_overlap=0)
    text_split_by_characters = character_splitter.split_text(text)

    token_splitter = SentenceTransformersTokenTextSplitter(
        chunk_overlap=chunk_overlap,
```

```
                tokens_per_chunk=embedding_model.max_input_length,
                model_name=embedding_model.model_id,
        )
        chunks_by_tokens = []
        for section in text_split_by_characters:
            chunks_by_tokens.extend(token_splitter.split_text(section))

        return chunks_by_tokens
```

To conclude, the function above returns a list of chunks that respect both the provided chunk parameters and the embedding model's max input length.

The embedding handlers

The embedding handlers differ slightly from the others as the EmbeddingDataHandler() interface contains most of the logic. We took this approach because, when calling the embedding model, we want to batch as many samples as possible to optimize the inference process. When running the model on a GPU, the batched samples are processed independently and in parallel. Thus, by batching the chunks, we can optimize the inference process by 10x or more, depending on the batch size and hardware we use.

We implemented an embed() method, in case you want to run the inference on a single data point, and an embed_batch() method. The embed_batch() method takes chunked documents as input, gathers their content into a list, passes them to the embedding model, and maps the results to an embedded chunk domain entity. The mapping is done through the map_model() abstract method, which has to be customized for every data category.

```
… # Other imports.
from typing import Generic, TypeVar, cast
from llm_engineering.application.networks import EmbeddingModelSingleton

ChunkT = TypeVar("ChunkT", bound=Chunk)
EmbeddedChunkT = TypeVar("EmbeddedChunkT", bound=EmbeddedChunk)

embedding_model = EmbeddingModelSingleton()

class EmbeddingDataHandler(ABC, Generic[ChunkT, EmbeddedChunkT]):
    """

    Abstract class for all embedding data handlers.
```

```
        All data transformations logic for the embedding step is done here
        """


    def embed(self, data_model: ChunkT) -> EmbeddedChunkT:
        return self.embed_batch([data_model])[0]


    def embed_batch(self, data_model: list[ChunkT]) ->
list[EmbeddedChunkT]:
        embedding_model_input = [data_model.content for data_model in
data_model]
        embeddings = embedding_model(embedding_model_input, to_list=True)


        embedded_chunk = [
            self.map_model(data_model, cast(list[float], embedding))
            for data_model, embedding in zip(data_model, embeddings,
strict=False)
        ]


        return embedded_chunk


    @abstractmethod
    def map_model(self, data_model: ChunkT, embedding: list[float]) ->
EmbeddedChunkT:
        pass
```

Let's look only at the implementation of the ArticleEmbeddingHandler(), as the other handlers are highly similar. As you can see, we only have to implement the map_model() method, which takes a chunk of input and computes the embeddings in batch mode. Its scope is to map this information to an EmbeddedArticleChunk Pydantic entity.

```
class ArticleEmbeddingHandler(EmbeddingDataHandler):
    def map_model(self, data_model: ArticleChunk, embedding: list[float])
-> EmbeddedArticleChunk:
        return EmbeddedArticleChunk(
            id=data_model.id,
            content=data_model.content,
            embedding=embedding,
            platform=data_model.platform,
            link=data_model.link,
```

```
                    document_id=data_model.document_id,
                    author_id=data_model.author_id,
                    author_full_name=data_model.author_full_name,
                    metadata={
                        "embedding_model_id": embedding_model.model_id,
                        "embedding_size": embedding_model.embedding_size,
                        "max_input_length": embedding_model.max_input_length,
                    },
                )
```

The last step is to understand how the `EmbeddingModelSingleton()` works. It is a wrapper over the `SentenceTransformer()` class from Sentence Transformers that initializes the embedding model. Writing a wrapper over external packages is often good practice. Thus, when you want to change the third-party tool, you have to modify only the internal logic of the wrapper instead of the whole code base.

The `SentenceTransformer()` class is initialized with the `model_id` defined in the `Settings` class, allowing us to quickly test multiple embedding models just by changing the configuration file and not the code. That is why I am not insisting at all on what embedding model to use. This differs constantly based on your use case, data, hardware, and latency. But by writing a generic class, which can quickly be configured, you can experiment with multiple embedding models until you find the best one for you.

```
from sentence_transformers.SentenceTransformer import SentenceTransformer
from llm_engineering.settings import settings
from .base import SingletonMeta


class EmbeddingModelSingleton(metaclass=SingletonMeta):
    def __init__(
        self,
        model_id: str = settings.TEXT_EMBEDDING_MODEL_ID,
        device: str = settings.RAG_MODEL_DEVICE,
        cache_dir: Optional[Path] = None,
    ) -> None:
        self._model_id = model_id
        self._device = device

        self._model = SentenceTransformer(
```

```
                self._model_id,
                device=self._device,
                cache_folder=str(cache_dir) if cache_dir else None,
            )
        self._model.eval()

    @property
    def model_id(self) -> str:
        return self._model_id

    @cached_property
    def embedding_size(self) -> int:
        dummy_embedding = self._model.encode("")

        return dummy_embedding.shape[0]

    @property
    def max_input_length(self) -> int:
        return self._model.max_seq_length

    @property
    def tokenizer(self) -> AutoTokenizer:
        return self._model.tokenizer

    def __call__(
        self, input_text: str | list[str], to_list: bool = True
    ) -> NDArray[np.float32] | list[float] | list[list[float]]:
        try:
            embeddings = self._model.encode(input_text)
        except Exception:
            logger.error(f"Error generating embeddings for {self._model_
id=} and {input_text=}")

            return [] if to_list else np.array([])

        if to_list:
```

```
        embeddings = embeddings.tolist()

    return embeddings
```

The embedding model class implements the singleton pattern (`https://refactoring.guru/design-patterns/singleton`), a creational design pattern that ensures a class has only one instance while providing a global access point to this instance. The `EmbeddingModelSingleton()` class inherits from the `SingletonMeta` class, which ensures that whenever an `EmbeddingModelSingleton()` is instantiated, it returns the same instance. This works well with ML models, as you load them once in memory through the singleton pattern, and afterward, you can use them anywhere in the code base. Otherwise, you risk loading the model in memory every time you use it or loading it multiple times, resulting in memory issues. Also, this makes it very convenient to access properties such as `embedding_size`, where you have to make a dummy forward pass into the embedding model to find the size of its output. As a singleton, you do this forward pass only once, and then you have it accessible all the time during the program's execution.

Summary

This chapter began with a soft introduction to RAG and why and when you should use it. We also understood how embeddings and vector DBs work, representing the cornerstone of any RAG system. Then, we looked into advanced RAG and why we need it in the first place. We built a strong understanding of what parts of the RAG can be optimized and proposed some popular advanced RAG techniques for working with textual data. Next, we applied everything we learned about RAG to designing the architecture of LLM Twin's RAG feature pipeline. We also understood the difference between a batch and streaming pipeline and presented a short introduction to the CDC pattern, which helps sync two DBs.

Ultimately, we went step-by-step into the implementation of the LLM Twin's RAG feature pipeline, where we saw how to integrate ZenML as an orchestrator, how to design the domain entities of the application, and how to implement an OVM module. Also, we understood how to apply some software engineering best practices, such as the abstract factory and strategy software patterns, to implement a modular and extendable layer that applies different cleaning, chunking, and embedding techniques based on the data category of each document.

This chapter focused only on implementing the ingestion pipeline, which is just one component of a standard RAG application. In *Chapter 9*, we will conclude the RAG system by implementing the retrieval and generation components and integrating them into the inference pipeline. But first, in the next chapter, we will explore how to generate a custom dataset using the data we collected and fine-tune an LLM with it.

References

- Kenton, J.D.M.W.C. and Toutanova, L.K., 2019, June. Bert: Pre-training of deep bidirectional transformers for language understanding. In *Proceedings of naacL-HLT* (Vol. 1, p. 2).

- Liu, Y., 2019. Roberta: A robustly optimized bert pretraining approach. *arXiv preprint arXiv:1907.11692.*

- Mikolov, T., 2013. Efficient estimation of word representations in vector space. *arXiv preprint arXiv:1301.3781.*

- Jeffrey Pennington, Richard Socher, and Christopher Manning. 2014. *GloVe: Global Vectors for Word Representation.* In *Proceedings of the 2014 Conference on Empirical Methods in Natural Language Processing* (*EMNLP*), pages 1532–1543, Doha, Qatar. Association for Computational Linguistics.

- He, K., Zhang, X., Ren, S. and Sun, J., 2016. Deep residual learning for image recognition. In *Proceedings of the IEEE conference on computer vision and pattern recognition* (pp. 770-778).

- Radford, A., Kim, J.W., Hallacy, C., Ramesh, A., Goh, G., Agarwal, S., Sastry, G., Askell, A., Mishkin, P., Clark, J. and Krueger, G., 2021, July. Learning transferable visual models from natural language supervision. In *International conference on machine learning* (pp. 8748-8763). PMLR.

- *What is Change Data Capture (CDC)? | Confluent.* (n.d.). Confluent. https://www.confluent.io/en-gb/learn/change-data-capture/

- Refactoring.Guru. (2024, January 1). *Singleton.* https://refactoring.guru/design-patterns/singleton

- Refactoring.Guru. (2024b, January 1). *Strategy.* https://refactoring.guru/design-patterns/strategy

- Refactoring.Guru. (2024a, January 1). *Abstract Factory.* https://refactoring.guru/design-patterns/abstract-factory

- Schwaber-Cohen, R. (n.d.). *What is a Vector Database & How Does it Work? Use Cases + Examples.* Pinecone. https://www.pinecone.io/learn/vector-database/

- Monigatti, L. (2024, February 19). *Advanced Retrieval-Augmented Generation: From Theory to LlaMaIndex Implementation. Medium.* https://towardsdatascience.com/advanced-retrieval-augmented-generation-from-theory-to-llamaindex-implementation-4de1464a9930

- Monigatti, L. (2023, December 6). A guide on 12 tuning Strategies for Production-Ready RAG applications. *Medium.* https://towardsdatascience.com/a-guide-on-12-tuning-strategies-for-production-ready-rag-applications-7ca646833439

- Monigatti, L. (2024b, February 19). *Advanced Retrieval-Augmented Generation: From Theory to LlaMaIndex Implementation. Medium.* `https://towardsdatascience.com/advanced-retrieval-augmented-generation-from-theory-to-llamaindex-implementation-4de1464a9930`

- Maameri, S. (2024, May 10). Routing in RAG-Driven applications - towards data science. *Medium.* `https://towardsdatascience.com/routing-in-rag-driven-applications-a685460a7220`

Join our book's Discord space

Join our community's Discord space for discussions with the authors and other readers:

`https://packt.link/llmeng`

5

Supervised Fine-Tuning

Supervised Fine-Tuning (SFT) is a crucial step in preparing LLMs for real-world applications. Following the initial pre-training phase, where an LLM learns to predict the next token in a sequence, SFT refines the model's capabilities using carefully curated pairs of instructions and corresponding answers. This process serves two primary purposes: it teaches the model to understand and follow a specific chat format, effectively transforming it into a conversational agent, and it allows the model to adapt its broad knowledge base to excel in targeted tasks or specialized domains.

The importance of SFT lies in its ability to bridge the gap between a model's general language understanding and its practical utility. By exposing the model to examples of desired input-output patterns, SFT shapes the LLM's behavior to align with specific goals, whether they involve task completion (such as summarization or translation) or domain expertise (like medical or legal knowledge). This tailored approach not only enhances the model's performance in intended areas but also improves its ability to follow instructions and generate more relevant and coherent responses.

In this chapter, we will cover the following topics:

- Creating a high-quality instruction dataset
- SFT techniques
- Implementing fine-tuning in practice

By the end of this chapter, you will be able to create your own instruction datasets and efficiently fine-tune LLMs on them.

All the code examples from this chapter can be found on GitHub at https://github.
com/PacktPublishing/LLM-Engineering.

Creating an instruction dataset

In most use cases, creating an instruction dataset is the most difficult part of the fine-tuning process. This is due to multiple factors. Most use cases can be connected to raw text, but it is rare to find natural pairs of instructions and answers. This raw text needs to be transformed into a format that includes both instructions and answers. Moreover, the quality of the data is also crucial. Because of this, a lot of time is invested in manually checking and verifying individual samples. This careful review helps ensure that the dataset is accurate and useful for training the model.

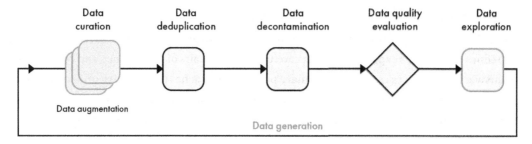

Figure 5.1 – Overview of the post-training data pipeline covered in this chapter

In this section, we will introduce a general framework to create your own instruction datasets, regardless of the final use case. We will then leverage the scraped data from *Chapter 3* and transform it into an instruction dataset. The different stages in our data generation pipeline are summarized in *Figure 5.1*.

General framework

Instruction datasets are defined as pairs of instructions and answers. The instructions are the inputs of the model, used as context during fine-tuning. The answers are the expected outputs of the model. During fine-tuning, you can choose to train the model on the instructions and answers, or on answers only. Pairs of instructions and answers follow a certain template. Some instruction templates, such as Alpaca, introduce additional fields like inputs and system. Both of them can be considered subfields of the instruction field. In this case, "inputs" contain the data the model needs to complete the instruction, and "system" is a meta-prompt to steer the general behavior of the model. Here is an example from the SlimOrca dataset, with "system" and "instruction":

System

You are a helpful assistant, who always provide explanation. Think like you are answering to a five year old.

Instruction

Concepts: building, shop, town

Write a sentence that includes all these words.

Output

In our little town, there is a shop inside a big building where people go to buy their favorite toys and candies.

Table 5.1 – Example of sample from the Open-Orca/SlimOrca dataset

This example illustrates how the "system" field is used to define specific behaviors for the model, such as being helpful, always providing explanations, and tailoring responses as if speaking to a five-year-old. The "instruction" field provides the necessary data (the concepts) and the task (constructing a sentence). The output field shows the expected answer, which, while not the only possible answer, represents a high-quality response.

To build an instruction dataset, we want to curate data that is representative of how the model will be used. Once we have gathered enough samples, our goal is to filter them to only keep high-quality data. In this context, high-quality data can be described through three main dimensions:

- **Accuracy**: It refers to the factual correctness and relevance of the samples. In the context of instruction datasets, this means ensuring that responses are not only factually accurate but also relevant to their corresponding instructions. High accuracy is essential for training models that can provide reliable and trustworthy information.

- **Diversity**: A high-quality dataset should encompass a wide range of use cases, covering the potential queries and tasks the deployed LLM might encounter. This diversity should span topics, contexts, text lengths, and writing styles. By sampling data in a representative manner, we allow models to develop robust instruction-following capabilities.

- **Complexity**: Trivial or overly simplistic samples do little to improve an LLM's capabilities. Instead, datasets should include complex, multi-step reasoning problems and challenging tasks that push the boundaries of what the model is expected to handle. This complexity helps in developing models capable of tackling complex real-world problems.

In the following sections, we will see techniques to filter and evaluate instruction samples according to these dimensions.

Data quantity

The Hugging Face Hub contains numerous instruction datasets, which can be general-purpose or designed for particular tasks or domains. When working on a new use case, it can be beneficial to look for related open-source datasets to leverage for fine-tuning. This is particularly important if your number of samples is too low (for example, fewer than 1,000), requiring you to augment it with high-quality data.

Figure 5.2 – Screenshot of the most-liked datasets on the Hugging Face Hub

Calculating an ideal number of samples is a difficult task, as both the quality of the data and the size of the model can have a dramatic impact. For large models (around 70 billion parameters, for example), this number can be as low as 1,000 high-quality samples (see the LIMA paper in the *References* section). This is not true for smaller models (around seven billion parameters, for instance), as they need more samples to simply learn the correct chat template. In any case, the quality of the data is a crucial factor, and a high number of samples is always desirable.

To provide additional numbers, we can look at the fine-tuned models developed by companies and the open-source community. We can distinguish two types of finetunes: general-purpose, aimed to reproduce the capabilities of models like GPT, and task- or domain-specific models, designed to optimize their performance for a particular application.

General-purpose models cover more topics, which requires additional samples. Among companies, we observe a wide range of values. For instance, Yi models from 01-ai rely on less than 10,000 samples. At the opposite range of the spectrum, Meta reported using 10 million samples for Llama 3 through the entire fine-tuning process (including preference alignment). In the open-source community, models like OpenHermes and Dolphin use around one million samples. Based on the quality of these finetunes, we recommend an instruction dataset of at least one million samples to create a good general-purpose instruct model. On the other hand, models fine-tuned for a specific purpose require fewer samples. Here, we differentiate task-specific models from domain-specific ones.

Task-specific and domain-specific models represent two distinct approaches to fine-tuning LLMs. Task-specific models are designed to excel at a particular function, such as translation, summarization, or sentiment analysis. These models benefit from a focused training approach on a single task, allowing for efficient performance even with smaller model sizes (typically less than 8 billion parameters). The data required for task-specific fine-tuning is generally more manageable, ranging from 100 to 100,000 samples. This makes task-specific fine-tuning an attractive option for many applications where resources may be limited.

Domain-specific models, on the other hand, aim to tweak the LLM with specialized knowledge and familiarity with the vocabulary and linguistic patterns of a particular field. These models are valuable in areas such as medicine, law, finance, e-commerce, engineering, and hospitality. The data requirements for domain-specific fine-tuning can vary widely depending on the complexity and breadth of the domain. Some fields, like medicine or law, may require as much data as general-purpose fine-tuning due to their vast technical corpora. Others, such as e-commerce or hospitality, might need fewer samples, more in line with task-specific fine-tuning.

The key factors determining the data needs for domain-specific models are the "size" of the domain (i.e., the extent of its specialized knowledge and vocabulary) and the representation of that domain in the model's pre-training data. Domains that are well-represented in the original training data may require less fine-tuning, while those that are more specialized or underrepresented may need more extensive datasets. Even with open-source LLMs, many pre-training datasets are closed-source, which requires making educated guesses to determine their composition (e.g., 30% code or 20% math).

Data curation

When it comes to procuring data for fine-tuning, the approaches differ between task-specific and domain-specific models. For task-specific models, data curation often involves collecting examples of the desired task from existing datasets or creating new ones. This might involve gathering pairs of original and summarized texts for a summarization model or collecting sentences in different languages for a translation model.

Domain-specific data curation can be more challenging. It often requires collaboration with subject matter experts to gather and validate relevant texts, research papers, technical documents, and other domain-specific content. In some cases, it may involve partnering with organizations or institutions that have access to large repositories of specialized information. The quality and relevance of this data is crucial, as it directly impacts the model's ability to understand and generate content in the target domain.

It's worth noting that few-shot prompting has emerged as an alternative strategy to fine-tuning, especially for task-specific applications. This approach leverages the capabilities of large, powerful models by providing a few examples of the desired task within the input prompt. While not a replacement for fine-tuning in all scenarios (e.g., when you want to learn a new domain), few-shot prompting can be an efficient way to adapt models to new tasks without the need for extensive additional training.

In practice, the line between task-specific and domain-specific models can sometimes blur. For instance, a model fine-tuned for medical diagnosis could be considered both task-specific (focused on diagnosis) and domain-specific (specialized in medical knowledge). The key is to understand the primary goal of the fine-tuning process and tailor the approach accordingly.

At this point in the process, we should have a collection of datasets suited for our use case. The next step consists of refining the quality of the samples through rule-based filtering, data duplication, data decontamination, and data quality evaluation.

Rule-based filtering

Rule-based filtering is a systematic approach to data quality control that relies on explicit, predefined rules to evaluate and filter data samples. These rules are typically designed to address common quality issues and can range from simple checks to more complex logical operations. The primary goal of rule-based filtering is to maintain a high standard of data quality by removing samples that do not meet specific criteria.

Length filtering is a straightforward yet effective rule-based filtering technique. This method involves setting thresholds for the acceptable length of responses in the dataset. Extremely short responses often lack sufficient information to be meaningful, while excessively long ones may contain irrelevant or redundant content. It's important to note that the appropriate length thresholds can vary significantly depending on the specific task and domain. For example, a dataset for generating concise summaries might have a lower maximum threshold compared to one for detailed explanations.

Keyword exclusion is another powerful rule-based filtering technique that focuses on the content of the samples rather than their structure. This method involves creating a list of keywords or phrases associated with low-quality or inappropriate content, and then filtering out any samples that contain these terms. The keyword list can include obvious indicators of low quality, such as profanities or spam-related terms, as well as domain-specific words that might indicate irrelevant or off-topic content. For instance, in a dataset for a professional writing assistant, you might exclude samples containing slang terms or informal expressions that don't align with the intended tone and style.

Format checking is recommended for datasets that include structured data or follow specific formatting requirements. This technique ensures that all samples adhere to the expected format, maintaining consistency and facilitating processing downstream. Format checking can be particularly important for datasets containing code samples, JSON structures, or other formatted text. For example, in a dataset of programming instructions and solutions, you might implement rules to verify that code samples are syntactically correct and follow specified style guidelines.

Rule-based filtering offers significant advantages in preparing instruction datasets. Its speed and efficiency allow for rapid application to large volumes of data, making it highly scalable. The consistency of rule application ensures uniform treatment of data, reducing human error and bias. Furthermore, the explicit definition of filtering criteria provides transparency and interpretability, facilitating easy understanding, auditing, and adjustment. The ability to automate rule-based filtering reduces the need for manual intervention and enables continuous data quality monitoring.

However, rule-based filtering also has limitations that must be considered. Predefined rules may lack the nuance required to capture the full complexity of language and context, potentially leading to the removal of valid but unusual samples. The typically binary nature of rules (pass/fail) may not always align with the nuanced nature of language and instruction quality. Additionally, as data patterns and quality standards evolve, rules need regular review and updates to remain effective. There's also a risk that poorly designed rules could inadvertently introduce or amplify biases in the dataset.

Data deduplication

Dataset diversity is fundamental to training models that can generalize well to new, unseen data. When a dataset contains duplicates or near-duplicates, it can lead to several issues:

- Overfitting: Models may memorize specific examples rather than learning general patterns.

- Biased performance: Overrepresented data points may skew the model's performance towards certain types of inputs.

- Inefficient training: Redundant data can increase training time without providing additional valuable information.

- Inflated evaluation metrics: Duplicate data in test sets may lead to overly optimistic performance estimates.

To deduplicate datasets, we distinguish between exact and fuzzy deduplication. **Exact deduplication** removes identical samples through a straightforward process involving data normalization, hash generation, and duplicate removal. Data normalization standardizes the format of entries, such as converting text to lowercase. Hash generation then creates unique hashes for each entry using algorithms like MD5 or SHA-256. These hashes are compared to find matches, and duplicates are removed, leaving only one instance of each. While effective for identical entries, exact deduplication does not detect near-duplicates or semantically similar content, requiring more advanced techniques for those cases.

The most popular approach to **fuzzy deduplication** is MinHash deduplication. Compared to other fuzzy techniques, it maintains high accuracy while significantly reducing computational complexity. MinHash operates by generating compact representations, or signatures, for each data item. These signatures serve as fingerprints that capture the essence of the data while drastically reducing its dimensionality. In practice, MinHash transforms data items (such as text documents) into sets of shingles, applies multiple hash functions to these sets, and selects the minimum hash values to form signature vectors. These signatures can then be compared using similarity measures like Jaccard similarity to efficiently identify near-duplicates.

In addition to exact and fuzzy deduplication, **semantic similarity** takes a different approach by focusing on the meaning of text for deduplication. This method involves converting words or entire samples into vector representations using various natural language processing techniques. Word embedding models such as Word2Vec, GloVe, and FastText transform individual words into dense vectors, capturing semantic relationships.

For more context-aware representations, language models like BERT, sentence transformers, or cross-encoders can generate embeddings for entire sentences or documents. Once these vector representations are obtained, deduplication can be performed by comparing the similarity between vectors. Common similarity measures include cosine similarity or Euclidean distance. Samples with high similarity scores above a predefined threshold can be considered duplicates. For large datasets, clustering techniques may be applied to group similar vectors. Methods like K-means, DBSCAN, or hierarchical clustering can efficiently organize the vector space, allowing for the identification of clusters that represent semantically similar content. Within each cluster, a representative sample can be retained while others are marked as duplicates.

Data decontamination

Data decontamination is the process of ensuring that the training dataset does not contain samples that are identical or highly similar to those in the evaluation or test sets. This step is important for ensuring the quality of the model evaluation and preventing overfitting or memorization of test data.

Data decontamination uses techniques from data deduplication. Exact matching can be used to remove any training samples that are identical to those in the evaluation sets. This can be done using hash functions or direct string comparisons. Next, we can also use near-duplicate detection methods to identify and remove training samples that are very similar to evaluation samples, even if they are not exactly the same. This often involves techniques like MinHash or computing similarity scores based on n-grams or embeddings.

 A simple way to perform data decontamination is to add your evaluation set to the instruction dataset during the data deduplication stage. In this case, we want to ensure that we only remove samples from the instruction dataset, which can be implemented in different ways (only filtering out the first duplicate, recording the indexes of the evaluation samples, etc.). Ideally, you can automatically add your evaluation sets in the data deduplication stage to fully automate this process. This is particularly efficient if you iterate over several versions of custom benchmarks.

Another aspect of data decontamination is filtering out samples that may have been derived from the same source as evaluation data. This can involve checking for overlapping phrases, similar sentence structures, or common metadata. Practitioners may also use provenance tracking (source the data they use) to identify and exclude data from specific sources that are known to be used in evaluation sets.

Data quality evaluation

Data quality evaluation is a critical aspect of machine learning, particularly for LLMs. The process involves assessing various characteristics of datasets, including accuracy, diversity, and complexity. While some aspects like mathematical accuracy can be easily verified using tools such as Python interpreters, evaluating subjective or open-ended content remains challenging.

Traditional methods of data quality assessment include human annotation, which generally provides high accuracy but is resource-intensive. To address scalability issues, machine learning techniques have been developed to automate the evaluation process. These include using LLMs as judges, reward models, and classifiers trained for quality prediction.

The LLM-as-a-judge strategy involves prompting LLMs to evaluate the quality of each sample. This approach has become popular due to its flexibility and ease of use, though it does present some challenges. Different LLMs have different levels of performance across tasks, and their evaluations often align more closely with those of non-experts. With domain-specific datasets, you might want to use domain-specific models instead of better, general-purpose LLMs. Comparative assessment methods (e.g., "Is answer A better than answer B?") generally outperform absolute scoring approaches (e.g., "Rate answer A between 1 and 4"), though both can be used at scale with sufficient prompt engineering. We recommend iterating through different prompts over a representative subset to manually verify the quality of the responses. *Table 5.2* shows an example of a custom prompt for a judge LLM.

Instruction

You are a data quality evaluator. Your goal is to assess an instruction and its corresponding answer, determining how effectively the answer addresses the given task.

In your evaluation, you will provide feedback detailing the strengths and weaknesses of the answer, followed by a score on a scale of 1 to 4.

A score of 1 means that the answer is terrible and irrelevant to the instruction.

A score of 2 means that the answer is not helpful and misses important aspects of the instruction.

A score of 3 means that the answer is helpful but could be improved in terms of relevance, accuracy, and depth.

A score of 4 means that the answer is excellent and fully addresses the task.

Provide your evaluation as follows:

Feedback: (strengths and weaknesses you find relevant)

Score: (number between 1 and 4)

Table 5.2 – Example of LLM-as-a-judge prompt for data quality evaluation

LLM-as-a-judge is known to have several biases. First, it has a position bias in comparative scoring, where the LLM judge favors the first answer. This can be addressed by randomizing the order of answers A and B. In addition, like humans, LLM judges favor long answers. Length normalization techniques can be applied to absolute scoring to mitigate this issue. Finally, LLM judges are known to have intra-model favoritism, meaning that they prefer models from the same family (GPT-4o with GPT-4 and GPT-4o mini, for example). This can be addressed by using several models instead of a single one.

In general, to improve evaluation reliability, strategies such as using multiple LLMs as a jury reduce bias and improve consistency. Leveraging a jury of smaller LLMs can also reduce costs while increasing accuracy and mitigating intra-model favoritism. For specific applications like chatbots, it's advisable to aim for high agreement between LLM judges and human evaluators (around 80%). Simple grading scales (with few-shot prompting) and task-specific benchmarks are also recommended to ensure relevant and interpretable evaluations.

Reward models are another way to re-purpose LLMs for data quality evaluation. The term "reward model" comes from Reinforcement Learning from Human Feedback (RLHF, see *Chapter 6*). They can be broadly defined as models that take an instruction and answer pair and return a score as output. Generally, reward models are created by adding a linear head on top of a decoder-only architecture like Gemma or Llama. They are then trained for this specific purpose, using either reinforcement learning or traditional fine-tuning. *Figure 5.3* shows ArmoRM-Llama3-8B-v0.1's architecture, which adds regression and gating layers on top of a Llama 3 8B model. This model outputs multiple scores to target specific dimensions, such as helpfulness, correctness, coherence, complexity, and verbosity. This allows for a more fine-grained approach to data quality evaluation.

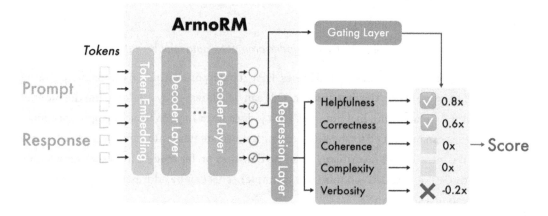

Figure 5.3 – Architecture of RLHFlow/ArmoRM-Llama3-8B-v0.1, based on Llama 3 (Source:
`https://doi.org/10.48550/arXiv.2406.12845`*)*

The Allen Institute for AI's RewardBench leaderboard, hosted on Hugging Face (allenai/reward-bench), is a good resource for comparing different reward models. It combines various types of reward models (generative, classifiers, DPO, etc.) and evaluates them on a curated set of chosen and rejected answers for each instruction. While this task is not directly related to instruction data quality, it is a good resource for finding models capable of differentiating between good and bad answers.

Classifiers or encoder-only models can be trained to perform data quality evaluation. A good example is HuggingFaceFW/fineweb-edu-classifier, a classifier designed to judge the educational value of web pages. This model was designed as a quality filter for pretraining data but a similar approach can be taken to evaluate instruction samples at scale. In practice, fineweb-edu-classifier adds a classification head to an embedding model (Snowflake/snowflake-arctic-embed-m) and trains it for 20 epochs on 450,000 samples that are annotated by Llama 3 70B Instruct.

This approach relies on encoder-only models, which are both smaller and better suited to classification tasks. Thanks to their low number of parameters, these models are faster to run and can scale to millions of samples. However, they are not as accurate as bigger models, particularly for complex reasoning tasks where they lack the ability to capture nuances. At smaller scale, encoder-only models are still valuable to filter out outliers or as part of an automated data pipeline, which requires faster processing.

Data exploration

Data exploration is a continuous process that requires practitioners to become familiar with the training data. It involves both manual inspection and automated analysis, each playing a crucial role in understanding the dataset's characteristics, strengths, and potential shortcomings.

Manual dataset exploration, though time-consuming, is an important step. It reveals errors and inconsistencies that automated processes might miss, including formatting issues, data entry mistakes, incoherent reasoning, and factual inaccuracies. This process provides qualitative insights into the dataset's content and style. To enhance efficiency, researchers can employ techniques like stratified sampling (selecting diverse samples), systematic review (using a criteria checklist), and collaborative review (involving multiple reviewers).

Figure 5.4 shows an example with Argilla, a collaborative platform for manual data quality evaluation and exploration.

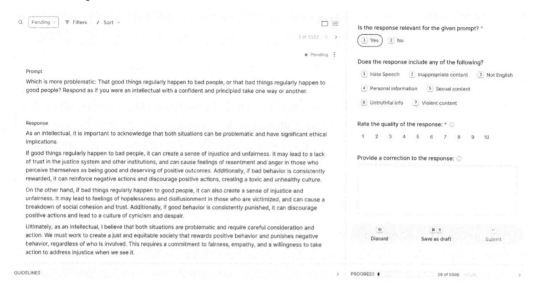

Figure 5.4 – Argilla's interface for collaborative data quality evaluation and exploration

Statistical analysis is a complementary technique that reveals vocabulary diversity, potential biases, and concept representation. This process utilizes natural language processing libraries like NLTK or spaCy for tokenization and analysis of large text volumes. Visualization tools such as Matplotlib or Seaborn create histograms and word clouds, enabling intuitive pattern recognition. These techniques provide insights into dataset composition, language breadth, and possible cultural or contextual preferences, which can influence model outputs.

Topic clustering automatically groups similar documents or pieces of text together, revealing underlying themes and patterns within the data. This process is especially important for understanding the content of large text corpora, identifying trends, and organizing information in a meaningful way. It is often associated with data visualization, with figures that show clusters of similar samples.

Let's consider the task of building an instruction dataset about various programming languages. You have collected a vast corpus of programming-related text from online forums, documentation, and tutorials. First, topic clustering can help identify the distinct programming languages present in the dataset (Python, JavaScript, etc.). Second, within each language cluster, you can further identify sub-topics like error handling, data structures, and web frameworks. This allows a balanced representation of each language and sub-topic in the corpus.

This makes sure that each topic is correctly covered for each programming language.

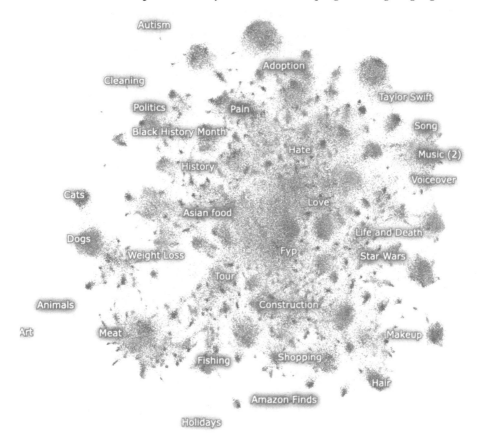

Figure 5.5 – Representation of the historical TikTok dataset made with Nomic Atlas

Several tools are available for performing topic clustering, each with its own strengths and approaches. For example, Hugging Face's text-clustering provides a simple pipeline with sentence transformers for embedding text into vector space, UMAP for dimensionality reduction, and DBSCAN for clustering. It also automatically labels clusters using an LLM and can output visualizations. Nomic Atlas (see *Figure 5.5*), BunkaTopics, and Lilac are alternatives proposing similar approaches with additional features.

Data generation

When the available instruction datasets are not sufficient, creating custom data becomes necessary. This is particularly relevant for specialized applications where publicly available data is scarce.

Additionally, it serves as a method to augment underrepresented areas in a dataset, like insufficient examples of JavaScript error-handling techniques in our previous example. While data can be generated manually by individuals or through crowdsourcing, these approaches often incur significant costs and time investments. Synthetic data generation using LLMs offers a more efficient and scalable alternative. This method, when combined with well-designed prompt engineering, can produce high-quality data at a much larger scale, effectively addressing the limitations of manual data creation processes.

The process of synthetic data generation typically begins with the preparation of a set of carefully designed prompts (sometimes called taxonomy). These serve as the foundation for generating new, diverse examples. Five seed prompts used in the original Alpaca dataset can be seen in *Table 5.3*. The quality of synthetically generated data largely depends on the prompts and techniques used in the generation process. Well-crafted prompts can guide the language model to produce diverse, relevant, and high-quality instruction-response pairs. These prompts often include specific instructions, examples, and constraints to ensure the generated data aligns with the desired format and content.

Seed instructions

- Is there anything I can eat for breakfast that doesn't include eggs, yet includes protein, and has roughly 700-1000 calories?

- What is the relation between the given pairs? Input: Night : Day :: Right : Left

- Generate a one-sentence description for each of the following people. Input: -Barack Obama\n- Elon Musk\n- Taylor Swift

- Describe a situation in which the given stereotype can harm you. Input: All Asians are smart!

- Generate an appropriate subjective title for the following email: Input: "Hi [person name],\n\nI'm writing to ask you if you are happy to be a panelist in our workshop on multimodality at CVPR. The workshop will be held on June 20, 2023. \n\nBest,\n[my name]

Table 5.3 – Examples of seed prompts used in the original Alpaca dataset

Many synthetic data generation pipelines incorporate multiple steps to ensure data quality. This may include generating an initial set of questions or instructions, followed by generating corresponding answers or responses. Some systems also implement validation steps, where another model or set of rules checks the generated pairs for accuracy, relevance, and adherence to specified criteria.

An important aspect of synthetic data generation is the ability to control various attributes of the generated data. This includes factors such as the complexity of the instructions, the length of the responses, the tone or style of the language used, and the specific topics or domains covered. By fine-tuning these parameters, it's possible to create datasets that are tailored to specific training objectives or that complement existing datasets in targeted ways. Structured generation using libraries like Outlines can also be beneficial to adhere to specific formats.

Furthermore, synthetic data generation can be particularly useful for addressing biases and gaps in existing datasets. By carefully designing the generation process, it's possible to create more balanced and inclusive datasets that represent a wider range of perspectives, topics, and language styles. This can help in training LLMs that are more equitable and capable of serving diverse user bases.

However, synthetic data generation also comes with challenges. One primary concern is the potential for the generated data to inherit biases or errors from the underlying language model used for generation. To mitigate this, many approaches incorporate human oversight, diverse prompts, and additional filtering mechanisms to ensure the quality and appropriateness of the generated data.

Another consideration is the need for the generated data to be sufficiently diverse and challenging. If the synthetic data is too simplistic or repetitive, it may not provide the level of complexity required to train a robust LLM. Advanced techniques in synthetic data generation often focus on creating varied and nuanced instruction-response pairs that can push the boundaries of what the model can learn.

Data augmentation

In this context, data augmentation refers to the process of increasing both the quantity and the quality of data samples. Unlike data generation, we use pre-existing instruction samples as inputs in this stage. While it is possible to upsample pairs of instructions and answers, data augmentation is mostly used to increase the quality of existing samples. In particular, it focuses on two aspects: diversity and complexity.

A pioneering approach in this field is the Evol-Instruct method, which uses LLMs to evolve simple instructions into more qualitative ones. The evolved instructions can then be used to generate answers using powerful LLMs. This method employs two main strategies: in-depth and in-breadth evolving.

In-depth evolving focuses on enhancing the complexity of existing instructions. It includes several techniques:

- **Constraints**: It involves introducing additional requirements or limitations to the original instruction, making it more challenging to fulfill.

- **Deepening**: Instead of shallow questions, it tries to find more deep questions, requiring more comprehensive responses.

- **Concretizing**: It replaces general concepts with more specific ones, adding detail and precision to the instruction.

- **Increasing reasoning steps**: It modifies instructions to explicitly request multiple-step reasoning, promoting more complex problem-solving.

- **Complicating input**: This involves adding more complex data formats or structures to the instruction, such as XML, JSON, or code snippets.

In-breadth evolving, on the other hand, aims to expand the diversity of the instruction dataset. It generates entirely new instructions inspired by existing ones, focusing on creating more rare or long-tailed examples within the same domain.

As an example of concrete implementation, in-depth evolving can be automated with the following prompt, from the AutoEvol paper. You simply need to provide the instruction you want to evolve as input, and a powerful model like GPT-4o will return a more complex version of the original instruction.

You are an Instruction Rewriter that rewrites the given #Instruction# into a more complex version. Please follow the steps below to rewrite the given "#Instruction#" into a more complex version.

- Step 1: Please read the "#Instruction#" carefully and list all the possible methods to make this instruction more complex (to make it a bit harder for well-known AI assistants such as ChatGPT and GPT4 to handle). Please do not provide methods to
- change the language of the instruction!
- Step 2: Please create a comprehensive plan based on the #Methods List# generated in Step 1 to make the #Instruction# more complex. The plan should include several methods from the #Methods List#.
- Step 3: Please execute the plan step by step and provide the #Rewritten Instruction#. #Rewritten Instruction# can only add 10 to 20 words into the "#Instruction#".
- Step 4: Please carefully review the #Rewritten Instruction# and identify any unreasonable parts. Ensure that the #Rewritten Instruction# is only a more complex version of the #Instruction#. Just provide the #Finally Rewritten Instruction# without anyexplanation.

Please reply strictly in the following format:

Step 1 #Methods List#:

Step 2 #Plan#:

Step 3 #Rewritten Instruction#:

Step 4 #Finally Rewritten Instruction#:

#Instruction#:

{Instruction}

Table 5.4 – Evol LLM prompt from the "Automatic Instruction Evolving for Large Language Models" paper by Zeng et al. (2024)

The UltraFeedback method is another innovative approach, focused on answer quality instead of instruction quality. It employs AI feedback to enhance the quality and diversity of model responses. Unlike Evol-Instruct, which evolves instructions, UltraFeedback uses a large pool of diverse instructions and models to generate a wide range of responses.

It then leverages advanced language models like GPT-4 to provide detailed critiques and numerical scores for these responses across multiple dimensions such as instruction-following, truthfulness, honesty, and helpfulness.

Based on these ideas, you can create your own augmentation techniques to create a more challenging and diverse instruction dataset. By refining and evolving existing instructions and answers, the resulting dataset can better train models to handle complex, multi-step tasks, and improve their performance across a wider range of applications.

Creating our own instruction dataset

In this section, we will create our own instruction dataset based on the crawled data from *Chapter 3*. To create a high-quality instruction dataset, we need to address two main issues: the unstructured nature of our data and the limited number of articles we can crawl.

This unstructured nature comes from the fact that we are dealing with raw text (articles), instead of pairs of instructions and answers. To address this issue, we will use an LLM to perform this transformation. Specifically, we will employ a combination of backtranslation and rephrasing. Backtranslation refers to the process of providing the expected answer as output and generating its corresponding instruction. However, using a chunk of text like a paragraph as an answer might not always be appropriate. This is why we want to rephrase the raw text to ensure we're outputting properly formatted, high-quality answers. Additionally, we can ask the model to follow the author's writing style to stay close to the original paragraph. While this process involves extensive prompt engineering, it can be automated and used at scale, as we will see in the following implementation.

Our second issue regarding the limited number of samples is quite common in real-world use cases. The number of articles we can retrieve is limited, which constrains the size of the instruction dataset we are able to create. In this example, the more samples we have, the better the model becomes at imitating the original authors. To address this problem, we will divide our articles into chunks and generate three instruction-answer pairs for each chunk. This will multiply the number of samples we create while maintaining diversity in the final dataset. For simplicity, we will do it using OpenAI's GPT-4o-mini model, but you can also use open-source models.

However, LLMs are not reliable when it comes to producing structured output. Even when given specific templates or instructions, there's no guarantee that the model will consistently adhere to them. This inconsistency often necessitates additional string parsing to ensure the output meets the desired format.

To simplify this process and ensure properly structured results, we can employ structured generation techniques. Structured generation is an effective method to force an LLM to follow a predefined template, such as JSON, pydantic classes, or regular expressions. In the following, we will use OpenAI's JSON mode feature, which provides a more robust way to return valid JSON objects and reduce the need for extensive post-processing.

Based on this description, the following figure summarizes every step of the synthetic data pipeline we want to build.

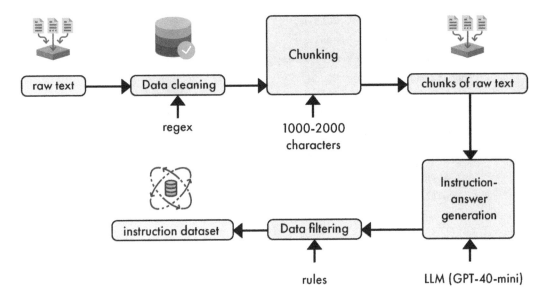

Figure 5.6 – Synthetic data generation pipeline from raw text to instruction dataset

Let's now implement it in Python. You can implement it as part of the LLMOps pipeline, or as a standalone script:

1. We want to make sure that the following libraries are installed. The OpenAI library will allow us to interact with a model to generate the instruction data, and datasets will format it into a Hugging Face-compatible format. The tqdm library is installed to visualize the progress during the data generation process.

```
openai==1.37.1
datasets==2.20.0
tqdm==4.66.4
```

2. We import all the required libraries as follows.

```
import concurrent.futures
import json
import random
import re
from concurrent.futures import ThreadPoolExecutor

from typing import List, Tuple
from datasets import Dataset
from openai import OpenAI
from pydantic import BaseModel, Field
from tqdm.auto import tqdm
```

3. The raw data we have is a JSON file. We create a Hugging Face dataset from this JSON file by extracting specific fields from each article: id, content, platform, author_id, author name, and link.

```
def load_articles_from_json(file_path: str) -> Dataset:
    with open(file_path, "r") as file:
        data = json.load(file)

    return Dataset.from_dict(
        {
            "id": [item["id"] for item in data["artifact_data"]],
            "content": [item["content"] for item in data["artifact_
data"]],
            "platform": [item["platform"] for item in
data["artifact_data"]],
            "author_id": [item["author_id"] for item in
data["artifact_data"]],
            "author_full_name": [item["author_full_name"] for item
in data["artifact_data"]],
            "link": [item["link"] for item in data["artifact_
data"]],
        }
    )
```

If we simply load our dataset as a pandas dataframe, it returns the following table.

	id	content	platform	author_id	author_ full_ name	link
0	ab2f9e2e- 5459-4dd6- 97d6- c291de4a7093	The Impor- tance of Data Pipelines in the Era of...	medium	e6b945ba- 6a9a- 4cde-b2bf- 0890af79732b	Alex Vesa	`https://medium. com/decodingml/ t h e - importance-o...`
1	ccfe70f3- d324- 40b6-ba38- 86e72786dcf4	Change Data Capture: Enabling Event-Driven Arc...	medium	e6b945ba- 6a9a- 4cde-b2bf- 0890af79732b	Alex Vesa	`https://medium. com/decodingml/ the-3nd-out- of-1...`
2	4c9f68ae- ec8b-4534- 8ad5- 92372bf8bb37	The Role of Feature Stores in Fine-Tun- ing LLMs...	medium	e6b945ba- 6a9a- 4cde-b2bf- 0890af79732b	Alex Vesa	`https://medium. com/decodingml/ the-role-of- feat...`
...	...	...	...	...	...	...
73	68795a4d- 26c2-43b7- 9900- 739a80b9b- 7dc	DML: 4 key ideas you must know to train an LLM...	decod- ingml. substack. com	1519b1d1- 1a5d-444c- a880-926c9e- b6539e	Paul Iusztin	`h t t p s : / / d e c o d i n g m l . substack.com/p/ dml-4-key-id...`
74	d91b17c0- 05d8- 4838-bf61- e2abc1573622	DML: How to add real-time monitoring & metrics...	decod- ingml. substack. com	1519b1d1- 1a5d-444c- a880-926c9e- b6539e	Paul Iusztin	`h t t p s : / / d e c o d i n g m l . substack.com/p/ dml-how-to-a...`
75	dcf55b28- 2814- 4480-a18b- a77d01d44f5f	DML: Top 6 ML Platform Features You Must Know ...	decod- ingml. substack. com	1519b1d1- 1a5d-444c- a880-926c9e- b6539e	Paul Iusztin	`h t t p s : / / d e c o d i n g m l . substack.com/p/ dml-top-6-ml...`

4. If we inspect the content of some articles a little further, we realize that some of them have special characters and redundant whitespaces. We can clean this with a simple regex.

First, we use `[^\w\s.,!?']` to remove non-alphanumeric characters except for apostro- phes, periods, commas, exclamation marks, and question marks. Then, we use `\s+` to replace multiple consecutive whitespace characters with a single space.

Finally, we implement `strip()` to remove any leading or trailing whitespace.

```python
def clean_text(text):
    text = re.sub(r"[^\w\s.,!?']", " ", text)
    text = re.sub(r"\s+", " ", text)
    return text.strip()
```

5. Now that we can load our articles, we need to chunk them before turning them into pairs of instructions and answers. Ideally, you would want to use headlines or paragraphs to produce semantically meaningful chunking.

However, in our example, like in the real world, raw data tends to be messy. Due to improper formatting, we cannot extract paragraphs or headlines for every article in our raw dataset. Instead, we will extract sentences using a regex to get chunks between 1,000 and 2,000 characters. This number can be optimized depending on the density of the information contained in the text.

The `extract_substrings` function processes each article in the dataset by first cleaning the text and then using a regex to split it into sentences. It then builds chunks of text by concatenating these sentences until each chunk is between 1,000 and 2,000 characters long.

```python
def extract_substrings(dataset: Dataset, min_length: int = 1000,
max_length: int = 2000) -> List[str]:
    extracts = []
    sentence_pattern = r"(?<!\w\.\w.)(?<![A-Z][a-z]\.)
(?<=\.|\?|\!)\s"

    for article in dataset["content"]:
        cleaned_article = clean_text(article)
        sentences = re.split(sentence_pattern, cleaned_article)

        current_chunk = ""
        for sentence in sentences:
            sentence = sentence.strip()
            if not sentence:
                continue

            if len(current_chunk) + len(sentence) <= max_length:
                current_chunk += sentence + " "
            else:
```

```
                    if len(current_chunk) >= min_length:
                        extracts.append(current_chunk.strip())
                    current_chunk = sentence + " "

            if len(current_chunk) >= min_length:
                extracts.append(current_chunk.strip())

        return extracts
```

6. Next, we want to create instruction-answer pairs from the extracted chunks of text. To manage these pairs effectively, we introduce the InstructionAnswerSet class. This class allows us to create instances directly from JSON strings, which is useful when parsing the output from the OpenAI API.

```
class InstructionAnswerSet:
    def __init__(self, pairs: List[Tuple[str, str]]):
        self.pairs = pairs

    @classmethod
    def from_json(cls, json_str: str) -> 'InstructionAnswerSet':
        data = json.loads(json_str)
        pairs = [(pair['instruction'], pair['answer'])
                    for pair in data['instruction_answer_pairs']]
        return cls(pairs)

    def __iter__(self):
        return iter(self.pairs)
```

7. Now that we have a set of extracts from the articles with a reasonable length, we can use an LLM to transform them into pairs of instructions and answers. Note that this step is model-agnostic and can be implemented with any open-source or closed-source model. Because this output is grounded in the context we provide, it doesn't require complex reasoning or high-performing models.

For convenience, we will use GPT-4o mini in this example. This choice is motivated by the low cost and good performance of this model. Prompt engineering is the most important aspect of this data transformation stage and requires several iterations to produce the expected outputs. We recommend starting with simple prompts and adding complexity when required to be more accurate, modify the style, or output multiple responses.

In our example, we want to create instructions like "Write a paragraph about X topic" and corresponding answers that are factual and imitate the writer's style. To implement this, we need to provide an extract that will ground the model's responses. For efficiency, we also choose to generate five instruction-answer pairs for each extract. Here's the beginning of our function for instruction generation, including our prompt.

```python
def generate_instruction_answer_pairs(
    extract: str, client: OpenAI
) -> List[Tuple[str, str]]:
    prompt = f"""Based on the following extract, generate five
instruction-answer pairs. Each instruction \
must ask to write about a specific topic contained in the context.
each answer \
must provide a relevant paragraph based on the information found in
the \
context. Only use concepts from the context to generate the
instructions. \
Instructions must never explicitly mention a context, a system, a
course, or an extract. \
Instructions must be self-contained and general. \
Answers must imitate the writing style of the context. \
Example instruction: Explain the concept of an LLM Twin. \
Example answer: An LLM Twin is essentially an AI character that
mimics your writing style, personality, and voice. \
It's designed to write just like you by incorporating these elements
into a language model. \
The idea is to create a digital replica of your writing habits using
advanced AI techniques. \
Provide your response in JSON format with the following structure:
{{
    "instruction_answer_pairs": [
        {{"instruction": "...", "answer": "..."}},
        ...
    ]
}}

Extract:
{extract}
"""
```

8. In addition to the user prompt, we can also specify a system prompt to guide the model into generating the expected instructions. Here, we repeat our high-level task in the system prompt.

The concatenation of the system and user prompts is fed to the OpenAI API, using the GPT-4o mini model in JSON mode and a maximum of 1,200 tokens in the answer. We also use a standard temperature of 0.7 to encourage diverse responses. The generated text is directly parsed using the InstructionAnswerSet class to return pairs of instructions and answers.

```python
completion = client.chat.completions.create(
    model="gpt-4o-mini",
    messages=[
        {
            "role": "system", "content": "You are a helpful
assistant who \
            generates instruction-answer pairs based on the given
context. \
            Provide your response in JSON format.",
        },
        {"role": "user", "content": prompt},
    ],
    response_format={"type": "json_object"},
    max_tokens=1200,
    temperature=0.7,
)

# Parse the structured output
result = InstructionAnswerSet.from_json(completion.choices[0].
message.content)

# Convert to list of tuples
return result.pairs
```

9. Let's create a main function to automate the process. It extracts substrings from the input dataset, then uses concurrent processing via Python's ThreadPoolExecutor to efficiently generate instruction-answer pairs for each extract.

We use a default max_workers value of 4 because higher values tend to exceed OpenAI's rate limits, potentially causing API request failures or throttling.

```python
def create_instruction_dataset(
    dataset: Dataset, client: OpenAI, num_workers: int = 4
) -> Dataset:
    extracts = extract_substrings(dataset)
    instruction_answer_pairs = []
    with concurrent.futures.ThreadPoolExecutor(max_workers=num_
workers) as executor:
        futures = [executor.submit(generate_instruction_answer_
pairs, extract, client)
            for extract in extracts
        ]
        for future in tqdm(concurrent.futures.as_completed(futures),
total=len(futures)
        ):
            instruction_answer_pairs.extend(future.result())

    instructions, answers = zip(*instruction_answer_pairs)
    return Dataset.from_dict(
        {"instruction": list(instructions), "output": list(answers)}
    )
```

10. We can create our instruction dataset by calling this function. Running it over the raw data with GPT-4o mini costs less than 0.5$.

11. We can now create a main function to orchestrate the entire pipeline. It loads the raw data, creates the instruction dataset, splits it into training and testing sets, and pushes the result to the Hugging Face Hub.

```python
def main(dataset_id: str) -> Dataset:
    client = OpenAI()

    # 1. Load the raw data
    raw_dataset = load_articles_from_json("cleaned_documents.json")
    print("Raw dataset:")
    print(raw_dataset.to_pandas())

    # 2. Create instructiondataset
```

```
instruction_dataset = create_instruction_dataset(raw_dataset,
client)
    print("Instruction dataset:")
    print(instruction_dataset.to_pandas())


    # 3. Train/test split and export
    filtered_dataset = instruction_dataset.train_test_split(test_
size=0.1)
    filtered_dataset.push_to_hub("mlabonne/llmtwin")


    return filtered_dataset

Dataset({
    features: ['instruction', 'output'],
    num_rows: 3335
})
```

We obtained 3,335 pairs with this process. You can find our version of the dataset at https://huggingface.co/datasets/mlabonne/llmtwin. The Hugging Face Hub provides a convenient dataset viewer (see *Figure 5.7*) to explore instructions and answers and make sure that there are no obvious mistakes in these samples. Due to the small size of the dataset, there is no need for comprehensive exploration and topic clustering.

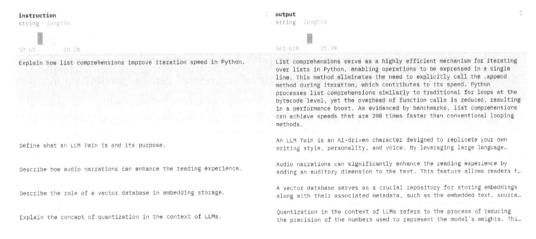

Figure 5.7 – The mlabonne/llmtwin instruction dataset on the Hugging Face Hub

As seen in the previous section, we could refine this instruction dataset by increasing the diversity and complexity of our samples. More advanced prompt engineering could also increase the quality of the generated data by providing examples of the expected results, for instance. Finally, quality evaluation could help filter out low-quality samples by reviewing them individually. For conciseness and simplicity, we will keep a straightforward approach for this instruction dataset and explore more advanced methods in *Chapter 6* when we create a preference dataset.

In the next section, we will introduce SFT techniques, as well as related concepts.

Exploring SFT and its techniques

SFT consists of re-training pre-trained models on a smaller dataset composed of pairs of instructions and answers. The goal of SFT is to turn a base model, which can only perform next-token prediction, into a useful assistant, capable of answering questions and following instructions. SFT can also be used to improve the general performance of the base model (general-purpose SFT), instill new knowledge (e.g., new languages, domains, etc.), focus on specific tasks, adopt a particular voice, and so on.

In this section, we will discuss when to use fine-tuning and explore related concepts with storage formats and chat templates. Finally, we will introduce three popular ways of implementing SFT: full-finetuning, **Low-Rank Adaptation (LoRA)** and **Quantization-aware Low-Rank Adaptation (QLoRA)**.

When to fine-tune

In most scenarios, it is recommended to start with prompt engineering instead of directly fine-tuning models. Prompt engineering can be used with either open-weight or closed-source models. By using techniques like few-shot prompting or **retrieval augmented generation (RAG)**, numerous problems can efficiently be tackled without SFT. Prompt engineering also allows us to build a robust evaluation pipeline, which measures metrics like accuracy, but also cost and latency. If these results do not match the requirements, we can explore the possibility of creating an instruction dataset, as illustrated in the previous section. If enough data is available, fine-tuning becomes an option.

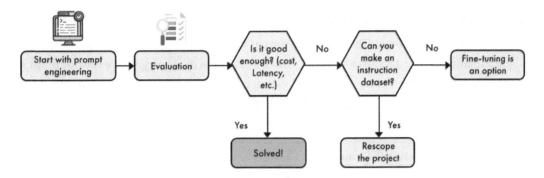

Figure 5.8 – Basic flowchart to determine when fine-tuning is an option on a technical level

Beyond these technical considerations, SFT answers common needs in terms of control ("know your data") and customizability (the fine-tuned model is unique). Instead of building applications around a chatbot, fine-tuning allows developers to create more diverse interactions with LLMs, like tool analytics, moderation, and additional context. Note that if we focus on open-weight models in this book, several LLM providers offer automated fine-tuning services. While they don't offer the same level of control and customizability as managing your own fine-tuning pipeline, it can be an interesting trade-off in specific scenarios (e.g., limited resources in terms of machine learning engineering).

Despite these advantages, fine-tuning also has limitations. It is generally understood that SFT leverages pre-existing knowledge in the base model's weights and refocuses the parameters for a specific purpose. This has several implications. First of all, knowledge that is too distant from what has been learned in the pre-training set (such as an unknown or rare language) can be difficult to learn effectively.

Even worse, a study showed that fine-tuning a model on new knowledge could result in more frequent hallucinations. Depending on the SFT technique that is used, we're also at risk of erasing knowledge that was present in the base model (a common issue referred to as "catastrophic forgetting").

Instruction dataset formats

Instruction datasets are stored in a particular format to organize instructions and answers. Typically, each sample in the dataset can be represented as a Python dictionary, where keys are prompt types like system, instruction, output, and values corresponding to the actual text. The three most standard formats are Alpaca, ShareGPT, and OpenAI. The following table shows how these data formats are generally organized.

Name	JSONL format
Alpaca	{"instruction": "...", "input": "...", "output": "..."} {"instruction": "...", "output": "..."}
ShareGPT	{"conversations": [{"from": "...", "value": "..."}, ...]}
OpenAI	{"conversations": [{"role": "...", "content": "..."}, ...]}
OASST	{"INSTRUCTION": "...", "RESPONSE": "..."}
Raw text	{"text": "..."}

Table 5.5 – Examples of instruction data storage format

Note that for Alpaca, the "input" key is optional. The content of the "input" key is only appended to the content of the "instruction" key when it exists. We also added the "raw text" data format to show that SFT is not inherently different from pre-training. If you choose to re-train a model on raw text, this is a type of fine-tuning generally called "continual pre-training."

The dataset we created in the previous section has two columns ("instruction" and "output") and corresponds to the Alpaca format. Alpaca is sufficient for single-turn instructions and answers, which means it is limited to one instruction and one answer. When you want to process conversations (multiple instructions and answers), formats like ShareGPT or OpenAI are a better fit. By storing each message as a dictionary in a list, they can represent an arbitrarily long conversation in each sample.

The choice of single-turn and multi-turn conversations directly impacts the storage type and depends on the end use case.

Chat templates

Once the instruction-answer pairs are parsed from the dataset format, we want to structure them in a chat template. Chat templates offer a unified way to present the instructions and answers to the model.

In general, they also include special tokens to identify the beginning and the end of a message, or who is the author of the message. Since base models are not designed to follow instructions, they don't have a chat template. This means that you can choose any template when you fine-tune a based model. If you want to fine-tune an instruct model (not recommended), you need to use the same template or it might degrade your performance.

Like instruction dataset formats, there are different chat templates: ChatML, Llama 3, Mistral, and many others. In the open-source community, the ChatML template (originally from OpenAI) is a popular option. It simply adds two special tokens (`<|im_start|>` and `<|im_end|>`) to indicate who is speaking. To give you an example, here is what we obtain when we apply the ChatML template to the instruction-answer pair shown in *Table 5.1*:

```
<|im_start|>system
You are a helpful assistant, who always provide explanation. Think like you
are answering to a five year old.<|im_end|>
<|im_start|>user
Concepts: building, shop, town
Write a sentence that includes all these words.<|im_end|>
<|im_start|>assistant
In our little town, there is a shop inside a big building where people go
to buy their favorite toys and candies.<|im_end|>
```

Table 5.6 – Sample from Table 5.1 with the ChatML chat template

As you can see, we still have three distinct parts: system, user, and assistant. Each part starts with the `<|im_start|>` token and ends with `<|im_end|>`. The current speaker is identified by a string (like "system") instead of a special token. This is the exact string that is tokenized and used as input by the model during fine-tuning.

However, during inference, we can't provide the expected answer. In this case, we provide the system and user part as shown in *Figure 5.6*, and prompt the model to answer by adding `<|im_start|>assistant\n`.

Because the model has been fine-tuned with this template, it understands that the next tokens should be an answer relevant to the user instruction and guided by the system prompt. This is how fine-tuned models acquire instruction-following capabilities.

A common issue with chat templates is that every single whitespace and line break is extremely important. Adding or removing any character would result in a wrong tokenization, which negatively impacts the performance of the model. For this reason, it is recommended to use reliable templates like Jinja, as implemented in the Transformers library. *Table 5.7* shows a few examples of such templates, including Alpaca, which is both the name of an instruction dataset format and a chat template.

Name	Jinja template

Alpaca	```### Instruction: What is the capital of France?```
	
	```### Response: The capital of France is Paris.<EOS>```

ChatML	```<|im_start|>user```
	```What is the capital of France?<|im_end|>```
	```<|im_start|>assistant```
	```The capital of France is Paris.<|im_end|>```

Llama 3	```<|begin_of_text|><|start_header_id|>user<|end_header_id|>```
	
	```What is the capital of France?<|eot_id|><|start_header_id|>assistant<|end_header_id|>```
	
	```The capital of France is Paris.<|eot_id|>```

Phi-3	```<|user|>```
	```What is the capital of France?<|end|>```
	```<|assistant|>```
	```The capital of France is Paris.<|end|>```

Gemma	```<bos><start_of_turn>user```
	```What is the capital of France?<end_of_turn>```
	```<start_of_turn>model```
	```The capital of France is Paris.<end_of_turn>```

Table 5.7 – Example of common chat templates

Jinja implements loops and conditions, which allow the same template to be used for training and inference (add_generation_prompt).

Parameter-efficient fine-tuning techniques

While many techniques exist in the literature, SFT has converged on three main techniques: full fine-tuning, LoRA, and QLoRA. We will introduce each technique individually, and weigh their pros and cons depending on your use cases.

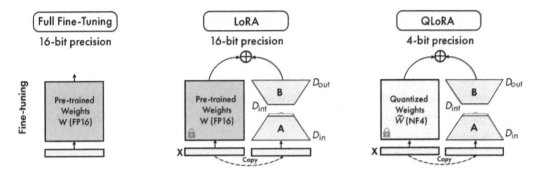

Figure 5.9 – Architectural differences of the three main SFT techniques at the module level

Full fine-tuning

Full fine-tuning refers to the most straightforward SFT technique, consisting of re-training every parameter in the base model. Like pre-training, SFT uses next-token prediction as its training objective. This means that the previously discussed structure of the dataset can be seen as the main difference between continual pre-training and full fine-tuning.

This method often provides the best results but requires significant computational resources. Memory usage depends on several factors, including model size, training techniques, and optimization methods. At its simplest, using a single-GPU setting, the memory required can be estimated using the following formula:

$$Memory = Parameters + Gradients + Optimizer\ States + Activations$$

For a basic setup using **32-bit floating point (fp32)** precision, we can estimate:

- **Parameters**: Learnable weights and biases within a neural network. In a large language model, these are typically the weights in the attention mechanisms, feed-forward layers, and embedding layers. Cost: 4 bytes/parameter (FP32) or 2 bytes/parameter (FP16/BF16).
- **Gradients**: Gradients are the partial derivatives of the loss function with respect to each model parameter. They indicate how much each parameter should be adjusted to minimize the loss. During training, gradients are computed for each parameter through backpropagation and are used to update the model parameters. Cost: 4 bytes/parameter.

- **Optimizer states:** Optimizer states are additional values maintained by optimization algorithms like Adam or AdamW. These typically include running averages of past gradients and past squared gradients for each parameter. They help in adapting the learning rate for each parameter and navigating the loss landscape more effectively. For instance, Adam maintains two additional values (momentum and variance) per parameter. Cost: 8 bytes/parameter (for Adam optimizer).

- **Activations:** Activations are the intermediate outputs of each layer in the neural network during the forward pass. For transformer-based models, this includes the outputs of attention mechanisms, feed-forward layers, and normalization layers. Activations need to be kept in memory during the forward pass to compute gradients in the backward pass, unless techniques like activation checkpointing are used. Cost: variable, but often negligible for small batch sizes.

This gives us a baseline of 16 bytes per parameter. This translates into 112 GB of VRAM for a 7 B model and 1,120 GB for a 70 B model. However, this is often an underestimate, as it doesn't account for additional memory needed for activations, temporary buffers, and overhead from various training techniques.

Several techniques can be employed to reduce memory usage during LLM fine-tuning. Model parallelism spreads the workload across multiple GPUs, though it adds some overhead. Gradient accumulation enables larger effective batch sizes without proportional memory increase. Memory-efficient optimizers like 8-bit Adam can reduce the footprint of optimizer states. Activation checkpointing trades computation for memory by recalculating certain activations. When combined, these techniques can significantly lower memory usage. For instance, using mixed precision with model parallelism might reduce costs to around 14-15 bytes per parameter, compared to the 16-byte baseline. However, memory requirements remain substantial for large models even with these optimizations.

In addition, full fine-tuning directly modifies the pre-training weights, which makes it destructive by nature. If training doesn't behave as expected, it might erase previous knowledge and skills – a phenomenon referred to as "catastrophic forgetting." The same phenomenon can happen with continual pre-training, which generally makes these techniques more difficult to use. Due to this additional complexity and its high computational requirements, parameter-efficient techniques are often preferred to full fine-tuning to create task and domain-specific models.

LoRA

LoRA is a parameter-efficient technique for fine-tuning LLMs. Developed to address the computational challenges associated with adapting massive neural networks, LoRA has quickly become a cornerstone technique in LLM fine-tuning.

The primary purpose of LoRA is to enable the fine-tuning of LLMs with significantly reduced computational resources. This is achieved by introducing trainable low-rank matrices that modify the behavior of the model without changing its original parameters. The key advantages of LoRA include:

- Dramatically reduced memory usage during training
- Faster fine-tuning process
- Preservation of pre-trained model weights (non-destructive)
- Ability to switch between tasks efficiently by swapping LoRA weights

These benefits have made LoRA particularly attractive for researchers and developers working with limited computational resources, effectively democratizing the process of LLM fine-tuning.

At its core, LoRA employs a low-rank decomposition technique to update model weights efficiently. Instead of directly modifying the original weight matrix W, LoRA introduces two smaller matrices, A and B, which together form a low-rank update to W.

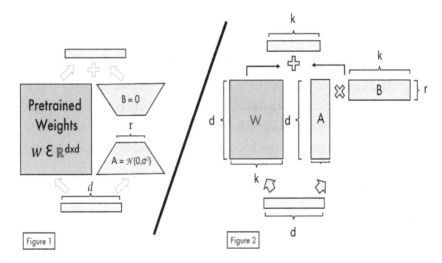

Figure 5.10 – LoRA adds the two trainable matrices A and B and keeps the pre-trained weights W frozen

Mathematically, this can be represented as:

$$W' = W + BA$$

Here, W is the original weight matrix, B and A are the LoRA matrices, and W' is the effective weight matrix used during inference.

The dimensions of matrices A and B are chosen such that their product has the same shape as W, but with a much lower rank. This rank, typically denoted as r, is a crucial hyperparameter in LoRA. During training, the original weights W remain frozen, while only A and B are updated. This approach significantly reduces the number of trainable parameters, leading to substantial memory savings and faster training times.

To implement LoRA effectively, we need to select the correct hyperparameters and target modules. LoRA comes with two hyperparameters:

- **Rank (r)**: Determines the size of the LoRA matrices. A common starting point is $r = 8$, but values up to 256 have shown good results in some cases. Larger ranks may capture more diverse tasks but could lead to overfitting.

- **Alpha (α)**: A scaling factor applied to the LoRA update. In practice, we update the frozen weights W by a factor of α/r. This is why a common heuristic is to set α to twice the value of r, effectively applying a scaling factor of 2 to the LoRA update. You can experiment with different ratios in case of overfitting or underfitting.

In addition, it is possible to add a drop-out layer to prevent overfitting. The dropout rate is usually set between 0 and 0.1 as an optional regularization factor, which slightly decreases training speed.

LoRA can be applied to various parts of the model architecture. Initially, LoRA was primarily focused on modifying the attention mechanism, specifically the **query (Q)** and **value (V)** matrices in transformer layers. However, experiments have demonstrated significant benefits in extending LoRA's application to other key components of the model. These additional target modules include:

- **Key (K)** matrices in attention layers
- Output projection layers (often denoted as O) in attention mechanisms
- Feed-forward or **Multi-Layer Perceptron (MLP)** blocks between attention layers
- Linear output layers

However, it's important to note that increasing the number of LoRA-adapted modules also increases the number of trainable parameters and, consequently, the memory requirements.

Using LoRA, it's possible to fine-tune a 7B parameter model on a single GPU with as little as 14-18 GB of VRAM, depending on the specific configuration. This is a dramatic reduction compared to full fine-tuning, which would typically require multiple high-end GPUs. In terms of trainable parameters, LoRA drastically reduces the number compared to full fine-tuning. For example, even when targeting every module with a rank of 16, a Llama 3 8 B model only has 42 million trainable LoRA parameters out of 8 billion parameters, which is 0.5196% of the model's parameters.

In terms of quality, LoRA can also achieve comparable or sometimes better results than full-fine-tuning. Multiple sets of LoRA weights can be combined for different tasks or domains, allowing flexible deployment and task switching without retraining. Different projects are specialized in multiple-LoRA serving, such as LoRAX. It's also a feature supported by Hugging Face's **Text Generation Inference (TGI)** and **Nvidia Inference Microservices (NIM)**.

QLoRA

Introduced by Dettmers et al., QLoRA is a method for fine-tuning LLMs that addresses the challenges of high computational costs. By combining quantization techniques with LoRA, QLoRA allows developers to fine-tune models on relatively small, widely available GPUs.

The core of QLoRA's approach involves quantizing the base model parameters to a custom **4-bit NormalFloat (NF4)** data type, which significantly reduces memory usage. Like LoRA, instead of updating all model parameters during fine-tuning, QLoRA introduces small, trainable low-rank matrices (adapters) to specific layers of the model. Only these adapters are updated during training, while the original model weights remain unchanged. To further reduce memory usage, QLoRA employs double quantization, which quantizes the quantization constants themselves. Additionally, it uses paged optimizers to manage memory spikes during training by leveraging Nvidia's unified memory feature.

QLoRA provides significant memory savings compared to LoRA, reducing peak GPU memory usage by up to 75%. For example, for a 7B model, QLoRA reduces peak memory usage from 14 GB to 9.1 GB during initialization, a 35% reduction. During fine-tuning, the memory savings increase to 40%, from 15.6 GB for LoRA to 9.3 GB for QLoRA. However, this memory efficiency comes at the cost of increased training time, with QLoRA being about 30% slower than LoRA. In terms of model performance, QLoRA shows only minor differences compared to LoRA.

In summary, QLoRA is particularly beneficial when memory constraints are the primary concern, such as when working with very large models or on hardware with limited GPU memory. However, if training speed is crucial and sufficient memory is available, LoRA might be the preferred choice.

The decision between QLoRA and LoRA should be based on the specific requirements of the project, available hardware, and the need to balance memory usage, training speed, and model performance.

Training parameters

When fine-tuning LLMs, several hyperparameters guide the training process and significantly impact the model's convergence, generalization, and overall effectiveness.

Learning rate and scheduler

The learning rate is the most important hyperparameter. It controls how much the model's parameters are updated during training. It typically ranges from very small values like 1e-6 to larger values like 1e-3. A common starting point for transformer models is often around 1e-5. If the learning rate is too low, training progresses slowly and may get stuck in suboptimal solutions. Conversely, if it's too high, training can become unstable or diverge, leading to poor performance. It's often beneficial to experiment with different learning rates to find the optimal value for your specific task and model.

The learning rate scheduler adjusts the learning rate throughout the training process. It typically starts with a higher learning rate to enable rapid initial progress, then gradually decreases it in later stages to fine-tune the model more precisely. The two most common types of schedulers are linear and cosine. A linear scheduler decreases the learning rate steadily over time, while a cosine scheduler follows a cosine curve, decreasing more slowly at first and then more rapidly toward the end of training. For example, you might start with a learning rate of 3e-4 and decrease it to 1e-7 over the course of training. The specific values and decay schedule depend on your model and dataset, but a common approach is to use a warmup period (e.g., 5% of total steps) where the learning rate increases from 0 to the initial value, followed by a decay period for the remaining 95% of steps. This approach helps stabilize early training and allows for more refined updates as the model converges. In general, linear and cosine schedulers provide the same level of performance.

Batch size

The batch size determines the number of samples processed before the model's weights are updated. Typical batch sizes for LLM fine-tuning range from 1 to 32, with common values being 1, 2, 4, 8, or 16. Larger batch sizes generally lead to more stable gradient estimates and can improve training speed, as they provide a better approximation of the true gradient of the entire dataset.

However, they also require more memory, which can be a limiting factor on GPUs with less VRAM. For instance, a batch size of 16 might work well on a high-end GPU with 24GB of memory, while a smaller GPU with 8 GB might only handle a batch size of 2 or 4.

To overcome memory constraints while still benefiting from larger batch sizes, a technique called gradient accumulation can be used. It works by performing multiple forward and backward passes with smaller mini-batches, accumulating the gradients over these steps before applying a single update to the model's parameters. This approach is particularly useful when working with large models or limited GPU memory. For example, if you want to achieve an effective batch size of 32 but your GPU can only handle 8 samples at a time, you can set the gradient accumulation steps to 4. This means you'll process 4 mini-batches of 8 samples each, accumulating the gradients, and then update the model as if you had processed all 32 samples at once.

The number of gradient accumulation steps typically ranges from 1 (no accumulation) to 8 or 16, depending on the desired effective batch size and available computational resources. When choosing the number of steps, consider the trade-off between training speed and memory usage. More accumulation steps allow for larger effective batch sizes but increase the time required for each update. Here's a simple formula to determine the effective batch size:

$$Effective\ Batch\ Size = Batch\ Size \times \#\ GPUs \times Gradient\ Accumulation\ Steps$$

For instance, if you're using 2 GPUs, each processing a batch of 4 samples, with 4 gradient accumulation steps, your effective batch size would be 4 * 2 * 4 = 32 samples.

Maximum length and packing

The maximum sequence length determines the longest input the model can process. It's typically set between 512 and 4,096 tokens but can go up to 128,000 or more, depending on the task and available GPU memory. For example, a maximum length of 2,048 tokens is common for many language generation tasks, while RAG applications might use up to 8,192 tokens or more. When processing input data, sequences longer than this limit are truncated, meaning excess tokens are removed. Truncation can occur at the beginning (left truncation) or end (right truncation) of the sequence. For instance, with a maximum length of 1,024 tokens, a 1,500-token input would have 476 tokens removed. This parameter directly impacts batch size and memory usage; a batch size of 12 with a max length of 1,024 would contain 12,288 tokens (12 * 1,024), while the same batch size with a max length of 512 would only contain 6,144 tokens. It's important to balance this parameter with your GPU capabilities and the nature of your training data to optimize performance and resource utilization.

Packing maximizes the utilization of each training batch. Instead of assigning one sample per batch, packing combines multiple smaller samples into a single batch, effectively increasing the amount of data processed in each iteration. For example, if your maximum sequence length is 1,024 tokens, but many of your samples are only 200-300 tokens long, packing could allow you to fit 3-4 samples into each batch slot. This approach can significantly improve training efficiency, especially when dealing with datasets containing many short sequences. However, packing requires careful implementation to ensure that model attention doesn't cross between packed samples. This is typically achieved by using attention masks that prevent the model from attending to tokens from different samples within the same packed sequence.

Number of epochs

The number of epochs is another important parameter, representing the number of complete passes through the entire training dataset. For LLM fine-tuning, the typical range is 1 to 10 epochs, with many successful runs using 2 to 5 epochs. The optimal number depends on factors such as task complexity, dataset size, and model architecture. More epochs allow the model to refine its learning, potentially improving performance. However, there's a crucial trade-off: too few epochs may lead to underfitting, while too many can cause overfitting. For example, a large model fine-tuned on a small dataset might only need 1-3 epochs, while a smaller model fine-tuned on a larger dataset could benefit from 5-10 epochs. It is helpful to monitor validation performance during training and implement early stopping if the model's performance plateaus or degrades. This approach helps determine the optimal number of epochs dynamically and prevents overfitting.

Optimizers

Optimizers adjust the model's parameters to minimize the loss function. For LLM fine-tuning, AdamW (Adaptive Moment Estimation with Weight Decay) is highly recommended, particularly its 8-bit version. AdamW 8-bit performs comparably to the 32-bit version while using less GPU memory (but it doesn't improve training speed). AdamW combines adaptive learning rates with weight decay regularization, often leading to better training stability and model performance.

For scenarios with severe memory constraints, AdaFactor presents an alternative designed for memory efficiency. It works well without explicit learning rate tuning, making it particularly useful in resource-constrained environments. However, it may not always match AdamW's performance in all cases. In situations involving extremely large models or limited GPU memory, paged versions of optimizers, such as paged AdamW 8-bit, can further reduce memory consumption by offloading to CPU RAM. If memory allows and maximum performance is the priority, the non-quantized `adamw_torch` optimizer may be the best choice.

Weight decay

Weight decay works by adding a penalty for large weights to the loss function, encouraging the model to learn simpler, more generalizable features. This helps the model avoid relying too heavily on any single input feature, which can improve its performance on unseen data. Typically, weight decay values range from 0.01 to 0.1, with 0.01 being a common starting point. For example, if you're using the AdamW optimizer, you might set the weight decay to 0.01.

While weight decay can be beneficial, setting it too high can impede learning by making it difficult for the model to capture important patterns in the data. Conversely, setting it too low may not provide sufficient regularization. The optimal weight decay value often depends on the specific model architecture and dataset, so it's generally a good practice to experiment with different values.

Gradient checkpointing

Gradient checkpointing is a technique that reduces memory consumption during training by storing only a subset of intermediate activations generated in the forward pass. In standard training procedures, all intermediate activations are retained in memory to facilitate gradient calculation during the backward pass. However, for very deep networks like LLMs, this approach can quickly become impractical due to hardware limitations, especially on GPUs with limited memory capacity.

Gradient checkpointing addresses this challenge by selectively saving activations at specific layers within the network. For layers where activations are not saved, they are recomputed during the backward pass as needed for gradient computation. This approach creates a trade-off between computation time and memory usage. While it significantly reduces memory requirements, it may increase overall computation time due to the need to recalculate some activations.

Other parameters and techniques exist but play a minor role compared to those previously discussed. In the next section, we will explore how to select and tune these parameters using a concrete example.

Fine-tuning in practice

Let's now fine-tune an open-source model on our custom dataset. In this section, we will show an example that implements LoRA and QLoRA for efficiency. Depending on the hardware you have available, you can select the technique that best corresponds to your configuration.

There are many efficient open-weight models we can leverage for task or domain-specific use cases. To select the most relevant LLM, we need to consider three main parameters:

- **License**: Some model licenses only allow non-commercial work, which is a problem if we want to fine-tune for a company. Custom licenses are common in this field, and can target companies with a certain number of users, for example.

- **Budget**: Models with smaller parameter sizes (<10 B) are a lot cheaper to fine-tune and deploy for inference than larger models. This is due to the fact that they can be run on cheaper GPUs and process more tokens per second.

- **Performance**: Evaluating the base model on general-purpose benchmarks or, even better, domain- or task-specific benchmarks relevant to the final use case, is crucial. This helps ensure that the model has the necessary capabilities to perform well on the intended tasks after fine-tuning.

In this chapter, we will choose Llama 3.1 8B, an open-weight model released by Meta. It has a permissive custom license ("Llama 3.1 Community License Agreement") that allows commercial use. With 8B parameters, it is small enough to fit on most GPUs while reaching a high level of performance compared to its competitors. We can verify this using the Open LLM Leaderboard, as well as other benchmarks detailed in the model card.

There are specialized tools and libraries to fine-tune models. In particular, we recommend the following:

- **TRL**: This is a library created and maintained by Hugging Face to train LLMs using SFT and preference alignment. It is a popular and reliable library that tends to be the most up-to-date in terms of algorithms. It works in single and multi-GPU settings with FSDP and DeepSpeed.

- **Axolotl**: Created by Wing Lian, this tool streamlines the fine-tuning of LLMs with reusable YAML configuration files. It is based on TRL but includes many additional features, such as automatically combining datasets stored in various formats. It also supports single- and multi-GPU settings with FSDP and DeepSpeed.

- **Unsloth**: Created by Daniel and Michael Han, Unsloth uses custom kernels to speed up training (2-5x) and reduce memory use (up to 80% less memory). It is based on TRL and provides many utilities, such as automatically converting models into the GGUF quantization format. At the time of writing, it is only available for single-GPU settings.

To maximize efficiency, we will perform fine-tuning using the Unsloth library. The following code is designed as part of our LLMOps pipeline, but can also be used as a stand-alone script. It can also be executed in different environments, like SageMaker, cloud GPUs (like Lambda Labs or RunPod), Google Colab, and many others. We tested it on different GPUs, like A40, A100, and L4.

To install the Unsloth library and its dependencies, we recommend directly installing from the GitHub repository of the book (`https://github.com/PacktPublishing/LLM-Engineering`) or Unsloth's repo (`https://github.com/unslothai/unsloth`). This approach is recommended because the installation steps are regularly updated to address potential conflicts with dependencies:

1. First, we want to access a gated model and (optionally) upload our fine-tuned model to Hugging Face (`https://huggingface.co/`). This requires being logged in to an account. If you don't have an account, you can create it and store your API key (**Settings | Access Tokens | Create new token**) in the .env file:

   ```
   HF_TOKEN = YOUR_API_KEY
   ```

2. Make sure that your Comet ML API key is also in the .env file:

   ```
   COMET_API_KEY = YOUR_API_KEY
   ```

3. Import all the necessary packages:

   ```
   import os
   import torch
   from trl import SFTTrainer
   from datasets import load_dataset, concatenate_datasets
   from transformers import TrainingArguments, TextStreamerfrom unsloth
   import FastLanguageModel, is_bfloat16_supported
   ```

4. Let's now load the model to fine-tune and its corresponding tokenizer. We use Unsloth's FastLaguageModel class with the `.from_pretrained()` method. In addition to the model name, we need to specify the max sequence length (2,048 in this example). Finally, the `load_in_4bit` argument indicates if we want to use **QLoRA (quantized pre-trained weights)** or LoRA.

   We'll use LoRA in this example because of faster training and higher quality, but you can easily switch to QLoRA if you don't meet the VRAM requirements.

   ```
   max_seq_length = 2048
   model, tokenizer = FastLanguageModel.from_pretrained(
       model_name="meta-llama/Meta-Llama-3.1-8B",
       max_seq_length=max_seq_length,
       load_in_4bit=False,
   )
   ```

5. Now that the model is loaded, we can define our LoRA configuration. Here, we use a rank of 32 that is large enough to imitate the writing style and copy the knowledge from our instruction samples. You can increase this value to 64 or 128 if your results are underwhelming. We also set an alpha of 32, without dropout and without bias, to speed up training. Finally, we target every linear layer to maximize the quality of the fine-tuning process.

```
model = FastLanguageModel.get_peft_model(
    model,
    r=32,
    lora_alpha=32,
    lora_dropout=0,
    target_modules=["q_proj", "k_proj", "v_proj", "up_proj", "down_
proj", "o_proj", "gate_proj"],
)
```

6. Next, we need to prepare the data in the right format for fine-tuning. In this example, we don't have a lot of samples in the llmtwin dataset (3,000 samples). This is an issue because the model might not correctly learn the chat template. To address this, we will upsample it with a high-quality general-purpose dataset called FineTome. This is a filtered version of arcee-ai/The-Tome using the fineweb-edu-classifier. Instead of using the 100,000 samples of this dataset, we will specify we only want 10,000 in the train split. We concatenate these two datasets to create our final set.

```
dataset1 = load_dataset("mlabonne/llmtwin")
dataset2 = load_dataset("mlabonne/FineTome-Alpaca-100k",
split="train[:10000]")
dataset = concatenate_datasets([dataset1, dataset2])
```

7. Now, we need to format this data using a chat template. Let's use the Alpaca template for convenience. This template doesn't require additional tokens, which makes it less error-prone (but can slightly impact performance compared to ChatML). Here, we map all the instructions and answers to the Alpaca template. We manually add the **end of sentence (EOS)** token at the end of each message to ensure that the model learns to output it. Without it, it will keep generating answers without ever stopping.

```
alpaca_template = """Below is an instruction that describes a task.
Write a response that appropriately completes the request.

### Instruction:
```

```
{}

### Response:
{}"""


EOS_TOKEN = tokenizer.eos_token
dataset = dataset.map(format_samples, batched=True, remove_
columns=dataset.column_names)
```

8. Once the dataset is ready, we can divide it into training (95%) and test (5%) sets for validation during training.

```
dataset = dataset.train_test_split(test_size=0.05)
```

9. The model is now ready to be trained. The SFTTrainer() class stores all the hyperparameters for our training. In addition, we provide the model, tokenizer, LoRA configuration, and datasets. Following the recommendations from the previous section, we set a learning rate of 3e-4 with a linear scheduler and a maximum sequence length of 2048. We train this model for three epochs with a batch size of 2 and 8 gradient accumulation steps (for an effective batch size of 16). We also choose the adamw_8bit optimizer with a weight_decay of 0.01. Depending on the GPU we use, it will automatically use FP16 or BF16 for the activations. Finally, we report our training run to Comet ML for experiment tracking.

```
trainer = SFTTrainer(
    model=model,
  tokenizer=tokenizer,
    train_dataset=dataset["train"],
    eval_dataset=dataset["test"],
    dataset_text_field="text",
    max_seq_length=max_seq_length,
    dataset_num_proc=2,
    packing=True,
    args=TrainingArguments(
        learning_rate=3e-4,
        lr_scheduler_type="linear",
        per_device_train_batch_size=2,
        gradient_accumulation_steps=8,
        num_train_epochs=3,
        fp16=not is_bfloat16_supported(),
```

```
        bf16=is_bfloat16_supported(),
        logging_steps=1,
        optim="adamw_8bit",
        weight_decay=0.01,
        warmup_steps=10,
        output_dir="output",
        report_to="comet_ml",
        seed=0,
    ),
)


trainer.train()
```

Training this model on our concatenated dataset can take a few hours. For example, it takes 50 minutes on an A100 GPU.

10. Once it's done, we can test it with a quick example. The goal is not to properly evaluate the fine-tuned model, but to make sure that there are no obvious errors related to the tokenizer or chat template.

    For fast inference, we can use FastLanguageModel.for_inference() from Unsloth. We directly format an instruction with the Alpaca format. Note that we provide an empty answer to append the assistant header (### Response): at the end of the user instruction. This forces the model to answer the instruction instead of completing it. We also use a text streamer to stream the generation instead of waiting for it to be complete before printing it.

    ```
    FastLanguageModel.for_inference(model)
    message = alpaca_prompt.format("Write a paragraph to introduce
    supervised fine-tuning.", "")
    inputs = tokenizer([message], return_tensors="pt").to("cuda")

    text_streamer = TextStreamer(tokenizer)
    _ = model.generate(**inputs, streamer=text_streamer, max_new_
    tokens=256, use_cache=True)
    ```

11. Here is the answer provided by our model:

    ```
    Supervised fine-tuning is a method used to enhance a language model
    by providing it with a curated dataset of instructions and their
    corresponding answers. This process is designed to align the model's
    ```

responses with human expectations, thereby improving its accuracy
and relevance. The goal is to ensure that the model can respond
effectively to a wide range of queries, making it a valuable tool
for applications such as chatbots and virtual assistants.

This is correct and properly formatted with the Alpaca chat template.

12. Now that our model has been successfully fine-tuned, we can save it locally and/or push
    it to the Hugging Face Hub using the following functions.

```
model.save_pretrained_merged("model", tokenizer, save_
method="merged_16bit")
model.push_to_hub_merged("mlabonne/TwinLlama-3.1-8B", tokenizer,
save_method="merged_16bit")
```

Congratulations on fine-tuning a base model from scratch! During training, you can access Comet
ML to monitor your training loss, validation loss, and many other metrics. You want to make sure
that these metrics correspond to what is expected. *Figure 5.11* shows the training run corresponding to the previous code in Comet ML.

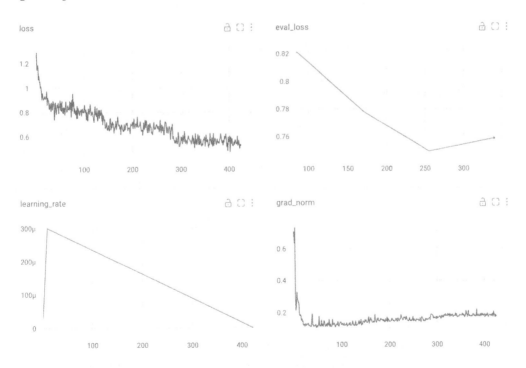

Figure 5.11 – Four monitored metrics during fine-tuning in Comet ML

In particular, three of these metrics are important to monitor:

- **Training loss**: It measures how well the model is performing on the task it's being trained for. The loss should continuously decrease on average, indicating improving performance. We expect a rapid decrease at the beginning of training, followed by a long plateau. Spikes and continuous increases in the loss value are signs that the training is failing. In this case, you might want to check the quality of your data, issues with the tokenizer, and tune parameters like learning rate and batch size. In *Figure 5.11* (loss), you can see three different phases corresponding to our three epochs.

- **Validation loss**: It measures the loss using the validation set instead of the training set; a well-fitted model typically shows both training and validation losses decreasing and eventually stabilizing, with a small gap between them. This gap should be minimal but is expected to exist as the model will always perform slightly better on the training data. If the training loss continues to decrease while the validation loss starts to increase, it's a sign of overfitting. Conversely, if both curves remain flat at a relatively high loss value, it indicates underfitting. There are no universal "recommended ranges" for loss values, as these depend on the specific problem and loss function used. However, you should look for convergence and stability in both curves. In *Figure 4.11* (eval_loss), we see a slight increase at step 340. This is still acceptable but might indicate that the model starts to overfit.

- **Gradient norm**: It represents the magnitude of the gradient vector during training. Large gradient norms can indicate training instability like overfitting, especially if accompanied by a divergence between training and validation losses. On the other hand, a stable or decreasing gradient norm generally means that the model is converging toward a local optimum. To mitigate issues associated with large gradient norms, gradient clipping can be employed. This technique involves setting a maximum threshold for the gradient norm, effectively limiting the size of parameter updates.

It is often interesting to try different learning rates and select the best model based on the minimal loss. Note that this is a proxy for real evaluations, which are covered in the next chapter.

Summary

This chapter covered essential aspects of LLM fine-tuning, both in theory and practice. We examined the instruction data pipeline and how to create high-quality datasets, from curation to augmentation. Each pipeline stage offers optimization opportunities, particularly in quality assessment, data generation, and enhancement. This flexible pipeline can be adapted to your use cases by selecting the most relevant stages and techniques.

We applied this framework to real-world data from *Chapter 3*, using an LLM to convert raw text into instruction-answer pairs. We then explored SFT techniques. This included an analysis of SFT's advantages and limitations, methods for storing and parsing instruction datasets with chat templates, and an overview of three primary SFT techniques: full fine-tuning, LoRA, and QLoRA. We compared these methods based on their impact on memory usage, training efficiency, and output quality. The chapter concluded with a practical demonstration that involved fine-tuning a Llama 3.1 8 B model on our custom instruction dataset. This example highlighted key steps and implementation details for successful fine-tuning.

In the next chapter, we will use preference alignment techniques to create a new version of Twin-Llama-3.1-8B. We will generate a new dataset with chosen and rejected answers that will help us calibrate the type of answers we expect from our model. We will detail many applications that can benefit from this framework and how to implement it.

References

- Tahori, Gulrajani, Zhang, Dubois, et al.. "*Alpaca: A Strong, Replicable Instruction-Following Model*" crfm.stanford.edu, March 13, 2023, https://crfm.stanford.edu/2023/03/13/alpaca.html.

- Subhabrata Mukherjee et al.. "*Orca: Progressive Learning from Complex Explanation Traces of GPT-4.*" arXiv preprint arXiv:2306.02707, June 2023.

- Wing Lian and Bleys Goodson and Eugene Pentland and Austin Cook and Chanvichet Vong and "Teknium". "*Open-Orca/OpenOrca.*" *huggingface.co*, 2023, https://huggingface.co/datasets/Open-Orca/OpenOrca.

- Weihao Zeng et al.. "*Automatic Instruction Evolving for Large Language Models.*" arXiv preprint arXiv:2406.00770, June 2024.

- Chunting Zhou et al.. "*LIMA: Less Is More for Alignment.*" arXiv preprint arXiv:2305.11206, May 2023

- 01. AI. "*Yi: Open Foundation Models by 01.AI.*" arXiv preprint arXiv:2403.04652, March 2024.

- Alex Birch. "*LLM finetuning memory requirements.*" blog.scottlogic.com, November 24, 2023, https://blog.scottlogic.com/2023/11/24/llm-mem.html.

- Quentin Anthony et al.. "*Transformer Math 101.*" blog.eleuther.ai, April 18, 2023, https://blog.eleuther.ai/transformer-math/.

- Edward J. Hu et al.. *"LoRA: Low-Rank Adaptation of Large Language Models."* arXiv preprint arXiv:2106.09685, June 2021.
- Tim Dettmers et al.. *"QLoRA: Efficient Finetuning of Quantized LLMs."* arXiv preprint arXiv:2305.14314, May 2023.

Join our book's Discord space

Join our community's Discord space for discussions with the authors and other readers:

`https://packt.link/llmeng`

6

Fine-Tuning with Preference Alignment

Supervised Fine-Tuning (SFT) has been crucial in adapting LLMs to perform specific tasks. However, SFT struggles to capture the nuances of human preferences and the long tail of potential interactions that a model might encounter. This limitation has led to the development of more advanced techniques for aligning AI systems with human preferences, grouped under the umbrella term *preference alignment*.

Preference alignment addresses the shortcomings of SFT by incorporating direct human or AI feedback into the training process. This method allows a more nuanced understanding of human preferences, especially in complex scenarios where simple supervised learning falls short. While numerous techniques exist for preference alignment, this chapter will primarily focus on **Direct Preference Optimization (DPO)** for simplicity and efficiency.

In this chapter, we will talk about the type of data that is required by preference alignment algorithms like DPO. We will build our own dataset to modify the writing style of our model, making it less artificial and more authentic. We will introduce the DPO algorithm and implement it to align the model trained in *Chapter 5*.

In this chapter, we will cover the following topics:

- Understanding preference datasets
- How to create our own preference dataset
- **Direct preference optimization (DPO)**
- Implementing DPO in practice to align our model

By the end of this chapter, you will be able to create your own preference datasets and align models with diverse techniques.

 All the code examples from this chapter can be found on GitHub at `https://github.com/PacktPublishing/LLM-Engineering`.

Understanding preference datasets

The principles for creating high-quality preference datasets are the same as those discussed in *Chapter 5* for instruction datasets. We want to maximize the accuracy, diversity, and complexity of our samples. To achieve this, we follow the same stages, as outlined in *Figure 6.1*: data curation, deduplication, decontamination, quality evaluation, exploration, generation, and augmentation.

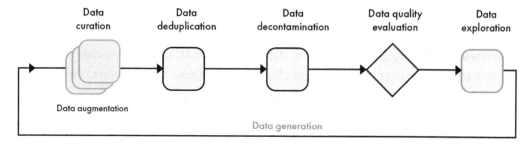

Figure 6.1 – Overview of the post-training data pipeline covered in this chapter

To avoid repetition, this section will focus on the main differences between instruction and preference datasets. We will introduce the structure of preference samples and the ideal size for preference datasets. Then, we will focus on the two stages that differ most from creating instruction datasets: data generation and evaluation.

Preference data

Preference datasets lack the standardization of instruction datasets due to varying data requirements across different training algorithms. Preference data comprises a collection of responses to a given instruction, ranked by humans or language models. This chapter focuses on DPO, so we will examine the specific data format required by this algorithm.

As illustrated in *Table 6.1*, the structure of DPO datasets is straightforward: each instruction is paired with one preferred answer and one rejected answer. The objective is to train the model to generate the preferred response rather than the rejected one.

Instruction	
Tell me a joke about octopuses.	
Chosen answer	**Rejected answer**
Why don't octopuses play cards in casinos? Because they can't count past eight.	How many tickles does it take to make an octopus laugh? Ten tickles.

Table 6.1 – Example of sample from the mlabonne/orpo-dpo-mix-40k dataset

In preference datasets, the rejected response is as important as the chosen one. Without the rejected response, the dataset would be a simple instruction set. Rejected responses represent the behavior we aim to eliminate from the model. This provides a lot of flexibility and allows us to use preference datasets in many contexts. Here is a list of examples where preference datasets are more beneficial to use compared to using SFT alone:

- **Chatbots**: In conversational AI, the quality of responses often depends on subjective factors like naturalness, engagement, and contextual appropriateness. A preference dataset allows the model to learn these nuanced aspects by comparing better and worse responses. Simple SFT might not capture the subtleties of what makes one response preferable over another in a given context.

- **Content moderation**: Determining whether content is appropriate or violates guidelines often involves nuanced judgments. Preference datasets can help the model learn to distinguish between borderline cases by comparing examples of content that is and isn't acceptable. This is more effective than binary classification through SFT, as it helps the model understand the reasoning behind moderation decisions.

- **Summarization**: The quality of a summary often depends on factors like conciseness, relevance, and coherence. By using preference datasets, models can learn to generate summaries that humans find more useful and informative. Simple SFT might result in summaries that are technically correct but less preferable to human readers.

- **Code generation**: In coding tasks, there are often multiple correct solutions, but some are more efficient or readable, or follow better practices than others. Preference datasets can help the model learn these qualitative aspects of code quality, which might not be captured by simple correctness-based SFT.

- **Creative writing**: For tasks like story generation or poetry writing, the quality of the output is highly subjective and multifaceted. Preference datasets can capture human judgments about style, creativity, and emotional impact better than instruction datasets, which might focus more on technical correctness or adherence to prompts.

- **Translation**: While traditional metrics like BLEU scores can measure translation accuracy, they don't always capture the fluency or naturalness of the translation. Preference datasets can help models learn to produce translations that native speakers prefer, even when multiple translations are technically correct.

In all these scenarios, preference datasets enable a more refined training approach. They capture subjective quality assessments and human preferences that extend beyond simple correctness or adherence to instructions. This method can produce models that generate output that is not only technically accurate but also better aligned with human judgment and preferences in complex, open-ended tasks.

Unlike instruction datasets, there are no standardized storage formats like Alpaca or ShareGPT. Most preference datasets follow a structure similar to that shown in *Table 6.1*, with columns for an instruction, a preferred answer, and a rejected answer. Multi-turn conversations are uncommon in preference alignment. At the time of writing, major fine-tuning libraries do not support multi-turn conversations and typically extract only the first or last message in a conversation.

Data quantity

DPO datasets typically require fewer samples than instruction datasets to significantly impact model behavior. As with instruction datasets, the required sample count depends on model size and task complexity. Larger models are more sample-efficient and thus require less data, while complex tasks demand more examples to capture the desired behavior. Once again, data quality is crucial, and a large number of preference pairs is generally beneficial.

General-purpose alignment is used by LLM providers to improve the overall performance of the fine-tuned models. This requires preference datasets with millions of samples. Major players in the AI industry, including Nvidia and Meta, are converging on similar post-training pipelines, involving multiple rounds of preference alignment, and extensive use of synthetic data. This consensus suggests that these methods are proving to be the most effective for pushing the boundaries of language model capabilities.

On a smaller scale, the open-source community uses datasets ranging from 10,000 to 100,000 samples to enhance model performance. This approach has proven effective not only in improving benchmark scores but also in healing networks after merging, pruning, and other modifications. Generally, DPO is less destructive than SFT and has a milder impact on the final model.

On the other hand, tasks like the ones previously described require fewer preference pairs. Task-specific alignment focuses on improving model performance for a particular function, such as modifying the writing style, refusing certain instructions, and so on. These alignments can often be achieved with smaller datasets, ranging from 100 to 10,000 preference pairs, depending on the task's complexity.

An example of an application that requires few samples is instructing the model to state that it wasn't trained by OpenAI, Meta, or another LLM provider. This can be achieved using a preference dataset, where the rejected answers are those claiming alternative origins, and the chosen answers are responses where the model correctly states that it was trained by you. A relatively small dataset of 200 to 500 pairs can be enough for this task.

Data generation and evaluation

When creating preference datasets, data generation and evaluation are closely linked. We first create answers and then rate them to make the final dataset. In the following, we introduce both steps as one process instead of two separate ones.

Generating preferences

Before making new preference data, it's good to look at relevant open-source datasets. There are fewer of these compared to instruction datasets, but you can find high-quality preference datasets on the Hugging Face Hub. These can be used for specific tasks or to add to your own dataset. Well-known preference datasets include the Anthropic HH-RLHF dataset, which has human preferences for helpful and harmless AI responses, and the OpenAI Summarize from Human Feedback dataset, which focuses on article summaries.

DPO datasets can be created using various methods, each with its own trade-offs between quality, cost, and scalability. These methods can be tailored to specific applications and require varying degrees of human feedback. We divide them into four main categories:

- **Human-generated, human-evaluated datasets**: This method involves hiring people to both create responses to prompts and evaluate the quality of these responses. While this approach can capture nuanced human preferences and is ideal for complex tasks, it's extremely resource-intensive and difficult to scale. As a result, it's primarily used by large AI companies with substantial resources.

- **Human-generated, LLM-evaluated datasets**: This method can be useful if you have a lot of existing human-generated content. However, it's rarely used in practice due to inefficiency, as it still requires significant human input for response generation while potentially missing nuanced preferences during the LLM evaluation stage.

- **LLM-generated, human-evaluated datasets:** This method offers a good balance between quality and efficiency. LLMs generate multiple responses to prompts, and humans rank these responses. This approach is often preferred because humans are generally better at judging answers than writing them from scratch. It allows the rapid generation of diverse responses while still capturing human preferences effectively. However, it may not provide creative or unexpected responses that humans might generate.

- **LLM-generated, LLM-evaluated datasets:** Fully synthetic datasets, where both generation and evaluation are done by LLMs, are becoming increasingly common due to their scalability and cost-effectiveness. This method can produce massive datasets quickly and improves as LLM capabilities advance. However, it requires careful prompt engineering to ensure quality and diversity, and may perpetuate biases or limitations of the generating LLM.

In practice, human-generated datasets are expensive, difficult to scale, and not necessarily of the highest quality. On the other hand, human evaluation is quite valuable but can be difficult to scale, which is why large datasets benefit from LLM evaluation. In addition to these high-level considerations, the way you obtain your data and how you plan to use it also need to be considered. For example, applications with many users can embed a feedback mechanism to provide preferences. This can be as simple as a `like` and `dislike` score, or something more in-depth with text.

Note that evaluation is not always required and preferences can emerge naturally from the generation process. For instance, it is possible to use a high-quality model to generate preferred outputs and a lower-quality or intentionally flawed model to produce less preferred alternatives. This creates a clear distinction in the preference dataset, allowing more effective training of AI systems to recognize and emulate high-quality outputs. The `Intel/orca_dpo_pairs` dataset available on the Hugging Face Hub was created with this process.

Another approach is to compare model-generated outputs with human-written responses, which can provide insights into how well the model aligns with actual human preferences and highlight areas where the model may be lacking. This can be used to copy a particular style and give a more authentic tone to the model.

Tips for data generation

The data generation is consistent between instruction and preference datasets. Prompts should be designed to encourage diversity and complexity in the model's responses. By crafting prompts that explicitly request different approaches or styles, we can ensure a wide range of outputs that capture the varied nature of human preferences.

For instance, when generating summaries, one might request variations such as concise summaries, detailed summaries, and summaries focusing on key points. This approach not only produces a diverse dataset but also helps in understanding how different styles and approaches align with human preferences.

Introducing variability in the outputs is another crucial aspect of generating synthetic preference datasets. This can be achieved by manipulating the temperature settings or employing other sampling methods in the LLM. Higher temperature settings tend to produce more creative and diverse responses, while lower settings result in more focused and deterministic outputs. This creates a trade-off between diversity and coherence, which depends on the kind of data we want to generate. For example, generating code requires low creativity, thus low temperature, while writing articles can be high temperature.

Using multiple LLMs to generate samples can be better than using just one model. Some LLMs are better at specific tasks, and this approach also adds more variety. This approach is used by popular open-source datasets like `argilla/Capybara-Preferences`, combining GPT-4 with open-weight models. The evaluation process then selects the chosen and the rejected answers.

Evaluating preferences

Data evaluation can be performed by human raters or automated with LLMs. **LLM evaluation** involves developing detailed criteria, creating a prompt that clearly communicates these guidelines to the LLM, and using the model to select preferred and rejected responses. While more scalable than human rating and allowing the consistent application of criteria, this quality of LLM evaluation depends directly on the model's performance and the provided guidelines. It may miss subtle human preferences or cultural nuances. However, as LLMs continue to improve, their ability to make nuanced judgments improves as well, potentially leading to higher-quality datasets over time.

Implementing LLM evaluation for preference datasets can be done through absolute scoring or pairwise ranking. In absolute scoring, the LLM assigns a numerical score or categorical rating to each response based on predefined criteria. This method is straightforward but may suffer from inconsistency across different prompts or evaluation sessions. Pairwise ranking, on the other hand, involves presenting the LLM with two responses and asking it to choose the better one or rank them. This approach more closely mimics the format of human evaluation and can lead to more consistent results.

For absolute scoring, you would create a prompt that outlines the evaluation criteria and asks the LLM to rate the response on a specific scale (e.g., 1-5 or poor/fair/good/excellent). The prompt might look like this: "Rate the following response on a scale of 1-5 based on relevance, coherence, and helpfulness: [INSERT RESPONSE]." For pairwise ranking, the prompt could be: "Compare the following two responses. Which one is better in terms of relevance, coherence, and helpfulness? Response A: [INSERT RESPONSE A] Response B: [INSERT RESPONSE B]."

The comparative nature of preference datasets makes pairwise ranking an ideal approach for evaluation. This method is generally more accurate and more closely correlated to human judgment than absolute scoring. Pairwise ranking mimics the natural way humans compare options, making it easier for both human raters and LLMs to provide consistent and meaningful evaluations.

We can further improve the accuracy of pairwise ranking by providing a ground-truth answer and using chain-of-thought reasoning. This approach encourages the evaluating LLM to consider multiple aspects of the responses and articulate its decision-making process, leading to more thorough and justified evaluations. When no ground-truth answer is available, we can prompt the LLM to create a grading note, which is a description of the expected answer. This technique works particularly well in scenarios where the LLM doesn't have extensive knowledge about a given topic, as it forces the model to establish clear criteria for evaluation before assessing the responses.

Here's a concrete implementation of an LLM-as-a-judge prompt to perform pairwise ranking:

Instruction

You are an answer judge. Your goal is to compare answer A and answer B. I want to know which answer does a better job of answering the instruction in terms of relevance, accuracy, completeness, clarity, structure, and conciseness.

Instruction: {instruction}

Answer A: {answer_a}

Answer B: {answer_b}

Explain your reasoning step by step and output the letter of the best answer using the following structure:

Reasoning: (compare the two answers)

Best answer: (A or B)

Table 6.2 – Example of LLM-as-a-judge prompt for pairwise ranking with one instruction and two answers

However, it's important to note that LLM-based evaluation can be subject to several types of bias:

- **Position bias**: In relative scoring, LLM judges tend to favor the first answer presented. This bias can skew results and lead to inaccurate preferences.

- **Length bias**: Similar to humans, LLM judges often show a preference for longer answers, potentially overlooking the quality of shorter, more concise responses.

- **Family bias**: LLM judges may favor responses that are generated by themselves or models from the same family, potentially due to similarities in language patterns or knowledge bases.

To mitigate these biases and enhance the quality of preference datasets, several solutions can be implemented. One key approach is to randomize the order of answer A and answer B in each comparison, which can counteract position bias by ensuring that the order of presentation doesn't consistently influence the evaluation. Another valuable strategy involves providing few-shot examples that demonstrate a balanced distribution of scores. These examples serve to calibrate the judge LLM's internal scoring mechanism and can effectively address both length and family bias by illustrating that shorter answers or those from different model families can also be of high quality. Additionally, employing multiple models as a jury, rather than relying on a single LLM judge, can significantly improve the robustness of the evaluation process. This multi-model approach helps to balance out individual biases that may be present in any single model, leading to a more comprehensive and accurate assessment of the responses.

In the next section, we will create our own preference dataset. We will rely on the data generation process to naturally create chosen (human-generated) and rejected (LLM-generated) answers.

Creating our own preference dataset

Our model can currently write paragraphs about topics related to machine learning, but it doesn't have the same writing style as the original authors. This is a typical use case for preference alignment, where we want to change the "voice" of the model to closely imitate the source data. It's important to note that, experimentally, DPO tends to make models more verbose and pushes them to use very formal language. Therefore, the training will need to use DPO surgically to avoid this pitfall and instead adopt the less formal style of these blog articles.

In this section, we will create a preference dataset where the chosen answers are extracts from the text, while rejected answers are generated by the model. To implement it, we will modify the code created in *Chapter 5*, which was designed to generate instruction datasets.

As seen in the previous section, preference and instruction datasets rely on the same principles. Instead of pairs of instructions and answers, we need triples (instruction, answer 1, answer 2). What's interesting in this setting is that we have ground-truth answers in the text chunks, which means we don't need complex evaluation processes like LLM judges. To make sure that these extracts are high-quality, we will implement two additional quality filters, based on length and punctuation. *Figure 6.2* summarizes the end-to-end process:

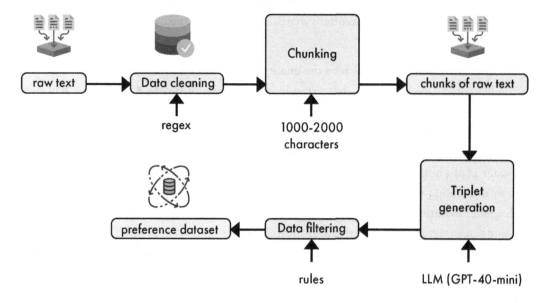

Figure 6.2 – Synthetic data generation pipeline from raw text to preference dataset

We are now ready to implement the preference data generation pipeline:

1. We start by importing the necessary libraries.

    ```python
    import concurrent.futures
    import json
    import re
    from typing import List, Tuple

    from datasets import Dataset
    from openai import OpenAI
    from tqdm.auto import tqdm
    ```

2. Instead of the `InstructionAnswerSet` class, we now have a `PreferenceSet` class. This class is designed to handle triples of instructions, generated answers (rejected), and extracted answers (chosen).

```python
class PreferenceSet:
    def __init__(self, triples: List[Tuple[str, str, str]]):
        self.triples = triples


    @classmethod
    def from_json(cls, json_str: str) -> 'PreferenceSet':
        data = json.loads(json_str)
        triples = [(triple['instruction'], triple['generated_
answer'], triple['extracted_answer'])
                    for triple in data['preference_triples']]
        return cls(triples)


    def __iter__(self):
        return iter(self.triples)
```

3. The `load_articles_from_json`, `clean_text`, and `extract_substrings` functions remain unchanged from the original code. Let's start with `load_articles_from_json`, which takes our JSON file (`cleaned_documents.json`) containing the articles as input and returns a Hugging Face dataset with the text and metadata (ID, platform, author ID, author full name, link).

```python
def load_articles_from_json(file_path: str) -> Dataset:
    with open(file_path, "r") as file:
        data = json.load(file)


    return Dataset.from_dict(
        {
            "id": [item["id"] for item in data["artifact_data"]],
            "content": [item["content"] for item in data["artifact_
data"]],
            "platform": [item["platform"] for item in
data["artifact_data"]],
            "author_id": [item["author_id"] for item in
data["artifact_data"]],
```

```
            "author_full_name": [item["author_full_name"] for item
    in data["artifact_data"]],
            "link": [item["link"] for item in data["artifact_
    data"]],
        }
    )
```

4. The `clean_text` function removes non-alphanumeric characters except for apostrophes,
    periods, commas, exclamation marks, and question marks. It also replaces multiple
    whitespaces with a single space to ensure proper formatting.

```
def clean_text(text: str) -> str:    text = re.sub(r"[^\w\s.,!?']",
" ", text)    text = re.sub(r"\s+", " ", text)
    return text.strip()
```

5. The `extract_substrings` function splits articles into chunks with a length between 1,000
    and 2,000 characters. To make sure that the splitting doesn't break sentences, which could
    modify their meanings, we use a regex to only split after the end of a sentence.

```
def extract_substrings(dataset: Dataset, min_length: int = 1000,
max_length: int = 2000) -> List[str]:
    extracts = []
    sentence_pattern = r"(?<!\w\.\w.)(?<![A-Z][a-z]\.)
(?<=\.|\?|\!)\s"

    for article in dataset["content"]:
        cleaned_article = clean_text(article)
        sentences = re.split(sentence_pattern, cleaned_article)

        current_chunk = ""
        for sentence in sentences:
            sentence = sentence.strip()
            if not sentence:
                continue

            if len(current_chunk) + len(sentence) <= max_length:
                current_chunk += sentence + " "
            else:
                if len(current_chunk) >= min_length:
                    extracts.append(current_chunk.strip())
```

```
                    current_chunk = sentence + " "

        if len(current_chunk) >= min_length:
            extracts.append(current_chunk.strip())

    return extracts
```

6. The generate_preference_triples function replaces the original generate_instruction_ answer_pairs function. The prompt is adapted from the instruction version and is designed to generate triples instead of pairs. It also provides general guidance about the type of instructions we're interested in, how to extract answers from articles, and how to style them:

```
def generate_preference_triples(extract: str, client: OpenAI) ->
List[Tuple[str, str, str]]:
    prompt = f"""Based on the following extract, generate five
instruction-answer triples. Each triple should consist of:
1. An instruction asking about a specific topic in the context.
2. A generated answer that attempts to answer the instruction based
on the context.
3. An extracted answer that is a relevant excerpt directly from the
given context.

Instructions must be self-contained and general, without explicitly
mentioning a context, system, course, or extract.

Important:
- Ensure that the extracted answer is a verbatim copy from the
context, including all punctuation and apostrophes.
- Do not add any ellipsis (...) or [...]  to indicate skipped text
in the extracted answer.
- If the relevant text is not continuous, use two separate sentences
from the context instead of skipping text.

Provide your response in JSON format with the following structure:
{{
    "preference_triples": [
        {{
            "instruction": "...",
```

```
                    "generated_answer": "...",
                    "extracted_answer": "..."
            }},
            ...
        ]
    }}

        Extract:
        {extract}
        """
```

7. In the same function, we use GPT-4o-mini to generate our answers using JSON mode. We specify in the system prompt that we want triples instead of pairs. The JSON answers are directly parsed by our `PreferenceSet` class to return the expected list of tuples.

```
        completion = client.chat.completions.create(
            model="gpt-4o-mini",
            messages=[
                {
                    "role": "system",
                    "content": "You are a helpful assistant who
        generates instruction-answer triples based on the given context.
        Each triple should include an instruction, a generated answer, and
        an extracted answer from the context. Provide your response in JSON
        format.",
                },
                {"role": "user", "content": prompt},
            ],
            response_format={"type": "json_object"},
            max_tokens=2000,
            temperature=0.7,
        )

        result = PreferenceSet.from_json(completion.choices[0].message.
    content)
        return result.triples
```

8. Two new filtering functions are introduced for the preference data pipeline: `filter_short_answers` and `filter_answer_format`. These functions filter out short answers and ensure that answers start with an uppercase letter and end with proper punctuation. We use them as heuristics to filter out samples with poor quality.

```python
def filter_short_answers(dataset: Dataset, min_length: int = 100) ->
Dataset:
    def is_long_enough(example):
        return len(example['chosen']) >= min_length

    return dataset.filter(is_long_enough)


def filter_answer_format(dataset: Dataset) -> Dataset:
    def is_valid_format(example):
        chosen = example['chosen']
        return (len(chosen) > 0 and
                chosen[0].isupper() and
                chosen[-1] in ('.', '!', '?'))

    return dataset.filter(is_valid_format)
```

9. The `create_preference_dataset` function replaces the original `create_instruction_dataset` function. This function now works with triples instead of pairs and uses different column names in the resulting dataset.

```python
def create_preference_dataset(dataset: Dataset, client: OpenAI, num_
workers: int = 4) -> Dataset:
    extracts = extract_substrings(dataset)
    preference_triples = []

    with concurrent.futures.ThreadPoolExecutor(max_workers=num_
workers) as executor:
        futures = [
            executor.submit(generate_preference_triples, extract,
client)
            for extract in extracts
        ]
        for future in tqdm(concurrent.futures.as_completed(futures),
total=len(futures)):
```

```
                preference_triples.extend(future.result())

        instructions, generated_answers, extracted_answers =
    zip(*preference_triples)
        return Dataset.from_dict(
            {
                "prompt": list(instructions),
                "rejected": list(generated_answers),
                "chosen": list(extracted_answers)
            }
        )
```

10. The main function is updated to include the new filtering steps and to use the preference dataset creation function:

```
def main(dataset_id: str) -> Dataset:
    client = OpenAI()

    # 1. Load the raw data
    raw_dataset = load_articles_from_json("cleaned_documents.json")
    print("Raw dataset:")
    print(raw_dataset.to_pandas())

    # 2. Create preference dataset
    dataset = create_preference_dataset(raw_dataset, client)
    print("Preference dataset:")
    print(dataset.to_pandas())

    # 3. Filter out samples with short answers
    dataset = filter_short_answers(dataset)

    # 4. Filter answers based on format
    dataset = filter_answer_format(dataset)

    # 5. Export
    dataset.push_to_hub(dataset_id)

    return dataset
```

The `create_preference_dataset()` function generated 2,970 samples. This dataset is then heavily filtered to only retain 1,467 samples by removing answers that are too short or not properly formatted (for example, answers that start with an uppercase letter or end with a period, exclamation mark, or question mark).

The final dataset is available on the Hugging Face Hub at the following address: `https://huggingface.co/datasets/mlabonne/llmtwin-dpo`. You can see in *Figure 6.3* an example that captures a subtle nuance in terms of writing style. Both answers are correct, but the **chosen** (extracted) answer sounds slightly more casual.

Figure 6.3 – Screenshot of the mlabonne/llmtwin-dpo preference dataset on the Hugging Face Hub

To produce this dataset, we iterated many times over the prompt to generate the data. This required some manual evaluation and experiments until we reached satisfying results. The quality of the prompt is fundamental in this process, which is why it is recommended to follow a similar process to generate your own preference datasets.

In the next section, we will introduce concepts related to **Reinforcement Learning from Human Feedback (RLHF)** and DPO. This will cover new parameters and ideas that are implemented in the final section of this chapter.

Preference alignment

Preference alignment regroups techniques to fine-tune models on preference data. In this section, we provide an overview of this field and then focus on the technique we will implement: **Direct Preference Optimization (DPO)**.

Reinforcement Learning from Human Feedback

Reinforcement Learning from Human Feedback (RLHF) combines **reinforcement learning (RL)** with human input to align models with human preferences and values. RLHF emerged as a response to challenges in traditional RL methods, particularly the difficulty of specifying reward functions for complex tasks and the potential for misalignment between engineered rewards and intended objectives.

The origins of RLHF can be traced back to the field of **preference-based reinforcement learning (PbRL)**, which was independently introduced by Akrour et al. and Cheng et al. in 2011. PbRL aimed to infer objectives from qualitative feedback, such as pairwise preferences between behaviors, rather than relying on quantitative reward signals. This approach addressed some of the limitations of conventional RL, where defining appropriate reward functions can be challenging and prone to reward hacking or unintended behaviors.

The term RLHF was coined later, around 2021-2022, as the approach gained prominence in the context of training LLMs. However, the core ideas had been developing for years prior. A seminal paper by Christiano et al. in 2017 demonstrated the effectiveness of learning reward models from human preferences and using them to train RL agents. This work showed that RLHF could match or exceed the performance of agents trained on hand-engineered rewards, but with significantly less human effort.

At its core, RLHF works by iteratively improving both a reward model and a policy:

- **Reward model learning**: Instead of using a pre-defined reward function, RLHF learns a reward model from human feedback. This is typically done by presenting humans with different answers and asking them to indicate which one they prefer. These preferences are used to train a reward model, often using a Bradley-Terry model or similar approaches that map preferences to underlying utility functions.

- **Policy optimization**: With the learned reward model, standard RL algorithms can be used to optimize a policy. This policy generates new behaviors that aim to maximize the predicted rewards from the learned model.

- **Iterative improvement**: As the policy improves, it generates new behaviors that can be evaluated by humans, leading to refinements in the reward model. This cycle continues, ideally resulting in a policy that aligns well with human preferences.

A key innovation in RLHF is its approach to handling the high cost of human feedback. Rather than requiring constant human oversight, RLHF allows for asynchronous and sparse feedback.

The learned reward model serves as a proxy for human preferences, enabling the RL algorithm to train continuously without direct human input for every action.

As an example, *Figure 6.4* shows a high-level view of the **Proximal Policy Optimization (PPO)** algorithm, which is one of the most popular RLHF algorithms. Here, the reward model is used to score the text that is generated by the trained model. This reward is regularized by an additional **Kullback–Leibler (KL)** divergence factor, ensuring that the distribution of tokens stays similar to the model before training (frozen model).

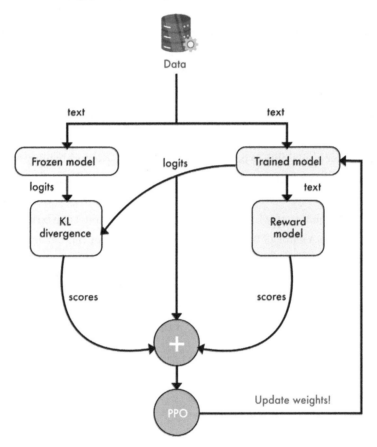

Figure 6.4 – High-level view of the PPO algorithm for preference alignment

While RLHF has proven effective for aligning AI systems with human preferences, it faces challenges due to its iterative nature and reliance on a separate reward model, which can be computationally expensive and potentially unstable. Despite theoretical superiority, RLHF algorithms have also experimentally underperformed compared to simpler approaches. One such approach that has gained significant attention is DPO.

Direct Preference Optimization

Introduced by Rafailov et al. in their 2023 paper *Direct Preference Optimization: Your Language Model is Secretly a Reward Model*, DPO offers a streamlined alternative to traditional RLHF methods.

DPO's core innovation lies in its reformulation of the preference learning problem. Unlike RLHF, which typically involves training a separate reward model and then using reinforcement learning algorithms like PPO to fine-tune the language model, DPO takes a more direct approach.

It derives a closed-form expression for the optimal policy under the standard RLHF objective of maximizing expected reward subject to a KL-divergence constraint with a reference policy. This mathematical insight allows DPO to express the preference learning problem directly in terms of the policy, eliminating the need for a separate reward model or complex reinforcement learning algorithms.

In practical terms, DPO can be implemented as a simple binary cross-entropy loss function that operates directly on the language model's output probabilities. This loss function encourages the model to assign higher probability to preferred responses and lower probability to non-preferred responses, while maintaining closeness to a reference (frozen) model. The importance of the reference model is directly controlled via a beta parameter between 0 and 1. The reference model is ignored when beta is equal to 0, which means that the trained model can be very different from the SFT one. In practice, a value of 0.1 is the most popular one, but this can be tweaked, as we'll see in the next section.

The simplicity of this approach allows optimization using standard gradient descent techniques, without the need for sampling from the model during training or implementing complex RL algorithms. *Figure 6.5* shows a high-level view of the DPO algorithm, greatly simplifying the training process compared to *Figure 6.4*.

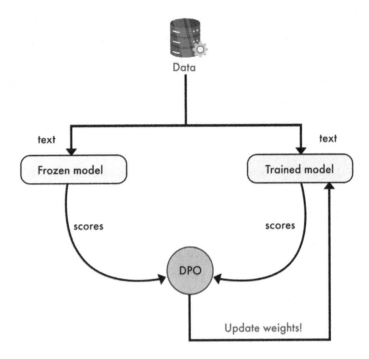

Figure 6.5 – High-level view of the DPO algorithm for preference alignment

DPO has several advantages over traditional RLHF methods. As previously mentioned, it significantly simplifies the preference learning pipeline, reducing the engineering complexity associated with RLHF methods. By eliminating the need for a separate reward model and RL algorithms, DPO is more computationally efficient than traditional RLHF approaches. Particularly when trained with adapters (LoRA, QLoRA), the frozen and trained models don't have to be separated. Indeed, since we're only training adapters, the trained model is not modified. This allows us to only load one model instead of two, which saves additional VRAM.

Despite its simplicity, DPO often matches the performance of more complex RLHF methods. It also tends to be more stable during training and less sensitive to hyperparameters. The simplified approach makes DPO easier to implement and scale, particularly for small teams without extensive RL knowledge.

While RLHF allows iterative improvement through multiple training rounds and can dynamically adapt to new preferences, DPO offers a more straightforward path to achieving similar results. The choice between DPO and PPO-based RLHF often comes down to a trade-off between ease of implementation and potential peak performance. For large-scale training runs with millions of preference samples, PPO-inspired methods still have a higher performance ceiling. However, for most applications, DPO provides the majority of the performance benefits at a lower computational and engineering cost.

Both RLHF and DPO benefit significantly from the integration of synthetic data. As LLMs become more capable, they can generate data that surpasses human-created content in quality and diversity. This enables a virtuous cycle where better models produce better training data, which in turn leads to further model improvements. The iterative nature of both approaches allows multiple rounds of model refinement, each focusing on different aspects of model performance and gradually enhancing capabilities across various domains.

Despite its advantages, DPO is not without drawbacks. Like RLHF, DPO still requires paired preference data, which can be expensive and time-consuming to collect. DPO lacks some of the theoretical guarantees associated with reinforcement learning approaches. There may be scenarios where the added flexibility of RLHF is beneficial, particularly for complex tasks or environments.

Nonetheless, DPO is ideal in most cases, including our twin LLM example. In the next section, we will implement it using Unsloth.

Implementing DPO

In this section, we will DPO fine-tune the **TwinLlama-3.1-8B** model we created in *Chapter 5*. For ease of use and to maximize performance, we will again use the Unsloth library for our DPO implementation. Depending on the available VRAM, you can choose between LoRA (higher quality, speed, and VRAM usage) and QLoRA (lower quality, speed, and VRAM usage). This technique, along with other preference alignment algorithms, is also available in TRL and Axolotl.

This example can be seen as an advanced application of DPO. Indeed, our objective of imitating a writing style conflicts with the natural tendency of DPO to encourage formal language. This is partly due to the fact that chosen answers are often more formal than rejected ones. In practice, this will force us to do light fine-tuning, with a low learning rate and number of epochs. To find the best hyperparameters, we trained over 20 models and compared their outputs on a set of questions, including "Write a paragraph to introduce supervised fine-tuning." This allowed us to select the model and parameters that worked best for this task.

The dependencies are the same as those in *Chapter 5* with SFT and can be found in the book's GitHub repository (`https://github.com/PacktPublishing/LLM-Engineering`) or in Unsloth's repo (`https://github.com/unslothai/unsloth`):

1. First, we want to access a gated model and (optionally) upload our fine-tuned model to Hugging Face (`https://huggingface.co/`). This requires us to log in to an account. If you don't have an account, you can create one and store your API key (**Settings | Access Tokens | Create new token**) in the `.env` file:

```
HF_TOKEN = YOUR_API_KEY
```

2. Make sure that your Comet ML API key is also in the `.env` file. Otherwise, the code will crash and raise an error when training starts.

```
COMET_API_KEY = YOUR_API_KEY
```

3. Before we import all the necessary packages, we want to apply a patch for the `DPOTrainer` class from TRL. This fixes the DPO logs in notebook environments.

```
from unsloth import PatchDPOTrainer
PatchDPOTrainer()
```

4. We can now import the other libraries. The main difference between DPO and SFT is the import of `DPOConfig` and `DPOTrainer` from TRL, which are specific to DPO training.

```
import os
import torch
from datasets import load_dataset
from transformers import TrainingArguments, TextStreamer
from unsloth import FastLanguageModel, is_bfloat16_supportedfrom trl
import DPOConfig, DPOTrainer
```

5. This step loads our fine-tuned model from *Chapter 5*. We use the same configuration with a `max_seq_length` of 2048. You can activate QLoRA by setting `load_in_4bit` to True. In the following, we will perform LoRA DPO fine-tuning for increased speed and quality.

```
max_seq_length = 2048
model, tokenizer = FastLanguageModel.from_pretrained(
    model_name="mlabonne/TwinLlama-3.1-8B",
    max_seq_length=max_seq_length,
    load_in_4bit=False,
)
```

6. Let's now prepare the model for PEFT with the LoRA configuration. We increase the rank
    (r) and `lora_alpha` from 32 (as it was in *Chapter 5*) to 64. This will allow more expressive
    fine-tuning. We keep a dropout of 0 for speed and we target every linear module as per
    usual.

```python
model = FastLanguageModel.get_peft_model(
    model,
    r=32,
    lora_alpha=32,
    lora_dropout=0,
    target_modules=["q_proj", "k_proj", "v_proj", "up_proj", "down_
proj", "o_proj", "gate_proj"],
)
```

7. We load the `llmtwin-dpo` dataset (training split), which contains our prompts, chosen,
    and rejected answers.

```python
dataset = load_dataset("mlabonne/llmtwin-dpo", split="train")
```

8. The data preparation is significantly different from the SFT example in *Chapter 5*. Here, we
    have triples with a prompt, a chosen answer, and a rejected answer. In the `format_samples`
    function, we apply the Alpaca chat template to each individual message. Note that the
    instruction is the only one that requires the chat format: chosen and rejected answers
    only need to be concatenated with the **end of sentence (EOS)** token. Finally, we create a
    train/test split with a 95%/5% ratio.

```python
alpaca_template = """Below is an instruction that describes a task.
Write a response that appropriately completes the request.

### Instruction:
{}

### Response:
"""

EOS_TOKEN = tokenizer.eos_token

def format_samples(example):
    example["prompt"] = alpaca_template.format(example["prompt"])
    example["chosen"] = example['chosen'] + EOS_TOKEN
```

```
        example["rejected"] = example['rejected'] + EOS_TOKEN
        return {"prompt": example["prompt"], "chosen":
    example["chosen"], "rejected": example["rejected"]}


    dataset = dataset.map(format_samples)


    dataset = dataset.train_test_split(test_size=0.05)
```

9. The model and data are now ready, so we can start fine-tuning. Compared to SFT, there are a few new parameters, like ref_model and beta. Since we're using LoRA (or QLoRA), we don't directly train the model but instead the adapters. This means we can use the original model (without adapters) as a reference, saving a lot of VRAM. The beta parameter controls the importance of the reference model. A standard value of 0.1 works well in most scenarios, but we decided to increase it to 0.5 based on our experiments. This is due to the fact that the trained model used formal language with lower values. Having it closer to the reference model helps to fix this issue.

   The learning rate is also lower (from 3e-4 for SFT to 2e-6 here). We train for 1 epoch instead of 3, and the max_seq_length parameter is now broken down into two new parameters: max_prompt_length (prompt only) and max_length (prompt and answer). Note that we also replaced the TrainingArguments class with DPOConfig.

```
    trainer = DPOTrainer(
        model=model,
        ref_model=None,
        tokenizer=tokenizer,
        beta=0.5,
        train_dataset=dataset["train"],
        eval_dataset=dataset["test"],
        max_length=max_seq_length//2,
        max_prompt_length=max_seq_length//2,
        args=DPOConfig(
            learning_rate=2e-6,
            lr_scheduler_type="linear",
            per_device_train_batch_size=2,
            per_device_eval_batch_size=2,
            gradient_accumulation_steps=8,
            num_train_epochs=1,
```

```
            fp16=not is_bfloat16_supported(),
            bf16=is_bfloat16_supported(),
            optim="adamw_8bit",
            weight_decay=0.01,
            warmup_steps=10,
            output_dir="output",
            eval_strategy="steps",
            eval_steps=0.2,
            logging_steps=1,
            report_to="comet_ml",
            seed=0,
        ),
    )
    trainer.train()
```

10. Once the model is trained, we can run it for a quick sanity check. This step is similar to the SFT example. It prepares the model for inference and generates a response to a prompt.

```
FastLanguageModel.for_inference(model)
message = alpaca_template.format("Write a paragraph to introduce
supervised fine-tuning.", "")
inputs = tokenizer([message], return_tensors="pt").to("cuda")

text_streamer = TextStreamer(tokenizer)
_ = model.generate(**inputs, streamer=text_streamer, max_new_
tokens=256, use_cache=True)
```

11. The trained DPO model returns the following response:

```
Supervised fine-tuning is a method used to enhance the performance
of pre-trained language models by utilizing labeled data. This
technique involves taking a pre-trained model and refining it on
a specific task, such as content creation or customer service. By
providing the model with relevant data and guidance, it can learn to
generate outputs that align more closely with the desired outcomes.
This approach allows for the creation of more specialized models
that can tackle complex tasks with greater accuracy and efficiency.
```

We can compare it with the answer provided by the SFT model:

```
Supervised fine-tuning is a method used to enhance a language model
by providing it with a curated dataset of instructions and their
corresponding answers. This process is designed to align the model's
responses with human expectations, thereby improving its accuracy
and relevance. The goal is to ensure that the model can respond
effectively to a wide range of queries, making it a valuable tool
for applications such as chatbots and virtual assistants.
```

The DPO model provides an answer that is both more accurate and closer to the desired writing style. It correctly identifies pre-training language models as source models for SFT. It also mentions domain or task-specific finetunes instead of alignment with "human expectations," which is closer to the preference alignment stage. The answer is also less formal and something we would use in a blog post.

12. Finally, the last step consists of saving the trained model locally and pushing it to the Hugging Face Hub.

```
model.save_pretrained_merged("model", tokenizer, save_
method="merged_16bit")
```

Congratulations! We have trained and exported our DPO model. It is now available on the Hugging Face Hub at https://huggingface.co/mlabonne/TwinLlama-3.1-8B-DPO. Compared to SFT, DPO has a few additional metrics that need to be tracked during training. *Figure 6.6* shows the Comet ML dashboard with the main metrics. You can publicly access it using the following URL: https://www.comet.com/mlabonne/llm-twin-training/

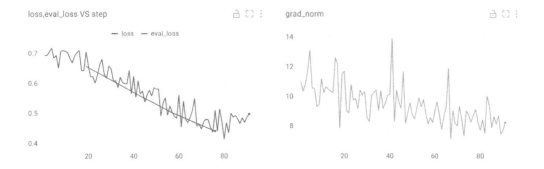

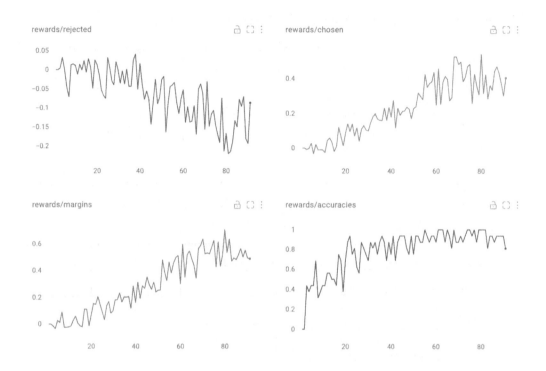

Figure 6.6 – Experiment tracking in Comet ML with DPO metrics

Let's review these metrics:

- **Training loss**: We still want the loss to continuously decrease on average. Note that it can rapidly fall to zero, meaning that the model is no longer learning anything. This behavior doesn't necessarily lead to overfitting or bad models but needs to be monitored closely.

- **Validation loss**: The same thing can be said about the validation loss. We expect a small gap compared to the training loss.

- **Gradient norm**: We expect small gradient norms with few spikes.

- **Rewards**: We have two different rewards: chosen and rejected. They correspond to the mean difference between the log probabilities output by the trained and reference models. Over time, we expect the model to choose the chosen answers and reject the rejected answers, which means that the gap between them should increase. This difference is directly tracked by the margins metric, defined as the difference between chosen and rejected rewards. A well-trained model's margin will quickly increase and then plateau.

- **Accuracies**: This metric represents the percentage of times the model correctly identifies the chosen answers. We want this accuracy to gradually increase during training, but it doesn't need to reach 100%. An accuracy of 100%, especially if it's achieved quickly, indicates that the preference dataset might be too easy for the model. While the LLM can still learn from such a dataset, it might be beneficial to add more challenging examples.

In general, DPO is slightly harder to monitor and debug than SFT because it's a more complex process, involving a reference model. However, it's also significantly easier to use than PPO and other RLHF algorithms. As long as you have a high-quality preference dataset and a strong fine-tuned model, you can experiment with different ranks, beta parameters, learning rates, and number of epochs to see which experiment best captures your preferences.

While this is not the purpose of this chapter, it is possible to automate the evaluation of models designed to imitate a writing style. A possible solution consists of comparing the distribution of words in the text generated by different models (SFT and DPO) with our ground-truth dataset. In this example, we expect the SFT model to output a lot of words that are overrepresented in GPT-4o-mini (like "delve into"). The distribution output by our DPO model should be a lot closer to the chosen answers.

Summary

This chapter explored preference alignment techniques for improving LLMs. It introduced the concept of preference datasets, explaining their structure and importance in capturing nuanced human preferences. We implemented our own custom preference data generation pipeline by comparing original and AI-generated text from real articles. This pipeline can be reused and customized based on your use case.

We also provided an overview of the evolution of RLHF, leading to the introduction of DPO as a simpler and more efficient alternative. Finally, we implemented DPO using the Unsloth library to fine-tune our TwinLlama-3.1-8B model from *Chapter 5*. Our step-by-step tutorial gave practical instructions for training the model, as well as highlighting key differences from SFT. The final model is available on the Hugging Face Hub.

In the next chapter, we will explore the crucial topic of LLM evaluation, addressing the challenges and current approaches in assessing LLM performance. We'll cover the creation of domain-specific evaluation sets, examine why evaluation remains a persistent problem in the field, and introduce the concept of using larger models to evaluate smaller ones (LLM-as-a-judge). The chapter will conclude with a comprehensive evaluation pipeline, providing a structured framework for consistent and effective LLM evaluation.

References

- Rafael Rafailov et al.. *"Direct Preference Optimization: Your Language Model is Secretly a Reward Model."* arXiv preprint arXiv:2305.18290, May 2023.

- Timo Kaufmann et al.. *"A Survey of Reinforcement Learning from Human Feedback."* arXiv preprint arXiv:2312.14925, December 2023.

- Anthropic. *"GitHub - anthropics/hh-rlhf: Human preference data for "Training a Helpful and Harmless Assistant with Reinforcement Learning from Human Feedback"."* github.com, 2022, `https://github.com/anthropics/hh-rlhf`.

- Nisan Stiennon et al.. *"Learning to summarize from human feedback."* arXiv preprint arXiv:2009.01325, September 2020.

- Intel(R) Neural Compressor. "Supervised Fine-Tuning and Direct Preference Optimization on Intel Gaudi2." medium.com, March 26, 2024, `https://medium.com/intel-analytics-software/the-practice-of-supervised-finetuning-and-direct-preference-optimization-on-habana-gaudi2-a1197d8a3cd3`.

- Argilla. *"GitHub - argilla-io/distilabel."* github.com, August 23, 2024, `https://github.com/argilla-io/distilabel`.

- Databricks. *"Enhancing LLM-as-a-Judge with Grading Notes."* databricks.com, July 22, 2024, `https://www.databricks.com/blog/enhancing-llm-as-a-judge-with-grading-notes`.

- Akrour, Riad & Schoenauer, Marc & Sebag, Michèle. (2011). Preference-Based Policy Learning. 12-27. 10.1007/978-3-642-23780-5_11.

- Cheng, Weiwei & Fürnkranz, Johannes & Hüllermeier, Eyke & Park, Sang-Hyeun. (2011). *Preference-Based Policy Iteration: Leveraging Preference Learning for Reinforcement Learning.* 312-327. 10.1007/978-3-642-23780-5_30.

- Paul Christiano et al.. *"Deep reinforcement learning from human preferences."* arXiv preprint arXiv:1706.03741, June 2017.

- Long Ouyang et al.. *"Training language models to follow instructions with human feedback."* arXiv preprint arXiv:2203.02155, March 2022.

- John Schulman et al.. *"Proximal Policy Optimization Algorithms."* arXiv preprint arXiv:1707.06347, July 2017.

- unslothai. *"GitHub - unslothai/unsloth: Finetune Llama 3.1, Mistral,* Phi & Gemma LLMs 2-5x faster with 80% less memory." github.com, August 21, 2024, `https://github.com/unslothai/unsloth`.

Join our book's Discord space

Join our community's Discord space for discussions with the authors and other readers:

https://packt.link/llmeng

7

Evaluating LLMs

LLM evaluation is a crucial process used to assess the performance and capabilities of LLM models. It can take multiple forms, such as multiple-choice question answering, open-ended instructions, and feedback from real users. Currently, there is no unified approach to measuring a model's performance but there are patterns and recipes that we can adapt to specific use cases.

While general-purpose evaluations are the most popular ones, with benchmarks like **Massive Multi-Task Language Understanding (MMLU)** or LMSYS Chatbot Arena, domain- and task-specific models benefit from more narrow approaches. This is particularly true when dealing with entire LLM systems (as opposed to models), often centered around a **retrieval-augmented generation (RAG)** pipeline. In these scenarios, we need to expand our evaluation framework to encompass the entire system, including new modules like retrievers and post-processors.

In this chapter, we will cover the following topics:

- Model evaluation
- RAG evaluation
- Evaluating TwinLlama-3.1-8B

By the end of this chapter, you will know the most popular LLM evaluations and how to evaluate models and RAG systems using different techniques.

Model evaluation

In model evaluation, the objective is to assess the capabilities of a single model without any prompt engineering, RAG pipeline, and so on.

This evaluation is essential for several reasons, such as selecting the most relevant LLM or making sure that the fine-tuning process actually improved the model. In this section, we will compare ML and LLM evaluation to understand the main differences between these two fields. We will then explore benchmarks for general-purpose, domain-specific, and task-specific models.

Comparing ML and LLM evaluation

ML evaluation is centered on assessing the performance of models designed for tasks like prediction, classification, and regression. Unlike the evaluation of LLMs, which often focuses on how well a model understands and generates language, ML evaluation is more concerned with how accurately and efficiently a model can process structured data to produce specific outcomes.

This difference comes from the nature of the tasks these models handle. ML models are generally designed for narrowly defined problems, such as predicting stock prices or detecting outliers, which often involve numerical or categorical data, making the evaluation process more straightforward. On the other hand, LLMs are tasked with interpreting and generating language, which adds a layer of subjectivity to the evaluation process. Instead of relying solely on numerical benchmarks, LLM evaluation requires a more nuanced approach and often incorporates qualitative assessments, examining how well the model produces coherent, relevant, and contextually accurate responses in natural language.

In particular, we can see three key differences in how these models work, which impact the evaluation process:

- **Numerical metrics**: Evaluating ML models typically involves measuring objective performance metrics, such as accuracy, precision, recall, or mean squared error, depending on the type of task at hand. This is less clear with LLMs, which can handle multiple tasks (hence, multiple evaluations) and can rarely rely on the same numerical metrics.

- **Feature engineering**: In traditional ML, a critical part of the process involves manually selecting and transforming relevant data features before training the model. Evaluating the success of this feature engineering often becomes part of the broader model evaluation. LLMs, however, are designed to handle raw text data directly, reducing the need for manual feature engineering.

- **Interpretability**: With ML models, it is easier to interpret why a model made certain predictions or classifications, and this interpretability can be a core part of their evaluation. This direct interpretation is not possible with LLMs. However, requesting explanations during the generation process can give insights into the model's decision-making process.

In the following section, we will see a more fine-grained exploration of different types of LLMs. While evaluating general-purpose models is fairly disconnected from ML evaluation, task-specific LLMs are more closely aligned with traditional ML.

General-purpose LLM evaluations

General-purpose evaluations refer to metrics dedicated to base and general-purpose fine-tuned models. They cover a breadth of capabilities that are correlated with knowledge and usefulness without focusing on specific tasks or domains. This allows developers to get an overview of these capabilities, compare themselves with competitors, and identify strengths and weaknesses. Based on these results, it is possible to tweak the dataset and hyperparameters, or even modify the architecture.

We can broadly categorize general-purpose evaluations in three phases: during pre-training, after pre-training, and after fine-tuning.

During pre-training, we closely monitor how the model learns, as shown at the end of *Chapter 5*. The most straightforward metrics are low-level and correspond to how models are trained:

- **Training loss**: Based on the cross-entropy loss, measures the difference between the model's predicted probability distribution and the true distribution of the next token
- **Validation loss**: Calculates the same loss as training loss, but on a held-out validation set to assess generalization
- **Perplexity**: Exponential of the cross-entropy loss, representing how "surprised" the model is by the data (lower is better)
- **Gradient norm**: Monitors the magnitude of gradients during training to detect potential instabilities or vanishing/exploding gradients

It's also possible to include benchmarks like HellaSwag (common sense reasoning) during this stage but there's a risk of overfitting these evaluations.

After pre-training, it is common to use a suite of evaluations to evaluate the base model. This suite can include internal and public benchmarks. Here's a non-exhaustive list of common public pre-training evaluations:

- **MMLU (knowledge)**: Tests models on multiple-choice questions across 57 subjects, from elementary to professional levels
- **HellaSwag (reasoning)**: Challenges models to complete a given situation with the most plausible ending from multiple choices

- **ARC-C (reasoning)**: Evaluates models on grade-school-level multiple-choice science questions requiring causal reasoning
- **Winogrande (reasoning)**: Assesses common sense reasoning through pronoun resolution in carefully crafted sentences
- **PIQA (reasoning)**: Measures physical common sense understanding through questions about everyday physical interactions

Many of these datasets are also used to evaluate general-purpose fine-tuned models. In this case, we focus on the difference in a given score between the base and the fine-tuned model. For example, bad fine-tuning can degrade the knowledge of the model, measured by MMLU. On the contrary, a good one might instill even more knowledge and increase the MMLU score.

This can also help identify any contamination issues, where the model might have been fine-tuned on data that is too close to a test set. For instance, improving the MMLU score of a base model by 10 points during the fine-tuning phase is unlikely. This is a sign that the instruction data might be contaminated.

In addition to these pre-trained evaluations, fine-tuned models also have their own benchmarks. Here, we use the term "fine-tuned model" to designate a model that has been trained with **supervised fine-tuning (SFT)** and preference alignment. These benchmarks target capabilities connected to the ability of fine-tuned models to understand and answer questions. In particular, they test instruction-following, multi-turn conversation, and agentic skills:

- **IFEval (instruction following)**: Assesses a model's ability to follow instructions with particular constraints, like not outputting any commas in your answer
- **Chatbot Arena (conversation)**: A framework where humans vote for the best answer to an instruction, comparing two models in head-to-head conversations
- **AlpacaEval (instruction following)**: Automatic evaluation for fine-tuned models that is highly correlated with Chatbot Arena
- **MT-Bench (conversation)**: Evaluates models on multi-turn conversations, testing their ability to maintain context and provide coherent responses
- **GAIA (agentic)**: Tests a wide range of abilities like tool use and web browsing, in a multi-step fashion

Understanding how these evaluations are designed and used is important to choose the best LLM for your application. For example, if you want to fine-tune a model, you want the best base model in terms of knowledge and reasoning for a given size. This allows you to compare the capabilities of different LLMs and pick the one that will offer the strongest foundation for your fine-tuning.

Even if you don't want to fine-tune a model, benchmarks like Chatbot Arena or IFEval are a good way to compare different instruct models. For instance, you want great conversational abilities if you're building a chatbot. However, this is not necessary if your end goal is something like information extraction from unstructured documents. In this case, you will benefit more from excellent instruction-following skills to understand and execute tasks.

While these benchmarks are popular and useful, they also suffer from inherent flaws. For example, public benchmarks can be gamed by training models on test data or samples that are very similar to benchmark datasets. Even human evaluation is not perfect and is often biased toward long and confident answers, especially when they're nicely formatted (e.g., using Markdown). On the other hand, private test sets have not been scrutinized as much as public ones and might have their own issues and biases.

This means that benchmarks are not a single source of truth but should be used as signals. Once multiple evaluations provide a similar answer, you can raise your confidence level about the real capabilities of a model.

Domain-specific LLM evaluations

Domain-specific LLMs don't have the same scope as general-purpose models. This is helpful to target more fine-grained capabilities with more depth than the previous benchmarks.

Within the category, the choice of benchmarks entirely depends on the domain in question. For common applications like a language-specific model or a code model, it is recommended to search for relevant evaluations and even benchmark suites. These suites encompass different benchmarks and are designed to be reproducible. By targeting different aspects of a domain, they often capture domain performance more accurately.

To illustrate this, here is a list of domain-specific evaluations with leaderboards on the Hugging Face Hub:

- **Open Medical-LLM Leaderboard**: Evaluates the performance of LLMs in medical question-answering tasks. It regroups 9 metrics, with 1,273 questions from the US medical license exams (MedQA), 500 questions from PubMed articles (PubMedQA), 4,183 questions from Indian medical entrance exams (MedMCQA), and 1,089 questions from 6 sub-categories of MMLU (clinical knowledge, medical genetics, anatomy, professional medicine, college biology, and college medicine).

- **BigCodeBench Leaderboard**: Evaluates the performance of code LLMs, featuring two main categories: BigCodeBench-Complete for code completion based on structured docstrings, and BigCodeBench-Instruct for code generation from natural language instructions. Models are ranked by their Pass@1 scores using greedy decoding, with an additional Elo rating for the Complete variant. It covers a wide range of programming scenarios that test LLMs' compositional reasoning and instruction-following capabilities.

- **Hallucinations Leaderboard**: Evaluates LLMs' tendency to produce false or unsupported information across 16 diverse tasks spanning 5 categories. These include *Question Answering* (with datasets like NQ Open, TruthfulQA, and SQuADv2), *Reading Comprehension* (using TriviaQA and RACE), *Summarization* (employing HaluEval Summ, XSum, and CNN/DM), *Dialogue* (featuring HaluEval Dial and FaithDial), and *Fact Checking* (utilizing MemoTrap, SelfCheckGPT, FEVER, and TrueFalse). The leaderboard also assesses instruction-following ability using IFEval.

- **Enterprise Scenarios Leaderboard**: Evaluates the performance of LLMs on six real-world enterprise use cases, covering diverse tasks relevant to business applications. The benchmarks include FinanceBench (100 financial questions with retrieved context), Legal Confidentiality (100 prompts from LegalBench for legal reasoning), Writing Prompts (creative writing evaluation), Customer Support Dialogue (relevance in customer service interactions), Toxic Prompts (safety assessment for harmful content generation), and Enterprise PII (business safety for sensitive information protection). Some test sets are closed-source to prevent gaming of the leaderboard. The evaluation focuses on specific capabilities such as answer accuracy, legal reasoning, creative writing, contextual relevance, and safety measures, providing a comprehensive assessment of LLMs' suitability for enterprise environments.

Leaderboards can have different approaches based on their domain. For example, BigCodeBench is significantly different from others because it relies on only two metrics that sufficiently capture the entire domain. On the other hand, the Hallucinations Leaderboard regroups 16 metrics, including many general-purpose evaluations. It shows that in addition to custom benchmarks, reusing general-purpose ones can complete your own suite.

In particular, language-specific LLMs often reuse translated versions of general-purpose benchmarks. This can be completed with original evaluations in the native language. While some of these benchmarks use machine translation, it is better to rely on human-translated evaluations to improve their quality. We selected the following three task-specific leaderboards and their respective evaluation suites to give you an idea of how to build your own:

- **OpenKo-LLM Leaderboard**: Evaluates the performance of Korean LLMs using nine metrics. These metrics are a combination of general-purpose benchmarks translated into Korean (GPQA, Winogrande, GSM8K, EQ-Bench, and IFEval) and custom evaluations (Knowledge, Social Value, Harmlessness, and Helpfulness).

- **Open Portuguese LLM Leaderboard**: Evaluates the performance of Portuguese language LLMs using nine diverse benchmarks. These benchmarks include educational assessments (ENEM with 1,430 questions, and BLUEX with 724 questions from university entrance exams), professional exams (OAB Exams with over 2,000 questions), language understanding tasks (ASSIN2 RTE and STS, FAQUAD NLI), and social media content analysis (HateBR with 7,000 Instagram comments, PT Hate Speech with 5,668 tweets, and tweetSentBR).

- **Open Arabic LLM Leaderboard**: Evaluates the performance of Arabic language LLMs using a comprehensive set of benchmarks, including both native Arabic tasks and translated datasets. The leaderboard features two native Arabic benchmarks: AlGhafa and Arabic-Culture-Value-Alignment. Additionally, it incorporates 12 translated benchmarks covering various domains, such as MMLU, ARC-Challenge, HellaSwag, and PIQA.

Both general-purpose and domain-specific evaluations are designed with three main principles. First, they should be complex and challenge models to distinguish good and bad outputs. Second, they should be diverse and cover as many topics and scenarios as possible. When one benchmark is not enough, additional ones can create a stronger suite. Finally, they should be practical and easy to run. This is more connected to evaluation libraries, which can be more or less complex to work with. We recommend lm-evaluation-harness (github.com/EleutherAI/lm-evaluation-harness) from Eleuther AI and lighteval (github.com/huggingface/lighteval) from Hugging Face to run your benchmarks.

Task-specific LLM evaluations

While general-purpose and domain-specific evaluations indicate strong base or instruct models, they cannot provide insights into how well these models work for a given task. This requires benchmarks specifically designed for this purpose, measuring downstream performance.

Because of their narrow focus, task-specific LLMs can rarely rely on pre-existing evaluation datasets. This can be advantageous because their outputs also tend to be more structured and easier to evaluate using traditional ML metrics. For example, a summarization task can leverage the **Recall-Oriented Understudy for Gisting Evaluation** (**ROUGE**) metric, which measures the overlap between the generated text and reference text using n-grams.

Likewise, classification tasks also benefit from it and use the following classic metrics, among others:

- **Accuracy**: Accuracy refers to the proportion of correctly predicted instances compared to the total instances. It's particularly useful for tasks with categorical outputs or where there is a clear distinction between right and wrong answers, such as **named entity recognition (NER)**.

- **Precision**: The ratio of true positive predictions to the total positive predictions made by the model.

- **Recall**: The ratio of true positive predictions to the total actual positive instances.

- **F1 Score**: The harmonic mean of precision and recall, used to balance both metrics. These are particularly useful in tasks such as classification or entity extraction.

When the task cannot be directly mapped to a traditional ML task, it is possible to create a custom benchmark. This benchmark can be inspired by general-purpose and domain-specific evaluation datasets. A common and successful pattern is the use of multiple-choice question answering. In this framework, the instruction consists of a question with several options. See the following example with a question from the MMLU dataset (abstract algebra):

Instruction

Find the degree for the given field extension Q(sqrt(2), sqrt(3)) over Q.

A. 0

B. 4

C. 2

D. 6

Output

B

Table 7.1: Example from the MMLU dataset

There are two main ways of evaluating models with this scheme—text generation and log-likelihood evaluations:

- The first approach involves having the model generate text responses and comparing those to predefined answer choices. For example, the model generates a letter (A, B, C, or D) as its answer, which is then checked against the correct answer. This method tests the model's ability to produce coherent and accurate responses in a format similar to how it would be used in real-world applications.

- Evaluation using probabilities, on the other hand, looks at the model's predicted probabilities for different answer options without requiring text generation. For MMLU, lm-evaluation-harness compares the probabilities for the full text of each answer choice. This approach allows for a more nuanced assessment of the model's understanding, as it can capture the relative confidence the model has in different options, even if it wouldn't necessarily generate the exact correct answer text.

For simplicity, we recommend the text-generation version of the evaluation that mimics human test-taking. It is easier to implement, and generally more discriminative, as low-quality models tend to overperform on probability-based evaluations. You can adapt this technique to quiz your models about a particular task, and even expand it to specific domains.

Conversely, if the task is too open-ended, traditional ML metrics and multiple-choice question answering might not be relevant. In this scenario, the LLM-as-a-judge technique introduced in *Chapter 5* can be used to evaluate the quality of the answers. If you have ground-truth answers, providing them as additional context improves the accuracy of the evaluation. Otherwise, defining different dimensions (such as relevance or toxicity, depending on your task) can also ground the evaluation in more interpretable categories.

It is recommended to use large models for evaluation and to iteratively refine your prompt. In this process, the explanations outputted by the model are important for understanding errors in its reasoning and fixing them through additional prompt engineering.

In order to easily parse answers, one can specify a structure in the instruction or use some kind of structured generation (like Outlines or OpenAI's JSON mode). Here is an example of an instruction with a structure:

```
You are an evaluator who assesses the quality of an answer to an
instruction.

Your goal is to provide a score that represents how well the answer
addresses the instruction.

You will use a scale of 1 to 4, where each number represents the following:

1. The answer is not relevant to the instruction.

2. The answer is relevant but not helpful.

3. The answer is relevant and helpful but could be more detailed.

4. The answer is relevant, helpful, and detailed.

Please provide your evaluation as follows:

##Evaluation##

Explanation: (analyze the relevant, helpfulness, and complexity of the
answer)

Total rating: (final score as a number between 1 and 4)
```

Instruction:

{instruction}

Answer:

{answer}

##Evaluation##

Explanation:

Table 7.2: Example of general-purpose LLM-as-a-judge prompt for answer evaluation

Naturally, you can tweak the scale, add a ground-truth answer to this prompt, and customize it for your own use cases.

However, judge LLMs can exhibit biases favoring assertive or verbose responses, potentially overrating answers that sound more confident but are less accurate. They may also lack domain expertise for specialized topics, leading to misjudgments. Consistency is also a concern, as LLMs might score similar responses differently. Additionally, they could have implicit preferences for certain writing styles unrelated to actual answer quality. To mitigate these issues, it's possible to combine LLM evaluations with other metrics, use multiple judges, and carefully design prompts to address biases.

Once a model has been properly evaluated and works as intended, it might be included within a broader system. In the next section, we will see how systems change the evaluation framework.

RAG evaluation

While traditional LLM evaluation focuses on the model's inherent capabilities, RAG evaluation requires a more comprehensive approach that considers both the model's generative abilities and its interaction with external information sources.

RAG systems combine the strengths of LLMs with information retrieval mechanisms, allowing them to generate responses that are not only coherent and contextually appropriate but also grounded in up-to-date, externally sourced information. This makes RAG particularly valuable in fields where current and accurate information is crucial, such as news reporting, research, and customer support.

The evaluation of RAG systems goes beyond assessing a standalone LLM. It requires examining the entire system's performance, including:

- **Retrieval accuracy**: How well does the system fetch relevant information?
- **Integration quality**: How effectively is the retrieved information incorporated into the generated response?
- **Factuality and relevance**: Does the final output address the query appropriately while seamlessly blending retrieved and generated content?

Key metrics for RAG evaluation include retrieval precision and recall, which measure the accuracy and comprehensiveness of the retrieved information. Additionally, the quality of integration between retrieved data and generated text is crucial, as is the overall factuality and coherence of the output.

To illustrate how these metrics are applied in practice, consider a RAG system designed for a customer support chatbot in an e-commerce setting. In this scenario, the user asks "What's your return policy for laptops purchased during the holiday sale?" The RAG pipeline finds relevant documents on the electronics return policy and documents on holiday sale terms. This additional context is appended at the end of the question, and the model uses it to respond:

```
For laptops purchased during our holiday sale, you have an extended return
period of 60 days from the date of purchase. This is longer than our
standard 30-day return policy for electronics. Please ensure the laptop is
in its original packaging with all accessories to be eligible for a full
refund.
```

Table 7.3: Example of output from a RAG pipeline designed for customer support

In this pipeline, we can evaluate if the retrieved documents correspond to what was expected (retrieval accuracy). We can also measure the difference between responses with and without additional context (integration quality). Finally, we can assess whether the output is relevant and grounded in the information provided by the documents (factuality and relevance).

In this section, we will cover two methods to evaluate how well RAG models incorporate external information into their responses.

Ragas

Retrieval-Augmented Generation Assessment (Ragas) is an open-source toolkit designed to provide developers with a comprehensive set of tools for RAG evaluation and optimization. It's designed around the idea of **metrics-driven development (MDD)**, a product development approach that relies on data to make well-informed decisions, involving the ongoing monitoring of essential metrics over time to gain valuable insights into an application's performance. By embracing this methodology, Ragas enables developers to objectively assess their RAG systems, identify areas for improvement, and track the impact of changes over time.

One of the key capabilities of Ragas is its ability to synthetically generate diverse and complex test datasets. This feature addresses a significant pain point in RAG development, as manually creating hundreds of questions, answers, and contexts is both time-consuming and labor-intensive. Instead, it uses an evolutionary approach paradigm inspired by works like Evol-Instruct to craft questions with varying characteristics such as reasoning complexity, conditional elements, and multi-context requirements. This approach ensures a comprehensive evaluation of different components within the RAG pipeline.

Additionally, Ragas can generate conversational samples that simulate chat-based question-and-follow-up interactions, allowing developers to evaluate their systems in more realistic scenarios.

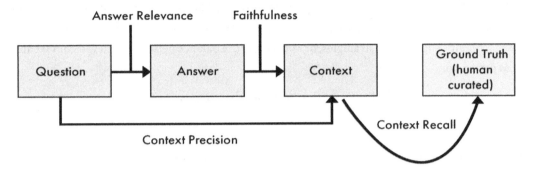

Figure 7.1: Overview of the Ragas evaluation framework

As illustrated in *Figure 7.1*, Ragas provides a suite of LLM-assisted evaluation metrics designed to objectively measure different aspects of RAG system performance. These metrics include:

- **Faithfulness:** This metric measures the factual consistency of the generated answer against the given context. It works by breaking down the answer into individual claims and verifying if each claim can be inferred from the provided context. The faithfulness score is calculated as the ratio of verifiable claims to the total number of claims in the answer.

- **Answer relevancy:** This metric evaluates how pertinent the generated answer is to the given prompt. It uses an innovative approach where an LLM is prompted to generate multiple questions based on the answer and then calculates the mean cosine similarity between these generated questions and the original question. This method helps identify answers that may be factually correct but off-topic or incomplete.

- **Context precision:** This metric evaluates whether all the ground-truth relevant items present in the contexts are ranked appropriately. It considers the position of relevant information within the retrieved context, rewarding systems that place the most pertinent information at the top.

- **Context recall:** This metric measures the extent to which the retrieved context aligns with the annotated answer (ground truth). It analyzes each claim in the ground truth answer to determine whether it can be attributed to the retrieved context, providing insights into the completeness of the retrieved information.

Finally, Ragas also provides building blocks for monitoring RAG quality in production environments. This facilitates continuous improvement of RAG systems. By leveraging the evaluation results from test datasets and insights gathered from production monitoring, developers can iteratively enhance their applications. This might involve fine-tuning retrieval algorithms, adjusting prompt engineering strategies, or optimizing the balance between retrieved context and LLM generation.

Ragas can be complemented with another approach, based on custom classifiers.

ARES

ARES (an automated evaluation framework for RAG systems) is a comprehensive tool designed to evaluate RAG systems. It offers an automated process that combines synthetic data generation with fine-tuned classifiers to assess various aspects of RAG performance, including context relevance, answer faithfulness, and answer relevance.

The ARES framework operates in three main stages: synthetic data generation, classifier training, and RAG evaluation. Each stage is configurable, allowing users to tailor the evaluation process to their specific needs and datasets.

In the synthetic data generation stage, ARES creates datasets that closely mimic real-world scenarios for robust RAG testing. Users can configure this process by specifying document file paths, few-shot prompt files, and output locations for the synthetic queries. The framework supports various pre-trained language models for this task, with the default being google/flan-t5-xxl. Users can control the number of documents sampled and other parameters to balance between comprehensive coverage and computational efficiency.

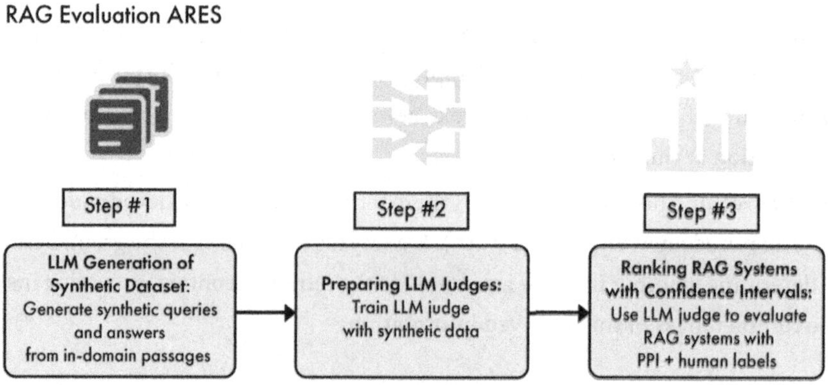

RAG Evaluation ARES

Step #1	Step #2	Step #3
LLM Generation of Synthetic Dataset: Generate synthetic queries and answers from in-domain passages	**Preparing LLM Judges:** Train LLM judge with synthetic data	**Ranking RAG Systems with Confidence Intervals:** Use LLM judge to evaluate RAG systems with PPI + human labels

Figure 7.2: Overview of the ARES evaluation framework

The classifier training stage involves creating high-precision classifiers to determine the relevance and faithfulness of RAG outputs. Users can specify the classification dataset (typically generated from the previous stage), test set for evaluation, label columns, and model choice. ARES uses microsoft/deberta-v3-large as the default model but supports other Hugging Face models. Training parameters such as the number of epochs, patience value for early stopping, and learning rate can be fine-tuned to optimize classifier performance.

The final stage, RAG evaluation, leverages the trained classifiers and synthetic data to assess the RAG model's performance. Users provide evaluation datasets, few-shot examples for guiding the evaluation, classifier checkpoints, and gold label paths. ARES supports various evaluation metrics and can generate confidence intervals for its assessments.

ARES offers flexible model execution options, supporting both cloud-based and local runs through vLLM integration. The framework also supports various artifact types (code snippets, documents, HTML, images, and so on), enabling comprehensive evaluation across different RAG system outputs.

In summary, Ragas and ARES complement each other through their distinct approaches to evaluation and dataset generation. Ragas's strength in production monitoring and LLM-assisted metrics can be combined with ARES's highly configurable evaluation process and classifier-based assessments. While Ragas may offer more nuanced evaluations based on LLM capabilities, ARES provides consistent and potentially faster evaluations once its classifiers are trained. Combining them offers a comprehensive evaluation framework, benefiting from quick iterations with Ragas and in-depth, customized evaluations with ARES at key stages.

In the next section, we will create our own evaluation framework to evaluate our task-specific TwinLlama-3.1-8B model.

Evaluating TwinLlama-3.1-8B

In the previous chapters, we created two models fine-tuned to generate high-quality posts and articles: TwinLlama-3.1-8B and TwinLlama-3.1-8B-DPO. Based on this summary, we want to assess their abilities to write text that is both accurate and well-written. In comparison, general-purpose fine-tuned models are accurate thanks to their extensive knowledge but often use overly formal and verbose language. With this fine-tuning, we want to adopt a more natural writing style, based on the original articles from the training set.

Due to the open-ended nature of this problem, we will leverage a judge LLM to evaluate the quality of the generated text. It will take both the instruction and the answer as inputs, and score it on a 1–3 scale based on two criteria:

- **Accuracy**: The degree of factual correctness and comprehensiveness of the information presented in the answer
- **Style**: The appropriateness of the tone and writing style for blog posts or social media content (no formal or academic expressions)

In our evaluation framework, we will use the test split of our instruction dataset to get test instructions. We will feed them to our models and generate answers. These answers will then be evaluated by our judge LLM (GPT-4o-mini), based on a prompt that specifies our criteria. Finally, we will analyze the scores and draw conclusions based on qualitative and quantitative evaluations.

Generating answers

The first step consists of efficiently generating answers for each instruction in our test set. In addition to our two models, we will also use meta-llama/Meta-Llama-3.1-8B-Instruct, the official instruct version of Llama-3.1-8B, as a reference point to better understand the trade-offs we made.

Let's start the first stage of the implementation:

1. We import the relevant libraries, including vLLM for fast generation. This library is a lot faster than transformers for batch generation with local models:

   ```
   from vllm import LLM, SamplingParams
   from datasets import load_dataset
   from tqdm.auto import tqdm
   import gc
   ```

2. We define a function called generate_answers that will process our dataset and generate responses using a specified model. It takes two inputs—the ID of the model we want to use and the name of the test dataset:

   ```
   def generate_answers(model_id, dataset_name):
       dataset = load_dataset(dataset_name, split="test")
   ```

3. We need to format the raw instructions using the chat template our models have been trained on. Note that Llama-3.1-8B-Instruct has been used with a different template, but it can follow this simple format. Here, we use the same chat template with every model for simplicity. We map the entire test set to this template with the format() function:

```
       def format(sample):
           return "Below is an instruction that describes a task.
    Write a response that appropriately completes the request.\n\n###
    Instruction:\n{}\n\n### Response:\n".format(sample["instruction"])
       dataset = dataset.map(lambda sample: {"prompt": format(sample)})
```

4. Let's initialize the LLM object used by vLLM with a maximum length of 4,096 tokens. We can also specify sampling parameters, which correspond to variables used in the decoding strategy. Here, we use parameters to encourage diversity (high temperature) while removing the most unlikely tokens (top_p and min_p). Finally, we start the generation by providing the list of prompts with dataset["prompt"]:

```
       llm = LLM(model=model_id, max_model_len=4096)
       sampling_params = SamplingParams(temperature=0.8, top_p=0.95,
    min_p=0.05, max_tokens=4096)
       outputs = llm.generate(dataset["prompt"], sampling_params)
```

5. This process should take a few minutes with our 334 prompts. Once this is done, we extract the answers from the object that is outputted by vLLM. We then add these answers as a new column to our dataset. This is useful to log the answers and review them later:

```
       answers = [output.outputs[0].text for output in outputs]
       dataset = dataset.add_column("answers", answers)
```

6. We save our results to the Hugging Face Hub for easy access later. Then, we clear our GPU memory to prevent running out of space when we process the next model:

```
       print(f"Uploading results for {model_id}")
       dataset.push_to_hub(f"mlabonne/{model_id.split('/')
    [-1]}-results")
       gc.collect()

       return dataset
```

7. We create a list of the three models we want to test. Then, we run our generate_answers() function for each of these models, one at a time. This will create and upload a separate set of results for each model:

```
    model_ids = [
        'mlabonne/TwinLlama-3.1-8B',
        'mlabonne/TwinLlama-3.1-8B-DPO',
```

```
        'meta-llama/Meta-Llama-3.1-8B-Instruct'
]
for model_id in model_ids:
    generate_answers(model_id, "mlabonne/llmtwin")
```

Now that we have the answer generation, we can move on to the evaluation process.

Evaluating answers

To evaluate our answers, we will rely on GPT-4o-mini as a judge. This strategy is similar to what we used for data generation. As a matter of fact, you could adapt it to filter out bad samples during the data generation process. Here, we will score every generated answer from every model in terms of accuracy and style. The average scores will inform us about the quality of our fine-tuning compared to Llama-3.1-8B-Instruct:

1. First, we import the required libraries, including openai:

    ```
    import json
    from typing import List
    from datasets import Dataset, load_dataset
    from openai import OpenAI
    from tqdm.auto import tqdm
    import concurrent.futures
    ```

2. We then define the evaluate_answer() function. This function contains our evaluation prompt, which sets up the context for evaluating answers based on accuracy and style:

    ```
    def evaluate_answer(
        instruction: str, answer: str, client: OpenAI
    ) -> dict:
        prompt = f"""You are an expert judge. Please evaluate the
    quality of a given answer to an instruction based on two criteria:
    1. Accuracy: How factually correct is the information presented in
    the answer? You are a technical expert in this topic.
    2. Style: Is the tone and writing style appropriate for a blog post
    or social media content? It should use simple but technical words
    and avoid formal or academic language.
    ```

3. In the same prompt, we define our scales for each metric. Those are three-point Likert scales with a precise definition for each score:

    ```
    Accuracy scale:
    ```

```
1 (Poor): Contains factual errors or misleading information
2 (Good): Mostly accurate with minor errors or omissions
3 (Excellent): Highly accurate and comprehensive


Style scale:
1 (Poor): Too formal, uses some overly complex words
2 (Good): Good balance of technical content and accessibility, but
still uses formal words and expressions
3 (Excellent): Perfectly accessible language for blog/social media,
uses simple but precise technical terms when necessary
```

4. Finally, we conclude the prompt with two examples to illustrate what we mean by "*complex words*" and "*formal or academic language.*" We provide the corresponding instruction-answer pair and ask the model to return a response in JSON:

```
Example of bad style: The Llama2 7B model constitutes a noteworthy
progression in the field of artificial intelligence, serving as the
successor to its predecessor, the original Llama architecture.
Example of excellent style: Llama2 7B outperforms the original Llama
model across multiple benchmarks.


Instruction: {instruction}


Answer: {answer}


Provide your evaluation in JSON format with the following structure:
{{
    "accuracy": {{
        "analysis": "...",
        "score": 0
    }},
    "style": {{
        "analysis": "...",
        "score": 0
    }}
}}
"""
```

5. This prompt is given as a user query to the GPT-4o-mini model. The system prompt reinforces that we are interested in answer evaluation based on accuracy and style:

```python
completion = client.chat.completions.create(
    model="gpt-4o-mini",
    messages=[
        {
            "role": "system",
            "content": "You are a helpful assistant who
evaluates answers based on accuracy and style. Provide your response
in JSON format with a short analysis and score for each criterion.",
        },
        {"role": "user", "content": prompt},
    ],
    response_format={"type": "json_object"},
    max_tokens=1000,
    temperature=0.8,
)
```

6. As in the previous chapters, we will batch our requests to speed up the process. This is why we create an evaluate_batch() function, which returns a list of parsed structured outputs with their corresponding indices. These indices are important to ensure a correct ordering of the evaluations:

```python
def evaluate_batch(batch, start_index):
    client = OpenAI(api_key=OPENAI_KEY)
    return [
        (i, evaluate_answer(instr, ans, client))
        for i, (instr, ans) in enumerate(batch, start=start_index)
    ]
```

7. We can now orchestrate the previous code in the evaluate_answers() function. It takes the model ID, number of threads, and batch size as inputs. First, we load the dataset with the generations we previously saved:

```python
def evaluate_answers(model_id: str, num_threads: int = 10, batch_
size: int = 5) -> Dataset:
    dataset = load_dataset(f"mlabonne/{model_id.split('/')
[-1]}-results", split="all")
```

8. We create batches of instruction-answer pairs from our dataset. Each batch contains batch_size number of pairs:

```
batches = [
    (i, list(zip(dataset["instruction"][i:i+batch_size],
dataset["answers"][i:i+batch_size])))
    for i in range(0, len(dataset), batch_size)
]
```

9. We perform parallel evaluation of batches of instruction-answer pairs using multiple threads. We use parallel processing to evaluate multiple batches simultaneously, speeding up the overall evaluation process. The ThreadPoolExecutor submits each batch to evaluate_batch(). The results are stored in the evaluations list:

```
evaluations = [None] * len(dataset)

with concurrent.futures.ThreadPoolExecutor(max_workers=num_
threads) as executor:
    futures = [executor.submit(evaluate_batch, batch, start_
index) for start_index, batch in batches]

    for future in tqdm(concurrent.futures.as_completed(futures),
total=len(futures)):
        for index, evaluation in future.result():
            evaluations[index] = evaluation
```

10. We create a new column with the result of the evaluation process. This column will store the raw JSON output of the judge model, including scores and explanations:

```
if 'evaluation' in dataset.column_names:
    dataset = dataset.remove_columns(['evaluation'])
dataset = dataset.add_column("evaluation", evaluations)
```

11. We can directly parse this JSON object with json.loads() and try to retrieve the accuracy and style scores that should have been generated. This generation is in best-effort mode, which means that scores are not guaranteed. If there's an error in parsing, we use None values as a fallback:

```
accuracy_scores = []
style_scores = []
```

```
    for evaluation in dataset['evaluation']:
        try:
            eval_dict = json.loads(evaluation) if
isinstance(evaluation, str) else evaluation
            accuracy_score = eval_dict['accuracy']['score']
            style_score = eval_dict['style']['score']
            accuracy_scores.append(accuracy_score)
            style_scores.append(style_score)
        except (json.JSONDecodeError, KeyError, TypeError):
            accuracy_scores.append(None)
            style_scores.append(None)
```

12. We add two new columns to store the accuracy and style scores for further analysis:

```
    if 'accuracy' in dataset.column_names:
        dataset = dataset.remove_columns(['accuracy'])
    dataset = dataset.add_column('accuracy', accuracy_scores)
    if 'style' in dataset.column_names:
        dataset = dataset.remove_columns(['style'])
    dataset = dataset.add_column('style', style_scores)
```

13. Let's push the final dataset with generated answers, evaluations, and scores to the Hugging Face Hub:

```
    dataset.push_to_hub(f"mlabonne/{model_id.split('/')
[-1]}-results")
    return dataset
```

14. We can now call the evaluate_answers() function with the three models we selected:

```
model_ids = [
    'mlabonne/TwinLlama-3.1-8B',
    'mlabonne/TwinLlama-3.1-8B-DPO',
    'meta-llama/Meta-Llama-3.1-8B-Instruct'
```

```
]
for model_id in model_ids:
    evaluate_answers(model_id)
```

By saving intermediate results, our evaluation framework becomes more robust to failures. It is also easily extendable to other models, datasets, and criteria.

Analyzing results

There are three elements we can review at the end of this evaluation process: model answers, explanations from evaluations, and scores.

While reviewing answers is not scalable, it is a crucial step that can help to identify a lot of common mistakes, such as a wrong chat template or incorrect model. Here, we will focus on a single instruction and read the answers provided by our two models and Llama-3.1-8B-Instruct.

Instruction

Discuss the concept of algorithm bias and its implications.

TwinLlama-3.1-8B

Algorithm bias refers to the tendency of algorithms to produce outcomes that are skewed or unfair due to underlying assumptions or programming biases. This can have significant implications, particularly in fields like machine learning and AI, where algorithms are relied upon to make critical decisions. If an algorithm is not properly vetted for bias, it may lead to discriminatory outcomes, such as lending practices that disproportionately affect certain demographic groups or recruitment processes that unfairly favor certain candidates. It is essential to ensure that algorithms are designed and implemented with fairness and accuracy in mind to mitigate these risks.

TwinLlama-3.1-8B-DPO

Algorithm bias refers to the tendency of algorithms to produce outcomes that are skewed or unfair due to underlying assumptions or programming biases. This can have significant implications, particularly in fields like machine learning and AI, where algorithms are relied upon to make critical decisions. If an algorithm is not properly vetted for bias, it could lead to discriminatory outcomes, such as denying loans to certain demographic groups or perpetuating stereotypes. Therefore, it is essential to address algorithmic bias proactively to ensure that the technology we develop is equitable and just.

Llama-3.1-8B-Instruct

Algorithm bias, also known as algorithmic bias, refers to the unintended or inherent bias in machine learning models that can affect their performance, accuracy, and fairness. This bias can be caused by various factors, including the data used to train the model, the algorithm itself, and the biases present in the society or culture. One of the most significant implications of algorithm bias is its potential to perpetuate and exacerbate existing social inequalities. For instance, facial recognition software has been shown to be less accurate for people of color, leading to wrongful arrests and discrimination. Similarly, language processing models have been found to be biased towards the language and dialect of the dominant group, making it difficult for marginalized communities to access information and services. Algorithm bias can also have severe consequences in areas such as healthcare, education, and employment. For example, a medical diagnosis algorithm that is biased towards certain demographics may misdiagnose or underdiagnose conditions in other groups, leading to delayed or inadequate treatment. In education, an algorithm that is biased towards certain learning styles may disproportionately affect students with different learning abilities, leading to unequal opportunities. To mitigate the effects of algorithm bias, it is essential to address the root causes of bias and implement measures to ensure fairness and transparency in machine learning models. This can be achieved through techniques such as data cleansing, regularization, and debiasing, as well as implementing diverse and representative datasets. Additionally, it is crucial to involve diverse stakeholders, including members of marginalized communities, in the development and testing of algorithms to ensure that they are fair and equitable. In conclusion, algorithm bias is a significant concern that can have far-reaching implications for individuals and society as a whole. It is essential to recognize the potential biases in machine learning models and take proactive steps to mitigate their effects. By doing so, we can create more equitable and just systems that benefit everyone, regardless of their background or demographic characteristics.

Table 7.4: Example of generated answers for a given instruction

Immediately, we can see that the answers from our models are very close to each other. This is not the case with Llama-3.1-8B-Instruct's answer, which is extremely verbose and lists many examples. This is typically the kind of answer that is correct but can feel artificial and unpleasant to read because of its length. On the other hand, the DPO model slightly simplifies the language of the SFT version, making it less academic. This is exactly the behavior we want to capture, modifying the writing style but not the actual content of the answer.

Let's now review the evaluations provided by GPT-4o-mini for each answer.

TwinLlama-3.1-8B

Accuracy

The answer accurately defines algorithm bias and highlights its implications in fields like machine learning and AI. It correctly identifies the risks of discriminatory outcomes due to biased algorithms. There are no apparent factual errors, making this a comprehensive response.

Score: 3

Style

The tone is informative and relatively accessible, though it tends towards a formal tone in some sections (e.g., 'underlying assumptions or programming biases'). While it does use some technical terms appropriately, it could be simplified further for a broader audience, especially for blog or social media content.

Score: 2

TwinLlama-3.1-8B-DPO

Accuracy

The answer accurately defines algorithm bias and outlines its implications in critical fields like machine learning and AI. It highlights the potential for discriminatory outcomes, making it a comprehensive overview of the topic without any factual errors.

Score: 3

Style

The writing style is clear, accessible, and effectively communicates the technical concept of algorithm bias without becoming overly formal. While it uses some technical terms, they are appropriate and explained well for a general audience.

Score: 3

Llama-3.1-8B-Instruct

Accuracy

The answer accurately defines algorithm bias and discusses its causes and implications in various domains such as facial recognition, healthcare, and education. It also correctly identifies methods to mitigate bias, such as involving diverse stakeholders and employing debiasing techniques. Overall, the information is factually correct and comprehensive.

Score: 3

Style

The tone is informative and accessible, with technical terms explained clearly. However, some phrases like 'unintended or inherent bias' and 'implementation of diverse and representative datasets' could be simplified for broader audience appeal. The writing is generally suitable for blog or social media content, but it could benefit from a more conversational tone.

Score: 2

Table 7.5: Evaluations of each answer made by GPT-4o-mini, according to style and accuracy

According to our judge LLM, there is no issue with the accuracy of the answers, which get a perfect score. However, the style is considered too formal for TwinLlama-3.1-8B (SFT) and Llama-3.1-8B-Instruct, with a score of 2. The judge LLM agreed with our previous analysis and assigned a perfect score to TwinLlama-3.1-8B-DPO's answer for communicating "the technical concept of algorithm bias without becoming overly formal."

This trend is confirmed by the average scores obtained by each model:

```
TwinLlama-3.1-8B - Accuracy: 2.45
TwinLlama-3.1-8B - Style: 2.04


TwinLlama-3.1-8B-DPO - Accuracy: 2.46
TwinLlama-3.1-8B-DPO - Style: 2.12


Llama-3.1-8B-Instruct - Accuracy: 2.62
Llama-3.1-8B-Instruct - Style: 1.86
```

In terms of accuracy, our two fine-tuned models get similar scores, while Llama-3.1-8B-Instruct achieves the highest accuracy score of 2.62. This suggests that the instruct-tuned Llama model may have a slight edge in providing factually correct information. This is probably due to its extensive post-training process with over 10 million samples (compared to 13,000 in our case).

However, when it comes to style, we see a different pattern. TwinLlama-3.1-8B-DPO leads with a score of 2.12, successfully achieving a more accessible and less formal writing style without sacrificing content quality. TwinLlama-3.1-8B (SFT) follows with 2.04, showing improvement but retaining some formality, while Llama-3.1-8B-Instruct trails with 1.86, tending toward verbosity.

Based on this feedback and the manual review of the generated answers, we can detect mistakes and identify areas for improvement. This is essential for refining the data generation process through additional filtering or augmenting the dataset with missing information. While this first version already shows promising results, iterating over different datasets and models will allow us to significantly outperform our baseline and create the best possible model for our use case.

Summary

In this chapter, we explored LLM evaluation with models and RAG systems. We saw how to interpret classic benchmarks like MMLU to select strong candidates to use or fine-tune. We also detailed how domain-specific and task-specific evaluations work, and how to create our own based on publicly available examples.

We focused on two techniques (multiple-choice question answering and LLM-as-a-judge) as the backbone of these custom evaluation frameworks.

However, models are commonly integrated into broader systems that provide additional context. We introduced two evaluation frameworks for RAG systems, Ragas and ARES. We saw both similarities (for example, synthetic data generation) and differences in how they evaluate RAG systems (context-based metrics versus trained classifiers). Finally, we evaluated TwinLlama-3.1-8B with a judge LLM according to three criteria: relevance, coherence, and conciseness. This provided insights into how we can improve it.

In the next chapter, we will explore inference optimization techniques to improve speed and reduce memory usage, without significantly compromising model performance. We will also delve into optimization methods, model parallelism techniques and examine different quantization approaches.

References

- Lianmin Zheng et al.. *"Judging LLM-as-a-Judge with MT-Bench and Chatbot Arena."* arXiv preprint arXiv:2306.05685, June 2023.

- Aymeric Roucher. *"Using LLM-as-a-judge for an automated and versatile evaluation - Hugging Face Open-Source AI Cookbook."* huggingface.co, No date found, `https://huggingface.co/learn/cookbook/en/llm_judge`.

- LangChain. *"Aligning LLM-as-a-Judge with Human Preferences."* blog.langchain.dev, June 26, 2024, `https://blog.langchain.dev/aligning-llm-as-a-judge-with-human-preferences/`.

- Dan Hendrycks et al.. *"Measuring Massive Multitask Language Understanding."* arXiv preprint arXiv:2009.03300, September 2020.

- Jeffrey Zhou et al.. *"Instruction-Following Evaluation for Large Language Models."* arXiv preprint arXiv:2311.07911, November 2023.

- Yann Dubois et al.. *"Length-Controlled AlpacaEval: A Simple Way to Debias Automatic Evaluators."* arXiv preprint arXiv:2404.04475, April 2024.

- Grégoire Mialon et al.. *"GAIA: a benchmark for General AI Assistants."* arXiv preprint arXiv:2311.12983, November 2023.

- Giwon Hong et al.. *"The Hallucinations Leaderboard -- An Open Effort to Measure Hallucinations in Large Language Models."* arXiv preprint arXiv:2404.05904, April 2024.

- Shahul Es et al.. *"RAGAS: Automated Evaluation of Retrieval Augmented Generation."* arXiv preprint arXiv:2309.15217, September 2023.

- Jon Saad-Falcon et al.. *"ARES: An Automated Evaluation Framework for Retrieval-Augmented Generation Systems."* arXiv preprint arXiv:2311.09476, November 2023.

Join our book's Discord space

Join our community's Discord space for discussions with the authors and other readers:

`https://packt.link/llmeng`

8

Inference Optimization

Deploying LLMs is challenging due to their significant computational and memory requirements. Efficiently running these models necessitates the use of specialized accelerators, such as GPUs or TPUs, which can parallelize operations and achieve higher throughput. While some tasks, like document generation, can be processed in batches overnight, others require low latency and fast generation, such as code completion. As a result, optimizing the inference process – how these models make predictions based on input data – is critical for many practical applications. This includes reducing the time it takes to generate the first token (latency), increasing the number of tokens generated per second (throughput), and minimizing the memory footprint of LLMs.

Indeed, naive deployment approaches lead to poor hardware utilization and underwhelming throughput and latency. Fortunately, a variety of optimization techniques have emerged to dramatically speed up inference. This chapter will explore key methods like speculative decoding, model parallelism, and weight quantization, demonstrating how thoughtful implementations can achieve speedups of 2–4X or more. We will also introduce three popular inference engines (Text Generation Inference, vLLM, and TensorRT-LLM) and compare their features in terms of inference optimization.

In this chapter, we will cover the following topics:

- Model optimization strategies
- Model parallelism
- Model quantization

By the end of this chapter, you will understand the core challenges in LLM inference and be familiar with state-of-the-art optimization techniques, including model parallelism and weight quantization.

 All the code examples from this chapter can be found on GitHub at https://github.com/PacktPublishing/LLM-Engineering.

Model optimization strategies

Most of the LLMs used nowadays, like GPT or Llama, are powered by a decoder-only Transformer architecture. The *decoder-only* architecture is designed for text-generation tasks. It predicts the next word in a sequence based on preceding words, making it effective for generating contextually appropriate text continuations.

In contrast, an *encoder-only* architecture, like BERT, focuses on understanding and representing the input text with detailed embeddings. It excels in tasks that require comprehensive context understanding, such as text classification and named entity recognition. Finally, the encoder-decoder architecture, like T5, combines both functionalities. The encoder processes the input text to generate a context-rich representation, which the decoder then uses to produce the output text. This dual structure is particularly powerful for sequence-to-sequence tasks like translation and summarization, where understanding the input context and generating a relevant output are equally important.

In this book, we only focus on the decoder-only architecture, which dominates the LLM field.

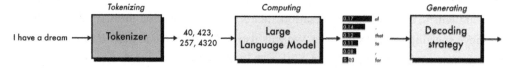

Figure 8.1 – Inference process with decoder-only models. We provide "I have a dream" as input and obtain "of" as output.

As shown in *Figure 8.1*, the basic inference process for a decoder-only model involves:

1. **Tokenizing** the input prompt and passing it through an embedding layer and positional encoding.

2. **Computing** key and value pairs for each input token using the multi-head attention mechanism.

3. **Generating** output tokens sequentially, one at a time, using the computed keys and values.

While *Steps 1* and *2* are computationally expensive, they consist of highly parallelizable matrix multiplication that can achieve high hardware utilization on accelerators like GPUs and TPUs.

The real challenge is that the token generation in *Step 3* is inherently sequential – to generate the next token, you need to have generated all previous tokens. This leads to an iterative process where the output sequence is grown one token at a time, failing to leverage the parallel computing capabilities of the hardware. Addressing this bottleneck is one of the core focuses of inference optimization.

In this section, we will detail several optimization strategies that are commonly used to speed up inference and reduce **Video Random-Access Memory (VRAM)** usage, such as implementing a (static) KV cache, continuous batching, speculative decoding, and optimized attention mechanisms.

KV cache

We saw that LLMs generate text token by token, which is slow because each new prediction depends on the entire previous context. For example, to predict the 100th token in a sequence, the model needs the context of tokens 1 through 99. When predicting the 101st token, it again needs the information from tokens 1 through 99, plus token 100. This repeated computation is particularly inefficient.

The **key-value (KV)** cache addresses this issue by storing key-value pairs produced by self-attention layers. Instead of recalculating these pairs for each new token, the model retrieves them from the cache, significantly speeding up the generation.

You can see an illustration of this technique in *Figure 8.2*:

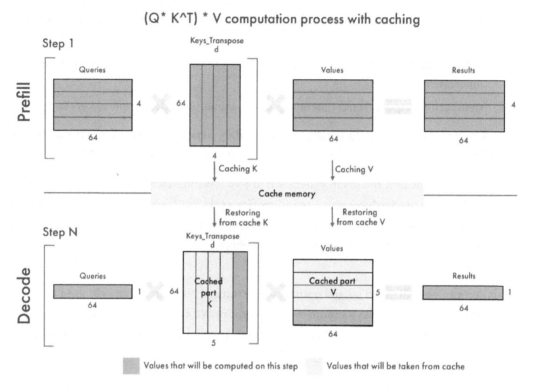

Figure 8.2 – Illustration of the KV cache

When a new token is generated, only the key and value for that single token need to be computed and added to the cache. The KV cache is an immediate optimization that is implemented in every popular tool and library. Some implementations maintain a separate KV cache for each layer of the model.

The size of the KV cache scales with the number of tokens (n_{tokens}) and several model dimensions, like the number of layers (n_{layers}), the number of attention heads (n_{heads}), their dimension ($\dim_{head}$), and the precision of the parameters in bytes (n_{bytes}):

$$size(KV\ cache) = 2n_{tokens}\ n_{layers}\ n_{heads}\ \dim_{head}\ n_{bytes}$$

For a typical 7B parameter model using 16-bit precision, this exceeds 2 GB for high sequence lengths (higher than 2,048 tokens). Larger models with more layers and higher embedding dimensions will see even greater memory requirements.

Since the KV cache grows with each generation step and is dynamic, it prevents you from taking advantage of torch.compile, a powerful optimization tool that fuses PyTorch code into fast and optimized kernels. The *static KV cache* solves this issue by pre-allocating the KV cache size to a maximum value, which allows you to combine it with torch.compile for up to a 4x speedup in the forward pass.

To configure a model to use a static KV cache with the transformers library, follow these steps:

1. We import the tokenizer and the model we want to optimize:

```
import torch
from transformers import AutoTokenizer, AutoModelForCausalLM

model_id = "google/gemma-2b-it"
tokenizer = AutoTokenizer.from_pretrained(model_id)
model = AutoModelForCausalLM.from_pretrained(model_id, device_
map="auto")
```

2. To implement the static cache, we change the cache implementation in the model's generation config to static:

```
model.generation_config.cache_implementation = "static"
```

3. Now that our KV cache is static, we can compile the model using torch.compile:

```
compiled_model = torch.compile(model, mode="reduce-overhead",
fullgraph=True)
```

4. We tokenize an input question, "What is 2+2?", and store it on a GPU if available (if not, we store it on the CPU):

```
device = "cuda" if torch.cuda.is_available() else "cpu"
inputs = tokenizer("What is 2+2?", return_tensors="pt").to(device)
```

5. Let's use the generate() method to get the model's output and decode it with batch_ decode() to print its answer:

```
outputs = model.generate(**inputs, do_sample=True, temperature=0.7,
max_new_tokens=64)
print(tokenizer.batch_decode(outputs, skip_special_tokens=True))
['What is 2+2?\n\nThe answer is 4. 2+2 = 4.']
```

This returns a list containing both the input and output, correctly answering our question.

 Note that the static cache doesn't work with all architectures. For details on which architectures are supported, check out the transformers documentation.

Efficiently managing the KV cache is essential, as it can quickly exhaust available GPU memory and limit the batch sizes that can be processed. This has motivated the development of memory-efficient attention mechanisms and other techniques, which we will cover in the last section.

Continuous batching

Batching, or processing multiple inference requests simultaneously, is a standard approach to achieve high throughput. Larger batch sizes spread out the memory cost of model weights and transfer more data to the GPU at once, better saturating its parallel compute capacity.

However, decoder-only models pose a particular challenge due to the high variability in input prompt lengths and desired output lengths. Some requests may have short prompts and only need a one-word answer, while others may input a lengthy context and expect a multi-paragraph response.

With traditional batching, we would have to wait for the longest request in a batch to complete before starting a new batch. This leads to under-utilization as the accelerator sits partly idle waiting for a straggling request to finish. *Continuous batching*, also known as in-flight batching, aims to prevent idle time by immediately feeding a new request into the batch as soon as one completes.

The batching process begins the same – by filling the batch with initial requests. But as soon as a request completes its generation, it is evicted from the batch and a new request takes its place. This way, the accelerator is always processing a full batch, leading to maximally efficient hardware utilization. An additional consideration is the need to periodically pause the generation process to run prefill, or the embedding and encoding of waiting requests. Finding the optimal balance between generation and prefill requires some tuning of the waiting-served ratio hyperparameter.

Continuous batching is natively implemented in most inference frameworks, like Hugging Face's **Text Generation Inference** (**TGI**), vLLM, and NVIDIA TensorRT-LLM.

Speculative decoding

Another powerful optimization technique is *speculative decoding*, also called assisted generation. The key insight is that even with continuous batching, the token-by-token generation process fails to fully saturate the parallel processing capabilities of the accelerator. Speculative decoding aims to use this spare compute capacity to predict multiple tokens simultaneously, using a smaller proxy model (see *Figure 8.3*).

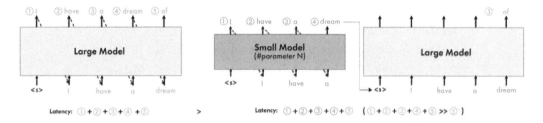

Figure 8.3 – Illustration of traditional decoding (left) and speculative decoding (right)

The general approach is:

- Apply a smaller model, like a distilled or pruned version of the main model, to predict multiple token completions in parallel. This could be 5–10 tokens predicted in a single step.

- Feed these speculative completions into the full model to validate which predictions match what the large model would have generated.

- Retain the longest matching prefix from the speculative completions and discard any incorrect tokens.

The result is that, if the small model approximates the large model well, multiple tokens can be generated in a single step. This avoids running the expensive large model for several iterations. The degree of speedup depends on the quality of the small model's predictions – a 90% match could result in a 3–4X speedup.

It is crucial that both models use the same tokenizer. If this is not the case, the tokens generated by the draft model will not align with those produced by the large model, making them incompatible. Let's implement this using the transformers library. In this example, we will use two Qwen1.5 models from Alibaba Cloud: a 1.8B version as the main model, and a 0.5B version as the draft model. Note that, if you have enough VRAM, you can use much larger models like 14B, 32B, 72B, or 110B as the main model.

Here, we're limited by the VRAM of the T4 GPU in Google Colab, but to get the maximum speedup, the assistant model should be much smaller than the large model.

Here's a step-by-step guide to implement speculative decoding:

1. We load the tokenizer and both models:

```
import torch
from transformers import AutoTokenizer, AutoModelForCausalLM


model_id = "Qwen/Qwen1.5-1.8B-Chat"
tokenizer = AutoTokenizer.from_pretrained(model_id)
model = AutoModelForCausalLM.from_pretrained(model_id, device_
map="auto")
draft_model = AutoModelForCausalLM.from_pretrained("Qwen/Qwen1.5-
0.5B-Chat", device_map="auto")
```

2. We then tokenize the same input and store it in the accelerator, if available:

```
device = "cuda" if torch.cuda.is_available() else "cpu"
inputs = tokenizer("What is 2+2?", return_tensors="pt").to(device)
```

3. We can now use `model.generate()` with the argument `assistant_model` to enable speculative decoding:

```
outputs = model.generate(**inputs, do_sample=True, assistant_
model=draft_model, temperature=0.7, max_new_tokens=64)
print(tokenizer.batch_decode(outputs, skip_special_tokens=True))
['What is 2+2? 2 + 2 equals 4!']
```

The speedup in this small example is not significant, but it is clearly noticeable with bigger models.

Prompt lookup decoding is a variant of speculative decoding, tailored to input-grounded tasks like summarization where there is often overlap between the prompt and output. Shared n-grams are used as the LLM candidate tokens. We can enable prompt lookup decoding by using the `prompt_lookup_num_tokens` parameter in `model.generate()`:

```
outputs = model.generate(**inputs, prompt_lookup_num_tokens=4)
```

By combining the static KV cache with torch.compile, implementing continuous batching, and leveraging speculative decoding techniques, LLMs can see inference speedups of 2–4x or more with no loss in quality.

Another approach to creating a small proxy model consists of jointly fine-tuning a small model alongside a large model for maximum fidelity. A representative technique here is Medusa, which inserts dedicated speculation heads into the main model. The Medusa-1 approach fine-tunes these speculation heads while freezing the large model, while the Medusa-2 approach jointly fine-tunes both the speculation heads and the large model. The Medusa method has demonstrated impressive results, enabling a 70M parameter model to closely approximate the performance of a 7B parameter model on a range of tasks. Speculative decoding is natively supported by TGI.

Optimized attention mechanisms

The Transformer architecture is based on the attention mechanism, which scales quadratically with the number of input tokens (or sequence length). This is particularly inefficient for longer sequences, where the size of the KV cache can blow up.

Introduced by Kwon, Li, et al. (2023), *PagedAttention* addresses these memory challenges by drawing inspiration from virtual memory and paging in operating systems. It partitions the KV cache into blocks, eliminating the need for contiguous memory allocation. Each block contains the keys and values for a fixed number of tokens. During attention computation, the PagedAttention kernel efficiently fetches these blocks, regardless of their physical memory location.

This partitioning allows for near-optimal memory utilization. This is useful for batching more sequences together, which increases throughput and GPU utilization. Moreover, `PagedAttention`'s block-based approach naturally supports memory sharing across multiple output sequences generated from the same prompt. This is particularly advantageous in parallel sampling and beam search, where the same prompt is used to generate multiple outputs. The shared memory blocks reduce redundant computations and memory usage, cutting the memory overhead by up to 55% and improving throughput by up to 2.2x, according to the authors. The vLLM library received the first implementation of PagedAttention. Since then, PagedAttention has also been implemented in TGI and TensorRT-LLM.

Another popular option is *FlashAttention-2*. Developed by Tri Dao (2023), it introduced several key innovations that are designed to address the quadratic runtime and memory constraints in traditional attention. By dividing input and output matrices into smaller blocks, FlashAttention-2 ensures that these blocks can fit into the GPU's on-chip SRAM, which is much faster than high-bandwidth memory. This approach significantly reduces the frequency of data transfers between the GPU's main memory and its processing units.

This is combined with online softmax, which computes the softmax function independently for each block of the attention scores matrix, rather than for the entire matrix at once. By maintaining a running maximum and a running sum of exponentials, FlashAttention-2 can calculate attention probabilities without needing to store large intermediate matrices.

Additionally, FlashAttention-2's online softmax computation enables block-wise processing, maintaining accuracy while significantly reducing memory requirements. This is particularly important for training, where the recomputation of intermediate values (instead of storing them) in the backward pass reduces memory usage from quadratic to linear, in relation to sequence length.

Unlike PagedAttention, FlashAttention-2 can easily be used with the transformers library through the `attn_implementation` parameter:

1. Install the `flash-attn` library with `--no-build-isolation` so that we don't install the dependencies:

    ```
    pip install flash-attn --no-build-isolation
    ```

2. To use FlashAttention-2 for inference, specify `flash_attention_2` in the `attn_implementation` parameter when loading a model. For example, this is how to load Mistral-7B-Instruct-v0.3 with FlashAttention-2:

    ```
    from transformers import AutoModelForCausalLM
    model = AutoModelForCausalLM.from_pretrained(
        "mistralai/Mistral-7B-Instruct-v0.3",
        attn_implementation="flash_attention_2",
    )
    ```

The techniques presented in this section focused on improving the model's efficiency in processing tokens. In the next section, we will discuss how to distribute our model and calculations across multiple GPUs.

Model parallelism

Model parallelism allows you to distribute the memory and compute requirements of LLMs across multiple GPUs. This enables the training and inference of models too large to fit on a single device, while also improving performance in terms of throughput (tokens per second).

There are three main approaches to model parallelism, each involving splitting the model weights and computation in different ways: *data parallelism*, *pipeline parallelism*, and *tensor parallelism*.

Although these approaches were originally developed for training, we can reuse them for inference by focusing on the forward pass only.

Data parallelism

Data parallelism (DP) is the simplest type of model parallelism. It involves making copies of the model and distributing these replicas across different GPUs (see *Figure 8.4*). Each GPU processes a subset of the data simultaneously. During training, the gradients calculated on each GPU are averaged and used to update the model parameters, ensuring that each replica remains synchronized. This approach is particularly beneficial when the batch size is too large to fit into a single machine or when aiming to speed up the training process.

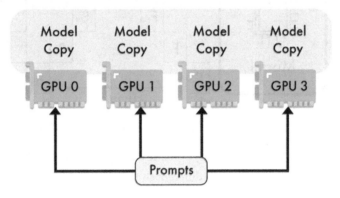

Figure 8.4 – Illustration of data parallelism with four GPUs

During inference, DP can be useful for processing concurrent requests. By distributing the workload across multiple GPUs, this approach helps reduce latency, as multiple requests can be handled simultaneously. This concurrent processing also increases throughput, since a higher number of requests can be processed at the same time.

However, the effectiveness of DP is limited by the model size and the communication overhead between GPUs. Indeed, replicating the model's parameters on each GPU is inefficient. This means that this technique only works when the model is small enough to fit into a single GPU, leaving less room for input data and thus limiting the batch size. For larger models or when memory is a constraint, this can be a significant drawback.

Typically, DP is mainly used for training, while pipeline and tensor parallelism are preferred for inference.

Pipeline parallelism

Introduced by Huang et al. in the GPipe paper (2019), **pipeline parallelism (PP)** is a strategy for distributing the computational load of training and running large neural networks across multiple GPUs.

Unlike traditional DP, which replicates the entire model on each GPU, pipeline parallelism partitions the model's layers across different GPUs. This approach allows each GPU to handle a specific portion of the model, thereby reducing the memory burden on individual GPUs.

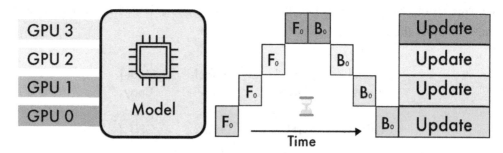

Figure 8.5 – Illustration of pipeline parallelism with four GPUs

As shown in *Figure 8.5*, in a typical four-way pipeline parallel split, the model is divided into four segments, with each segment assigned to a different GPU. The first 25% of the model's layers might be processed by GPU 1, the next 25% by GPU 2, and so on. During the forward pass, activations are computed and then passed along to the next GPU. For training, the backward pass follows a similar sequence in reverse, with gradients being propagated back through the GPUs. The number of GPUs is often referred to as the degree of parallelism.

The primary advantage of pipeline parallelism is its ability to significantly reduce the memory requirements per GPU. However, this approach introduces new challenges, particularly related to the sequential nature of the pipeline. One of the main issues is the occurrence of "pipeline bubbles." These bubbles arise when some GPUs are idle, waiting for activations from preceding layers. This idle time can reduce the overall efficiency of the process.

Micro-batching was developed to mitigate the impact of pipeline bubbles. By splitting the input batch into smaller sub-batches, micro-batching ensures that GPUs remain busier, as the next sub-batch can begin processing before the previous one is fully completed.

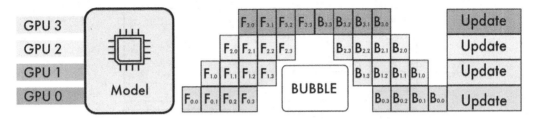

Figure 8.6 – Illustration of pipeline parallelism with micro-batching.

Figure 8.6 shows an example of pipeline parallelism with micro-batching. In this example, the pipeline has four stages (**F0, F1, F2, F3**), and the input batch is divided into four micro-batches. GPU 0 will process forward paths **F0**,0, **F0**,1, **F0**,2, and **F0**,3, sequentially. Once **F0**,0 is complete, GPU 1 can immediately start processing **F1**,0 and so on. After completing these forward passes, GPU 0 waits for the other GPUs to finish their respective forward computations before starting the backward paths (**B0**,3, **B0**,2, **B0**,1, and **B0**,0).

Pipeline parallelism is implemented in distributed training frameworks like Megatron-LM, Deep-Speed (ZeRO), and PyTorch through the dedicated **Pipeline Parallelism for PyTorch (PiPPy)** library. At the time of writing, only certain inference frameworks like TensorRT-LLM support pipeline parallelism.

Tensor parallelism

Introduced by Shoeby, Patwary, Puri et al. in the Megatron-LM paper (2019), **tensor parallelism (TP)** is another popular technique to distribute the computation of LLM layers across multiple devices. In contrast to pipeline parallelism, TP splits the weight matrices found in individual layers. This enables simultaneous computations, significantly reducing memory bottlenecks and increasing processing speed.

In TP, large matrices, such as the weight matrices in MLPs or the attention heads in self-attention layers, are partitioned across several GPUs. Each GPU holds a portion of these matrices and
performs computations on its respective slice.

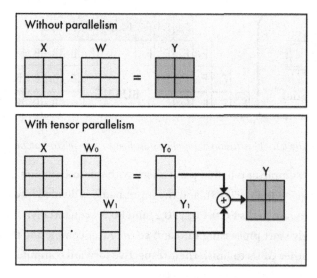

Figure 8.7 – Illustration of column-wise tensor parallelism in an MLP layer (W)

For instance, in an MLP layer, the weight matrix is divided so that each GPU processes only a subset
of the weights (see *Figure 8.7*). The inputs are broadcast to all GPUs, which then independently
compute their respective outputs. The partial results are then aggregated through an all-reduce
operation, combining them to form the final output.

In the context of self-attention layers, TP is particularly efficient due to the inherent parallelism
of attention heads. Each GPU can compute a subset of these heads independently, allowing the
model to process large sequences more effectively. This makes TP more efficient than pipeline
parallelism, which requires waiting for the completion of previous layers.

Despite its advantages, TP is not universally applicable to all layers of a neural network. Layers
like LayerNorm and Dropout, which have dependencies spanning the entire input, cannot be efficiently partitioned and are typically replicated across devices instead. However, these operations
can be split on the sequence dimension of the input instead (sequence parallelism). Different
GPUs can compute these layers on different slices of the input sequence, avoiding replication of
weights. This technique is limited to a few specific layers, but it can provide additional memory
savings, especially for very large input sequence lengths.

Moreover, TP necessitates high-speed interconnects between devices to minimize communication overhead, making it impractical to implement across nodes with insufficient interconnect bandwidth.

TP is also implemented in distributed training frameworks like Megatron-LM, DeepSpeed (ZeRO), and PyTorch (FSDP). It is available in most inference frameworks, like TGI, vLLM, and TensorRT-LLM.

Combining approaches

Data, tensor, and pipeline parallelisms are orthogonal techniques that can be combined. *Figure 8.8* illustrates how a given model can be split according to each approach:

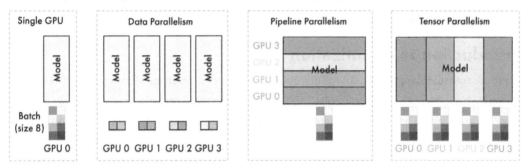

Figure 8.8 – Illustration of the different model parallelism techniques

Combining these techniques can mitigate their respective issues. Pipeline parallelism provides the greatest memory reduction but sacrifices efficiency, due to pipeline bubbles. This may be ideal if the primary constraint fits the model in the GPU memory. In contrast, if low latency is paramount, then prioritizing tensor parallelism and accepting a larger memory footprint may be the better trade-off. In practice, a model may be split depth-wise into a few pipeline stages, with tensor parallelism used within each stage.

Balancing these tradeoffs and mapping a given model architecture onto available hardware accelerators is a key challenge in deploying LLMs.

Model quantization

Quantization refers to the process of representing the weights and activations of a neural network using lower-precision data types. In the context of LLMs, quantization primarily focuses on reducing the precision of the model's weights and activations.

By default, weights are typically stored in a 16-bit or 32-bit floating-point format (FP16 or FP32), which provides high precision but comes at the cost of increased memory usage and computational complexity. Quantization is a solution to reduce the memory footprint and accelerate the inference of LLMs.

In addition to these benefits, larger models with over 30 billion parameters can outperform smaller models (7B–13B LLMs) in terms of quality when quantized to 2- or 3-bit precision. This means they can achieve superior performance while maintaining a comparable memory footprint.

In this section, we will introduce the concepts of quantization, GGUF with `llama.cpp`, GPTQ, and EXL2, along with an overview of additional techniques. In addition to the code provided in this section, you can refer to AutoQuant (`bit.ly/autoquant`) to quantize their models using a Google Colab notebook.

Introduction to quantization

There are two main approaches to weight quantization: **Post-Training Quantization (PTQ)** and **Quantization-Aware Training (QAT)**. PTQ is a straightforward technique where the weights of a pre-trained model are directly converted to a lower precision format without any retraining. While PTQ is easy to implement, it may result in some performance degradation. Conversely, QAT performs quantization during the training or fine-tuning stage, allowing the model to adapt to the lower precision weights. QAT often yields better performance compared to PTQ but requires additional computational resources and representative training data.

The choice of data type plays a crucial role in quantization. Floating-point numbers, such as **FP32**, **FP16** (half-precision), and **BF16** (brain floating-point), are commonly used in deep learning. These formats allocate a fixed number of bits to represent the `sign`, `exponent`, and `significand` (mantissa) of a number.

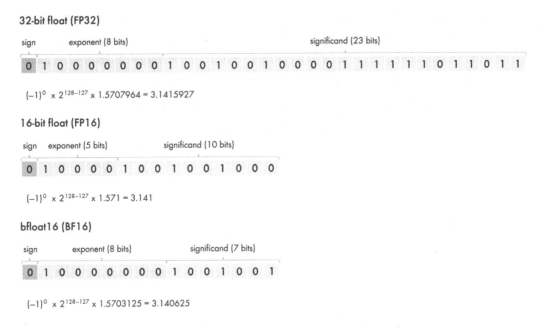

Figure 8.9 – Comparison the between FP32, FP16, and BF16 formats

A sign of 0 represents a positive number, while 1 indicates a negative number. Conversely, the exponent controls the range that is represented (big or small). Finally, the significand controls the precision of the number (the number of digits). The formula used to convert these representations into real numbers is:

$$(-1)^{\text{sign}} \times \text{base}^{\text{exponent}} \times \text{significand}$$

The data types shown in *Figure 7.7* display different tradeoffs, as illustrated with different representations of π (≈ 3.1415926535). FP32 uses 32 bits, providing high precision but also requiring more memory. Conversely, FP16 and BF16 use 16 bits, lowering the memory footprint at the cost of a lower precision. In general, neural networks prefer a bigger range than better precision, which is why BF16 is the most popular data type when the hardware supports it. For example, NVIDIA's Ampere architecture (A100, A30, etc.) supports BF16, but previous generations like Turing (T4, T40, etc.) do not.

However, we are not restricted to these three data types. Lower-precision data types, such as INT8 (8-bit integers), can be employed for quantization, further reducing the memory footprint. Naïve quantization techniques, such as *absolute maximum (absmax) quantization* and *zero-point quantization*, can be applied to convert FP32, FP16, or BF16 weights to INT8, as illustrated in *Figure 8.10*:

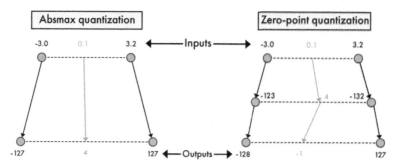

Figure 8.10 – Quantization of 0.1 in a [-3.0, 3.2] range with absmax quantization and zero-point quantization

Absmax quantization maps the original weights **x** to the range [-127, 127] by dividing them by the absolute maximum value of **x** and scaling them:

$$\mathbf{X}_{\text{quant}} = \text{round}\left(\frac{127 \cdot \mathbf{X}}{\max|\mathbf{X}|}\right)$$

For example, if our absolute maximum value is 3.2 (see *Figure 8.8*), a weight of 0.1 would be quantized to $\text{round}\left(\frac{127 \cdot 0.1}{3.2}\right) = 4$. To dequantize it, we do the inverse operation:

$$\mathbf{X}_{\text{dequant}} = \frac{\max|\mathbf{X}| \cdot \mathbf{X}_{\text{quant}}}{127}$$

This means that if we dequantize our weight, we obtain $\frac{3.2 \cdot 4}{127} \approx 0.1008$. We can see a rounding error of 0.0008 in this example. In Python, we can implement it as follows with the PyTorch library:

```python
import torch


def absmax_quantize(X):
    # Calculate scale
    scale = 127 / torch.max(torch.abs(X))

    # Quantize
    X_quant = (scale * X).round()

    return X_quant.to(torch.int8)
```

Zero-point quantization, on the other hand, considers asymmetric input distributions and maps the weights ⁀to the range [-128, 127] by introducing a zero-point offset:

$$\mathbf{X}_{quant} = round(scale \cdot \mathbf{X} + zeropoint)$$

Where $scale = \frac{255}{max(\mathbf{X})-min(\mathbf{X})}$ and $zeropoint = -round(scale \cdot min(\mathbf{X})) - 128$.

If we take the same example with a weight of 0.1, we get a scale of $\frac{255}{3.2+3.0} \approx 41.13$ and a zero-point value of $-round\left(\frac{255}{3.2+3.0} \cdot -3.0\right) - 128 = -5$. The weight of 0.1 would be quantized to $round(41.13 \cdot 0.1 - 5) = -1$, unlike the value of 4 provided by absmax.

We can easily get the dequantization by applying the inverse operation:

$$\mathbf{X}_{dequant} = \frac{\mathbf{X}_{quant} - zeropoint}{scale}$$

In Python, zero-point quantization can be implemented as follows:

```python
def zeropoint_quantize(X):
    # Calculate value range (denominator)
    x_range = torch.max(X) - torch.min(X)
    x_range = 1 if x_range == 0 else x_range

    # Calculate scale
    scale = 255 / x_range

    # Shift by zero-point
    zeropoint = (-scale * torch.min(X) - 128).round()

    # Scale and round the inputs
    X_quant = torch.clip((X * scale + zeropoint).round(), -128, 127)

    return X_quant.to(torch.int8)
```

However, naïve quantization methods have limitations, particularly when dealing with *outlier features* in LLMs. Outlier features are extreme weight values (about 0.1% of total values) that can significantly impact the quantization process, leading to reduced precision for other values.

Discarding these outliers is not feasible, as it would degrade a model's performance. You can see an example of outliers in *Figure 8.11*:

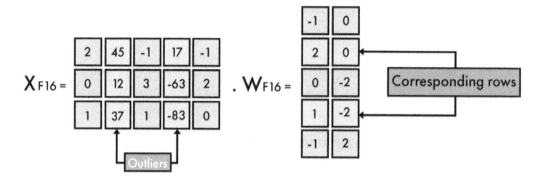

Figure 8.11 – Example of outliers in a weight matrix

To address the outlier problem, more advanced quantization techniques have been proposed. One notable example is LLM.int8(), introduced by Dettmers et al. (2022). LLM.int8() employs a mixed-precision quantization scheme, where outlier features are processed using FP16, while the remaining values are quantized to INT8. This approach effectively reduces the memory footprint of LLMs by nearly 2x while minimizing performance degradation.

LLM.int8() works by performing matrix multiplication in three steps. First, it extracts columns containing outlier features from the input hidden states using a custom threshold. Second, it performs separate matrix multiplications for the outliers (in FP16) and non-outliers (in INT8) using vector-wise quantization. Finally, it dequantizes the non-outlier results and combines them with the outlier results to obtain the final output in *FP16*.

The effectiveness of LLM.int8() has been demonstrated empirically, showing negligible performance degradation (<1%) compared to the original FP32 models. However, it does introduce an additional computational overhead, resulting in around 20% slower inference for large models. Models can be directly loaded in 8-bit precision with the transformer library, using LLM.int8(), as follows:

```
from transformers import AutoModelForCausalLM
model_name = "meta-llama/Meta-Llama-3-8B-Instruct"
model = AutoModelForCausalLM.from_pretrained(model_name, device_
map="auto", load_in_8bit=True)
```

Introduced by *Dettmers et al.* (2023), NF4 is a 4-bit precision format designed for QLoRA (discussed in *Chapter 5*). It is also integrated into the transformers library but requires the bitsandbytes library as a dependency. To load a model in NF4 (4-bit precision), you can use the `load_in_4bit` parameter, as follows:

```
from transformers import AutoModelForCausalLM
model_name = "meta-llama/Meta-Llama-3-8B-Instruct"
model = AutoModelForCausalLM.from_pretrained(model_name, device_
map="auto", load_in_4bit=True)
```

Quantization with GGUF and llama.cpp

The llama.cpp project is an open-source C++ software library created by Georgi Gerganov, designed to perform inference with various LLMs. It is the most popular quantization technique, with many quantized models available on the Hugging Face Hub.

Compared to other libraries that rely on hardware-specific closed-source libraries like CUDA, llama.cpp can run on a broader range of hardware. It has gained significant popularity, particularly among users without specialized hardware, as it can operate on CPUs and Android devices. Moreover, llama.cpp can also offload layers to the GPU, accelerating inference speed. It is compatible with different inference optimization techniques, such as FlashAttention-2 and speculative decoding.

This project features its own quantization format, GGUF, designed to simplify and speed up model loading. GGUF files store tensors and metadata, supporting various formats, from 1-bit to 8-bit precision. It follows a naming convention based on the number of bits used and specific variants, such as:

- IQ1_S and IQ1_M: 1-bit precision – very low quality
- IQ2_XXS/XS/S/M and Q2_K: 2-bit precision – generally low quality but IQ2 can be usable for large models
- IQ3_XXS/XS/S/M and Q3_K_S/M/L: 3-bit precision – low quality but usable for large models
- IQ4_XS/NL and Q4_K_S/M, Q4_0/1: 4-bit precision – good quality and usable for most models
- Q5_K_S/M and Q5_0/1: 5-bit precision – high quality
- Q6_K: 6-bit precision –very high quality
- Q8_0: 8-bit precision – highest quality

To provide a brief overview of GGUF quantization, llama.cpp groups values into blocks and rounds them to a lower precision. For instance, the legacy Q4_0 format handles 32 values per block, scaling and quantizing them based on the largest weight value in the block ($w = q \times block\_scale$). In Q4_1, the smallest Lvalue in the block is also added ($w = q \times block\_scale + block\_minimum$). In Q4_K, weights are divided into super-blocks, containing 8 blocks with 32 values. Block scales and minimum values are also quantized in higher precision with 6 bits ($w = q \times block\_scale(6bit) + block\_min(6bit)$). Finally, i-quants like IQ4_XS are inspired by another quantization technique called QuIP#. This ensures an even number of positive (or negative) quant signs in groups of eight and implements the E_8 lattice to store their magnitude.

Here is a practical example of how to quantize a model in the GGUF format. The following steps can be executed on a free T4 GPU in Google Colab:

1. Install llama.cpp and the required libraries:

```
!git clone https://github.com/ggerganov/llama.cpp
!cd llama.cpp && git pull && make clean && LLAMA_CUBLAS=1 make
!pip install -r llama.cpp/requirements.txt
```

2. Download the model to convert. We will provide the model ID from the Hugging Face Hub – for example, `mistralai/Mistral-7B-Instruct-v0.2`:

```
MODEL_ID = "mlabonne/EvolCodeLlama-7b"
MODEL_NAME = MODEL_ID.split('/')[-1]
!git lfs install
!git clone https://huggingface.co/{MODEL_ID}
```

3. First, we convert the model into FP16. This is an intermediary artifact that will be used for every GGUF quantization type. Note that different conversion scripts exist in llama. cpp and are compatible with different models:

```
fp16 = f"{MODEL_NAME}/{MODEL_NAME.lower()}.fp16.bin"
!python llama.cpp/convert.py {MODEL_NAME} --outtype f16 --outfile
{fp16}
```

4. We select a format (here, Q4_K_M) and start the quantization. This process can take an hour on a T4 GPU:

```
METHOD = "q4_k_m"
qtype = f"{MODEL_NAME}/{MODEL_NAME.lower()}.{method.upper()}.gguf"
!./llama.cpp/quantize {fp16} {qtype} {METHOD}
```

5. Once it's done, your quantized model is ready. You can download it locally, or upload it to the Hugging Face Hub using the following code:

```python
from huggingface_hub import create_repo, HfApi

hf_token = "" # Specify your token
username = "" # Specify your username

api = HfApi()

# Create empty repo
create_repo(
    repo_id = f"{username}/{MODEL_NAME}-GGUF",
    repo_type="model",
    exist_ok=True,
    token=hf_token
)

# Upload gguf files
api.upload_folder(
    folder_path=MODEL_NAME,
    repo_id=f"{username}/{MODEL_NAME}-GGUF",
    allow_patterns=f"*.gguf",
    token=hf_token
)
```

GGUF models can be used with backends such as llama-cpp-python and frameworks like Lang-Chain. This is useful if you want to integrate a quantized model into a broader system. You can also directly chat with the model using frontends, like llama.cpp's lightweight server, LM Studio, and the Text Generation Web UI. These tools enable easy interaction with the GGUF models, providing an experience similar to ChatGPT.

Quantization with GPTQ and EXL2

While GGUF and llama.cpp offer CPU inference with GPU offloading, GPTQ and EXL2 are two quantization formats dedicated to GPUs. This makes them both faster than llama.cpp during inference. In particular, EXL2 offers the highest throughput with its dedicated library, ExLlamaV2.

GPTQ and EXL2 quants are based on the GPTQ algorithm, introduced by Frantar et al. (2023). It optimizes weight quantization for LLMs by refining **the Optimal Brain Quantization (OBQ)** approach to handle extensive matrices efficiently. It begins with a Cholesky decomposition of the Hessian inverse, ensuring numerical stability. Instead of quantizing weights in a strict order, GPTQ processes them in batches, updating columns and associated blocks iteratively. This method leverages lazy batch updates, reducing computational redundancy and memory bottlenecks.

While GPTQ is limited to 4-bit precision, EXL2 offers more flexibility with a highly customizable precision that can mix different quantization levels. This allows for precise bitrates between 2 and 8 bits per weight, such as 2.3, 3.5, or 6.0. It can also apply multiple quantization levels to each linear layer, prioritizing more important weights with higher bit quantization. Parameters are selected automatically, by quantizing each matrix multiple times and choosing a combination that minimizes the quantization error while meeting a target bitrate. In practice, this allows 70B models to run on a single 24 GB GPU with 2.55-bit precision.

The inference itself is handled by the ExLlamaV2 library, which supports both the GPTQ and EXL2 models.

In the following example, let's quantize a model in the EXL2 format using ExLlamaV2. These steps can be executed on a free T4 GPU in Google Colab:

1. Install the ExLlamaV2 library from source:

```
!git clone https://github.com/turboderp/exllamav2
!pip install -e exllamav2
```

2. We download the model to quantize by cloning its repo from the Hugging Face Hub:

```
MODEL_ID = "meta-llama/Llama-2-7b-chat-hf"
MODEL_NAME = MODEL_ID.split('/')[-1]
!git lfs install
!git clone https://huggingface.co/{MODEL_ID}
```

3. Download the calibration dataset used to measure the quantization error. In this case, we will use WikiText-103, a standard calibration dataset with high-quality articles from Wikipedia:

```
!wget https://huggingface.co/datasets/wikitext/
resolve/9a9e482b5987f9d25b3a9b2883fc6cc9fd8071b3/wikitext-103-v1/
wikitext-test.parquet
```

4. Quantize the model at a given precision (for example, 4.5):

```
!mkdir quant
!python exllamav2/convert.py \
    -i {MODEL_NAME} \
    -o quant \
    -c wikitext-test.parquet \
    -b 4.5
```

The quantized model can then be uploaded to the Hugging Face Hub, as seen previously.

GPTQ and EXL2 quants are not as widely supported as GGUF. For example, frontends like LM Studio do not currently integrate them. You can use other tools instead, like oobabooga's Text Generation Web UI. It is also directly integrated into the transformers library and supported by TGI. GPTQ models are also supported in TensorRT-LLM.

While less popular than GGUF, you can find a lot of GPTQ and EXL2 models on the Hugging Face Hub.

Other quantization techniques

There is a variety of quantization techniques beyond GGUF, GPTQ, and EXL2. This subsection will briefly introduce **Activate-aware Weight Quantization (AWQ)** as well as extreme quantization techniques, like QuIP# (Quantization with Incoherence Processing) and HQQ (Half-Quadratic Quantization).

Introduced by Lin et al. (2023), AWQ is another popular quantization algorithm. It identifies and protects the most important weights, which are determined based on activation magnitude instead of weight magnitude. This approach involves applying optimal per-channel scaling to these salient weights, without relying on backpropagation or reconstruction, ensuring that the LLM does not overfit the calibration set. While it relies on a different paradigm, AWQ is quite close to the GPTQ and EXL2 versions, although slightly slower. They are well-supported by inference engines and integrated into TGI, vLLM, and TensorRT-LLM.

An interesting trend is the quantization of models into 1- or 2-bit precision. While some formats, like EXL2, allow extreme quantization, the quality of the models often suffers significantly. However, recent algorithms like QuIP# and HQQ have targeted this regime and offer quantization methods that better preserve the performance of the original models. This is particularly true for large models (over 30B parameters), which can end up taking less space than 7B or 13B parameter models while providing higher-quality outputs.

This trend is expected to continue, further optimizing these quantization methods.

To conclude this chapter, here is a table summarizing the features of the three main inference engines we covered in the previous sections:

Technique	TGI	vLLM	TensorRT-LLM
Continuous batching	✓	✓	✓
Speculative decoding	✓		
FlashAttention2	✓	✓	✓
PagedAttention	✓	✓	✓
Pipeline parallelism			✓
Tensor parallelism	✓	✓	✓
GPTQ	✓		✓
EXL2	✓		
AWQ	✓	✓	✓

Table 8.1 – Summary of features for TGI, vLLM, and TensorRT-LLM

Summary

In summary, inference optimization is a critical aspect of deploying LLMs effectively. This chapter explored various optimization techniques, including optimized generation methods, model parallelism, and weight quantization. Significant speedups can be achieved by leveraging techniques like predicting multiple tokens in parallel with speculative decoding, or using an optimized attention mechanism with FlashAttention-2. Additionally, we discussed how model parallelism methods, including data, pipeline, and tensor parallelism, distribute the computational load across multiple GPUs to increase throughput and reduce latency. Weight quantization, with formats like GGUF and EXL2, further reduces the memory footprint and accelerates inference, with some calculated tradeoff in output quality.

Understanding and applying these optimization strategies are essential for achieving high performance in practical applications of LLMs, such as chatbots and code completion. The choice of techniques and tools depends on specific requirements, including available hardware, desired latency, and throughput. By combining various approaches, such as continuous batching and speculative decoding, along with advanced attention mechanisms and model parallelism, users can tailor their deployment strategies to maximize efficiency.

Way back in *Chapter 4*, we focused only on implementing the ingestion pipeline, which is just one component of a standard RAG application. In the next chapter, we will conclude the RAG system by implementing the retrieval and generation components and integrating them into the inference pipeline.

References

- Hugging Face, Text Generation Inference, `https://github.com/huggingface/text-generation-inference`, 2022.

- *W. Kwon, Z. Li, S. Zhuang, Y. Sheng, L. Zheng, C.H. Yu, J.E. Gonzalez, H. Zhang, I. Stoica, Efficient Memory Management for Large Language Model Serving with PagedAttention, 2023.*

- Nvidia, *TensorRT-LLM,* `https://github.com/NVIDIA/TensorRT-LLM`, 2023.

- *Y. Leviathan, M. Kalman, Y. Matias, Fast Inference from Transformers via Speculative Decoding, 2023.*

- *T. Cai, Y. Li, Z. Geng, H. Peng, J.D. Lee, D. Chen, T. Dao, Medusa: Simple LLM Inference Acceleration Framework with Multiple Decoding Heads, 2024.*

- *W. Kwon, Z. Li, S. Zhuang, Y. Sheng, L. Zheng, C.H. Yu, J.E. Gonzalez, H. Zhang, I. Stoica, Efficient Memory Management for Large Language Model Serving with PagedAttention, 2023.*

- *R.Y. Aminabadi, S. Rajbhandari, M. Zhang, A.A. Awan, C. Li, D. Li, E. Zheng, J. Rasley, S. Smith, O. Ruwase, Y. He, DeepSpeed Inference: Enabling Efficient Inference of Transformer Models at Unprecedented Scale, 2022.*

- *Y. Huang, Y. Cheng, A. Bapna, O. Firat, M.X. Chen, D. Chen, H. Lee, J. Ngiam, Q.V. Le, Y. Wu, Z. Chen, GPipe: Efficient Training of Giant Neural Networks using Pipeline Parallelism, 2019.*

- *K. James Reed, PiPPy: Pipeline Parallelism for PyTorch,* `https://github.com/pytorch/PiPPy`, 2022.

- *M. Shoeybi, M. Patwary, R. Puri, P. LeGresley, J. Casper, B. Catanzaro, Megatron-LM: Training Multi-Billion Parameter Language Models Using Model Parallelism, 2020.*

- *Verma and Vaidya, Mastering LLM Techniques: Inference Optimization, NVIDIA Developer Technical Blog,* `https://developer.nvidia.com/blog/mastering-llm-techniques-inference-optimization/`, *2023.*

- *T. Dettmers, M. Lewis, Y. Belkada, L. Zettlemoyer, LLM.int8(): 8-bit Matrix Multiplication for Transformers at Scale, 2022.*

- *G. Gerganov, llama.cpp,* `https://github.com/ggerganov/llama.cpp`*, 2023.*

- *E. Frantar, S. Ashkboos, T. Hoefler, D. Alistarh, GPTQ: Accurate Post-Training Quantization for Generative Pre-trained Transformers, 2023.*

- *Tuboderp, exllamav2,* `https://github.com/turboderp/exllamav2`*, 2023.*

- *J. Lin, J. Tang, H. Tang, S. Yang, W.-M. Chen, W.-C. Wang, G. Xiao, X. Dang, C. Gan, S. Han, AWQ: Activation-aware Weight Quantization for LLM Compression and Acceleration, 2024.*

Join our book's Discord space

Join our community's Discord space for discussions with the authors and other readers:

`https://packt.link/llmeng`

RAG Inference Pipeline

Back in *Chapter 4*, we implemented the **retrieval-augmented generation** (**RAG**) feature pipeline to populate the vector **database** (**DB**). Within the feature pipeline, we gathered data from the data warehouse, cleaned, chunked, and embedded the documents, and, ultimately, loaded them to the vector DB. Thus, at this point, the vector DB is filled with documents and ready to be used for RAG.

Based on the RAG methodology, you can split your software architecture into three modules: one for retrieval, one to augment the prompt, and one to generate the answer. We will follow a similar pattern by implementing a retrieval module to query the vector DB. Within this module, we will implement advanced RAG techniques to optimize the search. Afterward, we won't dedicate a whole module to augmenting the prompt, as that would be overengineering, which we try to avoid. However, we will write an inference service that inputs the user query and context, builds the prompt, and calls the LLM to generate the answer. To summarize, we will implement two core Python modules, one for retrieval and one for calling the LLM using the user's input and context as input. When we glue these together, we will have an end-to-end RAG flow.

In *Chapters 5* and *6*, we fine-tuned our LLM Twin model, and in *Chapter 8*, we learned how to optimize it for inference. Thus, at this point, the LLM is ready for production. What is left is to build and deploy the two modules described above.

We will dedicate the next chapter entirely to deploying our fine-tuned LLM Twin model to AWS SageMaker, as an AWS SageMaker inference endpoint. Thus, the focus of this chapter is to dig into the advanced RAG retrieval module implementation. We have dedicated a whole chapter to the retrieval step because this is where the magic happens in an RAG system. At the retrieval step (and not when calling the LLM), you write most of the RAG inference code. This step is where you have to wrangle your data to ensure that you retrieve the most relevant data points from the vector DB. Hence, most of the advanced RAG logic goes within the retrieval step.

To sum up, in this chapter, we will cover the following topics:

- Understanding the LLM Twin's RAG inference pipeline
- Exploring the LLM Twin's advanced RAG techniques
- Implementing the LLM Twin's RAG inference pipeline

By the end of this chapter, you will know how to implement an advanced RAG retrieval module, augment a prompt using the retrieved context, and call an LLM to generate the final answer. Ultimately, you will know how to build a production-ready RAG inference pipeline end to end.

Understanding the LLM Twin's RAG inference pipeline

Before implementing the RAG inference pipeline, we want to discuss its software architecture and advanced RAG techniques. *Figure 9.1* illustrates an overview of the RAG inference flow. The inference pipeline starts with the input query, retrieves the context using the retrieval module (based on the query), and calls the LLM SageMaker service to generate the final answer.

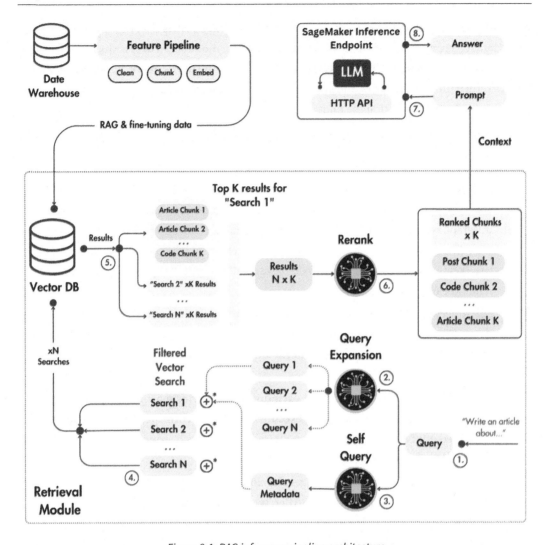

Figure 9.1: RAG inference pipeline architecture

The feature pipeline and the retrieval module, defined in *Figure 9.1*, are independent processes. The feature pipeline runs on a different machine on a schedule to populate the vector DB. At the same time, the retrieval module is called on demand, within the inference pipeline, on every user request.

By separating concerns between the two components, the vector DB is always populated with the latest data, ensuring feature freshness, while the retrieval module can access the latest features on every request. The input of the RAG retrieval module is the user's query, based on which we have to return the most relevant and similar data points from the vector DB, which will be used to guide the LLM in generating the final answer.

To fully understand the dynamics of the RAG inference pipeline, let's go through the architecture flow from *Figure 9.1* step by step:

1. **User query**: We begin with the user who makes a query, such as "Write an article about..."

2. **Query expansion**: We expand the initial query to generate multiple queries that reflect different aspects or interpretations of the original user query. Thus, instead of one query, we will use xN queries. By diversifying the search terms, the retrieval module increases the likelihood of capturing a comprehensive set of relevant data points. This step is crucial when the original query is too narrow or vague.

3. **Self-querying**: We extract useful metadata from the original query, such as the author's name. The extracted metadata will be used as filters for the vector search operation, eliminating redundant data points from the query vector space (making the search more accurate and faster).

4. **Filtered vector search**: We embed each query and perform a similarity search to find each search's top K data points. We execute xN searches corresponding to the number of expanded queries. We call this step a filtered vector search as we leverage the metadata extracted from the self-query step as query filters.

5. **Collecting results**: We get up to xK results closest to its specific expanded query interpretation for each search operation. Further, we aggregate the results of all the xN searches, ending up with a list of $N \times K$ results containing a mix of articles, posts, and repositories chunks. The results include a broader set of potentially relevant chunks, offering multiple relevant angles based on the original query's different facets.

6. **Reranking**: To keep only the top K most relevant results from the list of $N \times K$ potential items, we must filter the list further. We will use a reranking algorithm that scores each chunk based on the relevance and importance relative to the initial user query. We will leverage a neural cross-encoder model to compute the score, a value between 0 and 1, where 1 means the result is entirely relevant to the query. Ultimately, we sort the $N \times K$ results based on the score and pick the top K items. Thus, the output is a ranked list of K chunks, with the most relevant data points situated at the top.

7. **Build the prompt and call the LLM**: We map the final list of the most relevant K chunks to a string used to build the final prompt. We create the prompt using a prompt template, the retrieved context, and the user's query. Ultimately, the augmented prompt is sent to the LLM (hosted on AWS SageMaker exposed as an API endpoint).

8. **Answer**: We are waiting for the answer to be generated. After the LLM processes the prompt, the RAG logic finishes by sending the generated response to the user.

That wraps up the overview of the RAG inference pipeline. Now, let's dig deeper into the details.

Exploring the LLM Twin's advanced RAG techniques

Now that we understand the overall flow of our RAG inference pipeline, let's explore the advanced RAG techniques we used in our retrieval module:

- **Pre-retrieval step**: Query expansion and self-querying
- **Retrieval step**: Filtered vector search
- **Post-retrieval step**: Reranking

Before digging into each method individually, let's lay down the Python interfaces we will use in this section, which are available at `https://github.com/PacktPublishing/LLM-Engineers-Handbook/blob/main/llm_engineering/application/rag/base.py`.

The first is a prompt template factory that standardizes how we instantiate prompt templates. As an interface, it inherits from `ABC` and exposes the `create_template()` method, which returns a LangChain `PromptTemplate` instance. Even if we avoid being heavily reliant on LangChain, as we want to implement everything ourselves to understand the engineering behind the scenes, some objects, such as the `PromptTemplate` class, are helpful to speed up the development without hiding too much functionality:

```
from abc import ABC, abstractmethod

from langchain.prompts import PromptTemplate
from pydantic import BaseModel



class PromptTemplateFactory(ABC, BaseModel):
```

```
@abstractmethod
def create_template(self) -> PromptTemplate:
    pass
```

We also want to define a `RAGStep` interface used to standardize the interface of advanced RAG steps such as query expansion and self-querying. As these steps are often dependent on other LLMs, it has a mock attribute to reduce costs and debugging time during development:

```
from typing import Any


from llm_engineering.domain.queries import Query



class RAGStep(ABC):
    def __init__(self, mock: bool = False) -> None:
        self._mock = mock

    @abstractmethod
    def generate(self, query: Query, *args, **kwargs) -> Any:
        pass
```

Ultimately, we must understand how we modeled the `Query` domain entity to wrap the user's input with other metadata required for advanced RAG. Thus, let's look at its implementation. First, we import the necessary classes:

```
from pydantic import UUID4, Field


from llm_engineering.domain.base import VectorBaseDocument
from llm_engineering.domain.types import DataCategory
```

Next, we define the `Query` entity class, which inherits from the `VectorBaseDocument` **object-vector mapping (OVM)** class, discussed in *Chapter 4*. Thus, each query can easily be saved or retrieved from the vector DB:

```
class Query(VectorBaseDocument):
    content: str
    author_id: UUID4 | None = None
    author_full_name: str | None = None
    metadata: dict = Field(default_factory=dict)
```

```
class Config:
        category = DataCategory.QUERIES
```

What is essential to notice are the class's attributes used to combine the user's query with a bunch of metadata fields:

- content: A string containing input query.
- author_id: An optional UUID4 identifier extracted from the query used as a filter within the vector search operation to retrieve chunks written only by a specific author
- author_full_name: An optional string used to query the author_id
- metadata: A dictionary for any additional metadata, initialized as an empty dict by default

Besides the standard definition of a domain class, we also define a from_str() class method to create a Query instance directly from a string. This allows us to standardize how we clean the query string before constructing the query object, such as stripping any leading or trailing whitespace and newline characters:

```
@classmethod
def from_str(cls, query: str) -> "Query":
    return Query(content=query.strip("\n "))
```

Additionally, there's an instance method called replace_content() used to create a new Query instance with updated content while retaining the original query's id, author_id, author_full_name, and metadata:

```
def replace_content(self, new_content: str) -> "Query":
    return Query(
        id=self.id,
        content=new_content,
        author_id=self.author_id,
        author_full_name=self.author_full_name,
        metadata=self.metadata,
    )
```

This can be particularly useful when modifying the query text, for example, during preprocessing or normalization, without losing the associated metadata or identifiers. Following the Query class, we define the EmbeddedQuery class:

```
class EmbeddedQuery(Query):
```

```
        embedding: list[float]

    class Config:
        category = DataCategory.QUERIES
```

The EmbeddedQuery class extends Query by adding the embedding field. The EmbeddedQuery entity encapsulates all the data and metadata necessary to perform vector search operations on top of Qdrant (or another vector DB).

Now that we understand all the interfaces and new domain entities used within the RAG inference pipeline, let's move on to our advanced RAG pre-retrieval optimization techniques.

Advanced RAG pre-retrieval optimizations: query expansion and self-querying

We implemented two methods to optimize the pre-retrieval optimization step: query expansion and self-querying. The two methods work closely with the filtered vector search step, which we will touch on in the next section. For now, however, we will start with understanding the code for query expansion and move to implementing self-querying.

Within these two methods, we will leverage OpenAI's API to generate variations of the original query within the query expansion step and to extract the necessary metadata within the self-querying algorithm. When we wrote this book, we used GPT-4o-mini in all our examples, but as OpenAI's models quickly evolve, the model might get deprecated. But that's not an issue, as you can quickly change it in your .env file by configuring the OPENAI_MODEL_ID environment variable.

Query expansion

The *problem* in a typical retrieval step is that you query your vector DB using a single vector representation of your original question. This approach covers only a small area of the embedding space, which can be limiting. If the embedding doesn't contain all the required information or nuances of your query, the retrieved context may not be relevant. This means essential documents that are semantically related but not near the query vector might be overlooked.

The *solution* is based on query expansion, which offers a way to overcome this limitation. Using an LLM to generate multiple queries based on your initial question, you create various perspectives that capture different facets of your query. These expanded queries, when embedded, target other areas of the embedding space that are still relevant to your original question. This increases the likelihood of retrieving more relevant documents from the vector DB.

Implementing query expansion can be as straightforward as crafting a detailed zero-shot prompt to guide the LLM in generating these alternative queries. Thus, after implementing query expansion, instead of having only one query to search relevant context, you will have xN queries, hence xN searches.

Increasing the number of searches can impact your latency. Thus, you must experiment with the number of queries you generate to ensure the retrieval step meets your application requirements. You can also optimize the searches by parallelizing them, drastically reducing the latency, which we will do in the `ContextRetriever` class implemented at the end of this chapter.

> Query expansion is also known as multi-query, but the principles are the same. For example, this is an example of LangChain's implementation called `MultiQueryRetriver`: `https://python.langchain.com/docs/how_to/MultiQueryRetriever/`

Now, let's dig into the code. We begin by importing the necessary modules and classes required for query expansion:

```python
from langchain_openai import ChatOpenAI

from llm_engineering.domain.queries import Query
from llm_engineering.settings import settings

from .base import RAGStep
from .prompt_templates import QueryExpansionTemplate
```

Next, we define the `QueryExpansion` class, which generates expanded query versions. The class implementation can be found at `https://github.com/PacktPublishing/LLM-Engineers-Handbook/blob/main/llm_engineering/application/rag/query_expanison.py`:

```python
class QueryExpansion(RAGStep):
    def generate(self, query: Query, expand_to_n: int) -> list[Query]:
        assert expand_to_n > 0, f"'expand_to_n' should be greater than 0.
Got {expand_to_n}."

        if self._mock:
            return [query for _ in range(expand_to_n)]
```

In the generate method, we first ensure that the number of expansions requested (expand_to_n) is greater than zero. If the instance is in mock mode (self._mock is True), it simply returns a list containing copies of the original query to simulate expansion without actually calling the API. If not in mock mode, we proceed to create the prompt and initialize the language model:

```
query_expansion_template = QueryExpansionTemplate()
prompt = query_expansion_template.create_template(expand_to_n - 1)
model = ChatOpenAI(model=settings.OPENAI_MODEL_ID, api_
key=settings.OPENAI_API_KEY, temperature=0)
```

Here, we instantiate QueryExpansionTemplate and create a prompt tailored to generate expand_to_n - 1 new queries (excluding the original). We initialize the ChatOpenAI model with the specified settings and set the temperature to 0 for deterministic output. We then create a LangChain chain by combining the prompt with the model and invoke it with the user's question:

```
chain = prompt | model


response = chain.invoke({"question": query})
result = response.content
```

By piping the prompt into the model (prompt | model), we set up a chain that generates expanded queries when invoked with the original query. The response from the model is captured in the result object. After receiving the response, we parse and clean the expanded queries:

```
queries_content = result.strip().split(query_expansion_template.
separator)


queries = [query]
queries += [
    query.replace_content(stripped_content)
    for content in queries_content
    if (stripped_content := content.strip())
]


return queries
```

We split the result using the separator defined in the template to get individual queries. Starting with a list containing the original query, we append each expanded query after stripping any extra whitespace.

Finally, we define the `QueryExpansionTemplate` class, which constructs the prompt used for query expansion. The class and other prompt templates can be accessed at https://github.com/PacktPublishing/LLM-Engineers-Handbook/blob/main/llm_engineering/application/rag/prompt_templates.py:

```python
from langchain.prompts import PromptTemplate


from .base import PromptTemplateFactory



class QueryExpansionTemplate(PromptTemplateFactory):
    prompt: str = """You are an AI language model assistant. Your task is
to generate {expand_to_n}
    different versions of the given user question to retrieve relevant
documents from a vector
    database. By generating multiple perspectives on the user question,
your goal is to help
    the user overcome some of the limitations of the distance-based
similarity search.
    Provide these alternative questions separated by '{separator}'.
    Original question: {question}"""

    @property
    def separator(self) -> str:
        return "#next-question#"

    def create_template(self, expand_to_n: int) -> PromptTemplate:
        return PromptTemplate(
            template=self.prompt,
            input_variables=["question"],
            partial_variables={
                "separator": self.separator,
                "expand_to_n": expand_to_n,
            },
        )
```

This class defines a prompt instructing the language model to generate multiple versions of the user's question. It uses placeholders like {expand_to_n}, {separator}, and {question} to customize the prompt.

It takes expand_to_n as an input parameter to define how many queries we wish to generate while we build the `PromptTemplate` instance. The separator property provides a unique string to split the generated queries. The expand_to_n and separator variables are passed as partial_variables, making them immutable at runtime. Meanwhile, the {question} placeholder will be changed every time the LLM chain is called.

Now that we have finished studying the query expansion implementation, let's look at an example of how to use the `QueryExpansion` class. Let's run the following code using this python -m llm_engineering.application.rag.query_expansion command:

```
query = Query.from_str("Write an article about the best types of advanced
RAG methods.")
    query_expander = QueryExpansion()
    expanded_queries = query_expander.generate(query, expand_to_n=3)
    for expanded_query in expanded_queries:
        logger.info(expanded_query.content)
```

We get the following variations of the original query. As you can observe, the query expansion method was successful in providing more details and different perspectives of the initial query, such as highlighting the effectiveness of advanced RAG methods or the overview of these methods (remember that the first query is the original one):

```
2024-09-18 17:51:33.529 | INFO  - Write an article about the best types of
advanced RAG methods.
2024-09-18 17:51:33.529 | INFO  - What are the most effective advanced RAG
methods, and how can they be applied?
2024-09-18 17:51:33.529 | INFO  - Can you provide an overview of the top
advanced retrieval-augmented generation techniques?
```

Now, let's move to the next pre-retrieval optimization method: self-querying.

Self-querying

The *problem* when embedding your query into a vector space is that you cannot guarantee that all the aspects required by your use case are present with enough signal in the embedding vector. For example, you want to be 100% sure that your retrieval depends on the tags provided in the user's input. Unfortunately, you can't control the signal left within the embedding that emphasizes the tag. By embedding the query prompt alone, you can never be sure that the tags are sufficiently represented in the embedding vector or have enough signal when computing the distance against other vectors.

This problem stands for any other metadata you want to present during the search, such as IDs, names, or categories.

The *solution* is to use self-querying to extract the tags or other critical metadata within the query and use them alongside the vector search as filters. Self-querying uses an LLM to extract various metadata fields crucial for your business use case, such as tags, IDs, number of comments, likes, shares, etc. Afterward, you have complete control over how the extracted metadata is considered during retrieval. In our LLM Twin use case, we extract the author's name and use it as a filter. Self-queries work hand-in-hand with filtered vector searches, which we will explain in the next section.

Now, let's move on to the code. We begin by importing the necessary modules and classes on which our code relies:

```
from langchain_openai import ChatOpenAI

from llm_engineering.application import utils
from llm_engineering.domain.documents import UserDocument
from llm_engineering.domain.queries import Query
from llm_engineering.settings import settings

from .base import RAGStep
from .prompt_templates import SelfQueryTemplate
```

Next, we define the SelfQuery class, which inherits from RAGStep and implements the generate() method. The class can be found at https://github.com/PacktPublishing/LLM-Engineers-Handbook/blob/main/llm_engineering/application/rag/self_query.py:

```
class SelfQuery(RAGStep):
    def generate(self, query: Query) -> Query:
        if self._mock:
            return query
```

In the generate() method, we check if the _mock attribute is set to True. If it is, we will return the original query object unmodified. This allows us to bypass calling the model while testing and debugging. If not in mock mode, we create the prompt template and initialize the language model.

```
        prompt = SelfQueryTemplate().create_template()
        model = ChatOpenAI(model=settings.OPENAI_MODEL_ID, api_
key=settings.OPENAI_API_KEY, temperature=0)
```

Here, we instantiate the prompt using the SelfQueryTemplate factory class and create a ChatOpenAI model instance (similar to the query expansion implementation). We then combine the prompt and the model into a chain and invoke it with the user's query.

```
chain = prompt | model

response = chain.invoke({"question": query})
user_full_name = response.content.strip("\n ")
```

We extract the content from the LLM response and strip any leading or trailing whitespace to obtain the user_full_name value. Next, we check if the model was able to extract any user information.

```
if user_full_name == "none":
    return query
```

If the response is "none", it means no user name was found in the query, so we return the original query object. If a user name is found, we will split the user_full_name into the first_name and last_name variables using a utility function. Then, based on the user's details, we retrieve or create a UserDocument user instance:

```
first_name, last_name = utils.split_user_full_name(user_full_name)
user = UserDocument.get_or_create(first_name=first_name, last_
name=last_name)
```

Finally, we update the query object with the extracted author information and return it:

```
query.author_id = user.id
query.author_full_name = user.full_name

return query
```

The updated query now contains the author_id and author_full_name values, which can be used in subsequent steps of the RAG pipeline.

Let's look at the SelfQueryTemplate class, which defines the prompt to extract user information:

```
from langchain.prompts import PromptTemplate

from .base import PromptTemplateFactory
```

```
class SelfQueryTemplate(PromptTemplateFactory):
    prompt: str = """You are an AI language model assistant. Your task is
to extract information from a user question.
    The required information that needs to be extracted is the user name
or user id.
    Your response should consist of only the extracted user name (e.g.,
John Doe) or id (e.g. 1345256), nothing else.
    If the user question does not contain any user name or id, you should
return the following token: none.

    For example:
    QUESTION 1:
    My name is Paul Iusztin and I want a post about...
    RESPONSE 1:
    Paul Iusztin

    QUESTION 2:
    I want to write a post about...
    RESPONSE 2:
    none

    QUESTION 3:
    My user id is 1345256 and I want to write a post about...
    RESPONSE 3:
    1345256

    User question: {question}"""

    def create_template(self) -> PromptTemplate:
        return PromptTemplate(template=self.prompt, input_
variables=["question"])
```

In the SelfQueryTemplate class, we define a prompt instructing the AI model to extract the *user name* or *ID* from the input question. The prompt uses few-shot learning to guide the model on how to respond in different scenarios. When the template is invoked, the {question} placeholder will be replaced with the actual user question.

By implementing self-querying, we ensure that critical metadata required for our use case is explicitly extracted and used during retrieval. This approach overcomes the limitations of relying solely on the semantics of the embeddings to capture all necessary aspects of a query.

Now that we've implemented the `SelfQuery` class, let's provide an example. Run the following code using the `python -m llm_engineering.application.rag.self_query` CLI command:

```
query = Query.from_str("I am Paul Iusztin. Write an article about the
best types of advanced RAG methods.")
self_query = SelfQuery()
query = self_query.generate(query)
logger.info(f"Extracted author_id: {query.author_id}")
logger.info(f"Extracted author_full_name: {query.author_full_name}")
```

We get the following results where the author's full name and ID were extracted correctly:

```
2024-09-18 18:02:10.362 | INFO - Extracted author_id: 900fec95-d621-4315-
84c6-52e5229e0b96
2024-09-18 18:02:10.362 | INFO - Extracted author_full_name: Paul Iusztin
```

Now that we understand how self-querying works, let's explore how it can be used together with filtered vector search within the retrieval optimization step.

Advanced RAG retrieval optimization: filtered vector search

Vector search is pivotal in retrieving relevant information based on semantic similarity. A plain vector search, however, can introduce significant challenges that affect both the accuracy and latency of information retrieval. This is primarily because it operates solely on the numerical proximity of vector embeddings without considering the contextual or categorical nuances that might be crucial for relevance.

One of the primary issues with plain vector search is retrieving semantically similar but contextually irrelevant documents. Since vector embeddings capture general semantic meanings, they might assign high similarity scores to content that shares language patterns or topics but doesn't align with the specific intent or constraints of the query. For instance, searching for "Java" could retrieve documents about the programming language or the Indonesian island, depending solely on semantic similarity, leading to ambiguous or misleading results.

Moreover, as the size of the dataset increases, plain vector search can suffer from scalability issues. The lack of filtering means the search algorithm has to compute similarities across the entire vector space, which can significantly increase latency.

This exhaustive search slows response times and consumes more computational resources, making it inefficient for real-time or large-scale applications.

Filtered vector search emerges as a solution by filtering after additional criteria, such as metadata tags or categories, reducing the search space before computing vector similarities. By applying these filters, the search algorithm narrows the pool of potential results to those contextually aligned with the query's intent. This targeted approach enhances accuracy by eliminating irrelevant documents that might have otherwise been considered due to their semantic similarities alone.

Additionally, filtered vector search improves latency by reducing the number of comparisons the algorithm needs to perform. Working with a smaller, more relevant subset of data decreases the computational overhead, leading to faster response times. This efficiency is crucial for applications requiring real-time interactions or handling large queries.

As the metadata used within the filtered vector search is often part of the user's input, we have to extract it before querying the vector DB. That's precisely what we did during the self-query step, where we extracted the author's name to reduce the vector space only to the author's content. Thus, as we processed the query within the self-query step, it went into the pre-retrieval optimization category, whereas when the filtered vector search optimized the query, it went into the retrieval optimization bin.

For example, when using Qdrant, to add a filter that looks for a matching `author_id` within the metadata of each document, you must implement the following code:

```python
from qdrant_client.models import FieldCondition, Filter, MatchValue

records = qdrant_connection.search(
        collection_name="articles",
        query_vector=query_embedding,
        limit=3,
        with_payload=True,
        query_filter= Filter(
            must=[
                FieldCondition(
                    key="author_id",
                    match=MatchValue(
                        value=str("1234"),
                    ),
```

```
                    )
                ]
            ),
        )
```

In essence, while plain vector search provides a foundation for semantic retrieval, its limitations can slow performance in practical applications. Filtered vector search addresses these challenges by combining the strengths of vector embeddings with contextual filtering, resulting in more accurate and efficient information retrieval in RAG systems. The last step for optimizing our RAG pipeline is to look into reranking.

Advanced RAG post-retrieval optimization: reranking

The *problem* in RAG systems is that the retrieved context may contain irrelevant chunks that only:

- **Add noise:** The retrieved context might be irrelevant, cluttering the information and potentially confusing the language model.

- **Make the prompt bigger**: Including unnecessary chunks increases the prompt size, leading to higher costs. Moreover, language models are usually biased toward the context's first and last pieces. So, if you add a large amount of context, there's a big chance it will miss the essence.

- **Be come unaligned with your question**: Chunks are retrieved based on the similarity between the query and chunk embeddings. The issue is that the embedding model might not be tuned to your question, resulting in high similarity scores for chunks that aren't entirely relevant.

The *solution* is to use reranking to order all the N × K retrieved chunks based on their relevance relative to the initial question, where the first chunk will be the most relevant and the last the least. N represents the number of searches after query expansion, while K is the number of chunks retrieved per search. Hence, we retrieve a total of N x K chunks. In RAG systems, reranking serves as a critical post-retrieval step that refines the initial results obtained from the retrieval model.

We assess each chunk's relevance to the original query by applying the reranking algorithm, which often uses advanced models like neural cross-encoders. These models evaluate the semantic similarity between the query and each chunk more accurately than initial retrieval methods based on embeddings and the cosine similarity distance, as explained in more detail in *Chapter 4* in the *An overview of advanced RAG* section.

Ultimately, we pick the top K most relevant chunks from the sorted list of N x K items based on the reranking score. Reranking works well when combined with **query expansion**. First, let's understand how reranking works without query expansion:

1. **Search for > K chunks**: Retrieve more than K chunks to have a broader pool of potentially relevant information.

2. **Reorder using rerank**: Apply reranking to this larger set to evaluate the actual relevance of each chunk relative to the query.

3. **Take top K**: Select the top K chunks to use them as context in the final prompt.

Thus, when combined with query expansion, we gather potential valuable context from multiple points in space rather than just looking for more than K samples in a single location. Now the flow looks like this:

1. **Search for N × K chunks**: Retrieve multiple sets of chunks using the expanded queries.

2. **Reorder using rerank**: Rerank all the retrieved chunks based on their relevance.

3. **Take top K**: Select the most relevant chunks for the final prompt.

Integrating reranking into the RAG pipeline enhances the quality and relevance of the retrieved context and efficiently uses computational resources. Let's look at implementing the LLM Twin's reranking step to understand what we described above, which can be accessed on GitHub at `llm_engineering/application/rag/reranking.py`.

We begin by importing the necessary modules and classes for our reranking process:

```
from llm_engineering.application.networks import
CrossEncoderModelSingleton
from llm_engineering.domain.embedded_chunks import EmbeddedChunk
from llm_engineering.domain.queries import Query


from .base import RAGStep
```

Next, we define the `Reranker` class, which is responsible for reranking the retrieved documents based on their relevance to the query:

```
class Reranker(RAGStep):
    def __init__(self, mock: bool = False) -> None:
        super().__init__(mock=mock)

        self._model = CrossEncoderModelSingleton()
```

In the initializer of the Reranker class, we instantiate our cross-encoder model by creating an instance of `CrossEncoderModelSingleton`. This is the cross-encoder model used to score the relevance of each document chunk with respect to the query.

The core functionality of the Reranker class is implemented in the generate() method:

```
    def generate(self, query: Query, chunks: list[EmbeddedChunk], keep_
top_k: int) -> list[EmbeddedChunk]:
        if self._mock:
            return chunks

        query_doc_tuples = [(query.content, chunk.content) for chunk in
chunks]
        scores = self._model(query_doc_tuples)

        scored_query_doc_tuples = list(zip(scores, chunks, strict=False))
        scored_query_doc_tuples.sort(key=lambda x: x[0], reverse=True)

        reranked_documents = scored_query_doc_tuples[:keep_top_k]
        reranked_documents = [doc for _, doc in reranked_documents]

        return reranked_documents
```

The generate() method takes a query, a list of chunks (document segments), and the number of top documents to keep (keep_top_k). If we're in mock mode, it simply returns the original chunks. Otherwise, it performs the following steps:

1. Creates pairs of the query content and each chunk's content
2. Uses the cross-encoder model to score each pair, assessing how well the chunk matches the query
3. Zips the scores with the corresponding chunks to create a scored list of tuples
4. Sorts this list in descending order based on the scores
5. Selects the top keep_top_k chunks
6. Extracts the chunks from the tuples and returns them as the reranked documents

Before defining the CrossEncoder class, we import the necessary components:

```
from sentence_transformers.cross_encoder import CrossEncoder

from .base import SingletonMeta
```

We import the CrossEncoder class from the sentence_transformers library, which provides the functionality for scoring text pairs. We also import SingletonMeta from our base module to ensure our model class follows the singleton pattern, meaning only one instance of the model exists throughout the application. Now, we define the CrossEncoderModelSingleton class:

```python
class CrossEncoderModelSingleton(metaclass=SingletonMeta):
    def __init__(
        self,
        model_id: str = settings.RERANKING_CROSS_ENCODER_MODEL_ID,
        device: str = settings.RAG_MODEL_DEVICE,
    ) -> None:
        """
        A singleton class that provides a pre-trained cross-encoder model
for scoring pairs of input text.
        """

        self._model_id = model_id
        self._device = device

        self._model = CrossEncoder(
            model_name=self._model_id,
            device=self._device,
        )
        self._model.model.eval()
```

This class initializes the cross-encoder model using the specified model_id and device from the global settings loaded from the .env file. We set the model to evaluation mode using self._model.model.eval() to ensure the model is ready for inference.

The CrossEncoderModelSingleton class includes a callable method to score text pairs:

```python
    def __call__(self, pairs: list[tuple[str, str]], to_list: bool = True)
 -> NDArray[np.float32] | list[float]:
        scores = self._model.predict(pairs)

        if to_list:
            scores = scores.tolist()

        return scores
```

The __call__ method allows us to pass in a list of text pairs (each consisting of the query and a document chunk) and receive their relevance scores. The method uses the model's predict() function to call the model and compute the scores.

The CrossEncoderModelSingleton class is a wrapper over the CrossEncoder class, which we wrote for two purposes. The first one is for the singleton pattern, which allows us to easily access the same instance of the cross-encoder model from anywhere within the application without loading the model in memory every time we need it. The second reason is that by writing our wrapper, we defined our interface for a cross-encoder model (or any other model used for reranking). This makes the code future-proof as in case we need a different implementation or strategy for reranking, for example, using an API, we only have to write a different wrapper that follows the same interface and swap the old class with the new one. Thus, we can introduce new reranking methods without touching the rest of the code.

We now understand all the advanced RAG techniques used within our architecture. In the next section, we will examine the ContextRetriever class that connects all these methods and explain how to use the retrieval module with an LLM for an end-to-end RAG inference pipeline.

Implementing the LLM Twin's RAG inference pipeline

As explained at the beginning of this chapter, the RAG inference pipeline can mainly be divided into three parts: the retrieval module, the prompt creation, and the answer generation, which boils down to calling an LLM with the augmented prompt. In this section, our primary focus will be implementing the retrieval module, where most of the code and logic go. Afterward, we will look at how to build the final prompt using the retrieved context and user query.

Ultimately, we will examine how to combine the retrieval module, prompt creation logic, and the LLM to capture an end-to-end RAG workflow. Unfortunately, we won't be able to test out the LLM until we finish *Chapter 10*, as we haven't deployed our fine-tuned LLM Twin module to AWS SageMaker.

Thus, by the end of this section, you will learn how to implement the RAG inference pipeline, which you can test out end to end only after finishing *Chapter 10*. Now, let's start by looking at the implementation of the retrieval module.

Implementing the retrieval module

Let's dive into the `ContextRetriever` class implementation, which orchestrates the retrieval step in our RAG system by integrating all the advanced techniques we previously used: query expansion, self-querying, reranking, and filtered vector search. The class can be found on GitHub at https://github.com/PacktPublishing/LLM-Engineers-Handbook/blob/main/llm_engineering/application/rag/retriever.py.

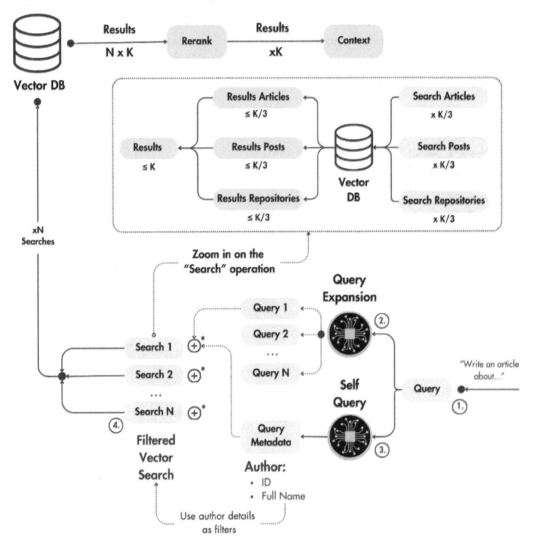

Figure 9.2: Search logic of the RAG retrieval module

The entry point function of the `ContextRetriever` class is the `search()` method, which calls all the advanced steps discussed in this chapter. *Figure 9.2* shows in more detail how the search method glues together all the steps required to search results similar to the user's query. It highlights how the extracted author details from the self-query step are used within the filtered vector search. Also, it zooms in on the search operation itself, where, for each query, we do three searches to the vector DB, looking for articles, posts, or repositories similar to the query. For each search (out of N searches), we want to retrieve a maximum of K results. Thus, we retrieve a maximum of K / 3 items for each data category (as we have three categories). Therefore, when summed up, we will have a list of ≤ K chunks. The retrieved list is ≤ K (and not equal to K) when a particular data category or more returns < K / 3 items after applying the author filters due to missing chunks for that specific author or data category.

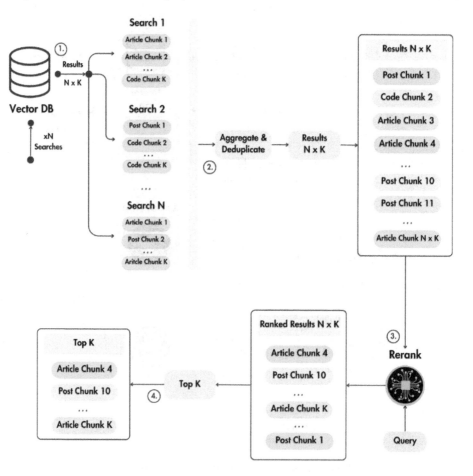

Figure 9.3: Processing the results flow of the RAG retrieval module

Figure 9.3 illustrates how we process the results returned by the xN searches. As each search returns ≤ K items, we will end up with ≤ N x K chunks that we aggregate into a single list. As some results might overlap between searchers, we must deduplicate the aggregated list to ensure each chunk is unique. Ultimately, we send the results to the rerank model, order them based on their reranking score, and pick the **most** relevant top **K** chunks we will use as context for RAG.

Let's understand how everything from *Figures 9.2* and *9.3* is implemented in the ContextRetriever class. First, we initialize the class by setting up instances of the QueryExpansion, SelfQuery, and Reranker classes:

```python
class ContextRetriever:
    def __init__(self, mock: bool = False) -> None:
        self._query_expander = QueryExpansion(mock=mock)
        self._metadata_extractor = SelfQuery(mock=mock)
        self._reranker = Reranker(mock=mock)
```

In the search() method, we convert the user's input string into a query object. We then use the SelfQuery instance to extract the author_id and author_full_name from the query:

```python
    def search(
        self,
        query: str,
        k: int = 3,
        expand_to_n_queries: int = 3,
    ) -> list:
        query_model = Query.from_str(query)

        query_model = self._metadata_extractor.generate(query_model)
        logger.info(
            "Successfully extracted the author_id from the query.",
            author_id=query_model.author_id,
        )
```

Next, we expand the query to generate multiple semantically similar queries using the QueryExpansion instance:

```python
        n_generated_queries = self._query_expander.generate(query_model,
    expand_to_n=expand_to_n_queries)
        logger.info(
            "Successfully generated queries for search.",
```

```
            num_queries=len(n_generated_queries),
    )
```

We then perform the search concurrently for all expanded queries using a thread pool. Each query is processed by the _search() method, which we'll explore shortly. The results are flattened, deduplicated, and collected into a single list:

```
        with concurrent.futures.ThreadPoolExecutor() as executor:
            search_tasks = [executor.submit(self._search, _query_model, k)
    for _query_model in n_generated_queries]

            n_k_documents = [task.result() for task in concurrent.futures.
    as_completed(search_tasks)]
            n_k_documents = utils.misc.flatten(n_k_documents)
            n_k_documents = list(set(n_k_documents))

        logger.info("All documents retrieved successfully.", num_
    documents=len(n_k_documents))
```

After retrieving the documents, we rerank them based on their relevance to the original query and keep only the top *k* documents:

```
        if len(n_k_documents) > 0:
            k_documents = self.rerank(query, chunks=n_k_documents, keep_
    top_k=k)
        else:
            k_documents = []

        return k_documents
```

The _search() method performs the filtered vector search across different data categories like posts, articles, and repositories. It uses the EmbeddingDispatcher to convert the query into an EmbeddedQuery, which includes the query's embedding vector and any extracted metadata:

```
    def _search(self, query: Query, k: int = 3) -> list[EmbeddedChunk]:
        assert k >= 3, "k should be >= 3"

        def _search_data_category(
            data_category_odm: type[EmbeddedChunk], embedded_query:
    EmbeddedQuery
        ) -> list[EmbeddedChunk]:
```

```
            if embedded_query.author_id:
                query_filter = Filter(
                    must=[
                        FieldCondition(
                            key="author_id",
                            match=MatchValue(
                                value=str(embedded_query.author_id),
                            ),
                        )
                    ]
                )
            else:
                query_filter = None

            return data_category_odm.search(
                query_vector=embedded_query.embedding,
                limit=k // 3,
                query_filter=query_filter,
            )

        embedded_query: EmbeddedQuery = EmbeddingDispatcher.
    dispatch(query)
```

We used the same `EmbeddingDispatcher` to embed the query as in the RAG feature pipeline to embed the document chunks stored in the vector DB. Using the same class ensures we use the same embedding model at ingestion and query time, which is critical for the retrieval step.

We search each data category separately by leveraging the local `_search_data_category()` function. Within the `_search_data_category()` function, we apply the filters extracted from the `embedded_query` object. For instance, if an `author_id` is present, we use it to filter the search results only to include documents from that author. The results from all categories are then combined:

```
        post_chunks = _search_data_category(EmbeddedPostChunk, embedded_
    query)
        articles_chunks = _search_data_category(EmbeddedArticleChunk,
    embedded_query)
        repositories_chunks = _search_data_
    category(EmbeddedRepositoryChunk, embedded_query)
```

```
        retrieved_chunks = post_chunks + articles_chunks + repositories_
chunks

        return retrieved_chunks
```

Finally, the `rerank()` method takes the original query and the list of retrieved documents to reorder them based on relevance:

```
    def rerank(self, query: str | Query, chunks: list[EmbeddedChunk],
keep_top_k: int) -> list[EmbeddedChunk]:
        if isinstance(query, str):
            query = Query.from_str(query)

        reranked_documents = self._reranker.generate(query=query,
chunks=chunks, keep_top_k=keep_top_k)

        logger.info("Documents reranked successfully.", num_
documents=len(reranked_documents))

        return reranked_documents
```

Leveraging the `ContextRetriever` class, we can retrieve context from any query with only a few lines of code. For example, let's take a look at the following code snippet, where we call the entire advanced RAG architecture with a simple call to the `search()` method:

```
from loguru import logger

from llm_engineering.application.rag.retriever import ContextRetriever


query = """
        My name is Paul Iusztin.

        Could you draft a LinkedIn post discussing RAG systems?
        I'm particularly interested in:
            - how RAG works
            - how it is integrated with vector DBs and large language
models (LLMs).
        """
```

```
retriever = ContextRetriever(mock=False)
documents = retriever.search(query, k=3)

logger.info("Retrieved documents:")
for rank, document in enumerate(documents):
    logger.info(f"{rank + 1}: {document}")
```

Calling the code from above using the following CLI command: poetry poe `call-rag-retrieval-module`. This outputs the following:

```
2024-09-18 19:01:50.588 | INFO - Retrieved documents:
2024-09-18 19:01:50.588 | INFO - 1: id=UUID('541d6c22-d15a-4e6a-924a-
68b7b1e0a330') content='4 Advanced RAG Algorithms You Must Know by
Paul Iusztin Implement 4 advanced RAG retrieval techniques to optimize
your vector DB searches. Integrate the RAG retrieval module into a
production LLM system…" platform='decodingml.substack.com' document_
id=UUID('32648f33-87e6-435c-b2d7-861a03e72392') author_id=UUID('900fec95-
d621-4315-84c6-52e5229e0b96') author_full_name='Paul Iusztin'
metadata={'embedding_model_id': 'sentence-transformers/all-MiniLM-L6-v2',
'embedding_size': 384, 'max_input_length': 256} link='https://decodingml.
substack.com/p/the-4-advanced-rag-algorithms-you?r=1ttoeh'
2024-09-18 19:01:50.588 | INFO - 2: id=UUID('5ce78438-1314-4874-8a5a-
04f5fcf0cb21') content='Overview of advanced RAG optimization techniquesA
production RAG system is split into 3 main components ingestion clean,
chunk, embed, and load your data to a vector DBretrieval query your vector
DB for …" platform='medium' document_id=UUID('bd9021c9-a693-46da-97e7-
0d06760ee6bf') author_id=UUID('900fec95-d621-4315-84c6-52e5229e0b96')
author_full_name='Paul Iusztin' metadata={'embedding_model_id': 'sentence-
transformers/all-MiniLM-L6-v2', 'embedding_size': 384, 'max_input_length':
256} link='https://medium.com/decodingml/the-4-advanced-rag-algorithms-
you-must-know-to-implement-5d0c7f1199d2'
2024-09-18 19:02:45.729 | INFO  - 3: id=UUID('0405a5da-4686-428a-91ca-
446b8e0446ff') content='Every Medium article will be its own lesson
An End to End Framework for Production Ready LLM Systems by Building
Your LLM TwinThe Importance of Data Pipelines in the Era of Generative
AIChange Data Capture Enabling Event Driven …" platform='medium' document_
id=UUID('bd9021c9-a693-46da-97e7-0d06760ee6bf') author_id=UUID('900fec95-
d621-4315-84c6-52e5229e0b96') author_full_name='Paul Iusztin'
metadata={'embedding_model_id': 'sentence-transformers/all-MiniLM-L6-v2',
'embedding_size': 384, 'max_input_length': 256} link='https://medium.
```

```
com/decodingml/the-4-advanced-rag-algorithms-you-must-know-to-implement-
5d0c7f1199d2'
```

As you can observe in the output above, along with the retrieved content, we have access to all kinds of metadata, such as the embedding model used for retrieval or the link from which the chunk was taken. These can quickly be added to a list of references when generating the result for the user, increasing trust in the final results.

Now that we understand how the retrieval module works, let's take a final step and examine the end-to-end RAG inference pipeline.

Bringing everything together into the RAG inference pipeline

To fully implement the RAG flow, we still have to build the prompt using the context from the retrieval model and call the LLM to generate the answer. This section will discuss these two steps and wrap everything together into a single rag() function. The functions from this section can be accessed on GitHub at https://github.com/PacktPublishing/LLM-Engineers-Handbook/blob/main/llm_engineering/infrastructure/inference_pipeline_api.py.

Let's start by looking at the call_llm_service()function, responsible for interfacing with the LLM service. It takes in a user's query and an optional context, sets up the language model endpoint, executes the inference, and returns the generated answer. The context is optional; you can call the LLM without it, as you would when interacting with any other LLM:

```
def call_llm_service(query: str, context: str | None) -> str:
    llm = LLMInferenceSagemakerEndpoint(
        endpoint_name=settings.SAGEMAKER_ENDPOINT_INFERENCE, inference_
component_name=None
    )
    answer = InferenceExecutor(llm, query, context).execute()

    return answer
```

This function makes an HTTP request to our fine-tuned LLM Twin model, which is hosted as an AWS SageMaker inference endpoint. We will explore all the SageMaker details in the next chapter, where we will dig into the LLMInferenceSagemakerEndpoint and InferenceExecutor classes. For now, what is essential to know is that we use this function to call our fine-tuned LLM. Still, we must highlight how the query and context, passed to the InferenceExecutor class, are transformed into the final prompt. We do that using a simple prompt template that is customized using the user query and retrieved context:

```
prompt = f"""
You are a content creator. Write what the user asked you to while using
the provided context as the primary source of information for the content.
User query: {query}
Context: {context}
        """
```

Moving on to the rag() function, this is where the RAG logic comes together. It handles retrieving relevant documents based on the query, mapping the documents to the context that will be injected into the prompt, and obtaining the final answer from the LLM:

```
def rag(query: str) -> str:
    retriever = ContextRetriever(mock=False)
    documents = retriever.search(query, k=3)
    context = EmbeddedChunk.to_context(documents)

    answer = call_llm_service(query, context)

    return answer
```

As we modularized all the RAG steps into independent classes, we reduced the high-level rag() function to five lines of code (encapsulating all the complexities of the system) similar to what we see in tools such as LangChain, LlamaIndex, or Haystack. Instead of their high-level implementation, we learned how to build an advanced RAG service from scratch. Also, by clearly separating the responsibility of each class, we can use them like LEGOs. Thus, you can quickly call the LLM independently without context or use the retrieval module as a query engine on top of your vector DB. In the next chapter, we will see the rag() function in action after we deploy our fine-tuned LLM to an AWS SageMaker inference endpoint.

Before ending this chapter, we want to discuss potential improvements you could add to the RAG inference pipeline. As we are building a chatbot, the first one is to add a conversation memory that stores all the user prompts and generated answers in memory. Thus, when interacting with the chatbot, it will be aware of the whole conversation, not only the latest prompt. When prompting the LLM, along with the new user input and context, we also pass the conversation history from the memory. As the conversation history can get long, to avoid exceeding the context window or higher costs, you have to implement a way to reduce the size of your memory. As illustrated in *Figure 9.4*, the simplest one is to keep only the latest K items from your chat history. Unfortunately, using this strategy, the LLM will never be aware of the whole conversation.

Therefore, another way to add the chat history to your prompt is to keep a summary of the conversation along with the latest K replies. There are multiple ways to compute this summary, which might defeat the purpose of this book if we get into them all, but the simplest way is to always update the summary on every user prompt and generate an answer.

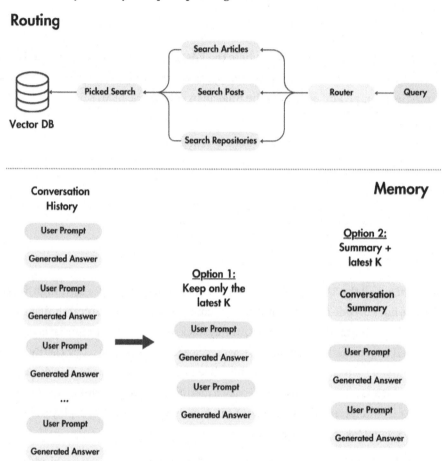

Figure 9.4: Routing and memory examples

As for each search, we send three queries to the vector DB, one for each data category. Thus, the second improvement is to add a router between the query and the search. The router will be a multi-category classifier that predicts the data categories we must retrieve for that specific query. Hence, instead of making three requests for every search, we can often reduce it to one or two. For example, if the user wants to write a theoretical paragraph about RAG for an article, then most probably, it's valuable to query only the article's collection. In this case, the router will predict the article class, which we can use to decide what collection we must query.

Another example would be if we want to illustrate a piece of code that shows how to build a RAG pipeline. In this case, the router would have to predict the article and repository data category, as we need to look up examples in both collections for an exhaustive context.

Usually, the router strategy decides what model to call based on a user's input, such as whether to use GPT-4 or a self-hosted Llama 3.1 model for that specific query. However, in our particular use case, we can adapt the router algorithm to optimize the retrieval step.

We can further optimize the retrieval using a hybrid search algorithm that combines the vector search (based on embeddings) with a keyword search algorithm, such as BM25. Search algorithms used BM25 (or similar methods) to find similar items in a DB before vector search algorithms became popular. By merging the methods, hybrid search retrieves results that match the exact terms, such as RAG, LLM, or SageMaker, and the query semantics, increasing the accuracy and relevance of your retrieved results. Fundamentally, the hybrid search algorithms follow the next mechanics:

1. **Parallel processing**: The search query is processed simultaneously through both the vector search and BM25 algorithms. Each algorithm retrieves a set of relevant documents based on its criteria.

2. **Score normalization**: The results from both searches are assigned relevance scores, which are then normalized to ensure comparability. This step is crucial because vector search and BM25 scoring mechanisms work at different scales. Thus, they can't be compared or merged without normalization.

3. **Result merging**: The normalized scores are combined, often through a weighted sum, to produce a final ranking of documents. Adjusting the weights allows for fine-tuning the emphasis on the semantic or keyword search algorithm.

To conclude, by combining the semantic and exact keyword search algorithms, you can improve the accuracy of your retrieval step. Vector search helps recognize synonyms or related concepts, ensuring that relevant information isn't overlooked due to vocabulary differences. Keyword search ensures that documents containing critical keywords are emphasized appropriately, particularly in technical fields with specific terminology.

One last improvement we can make to our RAG system is to use multi-index vector structures instead of indexing based only on the content's embedding. Let's detail how multi-indexing works. Instead of using the embeddings of a single field to do the vector search for a particular collection, it combines multiple fields.

For example, in our LLM Twin use case, we used only the content field of our articles, posts, or repositories to query the vector DB. When using a multi-index strategy, along with the content field, we could index the embeddings of the platform where the content was posted or when the content was published. This could impact the final accuracy of your retrieval as different platforms have different types of content, or more recent content is usually more relevant. Frameworks such as Superlinked make multi-indexing easy. For example, in the code snippet below, using Superlinked, we defined a multi-index on the content and platform for our article collection in just a few lines of code:

```python
from superlinked.framework.common.schema.id_schema_object import IdField
from superlinked.framework.common.schema.schema import schema
from superlinked.framework.common.schema.schema_object import String
… # Other Superlinked imports.


@schema
class ArticleSchema:
    id: IdField
    platform: String
    content: String


article = ArticleSchema()

articles_space_content = TextSimilaritySpace(
    text=chunk(article.content, chunk_size=500, chunk_overlap=50),
    model=settings.EMBEDDING_MODEL_ID,
)
articles_space_plaform = CategoricalSimilaritySpace(
    category_input=article.platform,
    categories=["medium", "substack", "wordpress"],
    negative_filter=-5.0,
)


article_index = Index(
    [articles_space_content, articles_space_plaform],
    fields=[article.author_id],
)
```

Superlinked is a powerful Python tool for any use case that includes vector computing, such as RAG, recommender systems, and semantic search. It offers an ecosystem where you can quickly ingest data into a vector DB, write complex queries on top of it, and deploy the service as a RESTful API.

The world of LLMs and RAG is experimental, similar to any other AI domain. Thus, when building real-world products, it's important to quickly build an end-to-end solution that works but is not necessarily the best. Then, you can reiterate with various experiments until you completely optimize it for your use case. This is standard practice in the industry and lets you iterate fast while providing value to the business and gathering user feedback as quickly as possible in the product's lifecycle.

Summary

This chapter taught us how to build an advanced RAG inference pipeline. We started by looking into the software architecture of the RAG system. Then, we zoomed in on the advanced RAG methods we used within the retrieval module, such as query expansion, self-querying, filtered vector search, and reranking. Afterward, we saw how to write a modular `ContextRetriever` class that glues all the advanced RAG components under a single interface, making searching for relevant documents a breeze. Ultimately, we looked into how to connect all the missing dots, such as the retrieval, the prompt augmentation, and the LLM call, under a single RAG function that will serve as our RAG inference pipeline.

As highlighted a few times in this chapter, we couldn't test our fine-tuned LLM because we haven't deployed it yet to AWS SageMaker as an inference endpoint. Thus, in the next chapter, we will learn how to deploy the LLM to AWS SageMaker, write an inference interface to call the endpoint, and implement a FastAPI web server to serve as our business layer.

References

- *A real-time retrieval system for social media data | VectorHub by SuperLinked.* (n.d.). https://superlinked.com/vectorhub/articles/real-time-retrieval-system-social-media-data
- *Building a Router from Scratch - LlamaIndex.* (n.d.). https://docs.llamaindex.ai/en/stable/examples/low_level/router/
- *How to add memory to chatbots | LangChain.* (n.d.). https://python.langchain.com/docs/how_to/chatbots_memory/#summary-memory

- *How to do "self-querying" retrieval | LangChain.* (n.d.). `https://python.langchain.com/docs/how_to/self_query/`

- *How to route between sub-chains | LangChain.* (n.d.). `https://python.langchain.com/docs/how_to/routing/#routing-by-semantic-similarity`

- *How to use the MultiQueryRetriever | LangChain.* (n.d.). `https://python.langchain.com/docs/how_to/MultiQueryRetriever/`

- *Hybrid Search explained.* (2023, January 3). Weaviate. `https://weaviate.io/blog/hybrid-search-explained`

- Iusztin, P. (2024, August 20). 4 Advanced RAG Algorithms You Must Know | Decoding ML. *Medium.* `https://medium.com/decodingml/the-4-advanced-rag-algorithms-you-must-know-to-implement-5d0c7f1199d2`

- Monigatti, L. (2024, February 19). Advanced Retrieval-Augmented Generation: From Theory to LlamaIndex Implementation. *Medium.* `https://towardsdatascience.com/advanced-retrieval-augmented-generation-from-theory-to-llamaindex-implementation-4de1464a9930`

- *Multi-attribute search with vector embeddings | VectorHub by Superlinked.* (n.d.). `https://superlinked.com/vectorhub/articles/multi-attribute-semantic-search`

- *Optimizing RAG with Hybrid Search & Reranking | VectorHub by Superlinked.* (n.d.). `https://superlinked.com/vectorhub/articles/optimizing-rag-with-hybrid-search-reranking`

- Refactoring.Guru. (2024, January 1). *Singleton.* `https://refactoring.guru/design-patterns/singleton`

- Stoll, M. (2024, September 7). Visualize your RAG Data—Evaluate your Retrieval-Augmented Generation System with Ragas. *Medium.* `https://towardsdatascience.com/visualize-your-rag-data-evaluate-your-retrieval-augmented-generation-system-with-ragas-fc2486308557`

- *Using LLM's for retrieval and reranking—LlamaIndex, data framework for LLM applications.* (n.d.). `https://www.llamaindex.ai/blog/using-llms-for-retrieval-and-reranking-23cf2d3a14b6`

Join our book's Discord space

Join our community's Discord space for discussions with the authors and other readers:

`https://packt.link/llmeng`

10

Inference Pipeline Deployment

Deploying the inference pipeline for the **large language model (LLM)** Twin application is a critical stage in the **machine learning (ML)** application life cycle. It's where the most value is added to your business, making your models accessible to your end users. However, successfully deploying AI models can be challenging, as the models require expensive computing power and access to up-to-date features to run the inference. To overcome these constraints, it's crucial to carefully design your deployment strategy. This ensures that it meets the application's requirements, such as latency, throughput, and costs. As we work with LLMs, we must consider the inference optimization techniques presented in *Chapter 8*, such as model quantization. Also, to automate the deployment processes, we must leverage MLOps best practices, such as model registries that version and share our models across our infrastructure.

To understand how to design the deployment architecture of the LLM Twin, we will first look at three deployment types we can choose from: online real-time inference, asynchronous inference, and offline batch transform. Also, to better understand which option to choose for our LLM Twin use case, we will quickly walk you through a set of critical criteria we must consider before making an architectural decision, such as latency, throughput, data, and infrastructure. Also, we'll weigh the pros and cons of monolithic and microservices architecture in model serving, a decision that can significantly influence the scalability and maintainability of your service.Once we've grasped the various design choices available, we'll focus on understanding the deployment strategy for the LLM Twin's inference pipeline. Subsequently, we will walk you through an end-to-end tutorial on deploying the LLM Twin service, including deploying our custom fine-tuned LLM to AWS SageMaker endpoints and implementing a FastAPI server as the central entry point for our users. We will then wrap up this chapter with a short discussion on autoscaling strategies and how to use them on SageMaker.

Hence, in this chapter, we will cover the following topics:

- Criteria for choosing deployment types
- Understanding inference deployment types
- Monolithic versus microservices architecture in model serving
- Exploring the LLM Twin's inference pipeline deployment strategy
- Deploying the LLM Twin service
- Autoscaling capabilities to handle spikes in usage

Criteria for choosing deployment types

When it comes to deploying ML models, the first step is to understand the four requirements present in every ML application: throughput, latency, data, and infrastructure.

Understanding them and their interaction is essential. When designing the deployment architecture for your models, there is always a trade-off between the four that will directly impact the user's experience. For example, should your model deployment be optimized for low latency or high throughput?

Throughput and latency

Throughput refers to the number of inference requests a system can process in a given period. It is typically measured in **requests per second** (**RPS**). Throughput is crucial when deploying ML models when you expect to process many requests. It ensures the system can handle many requests efficiently without becoming a bottleneck.

High throughput often requires scalable and robust infrastructure, such as machines or clusters with multiple high-end GPUs.**Latency** is the time it takes for a system to process a single inference request from when it is received until the result is returned. Latency is critical in real-time applications where quick response times are essential, such as in live user interactions, fraud detection, or any system requiring immediate feedback. For example, the average latency of OpenAI's API is the average response time from when a user sends a request, and the service provides a result that is accessible within your application.

The latency is the sum of the network I/O, serialization and deserialization, and the LLM's inference time. Meanwhile, the throughput is the average number of requests the API processes and serves a second.

Low-latency systems require optimized and often more costly infrastructure, such as faster processors, lower network latency, and possibly edge computing to reduce the distance data needs to travel.

A lower latency translates to higher throughput when the service processes multiple queries in parallel successfully. For example, if the service takes 100 ms to process requests, this translates to a throughput of 10 requests per second. If the latency reaches 10 ms per request, the throughput rises to 100 requests per second.

However, to complicate things, most ML applications adopt a batching strategy to simultaneously pass multiple data samples to the model. In this case, a lower latency can translate into lower throughput; in other words, a higher latency maps to a higher throughput. For example, if you process 20 batched requests in 100 ms, the latency is 100 ms, while the throughput is 200 requests per second. If you process 60 requests in 200 ms, the latency is 200 ms, while the throughput rises to 300 requests per second. Thus, even when batching requests at serving time, it's essential to consider the minimum latency accepted for a good user experience.

Data

As we know, data is everywhere in an ML system. But when talking about model serving, we mostly care about the model's input and output. This includes the format, volume, and complexity of the processed data. Data is the foundation of the inference process. The characteristics of the data, such as its size and type, determine how the system needs to be configured and optimized for efficient processing.

The type and size of the data directly impact latency and throughput, as more complex or extensive data can take longer to process. For example, designing a model that takes input structured data and outputs a probability differs entirely from an LLM that takes input text (or even images) and outputs an array of characters.

Infrastructure

Infrastructure refers to the underlying hardware, software, networking, and system architecture that supports the deployment and operation of the ML models. The infrastructure provides the necessary resources for deploying, scaling, and maintaining ML models. It includes computing resources, memory, storage, networking components, and the software stack:

- For **high throughput**, the systems require scalable infrastructure to manage large data volumes and high request rates, possibly through parallel processing, distributed systems, and high-end GPUs.

- Infrastructure must be optimized to reduce processing time to achieve **low latency**, such as using faster CPUs, GPUs, or specialized hardware. While optimizing your system for low latency while batching your requests, you often have to sacrifice high throughput in favor of lower latency, which can result in your hardware not being utilized at total capacity. As you process fewer requests per second, it results in idle computing, which increases the overall cost of processing a request. Thus, picking the suitable machine for your requirements is critical in optimizing costs.

It is crucial to design infrastructure to meet specific data requirements. This includes selecting storage solutions to handle large datasets and implementing fast retrieval mechanisms to ensure efficient data access. For example, we mostly care about optimizing throughput for offline training, while for online inference, we generally care about latency.

With this in mind, before picking a specific deployment type, you should ask yourself questions such as:

- What are the throughput requirements? You should make this decision based on the throughput's required minimum, average, and maximum statistics.
- How many requests the system must handle simultaneously? (1, 10, 1,000, 1 million, etc.)
- What are the latency requirements? (1 millisecond, 10 milliseconds, 1 second, etc.)
- How should the system scale? For example, we should look at the CPU workload, number of requests, queue size, data size, or a combination of them.
- What are the cost requirements?With what data do we work with? For example, do we work with images, text, or tabular data?
- What is the size of the data we work with? (100 MB, 1 GB, 10 GB)

Deeply thinking about these questions directly impacts the user experience of your application, which ultimately makes the difference between a successful product and not. Even if you ship a mind-blowing model, if the user needs to wait too long for a response or it often crashes, the user will switch your production to something less accurate that works reliably. For example, Google found in a 2016 study that 53% of visits are abandoned if a mobile site takes longer than three seconds to load: `https://www.thinkwithgoogle.com/consumer-insights/consumer-trends/mobile-site-load-time-statistics/`.

Let's move on to the three deployment architectures we can leverage to serve our models.

Understanding inference deployment types

As illustrated in *Figure 10.1*, you can choose from three fundamental deployment types when serving models:

- Online real-time inference
- Asynchronous inference
- Offline batch transform

When selecting one design over the other, there is a trade-off between latency, throughput, and costs. You must consider how the data is accessed and the infrastructure you are working with. Another criterion you have to consider is how the user will interact with the model. For example, will the user use it directly, like a chatbot, or will it be hidden within your system, like a classifier that checks if an input (or output) is safe?

You have to consider the freshness of the predictions as well. For example, serving your model in offline batch mode might be easier to implement if, in your use case, it is OK to consume delayed predictions. Otherwise, you have to serve your model in real-time, which is more infrastructure-demanding. Also, you have to consider your application's traffic. Ask yourself questions such as, "Will the application be constantly used, or will there be spikes in traffic and then flatten out?"

With that in mind, let's explore the three major ML deployment types.

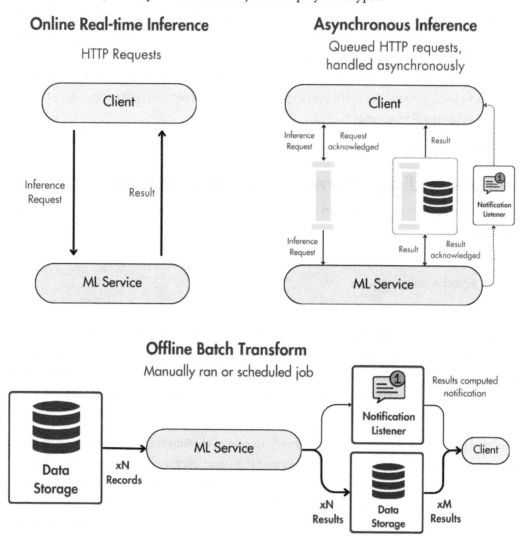

Figure 10.1: The three fundamental architectures of inference deployment types

Online real-time inference

In real-time inference, we have a simple architecture based on a server that can be accessed through HTTP requests. The most popular options are to implement a REST API or gRPC server. The REST API is more accessible but slower, using JSON to pass data between the client and server.

This approach is usually taken when serving models outside your internal network to the broader public. For example, OpenAI's API implements a REST API protocol.

On the other hand, implementing a gRPC makes your ML server faster, though it may reduce its flexibility and general applicability. You have to implement protobuf schemas in your client application, which are more tedious to work with than JSON structures. The benefit, however, is that protobuf objects can be compiled into bites, making the network transfers much faster. Thus, this protocol is often adopted for internal services within the same ML system.

Using the real-time inference approach, the client sends an HTTP request to the ML service, which immediately processes the request and returns the result in the same response. This synchronous interaction means the client waits for the result before moving on.

To make this work efficiently, the infrastructure must support low-latency, highly responsive ML services, often deployed on fast, scalable servers. Load balancing is crucial to evenly distribute incoming traffic evenly, while autoscaling ensures the system can handle varying loads. High availability is also essential to keeping the service operational at all times.

For example, this architecture is often present when interacting with LLMs, as when sending a request to a chatbot or API (powered by LLMs), you expend the predictions right ahead. LLM services, such as ChatGPT or Claude, often use WebSockets to stream each token individually to the end user, making the interaction more responsive. Other famous examples are AI services such as embedding or reranking models used for **retrieval-augmented generation (RAG)** or online recommendation engines in platforms like TikTok.

The simplicity of real-time inference, with its direct client-server interaction, makes it an attractive option for applications that require immediate responses, like chatbots or real-time recommendations. However, this approach can be challenging to scale and may lead to underutilized resources during low-traffic periods.

Asynchronous inference

In asynchronous inference, the client sends a request to the ML service, which acknowledges the request and places it in a queue for processing. Unlike real-time inference, the client doesn't wait for an immediate response. Instead, the ML service processes the request asynchronously. This requires a robust infrastructure that queues the messages to be processed by the ML service later on.

When the results are ready, you can leverage multiple techniques to send them to the client. For example, depending on the size of the result, you can put it either in a different queue or an object storage dedicated to storing the results.

The client can either adopt a polling mechanism that checks on a schedule if there are new results or adopt a push strategy and implement a notification system to inform the client when the results are ready.

Asynchronous inference uses resources more efficiently. It doesn't have to process all the requests simultaneously but can define a maximum number of machines that run in parallel to process the messages. This is possible because the requests are stored in the queue until a machine can process them. Another huge benefit is that it can handle spikes in requests without any timeouts. For example, let's assume that on an e-shop site, we usually have 10 requests per second handled by two machines. Because of a promotion, many people started to visit the site, and the number of requests spiked to 100 requests per second. Instead of scaling the number of **virtual machines (VMs)** by 10, which can add drastic costs, the requests are queued, and the same two VMs can process them in their rhythm without any failures.

Another popular advantage for asynchronous architectures is when the requested job takes significant time to complete. For example, if the job takes over five minutes, you don't want to block the client waiting for a response.

While asynchronous inference offers significant benefits, it does come with trade-offs. It introduces higher latency, making it less suitable for time-sensitive applications. Additionally, it adds complexity to the implementation and infrastructure. Depending on your design choices, this architecture type falls somewhere between online and offline, offering a balance of benefits and trade-offs.

For example, this is a robust design where you don't care too much about the latency of the inference but want to optimize costs heavily. Thus, it is a popular choice for problems such as extracting keywords from documents, summarizing them using LLMs, or running deep-fake models on top of videos. But suppose you carefully design the autoscaling system to process the requests from the queue at decent speeds. In that case, you can leverage this design for other use cases, such as online recommendations for e-commerce. In the end, it sums up how much computing power you are willing to pay to meet the expectations of your application.

Offline batch transform

Batch transform is about processing large volumes of data simultaneously, either on a schedule or triggered manually. In a batch transform architecture, the ML service pulls data from a storage system, processes it in a single operation, and then stores the results in storage. The storage system can be implemented as an object storage like AWS S3 or a data warehouse like GCP BigQuery.

Unlike the asynchronous inference architecture, a batch transform design is optimized for high throughput with permissive latency requirements. When real-time predictions are unnecessary, this approach can significantly reduce costs, as processing data in big batches is the most economical method. Moreover, the batch transform architecture is the simplest way to serve a model, accelerating development time.

The client pulls the results directly from data storage, decoupling its interaction with the ML service. Taking this approach, the client never has to wait for the ML service to process its input, but at the same time, it doesn't have the flexibility to ask for new results at any time. You can see the data storage, where the results are stored as a large cache, from where the client can take what is required. If you want to make your application more responsive, the client can be notified when the processing is complete and can retrieve the results.

Unfortunately, this approach will always introduce a delay between the time the predictions were computed and consumed. That's why not all applications can leverage this design choice. For example, if we implement a recommender system for a video streaming application, having a delay of one day for the predicted movies and TV shows might work because you don't consume these products at a high frequency. But suppose you make a recommender system for a social media platform. In that case, delaying one day or even one hour is unacceptable, as you constantly want to provide fresh content to the user.

Batch transform shines in scenarios where high throughput is needed, like data analytics or periodic reporting. However, it's unsuitable for real-time applications due to its high latency and requires careful planning and scheduling to manage large datasets effectively. That's why it is an offline serving method.

To conclude, we examined the three most common architectures for serving ML models. We started with online real-time inference, which serves clients when they request a prediction. Then, we looked at the asynchronous inference method, which sits between online and offline. Ultimately, we presented the offline batch transform, which is used to process large amounts of data and store them in data storage, from where the client later consumes them.

Monolithic versus microservices architecture in model serving

In the previous section, we saw three different methods of deploying the ML service. The differences in architecture were mainly based on the interaction between the client and the ML service, such as the communication protocol, the ML service responsiveness, and prediction freshness.

But another aspect to consider is the architecture of the ML service itself, which can be implemented as a monolithic server or as multiple microservices. This will impact how the ML service is implemented, maintained, and scaled. Let's explore the two options.

Monolith

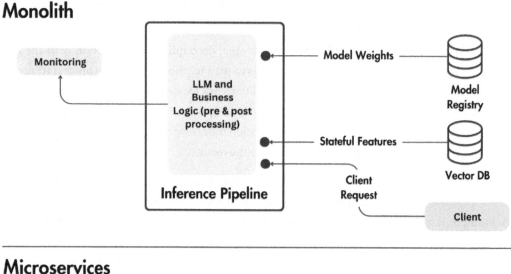

Microservices

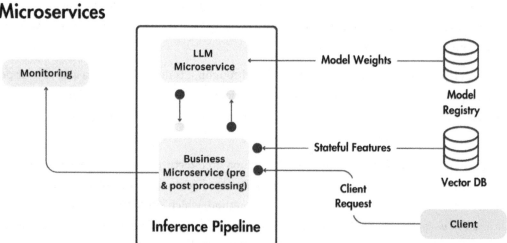

Figure 10.2: Monolithic versus microservices architecture in model serving

Monolithic architecture

The LLM (or any other ML model) and the associated business logic (preprocessing and post-processing steps) are bundled into a single service in a monolithic architecture. This approach is straightforward to implement at the beginning of a project, as everything is placed within one code base. Simplicity makes maintenance easy when working on small to medium projects, as updates and changes can be made within a unified system.

One key challenge of a monolithic architecture is the difficulty of scaling components independently. The LLM typically requires GPU power, while the rest of the business logic is CPU and I/O-bound. As a result, the infrastructure must be optimized for both GPU and CPU. This can lead to inefficient resource use, with the GPU being idle when the business logic is executed and vice versa. Such inefficiency can result in additional costs that could be avoided.

Moreover, this architecture can limit flexibility, as all components must share the same tech stack and runtime environment. For example, you might want to run the LLM using Rust or C++ or compile it with ONNX or TensorRT while keeping the business logic in Python. Having all the code in one system makes this differentiation difficult. Finally, splitting the work across different teams is complex, often leading to bottlenecks and reduced agility.

Microservices architecture

A microservices architecture breaks down the inference pipeline into separate, independent services—typically splitting the LLM service and the business logic into distinct components. These services communicate over a network using protocols such as REST or gRPC.

As illustrated in *Figure 10.3*, the main advantage of this approach is the ability to scale each component independently. For instance, since the LLM service might require more GPU resources than the business logic, it can be scaled horizontally without impacting the other components. This optimizes resource usage and reduces costs, as different types of machines (e.g., GPU versus CPU) can be used according to each service's needs.

For example, let's assume that the LLM inference takes longer, so you will need more ML service replicas to meet the demand. But remember that GPU VMs are expensive. By decoupling the two components, you will run only what is required on the GPU machine and not block the GPU VM with other computing that can be done on a much cheaper machine.

Thus, by decoupling the components, you can scale horizontally as required, with minimal costs, providing a cost-effective solution to your system's needs.

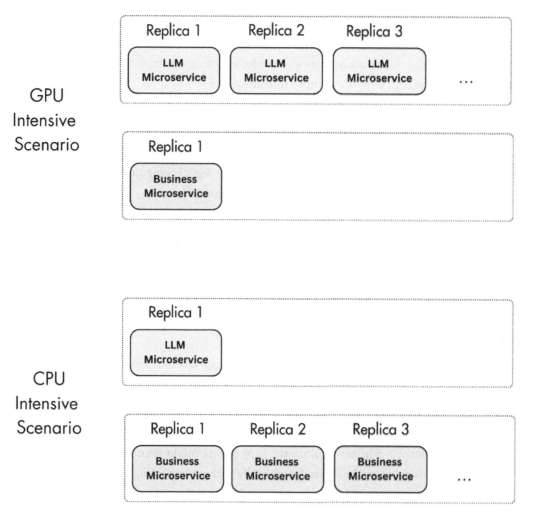

Figure 10.3: Scaling microservices independently based on compute requirements

Additionally, each microservice can adopt the most suitable technology stack, allowing teams to innovate and optimize independently.

However, microservices introduce complexity in deployment and maintenance. Each service must be deployed, monitored, and maintained separately, which can be more challenging than managing a monolithic system.

The increased network communication between services can also introduce latency and potential points of failure, necessitating robust monitoring and resilience mechanisms.

Note that the proposed design for decoupling the ML model and business logic into two services can be extended if necessary. For example, you can have one service for preprocessing the data, one for the model, and another for post-processing the data. Depending on the four pillars (latency, throughput, data, and infrastructure), you can get creative and design the most optimal architecture for your application needs.

Choosing between monolithic and microservices architectures

The choice between monolithic and microservices architectures for serving ML models largely depends on the application's specific needs. A monolithic approach might be ideal for smaller teams or more straightforward applications where ease of development and maintenance is a priority. It's also a good starting point for projects without frequent scaling requirements. Also, if the ML models are smaller, don't require a GPU, or don't require smaller and cheaper GPUs, the trade-off between reducing costs and complicating your infrastructure is worth considering.

On the other hand, microservices, with their adaptability and scalability, are well suited for larger, more complex systems where different components have varying scaling needs or require distinct tech stacks. This architecture is particularly advantageous when scaling specific system parts, such as GPU-intensive LLM services. As LLMs require powerful machines with GPUs, such as Nvidia A100, V100, or A10g, which are incredibly costly, microservices offer the flexibility to optimize the system for keeping these machines busy all the time or quickly scaling down when the GPU is idle. However, this flexibility comes at the cost of increased complexity in both development and operations.

A common strategy is to start with a monolithic design and further decouple it into multiple services as the project grows. However, to successfully do so without making the transition too complex and costly, you must design the monolith application with this in mind. For instance, even if all the code runs on a single machine, you can completely decouple the modules of the application at the software level. This makes it easier to move these modules to different microservices when the time comes. When working with Python, for example, you can implement the ML and business logic into two different Python modules that don't interact with each other. Then, you can glue these two modules at a higher level, such as through a service class, or directly into the framework you use to expose your application over the internet, such as FastAPI.

Another option is to write the ML and business logic as two different Python packages that you glue together in the same ways as before. This is better because it completely enforces a separation between the two but adds extra complexity at development time. The main idea, therefore, is that if you start with a monolith and down the line you want to move to a microservices architecture, it's essential to design your software with modularity in mind. Otherwise, if the logic is mixed, you will probably have to rewrite everything from scratch, adding tons of development time, which translates into wasted resources.

In summary, monolithic architectures offer simplicity and ease of maintenance but at the cost of flexibility and scalability. At the same time, microservices provide the agility to scale and innovate but require more sophisticated management and operational practices.

Exploring the LLM Twin's inference pipeline deployment strategy

Now that we've understood all the design choices available for implementing the deployment strategy of the LLM Twin's inference pipeline, let's explore the concrete decisions we made to actualize it.

Our primary objective is to develop a chatbot that facilitates content creation. To achieve this, we will process requests sequentially, with a strong emphasis on low latency. This necessitates the selection of an online real-time inference deployment architecture.

On the monolith versus microservice aspect, we will split the ML service between a REST API server containing the business logic and an LLM microservice optimized for running the given LLM. As the LLM requires a powerful machine to run the inference, and we can further optimize it with various engines to speed up the latency and memory usage, it makes the most sense to go with the microservice architecture. By doing so, we can quickly adapt the infrastructure based on various LLM sizes. For example, if we run an 8B parameter model, the model can run on a single machine with a Nivida A10G GPU after quantization. But if we want to run a 30B model, we can upgrade to an Nvidia A100 GPU. Doing so allows us to upgrade only the LLM microservice while keeping the REST API untouched.

As illustrated in *Figure 10.4*, most business logic is centered around RAG in our particular use case. Thus, we will perform RAG's retrieval and augmentation parts within the business microservice. It will also include all the advanced RAG techniques presented in the previous chapter to optimize the pre-retrieval, retrieval, and post-retrieval steps.

The LLM microservice is strictly optimized for the RAG generation component. Ultimately, the business layer will send the prompt trace consisting of the user query, prompt, answer, and other intermediary steps to the prompt monitoring pipeline, which we will detail in *Chapter 11*.

In summary, our approach involves implementing an online real-time ML service using a microservice architecture, which effectively splits the LLM and business logic into two distinct services.

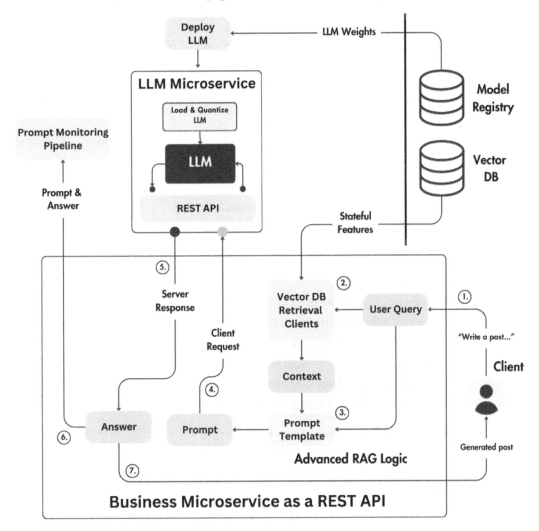

Figure 10.4: Microservice deployment architecture of the LLM Twin's inference pipeline

Let's review the interface of the inference pipeline, which is defined by the **feature/training/ inference (FTI)** architecture. For the pipeline to run, it needs two things:

- Real-time features used for RAG, generated by the feature pipeline, which is queried from our online feature store, more concretely from the Qdrant vector database (DB)
- A fine-tuned LLM generated by the training pipeline, which is pulled from our model registry

With that in mind, the flow of the ML service looks as follows, as illustrated in *Figure 10.4*:

1. A user sends a query through an HTTP request.

2. The user's input retrieves the proper context by leveraging the advanced RAG retrieval module implemented in *Chapter 4*.

3. The user's input and retrieved context are packed into the final prompt using a dedicated prompt template.

4. The prompt is sent to the LLM microservice through an HTTP request.

5. The business microservices wait for the generated answer.

6. After the answer is generated, it is sent to the prompt monitoring pipeline along with the user's input and other vital information to monitor.

7. Ultimately, the generated answer is sent back to the user.

Now, let's explore what tech stack we used to implement the architecture presented in *Figure 10.4*. As we know, we use Qdrant for the vector DB. We will leverage Hugging Face for the model registry. By doing so, we can publicly share our model with everyone who is testing the code from this book. Thus, you can easily use the model we provided if you don't want to run the training pipeline, which can cost up to 100 dollars. As you can see, shareability and accessibility are some of the most beautiful aspects of storing your model in a model registry.

We will implement the business microservice in FastAPI because it's popular, easy to use, and fast. The LLM microservice will be deployed on AWS SageMaker, where we will leverage SageMaker's integration with Hugging Face's **Deep Learning Containers (DLCs)** to deploy the model. We will discuss Hugging Face's DLCs in the next section, but intuitively, it is an inference engine used to optimize LLMs at serving time. The prompt monitoring pipeline is implemented using Comet, but we will look over that module only in *Chapter 11*.

The SageMaker Inference deployment is composed of the following components that we will show you how to implement:

- **SageMaker endpoint**: An endpoint is a scalable and secure API that SageMaker hosts to enable real-time predictions from deployed models. It's essentially the interface through which applications interact with your model. Once deployed, an application can make HTTP requests to the endpoint to receive real-time predictions.

- **SageMaker model**: In SageMaker, a model is an artifact that results from training an algorithm. It contains the information required to make predictions, including the weights and computation logic. You can create multiple models and use them in different configurations or for various predictions.

- **SageMaker configuration**: This configuration specifies the hardware and software set up to host the model. It defines the resources required for the endpoint, such as the type and number of ML compute instances. Endpoint configurations are used when creating or updating an endpoint. They allow for flexibility in the deployment and scalability of the hosted models.

- **SageMaker Inference component**: This is the last piece of the puzzle that connects the model and configuration to an endpoint. You can deploy multiple models to an endpoint, each with its resource configuration. Once deployed, models are easily accessible via the InvokeEndpoint API in Python.

Together, these components create a robust infrastructure for deploying and managing ML models in SageMaker, enabling scalable, secure, and efficient real-time predictions.

Other popular cloud platforms offer the exact solutions. For example, you have Azure OpenAI instead of Bedrock and Azure ML instead of SageMaker on Azure. The list of ML deployment tools, such as Hopsworks, Modal, Vertex AI, Seldon, BentoML, and many more, is endless and will probably change. What is essential though is to understand your use case requirements and find a tool that fits your needs.

The training versus the inference pipeline

Understanding the nuances between the training and inference pipelines is crucial before we deploy the inference pipeline. While it might seem straightforward that the training pipeline is for training and the inference pipeline is for inference, there are significant differences that we need to grasp to comprehend the technical aspects of our discussion fully.

One key difference lies in how data is handled and accessed within each pipeline. During training, data is typically accessed from offline storage in batch mode, optimized for throughput and ensuring data lineage. For example, our LLM Twin architecture uses ZenML artifacts to access, version, and track data fed to the training loop in batches. In contrast, the inference pipeline requires an online DB optimized for low latency. We will leverage the Qdrant vector DB to grab the necessary context for RAG. In this context, the focus shifts from data lineage and versioning to quick data access, ensuring a seamless user experience. Additionally, the outputs of these pipelines also differ significantly. The training pipeline outputs trained model weights stored in the model registry. Meanwhile, the inference pipeline outputs predictions served directly to the user.

Also, the infrastructure required for each pipeline is different. The training pipeline demands more powerful machines equipped with as many GPUs as possible. This is because training involves batching data and holding all the necessary gradients in memory for optimization steps, making it highly compute-intensive. More computational power and VRAM allow larger batches (or throughput), reducing training time and enabling more extensive experimentation. On the other hand, the inference pipeline typically requires less computation. Inference often involves passing a single sample or smaller batches to the model without the need for optimization steps.

Despite these differences, there is some overlap between the two pipelines, particularly regarding preprocessing and post-processing steps. Applying the same preprocessing and post-processing functions and hyperparameters during training and inference is crucial. Any discrepancies can lead to what is known as training-serving skew, where the model's performance during inference deviates from its performance during training.

Deploying the LLM Twin service

The last step is implementing the architecture presented in the previous section. More concretely, we will deploy the LLM microservice using AWS SageMaker and the business microservice using FastAPI. Within the business microservice, we will glue the RAG logic written in *Chapter 9* with our fine-tuned LLM Twin, ultimately being able to test out the inference pipeline end to end.

Serving the ML model is one of the most critical steps in any ML application's life cycle, as users can only interact with our model after this phase is completed. If the serving architecture isn't designed correctly or if the infrastructure isn't working properly, it doesn't matter that you have implemented a powerful and excellent model. As long as the user cannot appropriately interact with it, it has near zero value from a business point of view. For example, if you have the best code assistant on the market, but the latency to use it is too high, or the API calls keep crashing, the user will probably switch to a less performant code assistant that works faster and is more stable.

Thus, in this section, we will show you how to:

- Deploy our fined-tuned LLM Twin model to AWS SageMaker
- Write an inference client to interact with the deployed model
- Write the business service in FastAPI
- Integrate our RAG logic with our fine-tuned LLM
- Implement autoscaling rules for the LLM microservice

Implementing the LLM microservice using AWS SageMaker

We aim to deploy the LLM Twin model, stored in Hugging Face's model registry, to Amazon SageMaker as an online real-time inference endpoint. We will leverage Hugging Face's specialized inference container, known as the Hugging Face LLM **DLC**, to deploy our LLM.

What are Hugging Face's DLCs?

DLCs are specialized Docker images that come pre-loaded with essential deep-learning frameworks and libraries, including popular tools like transformers, datasets, and tokenizers from Hugging Face. These containers are designed to simplify the process of training and deploying models by eliminating the need for complex environment setup and optimization. The Hugging Face Inference DLC, in particular, includes a fully integrated serving stack, significantly simplifying the deployment process and reducing the technical expertise needed to serve deep learning models in production.

When it comes to serving models, the DLC is powered by the **Text Generation Inference (TGI)** engine, made by Hugging Face: https://github.com/huggingface/text-generation-inference.

TGI is an open-source solution for deploying and serving LLMs. It offers high-performance text generation using tensor parallelism and dynamic batching for the most popular open-source LLMs available on Hugging Face, such as Mistral, Llama, and Falcon. To sum up, the most powerful features the DLC image provides are:

- **Tensor parallelism**, thus enhancing the computational efficiency of model inference
- **Optimized transformers code for inference**, leveraging flash-attention to maximize performance across the most widely used architectures: https://github.com/Dao-AILab/flash-attention
- **Quantization with** bitsandbytes that reduces the model size while maintaining performance, making deployments more efficient: https://github.com/bitsandbytes-foundation/bitsandbytes

- **Continuous batching of incoming requests**, thus improving throughput by dynamically batching requests as they arrive

- **Accelerated weight loading** by utilizing `safetensors` for faster model initialization, reducing start-up time: `https://github.com/huggingface/safetensors`

- **Token streaming** that supports real-time interactions through **Server-Sent Events (SSE)**

To summarize, our LLM Twin model will run inside DLC Docker images, listening to requests, optimizing the LLM for inference, and serving the results in real time. The DLC's Docker images will be hosted on AWS SageMaker under inference endpoints that can be accessed through HTTP requests. With that in mind, let's move on to the implementation. We will start by deploying the LLM and then writing a wrapper class to interact with the SageMaker Inference endpoint.

Configuring SageMaker roles

The first step is to create the proper AWS **Identity and Access Management (IAM)** users and roles to access and deploy the SageMaker infrastructure. AWS IAM controls who can authenticate and what any actor has access to. You can create new users (assigned to people) and new roles (assigned to other actors within your infrastructure, such as EC2 VMs) through IAM.

The whole deployment process is automated. We will have to run a few CLI commands, but first, ensure that you have correctly configured the `AWS_ACCESS_KEY`, `AWS_SECRET_KEY`, and `AWS_REGION` environmental variables in the `.env` file. At this step, the easiest way is to use the credentials attached to an admin role as, in the following steps, we will create a set of narrower IAM roles used in the rest of the chapter.

After you configured your `.env` file, we have to:

1. Create an IAM user restricted to creating and deleting only the resources we need for the deployment, such as SageMaker itself, **Elastic Container Registry (ECR)**, and S3. To make it, run the following:

    ```
    poetry poe create-sagemaker-role
    ```

    This command will generate a JSON file called `sagemaker_user_credentials.json` that contains a new AWS access and secret key. From now on, we will use these credentials to deploy everything related to SageMaker to ensure we modify only the resources associated with SageMaker. Otherwise, we could accidentally modify other AWS resources using an admin account, resulting in additional costs or altering other existing projects. Thus, having a narrow role only to your use case is good practice.

The last step is to take the new credentials from the JSON file and update the AWS_ACCESS_KEY and AWS_SECRET_KEY variables in your .env file. You can check out the implementation at https://github.com/PacktPublishing/LLM-Engineers-Handbook/blob/main/llm_engineering/infrastructure/aws/roles/create_sagemaker_role.py.

2. Create an IAM execution role. We will attach this role to the SageMaker deployment, empowering it to access other AWS resources on our behalf. This is standard practice for cloud deployments, as instead of authenticating every machine within your credentials, you attach a role that allows them to access only what is necessary from your infrastructure. In our case, we will provide SageMaker access to AWS S3, CloudWatch, and ECR. To create the role, run the following:

```
poetry poe create-sagemaker-execution-role
```

This command will generate a JSON file called sagemaker_execution_role.json that contains the **Amazon Resource Name (ARN)** of the newly created role. The ARN is an ID attached to any AWS resource to identify it across your cloud infrastructure. Take the ARN value from the JSON file and update the AWS_ARN_ROLE variable from your .env file with it. You can check out the implementation at https://github.com/PacktPublishing/LLM-Engineers-Handbook/blob/main/llm_engineering/infrastructure/aws/roles/create_execution_role.py.

 If you have issues, configure the AWS CLI with the same AWS credentials as in the .env file and repeat the process. Official documentation for installing the AWS CLI: https://docs.aws.amazon.com/cli/latest/userguide/install-cliv2.html.

By setting the IAM user and role in your .env file, we will automatically load them in the settings Python object and use them throughout the following steps. Now, let's move on to the actual deployment.

Deploying the LLM Twin model to AWS SageMaker

The deployment of AWS SageMaker is fully automated through a set of Python classes, which we will cover in this chapter. This section aims to understand how we configure the SageMaker infrastructure directly from Python. Thus, you don't have to run everything step by step, as in a standard tutorial, but only to understand the code.

We can initiate and finalize the entire SageMaker deployment using a simple CLI command: poe deploy-inference-endpoint. This command will initialize all the steps presented in *Figure 10.5*, except for creating the SageMaker AWS IAMs we created and configured in the previous step.

In this section, we will walk you through the code presented in *Figure 10.5* that helps us fully automate the deployment process, starting with the create_endpoint() function. Ultimately, we will test the CLI command and check the AWS console to see whether the deployment was successful. The SageMaker deployment code is available at https://github.com/PacktPublishing/LLM-Engineers-Handbook/tree/main/llm_engineering/infrastructure/aws/deploy.

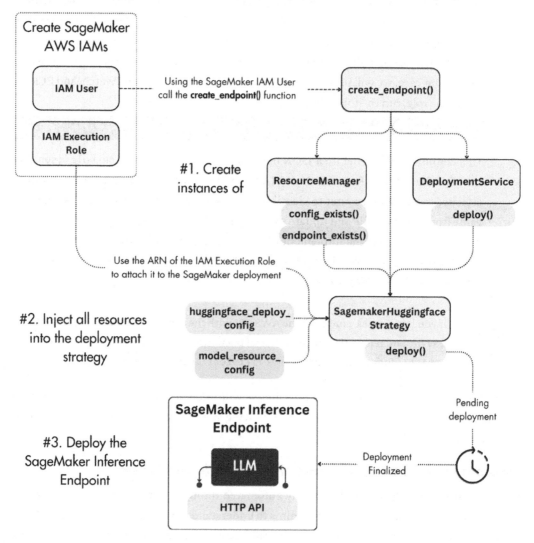

Figure 10.5: AWS SageMaker deployment steps

We will take a top-down approach to walk you through the implementation, starting with the main function that deploys the LLM Twin model to AWS SageMaker. In the function below, we first take the latest version of the Docker DLC image using the get_huggingface_llm_image_uri() function, which is later passed to the deployment strategy class, along with an instance of the resource manager and deployment service:

```python
def create_endpoint(endpoint_type=EndpointType.INFERENCE_COMPONENT_BASED):
    llm_image = get_huggingface_llm_image_uri("huggingface", version=None)

    resource_manager = ResourceManager()
    deployment_service = DeploymentService(resource_manager=resource_
manager)

    SagemakerHuggingfaceStrategy(deployment_service).deploy(
        role_arn=settings.ARN_ROLE,
        llm_image=llm_image,
        config=hugging_face_deploy_config,
        endpoint_name=settings.SAGEMAKER_ENDPOINT_INFERENCE,
        endpoint_config_name=settings.SAGEMAKER_ENDPOINT_CONFIG_INFERENCE,
        gpu_instance_type=settings.GPU_INSTANCE_TYPE,
        resources=model_resource_config,
        endpoint_type=endpoint_type,
    )
```

We must review the three classes used in the create_endpoint() function to fully understand the deployment process. Let's start with the ResourceManager class. The class begins with the initialization method, establishing the connection to AWS SageMaker using boto3, the AWS SDK for Python, which provides the necessary functions to interact with various AWS services, including SageMaker.

```python
class ResourceManager:
    def __init__(self) -> None:
        self.sagemaker_client = boto3.client(
            "sagemaker",
            region_name=settings.AWS_REGION,
            aws_access_key_id=settings.AWS_ACCESS_KEY,
            aws_secret_access_key=settings.AWS_SECRET_KEY,
        )
```

Next, we implement the endpoint_config_exists method, checking whether a specific Sage-Maker endpoint configuration exists:

```python
def endpoint_config_exists(self, endpoint_config_name: str) -> bool:
    try:
        self.sagemaker_client.describe_endpoint_
config(EndpointConfigName=endpoint_config_name)
        logger.info(f"Endpoint configuration '{endpoint_config_name}'
exists.")
        return True
    except ClientError:
        logger.info(f"Endpoint configuration '{endpoint_config_name}'
does not exist.")
        return False
```

The class also includes the endpoint_exists method, which checks the existence of a specific SageMaker endpoint:

```python
def endpoint_exists(self, endpoint_name: str) -> bool:
    try:
        self.sagemaker_client.describe_endpoint(EndpointName=endpoint_
name)
        logger.info(f"Endpoint '{endpoint_name}' exists.")
        return True
    except self.sagemaker_client.exceptions.ResourceNotFoundException:
        logger.info(f"Endpoint '{endpoint_name}' does not exist.")
        return False
```

Let's move to the DeploymentService. Within the constructor, we set up the sagemaker_client, which will interface with AWS SageMaker and an instance of the ResourceManager class we talked about earlier:

```python
class DeploymentService:
    def __init__(self, resource_manager):
        self.sagemaker_client = boto3.client(
            "sagemaker",
            region_name=settings.AWS_REGION,
            aws_access_key_id=settings.AWS_ACCESS_KEY,
            aws_secret_access_key=settings.AWS_SECRET_KEY,
```

```
            )
        self.resource_manager = resource_manager
```

The deploy() method is the heart of the DeploymentService class. This method orchestrates the entire process of deploying a model to a SageMaker endpoint. It checks whether the necessary configurations are already in place and, if not, it triggers the deployment:

```
def deploy(
    self,
    role_arn: str,
    llm_image: str,
    config: dict,
    endpoint_name: str,
    endpoint_config_name: str,
    gpu_instance_type: str,
    resources: Optional[dict] = None,
    endpoint_type: enum.Enum = EndpointType.MODEL_BASED,
) -> None:
    try:
        if self.resource_manager.endpoint_config_exists(endpoint_config_
name=endpoint_config_name):
            logger.info(f"Endpoint configuration {endpoint_config_name}
exists. Using existing configuration...")
        else:
            logger.info(f"Endpoint configuration{endpoint_config_name}
does not exist.")

        self.prepare_and_deploy_model(
            role_arn=role_arn,
            llm_image=llm_image,
            config=config,
            endpoint_name=endpoint_name,
            update_endpoint=False,
            resources=resources,
            endpoint_type=endpoint_type,
            gpu_instance_type=gpu_instance_type,
        )
```

```
        logger.info(f"Successfully deployed/updated model to endpoint
    {endpoint_name}.")
        except Exception as e:
            logger.error(f"Failed to deploy model to SageMaker: {e}")
            raise
```

The deploy method begins by checking whether the endpoint configuration already exists using the resource_manager. This step is crucial because it avoids unnecessary redeployment if the configuration is already set up. The deployment itself is handled by calling the prepare_and_deploy_model() method, which is responsible for the actual deployment of the model to the specified SageMaker endpoint.

The prepare_and_deploy_model() method is a static method within the DeploymentService class. This method is focused on setting up and deploying the Hugging Face model to SageMaker:

```
@staticmethod
def prepare_and_deploy_model(
    role_arn: str,
    llm_image: str,
    config: dict,
    endpoint_name: str,
    update_endpoint: bool,
    gpu_instance_type: str,
    resources: Optional[dict] = None,
    endpoint_type: enum.Enum = EndpointType.MODEL_BASED,
) -> None:
    huggingface_model = HuggingFaceModel(
        role=role_arn,
        image_uri=llm_image,
        env=config,
        transformers_version="4.6",
        pytorch_version="1.13",
        py_version="py310",
    )

    huggingface_model.deploy(
        instance_type=gpu_instance_type,
        initial_instance_count=1,
```

```
            endpoint_name=endpoint_name,
            update_endpoint=update_endpoint,
            resources=resources,
            tags=[{"Key": "task", "Value": "model_task"}],
            endpoint_type=endpoint_type,
    )
```

This method begins by creating an instance of HuggingFaceModel, a specialized model class from SageMaker designed to handle Hugging Face models. The constructor for HuggingFaceModel takes several essential parameters, such as the role ARN (which gives SageMaker the necessary permissions), the URI of the LLM DLC Docker image, and the LLM configuration that specifies what LLM to load from Hugging Face and its inference parameters, such as the maximum total of tokens.

Once HuggingFaceModel is instantiated, the method deploys it to SageMaker using the deploy function. This deployment process involves specifying the type of instance used, the number of instances, and whether to update an existing endpoint or create a new one. The method also includes optional resources for more complex deployments, such as the initial_instance_count parameter for multi-model endpoints and tags for tracking and categorization.

The last step is to walk you through the SagemakerHuggingfaceStrategy class, which aggregates everything we have shown. The class is initialized only with an instance of a deployment service, such as the one shown above.

```
class SagemakerHuggingfaceStrategy(DeploymentStrategy):
def __init__(self, deployment_service):
    self.deployment_service = deployment_service
```

The core functionality of the SagemakerHuggingfaceStrategy class is encapsulated in its deploy() method. This method orchestrates the deployment process, taking various parameters that define how the Hugging Face model should be deployed to AWS SageMaker:

```
def deploy(
    self,
    role_arn: str,
    llm_image: str,
    config: dict,
    endpoint_name: str,
    endpoint_config_name: str,
    gpu_instance_type: str,
```

```
    resources: Optional[dict] = None,
    endpoint_type: enum.Enum = EndpointType.MODEL_BASED,
) -> None:
    logger.info("Starting deployment using Sagemaker Huggingface
Strategy...")
    logger.info(
        f"Deployment parameters: nb of replicas: {settings.COPIES}, nb of
gpus:{settings.GPUS}, instance_type:{settings.GPU_INSTANCE_TYPE}"
    )
```

The parameters passed into the method are crucial to the deployment process:

- role_arn: The AWS IAM role that provides permissions for the SageMaker deployment.

- llm_image: The URI of the DLC Docker image

- config: A dictionary containing configuration settings for the model environment.

- endpoint_name and endpoint_config_name: Names for the SageMaker endpoint and its configuration, respectively.

- gpu_instance_type: The type of the GPU EC2 instances used for the deployment.

- resources: Optional resources dictionary used for multi-model endpoint deployments.

- endpoint_type: This can either be MODEL_BASED or INFERENCE_COMPONENT, determining whether the endpoint includes an inference component.

The method delegates the actual deployment process to the deployment_service. This delegation is a critical aspect of the strategy pattern, allowing for flexibility in how the deployment is carried out without altering the high-level deployment logic.

```
try:
    self.deployment_service.deploy(
        role_arn=role_arn,
        llm_image=llm_image,
        config=config,
        endpoint_name=endpoint_name,
        endpoint_config_name=endpoint_config_name,
        gpu_instance_type=gpu_instance_type,
        resources=resources,
        endpoint_type=endpoint_type,
    )
    logger.info("Deployment completed successfully.")
```

```
except Exception as e:
    logger.error(f"Error during deployment: {e}")
    raise
```

Also, let's review the resource configuration to understand the infrastructure better. These resources are leveraged when setting up multi-endpoint configurations that use multiple replicas to serve clients while respecting the latency and throughput requirements of the application. The ResourceRequirements object is initialized with a dictionary that specifies various resource parameters. These parameters include the number of replicas (copies) of the model to be deployed, the number of GPUs required, the number of CPU cores, and the memory allocation in megabytes. Each of these parameters plays a crucial role in the performance and scalability of the deployed model.

```
from sagemaker.compute_resource_requirements.resource_requirements import
ResourceRequirements

    model_resource_config = ResourceRequirements(
    requests={
        "copies": settings.COPIES,
        "num_accelerators": settings.GPUS
        "num_cpus": settings.CPUS,
        "memory": 5 * 1024
    },
)
```

In the preceding snippet, ResourceRequirements is configured with four key parameters:

- **copies**: This parameter determines how many instances or replicas of the model should be deployed. Having multiple replicas can help in reducing latency and increasing throughput.

- **num_accelerators**: This parameter specifies the number of GPUs to allocate. Since LLMs are computationally intensive, multiple GPUs are typically required to accelerate inference processes.

- **num_cpus:** This defines the number of CPU cores the deployment should have. The number of CPUs impacts the model's ability to handle data preprocessing, post-processing, and other tasks that are less GPU-dependent but still essential.

- **memory:** The memory parameter sets the minimum amount of RAM required for the deployment. Adequate memory is necessary to ensure the model can load and operate without running into memory shortages.

By setting these parameters, the class ensures that it has sufficient resources to operate efficiently when the model is deployed to a SageMaker endpoint. The precise tuning of these values will vary depending on the LLM's specific requirements, such as its size, the complexity of the tasks it will perform, and the expected load. To get a better understanding of how to use them, after deploying the endpoint, we suggest modifying them and seeing how the performance of the LLM microservice changes.

Ultimately, let's review the settings configuring the LLM engine. The HF_MODEL_ID identifies which Hugging Face model to deploy. For example, in the settings class, we set it to mlabonne/TwinLlama-3.1-8B-13 to load our custom LLM Twin model stored in Hugging Face. SM_NUM_GPUS specifies the number of GPUs allocated per model replica, which is crucial for fitting your model into the GPU's VRAM. HUGGING_FACE_HUB_TOKEN provides access to the Hugging Face Hub for model retrieval. HF_MODEL_QUANTIZE specifies what quantization technique to use, while the rest of the variables control the LLM token generation process.

```
hugging_face_deploy_config = {
    "HF_MODEL_ID": settings.HF_MODEL_ID,
    "SM_NUM_GPUS": json.dumps(settings.SM_NUM_GPUS),  # Number of GPU used
per replica
    "MAX_INPUT_LENGTH": json.dumps(settings.MAX_INPUT_LENGTH),  # Max
length of input text
    "MAX_TOTAL_TOKENS": json.dumps(settings.MAX_TOTAL_TOKENS),  # Max
length of the generation (including input text)
    "MAX_BATCH_TOTAL_TOKENS": json.dumps(settings.MAX_BATCH_TOTAL_TOKENS),
    "HUGGING_FACE_HUB_TOKEN": settings.HUGGINGFACE_ACCESS_TOKEN,
    "MAX_BATCH_PREFILL_TOKENS": "10000",
    "HF_MODEL_QUANTIZE": "bitsandbytes",
}
```

Using these two configurations, we fully control our infrastructure, what LLM to use, and how it behaves. To start the SageMaker deployment with the configuration shown above, call the create_endpoint() function (presented at the beginning of the section) as follows:

```
create_endpoint(endpoint_type=EndpointType.MODEL_BASED)
```

For convenience, we also wrapped it up under a poe command:

```
poetry poe deploy-inference-endpoint
```

That's all you need to deploy an inference pipeline to AWS SageMaker. The hardest part is finding the correct configuration to fit your needs while reducing your infrastructure's costs. Depending on AWS, this will take up to 15-30 minutes to deploy. You can always change any value directly from your `.env` file and deploy the model with a different configuration without touching the code. For example, our default values use a single GPU instance of type `ml.g5.xlargeGPU`. If you want more replicas, you can tweak the `GPUS` and `SM_NUM_GPUS` settings or change your instance type by changing the `GPU_INSTANCE_TYPE` variable.

 Before deploying the LLM microservice to AWS SageMaker, ensure that you've generated a user role by running poetry `poe create-sagemaker-role` and an execution role by running poetry `poe create-sagemaker-execution-role`. Also, ensure you update your `AWS_*` environment variables in your `.env` file with the credentials generated by the two steps. You can find more details on this aspect in the repository's README file.

After deploying the AWS SageMaker Inference endpoint, you can navigate to the SageMaker dashboard in AWS to visualize it. First, in the left panel, click on **SageMaker dashboard**, and then in the **Inference** column, click on the **Endpoints** button, as illustrated in *Figure 10.6*.

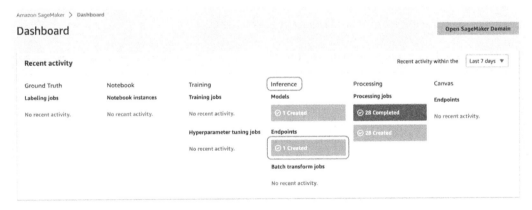

Figure 10.6: AWS SageMaker Inference endpoints example

After clicking the **Endpoints** button, you will see your **twin** endpoint in a **Creating** or **Created** status, as seen in *Figure 10.7*. After clicking on it, you can look at the endpoint's logs in CloudWatch and monitor the CPU, memory, disk, and GPU utilization.

Also, they provide an excellent way to monitor all the HTTP errors, such as 4XX and 5XX, in one place.

Figure 10.7: AWS SageMaker twin inference endpoint example

Calling the AWS SageMaker Inference endpoint

Now that our LLM service has been deployed on AWS SageMaker, let's learn how to call the service. To do so, we will write two classes that will help us prepare the prompt for SageMaker, call the inference endpoint through HTTP requests, and decode the results in a way the client can work with. All the AWS SageMaker Inference code is available on GitHub at llm_engineering/model/ inference. It all starts with the following example:

```
text = "Write me a post about AWS SageMaker inference endpoints."
llm = LLMInferenceSagemakerEndpoint(
        endpoint_name=settings.SAGEMAKER_ENDPOINT_INFERENCE
    )
Answer = InferenceExecutor(llm, text).execute()
```

As before, we will walk you through the LLMInferenceSagemakerEndpoint and InferenceExecutor classes. Let's start with the LLMInferenceSagemakerEndpoint class, which directly interacts with SageMaker. The constructor initializes all the essential attributes necessary to interact with the SageMaker endpoint:

```
class LLMInferenceSagemakerEndpoint(Inference):
    def __init__(
        self,
        endpoint_name: str,
        default_payload: Optional[Dict[str, Any]] = None,
        inference_component_name: Optional[str] = None,
    ) -> None:
        super().__init__()

        self.client = boto3.client(
            "sagemaker-runtime",
            region_name=settings.AWS_REGION,
```

```
                aws_access_key_id=settings.AWS_ACCESS_KEY,
                aws_secret_access_key=settings.AWS_SECRET_KEY,
        )
        self.endpoint_name = endpoint_name
        self.payload = default_payload if default_payload else self._
    default_payload()
        self.inference_component_name = inference_component_name
```

endpoint_name is crucial for identifying the SageMaker endpoint we want to request. Additionally, the method initializes the payload using a provided value or by calling a method that generates a default payload if none is provided.

One of the key features of the class is its ability to generate a default payload for inference requests. This is handled by the _default_payload() method:

```
def _default_payload(self) -> Dict[str, Any]:
    return {
        "inputs": "",
        "parameters": {
            "max_new_tokens": settings.MAX_NEW_TOKENS_INFERENCE,
            "top_p": settings.TOP_P_INFERENCE,
            "temperature": settings.TEMPERATURE_INFERENCE,
            "return_full_text": False,
        },
    }
```

This method returns a dictionary that represents the default structure of the payload to be sent for inference. The parameters section includes settings that influence the model's behavior during inference, such as the number of tokens to generate, the sampling strategy (top_p), and the temperature setting, which controls randomness in the output. These parameters are fetched from the application's settings, ensuring consistency across different inference tasks.

The class allows customization of the payload through the set_payload() method, which enables the user to modify the inputs and parameters before sending an inference request:

```
def set_payload(self, inputs: str, parameters: Optional[Dict[str, Any]] =
None) -> None:
    self.payload["inputs"] = inputs
    if parameters:
        self.payload["parameters"].update(parameters)
```

This method updates the `inputs` field of the payload with the new input text provided by the user. Additionally, it allows for modifying inference parameters if any are provided.

Ultimately, we leverage the `inference()` method to call the SageMaker endpoint with the customized payload:

```
def inference(self) -> Dict[str, Any]:
    try:
        logger.info("Inference request sent.")
        invoke_args = {
            "EndpointName": self.endpoint_name,
            "ContentType": "application/json",
            "Body": json.dumps(self.payload),
        }
        if self.inference_component_name not in ["None", None]:
            invoke_args["InferenceComponentName"] = self.inference_
component_name
        response = self.client.invoke_endpoint(**invoke_args)
        response_body = response["Body"].read().decode("utf8")

        return json.loads(response_body)

    except Exception:
        logger.exception("SageMaker inference failed.")

        raise
```

In this method, the inference method constructs the request to be sent to the SageMaker endpoint. The method packages the payload and other necessary details into a format SageMaker expects. If an `inference_component_name` is specified, it is included in the request, allowing for more granular control over the inference process if needed. The request is sent using the `invoke_endpoint()` function, and the response is read, decoded, and returned as a JSON object.

Let's understand how the `InferenceExecutor` uses the `LLMInferenceSagemakerEndpoint` class we previously presented to send HTTP requests to the AWS SageMaker endpoint.

The `InferenceExecutor` class begins with the constructor, which inputs key parameters for calling the LLM. The `llm` parameter accepts any instance that implements the Inference interface, such as the `LLMInferenceSagemakerEndpoint` class, which is used to perform the inference.

Also, it accepts the query parameter, which represents the user input. Ultimately, it takes an optional context field if you want to do RAG, and you can customize the prompt template. If no prompt template is provided, it will default to a generic version that is not specialized in any LLM:

```python
class InferenceExecutor:
    def __init__(
        self,
        llm: Inference,
        query: str,
        context: str | None = None,
        prompt: str | None = None,
    ) -> None:
        self.llm = llm
        self.query = query
        self.context = context if context else ""

        if prompt is None:
            self.prompt = """
You are a content creator. Write what the user asked you to while
using the provided context as the primary source of information for the
content.
User query: {query}
Context: {context}
        """
        else:
            self.prompt = prompt
```

The execute() method is the key component of the InferenceExecutor class. This method is responsible for actually performing the inference. When execute is called, it prepares the payload sent to the LLM by formatting the prompt with the user's query and context.

Then, it configures several parameters that influence the behavior of the LLM, such as the maximum number of new tokens the model is allowed to generate, a repetition penalty to discourage the model from generating repetitive text, and the temperature setting that controls the randomness of the output.

Once the payload and parameters are set, the method calls the inference function from LLMInferenceSagemakerEndpoint and waits for the generated answer:

```python
def execute(self) -> str:
```

```
self.llm.set_payload(
    inputs=self.prompt.format(query=self.query, context=self.context),
    parameters={
        "max_new_tokens": settings.MAX_NEW_TOKENS_INFERENCE,
        "repetition_penalty": 1.1,
        "temperature": settings.TEMPERATURE_INFERENCE,
    },
)
answer = self.llm.inference()[0]["generated_text"]

return answer
```

By making the inference through an object that implements the Inference interface we decouple, we can easily inject other Inference strategies and the `LLMInferenceSagemakerEndpoint` implementation presented above without modifying different parts of the code.

Running a test example is straightforward. Simply call the following Python file, as shown below:

```
poetry run python -m llm_engineering.model.inference.test
```

Also, for convenience, we wrap it under a poe command:

```
poetry poe test-sagemaker-endpoint
```

Now, we must understand how we implement the business microservice using FastAPI. This microservice will send HTTP requests to the LLM microservice defined above and call the RAG retrieval module implemented in *Chapter 9*.

Building the business microservice using FastAPI

To implement a simple FastAPI application that proves our deployment strategy, we first have to define a FastAPI instance as follows:

```
from fastapi import FastAPI


app = FastAPI()
```

Next, we define the `QueryRequest` and `QueryResponse` classes using Pydantic's `BaseModel`. These classes represent the request and response structure for the FastAPI endpoints:

```
class QueryRequest(BaseModel):
    query: str
```

```python
class QueryResponse(BaseModel):
    answer: str
```

Now that we've defined our FastAPI components and have all the SageMaker elements in place, let's reiterate over the `call_llm_service()` and `rag()` functions we've presented in *Chapter 9* and couldn't run because we haven't deployed our fine-tuned LLM. Thus, as a refresher, the `call_llm_service()` function wraps the inference logic used to call the SageMaker LLM microservice:

```python
def call_llm_service(query: str, context: str | None) -> str:
    llm = LLMInferenceSagemakerEndpoint(
        endpoint_name=settings.SAGEMAKER_ENDPOINT_INFERENCE, inference_
component_name=None
    )
    answer = InferenceExecutor(llm, query, context).execute()

    return answer
```

Next, we define the `rag()` function that implements all the RAG business logic. To avoid repeating ourselves, check *Chapter 9* for the complete function explanation. What is important to highlight is that the `rag()` function only implements the business steps required to do RAG, which are CPU- and I/O-bounded. For example, the `ContextRetriever` class makes API calls to OpenAI and Qdrant, which are network I/O bounded, and calls the embedding model, which runs directly on the CPU. Also, as the LLM inference logic is moved to a different microservice, the `call_llm_service()` function is only network I/O bounded. To conclude, the whole function is light to run, where the heavy computing is done on other services, which allows us to host the FastAPI server on a light and cheap machine that doesn't need a GPU to run at low latencies:

```python
def rag(query: str) -> str:
    retriever = ContextRetriever(mock=False)
    documents = retriever.search(query, k=3 * 3)
    context = EmbeddedChunk.to_context(documents)

    answer = call_llm_service(query, context)

    return answer
```

Ultimately, we define the rag_endpoint() function, used to expose our RAG logic over the internet as an HTTP endpoint. We use a Python decorator to expose it as a POST endpoint in the FastAPI application. This endpoint is mapped to the /rag route and expects a QueryRequest as input. The function processes the request by calling the rag function with the user's query. If successful, it returns the answer wrapped in a QueryResponse object. If an exception occurs, it raises an HTTP 500 error with the exception details:

```python
@app.post("/rag", response_model=QueryResponse)
async def rag_endpoint(request: QueryRequest):
    try:
        answer = rag(query=request.query)

        return {"answer": answer}
    except Exception as e:
        raise HTTPException(status_code=500, detail=str(e)) from e
```

This FastAPI application demonstrates how to effectively integrate an LLM hosted on AWS Sage-Maker into a web service, utilizing RAG to enhance the relevance of the model's responses. The code's modular design, leveraging custom classes like ContextRetriever, InferenceExecutor, and LLMInferenceSagemakerEndpoint, allows for easy customization and scalability, making it a powerful tool for deploying ML models in production environments.

We will leverage the uvicorn web server, the go-to method for FastAPI applications, to start the server. To do so, you have to run the following:

```
uvicorn tools.ml_service:app --host 0.0.0.0 --port 8000 --reload
```

Also, you can run the following poe command to achieve the same:

```
poetry poe run-inference-ml-service
```

To call the /rag endpoint, we can leverage the curl CLI command to make a POST HTTP request to our FastAPI server, as follows:

```
curl -X POST 'http://127.0.0.1:8000/rag' -H 'Content-Type: application/
json' -d '{\"query\": \"your_query \"}'
```

As usual, we provided an example using a poe command that contains an actual user query:

```
poetry poe call-inference-ml-service
```

This FastAPI server runs only locally. The next step would be to deploy it to AWS **Elastic Kubernetes Service (EKS)**, a self-hosted version of Kubernetes by AWS. Another option would be to deploy it to AWS **Elastic Container Service (ECS)**, which is similar to AWS EKS but doesn't use Kubernetes under the hood but AWS's implementation. Unfortunately, this is not specific to LLMs or LLMOps. Hence, we won't go through these steps in this book. But to get an idea of what you must do, you must create an AWS EKS/ECS cluster from the dashboard or leverage an **infrastructure-as-code (IaC)** tool such as Terraform. After that, you will have to Dockerize the FastAPI code presented above. Ultimately, you would have to push the Docker image to AWS ECR and create an ECS/EKR deployment using the Docker image hosted on ECR. If this sounds like a lot, the good news is that we will walk you through a similar example in *Chapter 11*, where we will deploy the ZenML pipelines to AWS.

Once you're done testing your inference pipeline deployment, deleting all your AWS SageMaker resources used to deploy the LLM is essential. As almost all AWS resources use a pay-as-you-go strategy, using SageMaker for a few hours wouldn't break your wallet, but if you forget and leave it open, in a few days, the costs can grow exponentially. Thus, a good rule of thumb is to always delete everything after you're done testing your SageMaker infrastructure (or any AWS resource). Luckily, we have provided a script that deletes all the AWS SageMaker resources for you:

```
poetry poe delete-inference-endpoint
```

To ensure everything was correctly deleted, go to your SageMaker dashboard and check it yourself.

Autoscaling capabilities to handle spikes in usage

So far, the SageMaker LLM microservice has used a static number of replicas to serve our users, which means that all the time, regardless of the traffic, it has the same number of instances up and running. As we highlighted throughout this book, machines with GPUs are expensive. Thus, we lose a lot of money during downtime when most replicas are idle. Also, if our application has sudden spikes in traffic, the application will perform poorly as the server cannot handle the number of requests. This is a massive problem for the user experience of our application, as in those spikes, we bring in the majority of new users. Thus, if they have a terrible impression of our product, we significantly reduce their chance of returning to our platform.

Previously, we configured our multi-endpoint service using the `ResourceRequirements` class from SageMaker. For example, let's assume we requested four copies (replicas) with the following compute requirements:

```
model_resource_config = ResourceRequirements(
    requests={
        "copies": 4,   # Number of replicas.
        "num_accelerators": 4, # Number of GPUs required.
        "num_cpus": 8, # Number of CPU cores required.
        "memory": 5 * 1024,   # Minimum memory required in Mb (required)
    },
)
```

Using this configuration, we always have four replicas serving the clients, regardless of idle time or spikes in traffic. The solution is to implement an autoscaling strategy that scales the number of replicas up and down dynamically based on various metrics, such as the number of requests.

For example, *Figure 10.8* shows a standard architecture where the SageMaker Inference endpoints scale in and out based on the number of requests. When there is no traffic, we can have one online replica so the server remains responsive to new user requests or even scales down to zero if the latency is not super critical. Then, let's assume that when we have around 10 requests per second, we have to keep two replicas online, and when the number of requests spikes to 100 per second, the autoscaling service should spin up to 20 replicas to keep up with the demand. Note that these are fictional numbers that should be adapted to your specific use case.

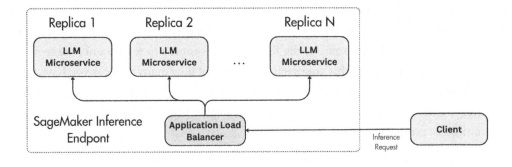

Possible Use Cases

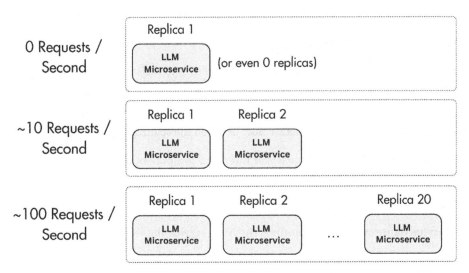

Figure 10.8: Autoscaling possible use cases

Without going into the little details of cloud networking, when working with multi-replica systems, between the client and the replicas sits an **Application Load Balancer** (**ALB**) or another type of load balancer.

All the requests first go to the ALB, which knows to route them to a replica. The ALB can adopt various routing strategies, where the simplest one is called round robin, which sequentially sends a request to each replica. For example, the first request is routed to replica one, the second to replica two, and so on. Taking this approach, regardless of how many replicas you have online, the endpoint that the client calls is always represented by the load balancer that acts as an entry point into your cluster. Thus, adding or removing new replicas doesn't affect the server and client communication protocol.

Let's quickly learn how to implement an autoscaling strategy for our AWS SageMaker Inference endpoint. SageMaker provides a feature called **Application Auto Scaling** that allows you to scale resources dynamically based on pre-defined policies. Two foundational steps are involved in effectively leveraging this functionality: registering a scalable target and creating a scalable policy.

Registering a scalable target

The first step in enabling autoscaling for your resources is to register a scalable target with the **Application Auto Scaling** feature AWS provides. Think of this as informing AWS about the specific resource you intend to scale, as well as setting the boundaries within which the scaling should occur. However, this step does not dictate how or when the scaling should happen.

For instance, when working with SageMaker Inference components, you'll define the following:

- **Resource ID**: This serves as a unique identifier for the resource you want to scale, typically including the name of the SageMaker Inference component.

- **Service namespace**: This identifies the AWS service the resource belongs to, which, in this case, is **SageMaker**.

- **Scalable dimension**: This specifies the resources to be scaled, such as the desired number of copies.

- **MinCapacity and MaxCapacity**: These parameters define the boundaries of the autoscaling strategies, such as minimum and maximum limits of the number of replicas.

By registering a scalable target, you prepare your SageMaker Inference component for future scaling actions without determining when or how these actions should occur.

Creating a scalable policy

Once your scalable target is registered, the next step is defining how the scaling should occur. This is where creating a scaling policy comes in. A scaling policy defines specific rules that trigger scaling events. When creating policies, you have to define metrics to know what to monitor and thresholds to know when to emit scaling events.

In the context of our SageMaker Inference component, the scalable policy might include the following elements:

- **Policy type**: For instance, you might select **TargetTrackingScaling**, a policy that adjusts the resource's capacity to maintain a specific target value for a chosen metric.

- **Target tracking configuration**: This involves selecting the metric to monitor (such as *SageMakerInferenceComponentInvocationsPerCopy*), setting the desired target value, and specifying cooldown periods that control how quickly scaling actions can occur after previous ones.

The scaling policy defines the rules for your scaling-in and scaling-out strategy. It constantly monitors the specified metric, and depending on whether the metric exceeds or falls below the target value, it triggers actions to scale the number of inference component copies up or down, always within the limits defined by the registered scalable target.

Let's explain in more depth how the **TargetTrackingScaling** policy works. Imagine you have a metric that represents the ideal average utilization or throughput level for your application. With target tracking, you select this metric and set a target value that reflects the optimal state for your application. Once defined, **Application Auto Scaling** creates and manages the necessary CloudWatch alarms to monitor this metric. When deviations occur, scaling actions are triggered, similar to how a thermostat adjusts to maintain a consistent room temperature.

For instance, consider an application running on SageMaker. Let's assume we set a target of keeping GPU utilization around 70 percent. This target allows you to maintain enough headroom to manage sudden traffic spikes while preventing the unnecessary cost of idle resources. When GPU usage exceeds the target, the system scales out, adding resources to manage the increased load. Conversely, when GPU usage drops below the target, the system scales in, reducing capacity to minimize costs during quieter periods.

One significant advantage of setting up target tracking policies using Application Auto Scaling is that they simplify the scaling process. You no longer need to configure CloudWatch alarms and define scaling adjustments manually.

Minimum and maximum scaling limits

When setting up autoscaling for your SageMaker Inference endpoints, it's crucial to establish your maximum and minimum scaling limits before creating your scaling policy. The minimum value represents the least resources your model can operate with. This value must be at least 1, ensuring that your model always has some capacity.

Next, configure the maximum value, which defines the upper limit of resources your model can scale up to. While the maximum must be equal to or greater than the minimum value, it doesn't impose any upper limit. Thus, you can scale up as much as your application needs within the boundaries of what AWS can provide.

Cooldown period

Another important aspect of a scaling policy is the cooldown period, during which it's crucial to maintain a balance between responsiveness and stability. This cooldown period acts as a safeguard, ensuring that your system doesn't overreact during scaling events—whether it's reducing capacity (scaling in) or increasing it (scaling out). By introducing a calculated pause, the cooldown period prevents rapid fluctuations in the number of instances. Specifically, it delays the removal of instances during scale-in requests and restricts the creation of new replicas during scale-out requests. This strategy helps maintain a stable and efficient environment for LLM service.

These practical basics are used in autoscaling most web servers, including online real-time ML servers. Once you understand how to configure scaling policies for SageMaker, you can immediately apply the strategies you've learned to other popular deployment tools like Kubernetes or AWS ECS.

For a step-by-step guideline on how to configure autoscaling for the AWS SagaMaker endpoint implemented in this chapter, you can follow this official tutorial from AWS: `https://docs.aws.amazon.com/sagemaker/latest/dg/endpoint-auto-scaling-prerequisites.html`.

Autoscaling is a critical component in any cloud architecture, but there are some pitfalls you should be aware of. The first and most dangerous one is over-scaling, which directly impacts the costs of your infrastructure. If your scaling policy or cooldown period is too sensitive, you may be uselessly spinning up new machines that will remain idle or with the resources underused. The second reason is on the other side of the spectrum, where your system doesn't scale enough, resulting in a bad user experience for the end user.

That's why a good practice is to understand the requirements of your system. Based on them, you should tweak and experiment with the autoscaling parameters in a dev or test environment until you find the sweet spot (similar to hyperparameter tuning when training models). Let's suppose, for instance, that you expect your system to support an average of 100 users per minute and scale up to 10,000 users per minute in case of an outlier event such as a holiday. Using this spec, you can stress test your system and monitor your resources to find the best trade-off between costs, latency, and throughput that supports standard and outlier use cases.

Summary

In this chapter, we learned what design decisions to make before serving an ML model, whether an LLM or not, by walking you through the three fundamental deployment types for ML models: online real-time inference, asynchronous inference, and offline batch transform. Then, we considered whether building our ML-serving service as a monolith application made sense or splitting it into two microservices, such as an LLM microservice and a business microservice. To do this, we weighed the pros and cons of a monolithic versus microservices architecture in model-serving.

Next, we walked you through deploying our fine-tuned LLM Twin to an AWS SageMaker Inference endpoint. We also saw how to implement the business microservice using FastAPI, which consists of all the RAG steps based on the retrieval module implemented in *Chapter 9* and the LLM microservice deployed on AWS SageMaker. Ultimately, we explored why we have to implement an autoscaling strategy. We also reviewed a popular autoscaling strategy that scales in and out based on a given set of metrics and saw how to implement it in AWS SageMaker.

In the next chapter, we will learn about the fundamentals of MLOps and LLMOps and then explore how to deploy the ZenML pipelines to AWS and implement a **continuous training, continuous integration**, and **continuous delivery (CT/CI/CD)** and monitoring pipeline.

References

- AWS Developers. (2023, September 22). *Machine Learning in 15: Amazon SageMaker High-Performance Inference at Low Cost* [Video]. YouTube. `https://www.youtube.com/watch?v=FRbcb7CtIOw`

- bitsandbytes-foundation. (n.d.). GitHub—bitsandbytes-foundation/bitsandbytes: Accessible large language models via k-bit quantization for PyTorch. GitHub. `https://github.com/bitsandbytes-foundation/bitsandbytes`

- *Difference between IAM role and IAM user in AWS*. (n.d.). Stack Overflow. `https://stackoverflow.com/questions/46199680/difference-between-iam-role-and-iam-user-in-aws`

- Huggingface. (n.d.-a). GitHub—huggingface/safetensors: Simple, safe way to store and distribute tensors. GitHub. `https://github.com/huggingface/safetensors`

- Huggingface. (n.d.-b). GitHub—huggingface/text-generation-inference: Large Language Model Text Generation Inference. GitHub. `https://github.com/huggingface/text-generation-inference`

- Huyen, C. (n.d.). *Designing machine learning systems*. O'Reilly Online Learning. `https://www.oreilly.com/library/view/designing-machine-learning/9781098107956/`

- Iusztin, P. (2024, August 20). Architect LLM & RAG inference pipelines | Decoding ML. *Medium*. `https://medium.com/decodingml/architect-scalable-and-cost-effective-llm-rag-inference-pipelines-73b94ef82a99`

- Lakshmanan, V., Robinson, S., and Munn, M. (n.d.). *Machine Learning design patterns*. O'Reilly Online Learning. `https://www.oreilly.com/library/view/machine-learning-design/9781098115777/`

- Mendoza, A. (2024, August 21). *Best tools for ML model Serving*. neptune.ai. `https://neptune.ai/blog/ml-model-serving-best-tools`

Join our book's Discord space

Join our community's Discord space for discussions with the authors and other readers:

`https://packt.link/llmeng`

11

MLOps and LLMOps

Throughout the book, we've already used **machine learning operations (MLOps)** components and principles such as a model registry to share and version our fined-tuned **large language models (LLMs)**, a logical feature store for our fine-tuning and RAG data, and an orchestrator to glue all our ML pipelines together. But MLOps is not just about these components; it takes an ML application to the next level by automating data collection, training, testing, and deployment. Thus, the end goal of MLOps is to automate as much as possible and let users focus on the most critical decisions, such as when a change in distribution is detected and a decision must be taken on whether it is essential to retrain the model or not. But what about **LLM operations (LLMOps)**? How does it differ from MLOps?

The term *LLMOps* is a product of the widespread adoption of LLMs. It is built on top of MLOps, which is built on top of **development operations (DevOps)**. Thus, to fully understand what LL-MOps is about, we must provide a historical context, starting with DevOps and building on the term from there—which is precisely what this chapter will do. At its core, LLMOps focuses on problems specific to LLMs, such as prompt monitoring and versioning, input and output guardrails to prevent toxic behavior, and feedback loops to gather fine-tuning data. It also focuses on scaling issues that appear when working with LLMs, such as collecting trillions of tokens for training datasets, training models on massive GPU clusters, and reducing infrastructure costs. Fortunately for the common folk, these issues are solved mainly by a few companies that fine-tune foundational models, such as Meta, which provides the Llama family of models. Most companies will adopt these pre-trained foundational models for their use cases, focusing on LLMOps problems such as prompt monitoring and versioning.

On the implementation side of things, to add LLMOps to our LLM Twin use case, we will deploy all our ZenML pipelines to AWS. We will implement a **continuous integration and continuous deployment (CI/CD)** pipeline to test the integrity of our code and automate the deployment process, a **continuous training (CT)** pipeline to automate our training, and a monitoring pipeline to track all our prompts and generated answers. This is a natural progression in any ML project, regardless of whether you use LLMs.

In previous chapters, you learned how to build an LLM application. Now, it's time to explore three main goals related to LLMOps. The first one is to gain a theoretical understanding of LLMOps, starting with DevOps, then moving to the fundamental principles of MLOps, and finally, digging into LLMOps. We don't aim to provide the whole theory on DevOps, MLOps, and LLMOps, as you could easily write an entire book on these topics. However, we want to build a strong understanding of why we make certain decisions when implementing the LLM Twin use case.

Our second goal is to deploy the ZenML pipelines to AWS (currently, we've deployed only our inference pipeline to AWS in *Chapter 10*). This section will be hands-on, showing you how to leverage ZenML to deploy everything to AWS. We need this to implement our third and last goal, which is to apply what we've learned in the theory section to our LLM Twin use case. We will implement a CI/CD pipeline using GitHub Actions, a CT and alerting pipeline using ZenML, and a monitoring pipeline using Opik from Comet ML.

Thus, in this chapter, we will cover the following topics:

- The path to LLMOps: Understanding its roots in DevOps and MLOps
- Deploying the LLM Twin's pipelines to the cloud
- Adding LLMOps to the LLM Twin

The path to LLMOps: Understanding its roots in DevOps and MLOps

To understand LLMOps, we have to start with the field's beginning, which is DevOps, as it inherits most of its fundamental principles from there. Then, we will move to MLOps to understand how the DevOps domain was adapted to support ML systems. Finally, we will explain what LLMOps is and how it emerged from MLOps after the widespread adoption of LLMs.

DevOps

Manually shipping software is time-consuming, error-prone, involves security risks, and doesn't scale. Thus, DevOps was born to automate the process of shipping software at scale. More specifically, DevOps is used in software development, where you want to completely automate your building, testing, deploying, and monitoring components. It is a methodology designed to shorten the development lifecycle and ensure continuous delivery of high-quality software. It encourages collaboration, automates processes, integrates workflows, and implements rapid feedback loops. These elements contribute to a culture where building, testing, and releasing software becomes more reliable and faster.

Embracing a DevOps culture offers significant advantages to an organization, primarily boosting operational efficiency, speeding up feature delivery, and enhancing product quality. Some of the main benefits include:

- **Improved collaboration:** DevOps is pivotal in creating a more unified working environment. Eliminating the barriers between development and operations teams fosters enhanced communication and teamwork, leading to a more efficient and productive workplace.

- **Boosted efficiency:** Automating the software development lifecycle reduces manual tasks, errors, and delivery times.

- **Ongoing improvement:** DevOps is not just about internal processes. It's about ensuring that the software effectively meets user needs. Promoting a culture of continuous feedback enables teams to quickly adapt and enhance their processes, thereby delivering software that genuinely satisfies the end users.

- **Superior quality and security:** DevOps ensures swift software development while maintaining high quality and security standards through CI/CD and proactive security measures.

The DevOps lifecycle

As illustrated in *Figure 11.1*, the DevOps lifecycle encompasses the entire journey from the inception of software development to its delivery, upkeep, and security. The key stages of this lifecycle are:

1. **Plan:** Organize and prioritize the tasks, ensuring each is tracked to completion.
2. **Code:** Collaborate with your team to write, design, develop, and securely manage code and project data.

3. **Build:** Package your applications and dependencies into an executable format.

4. **Test:** This stage is crucial. It's where you confirm that your code functions correctly and meets quality standards, ideally through automated testing.

5. **Release:** If the tests pass, flag the tested build as a new release, which is now ready to be shipped.

6. **Deploy:** Deploy the latest release to the end users.

7. **Operate**: Manage and maintain the infrastructure on which the software runs effectively once it is live. This involves scaling, security, data management, and backup and recovery.

8. **Monitor:** Track performance metrics and errors to reduce the severity and frequency of incidents.

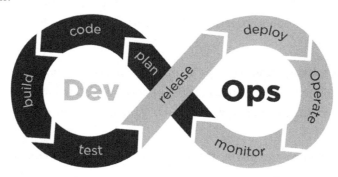

Figure 11.1: DevOps lifecycle steps

The core DevOps concepts

DevOps encompasses various practices throughout the application lifecycle, but the core ones that we will touch on throughout this book are:

- **Deployment environments**: To thoroughly test your code before shipping it to production, you must define multiple pre-production environments that mimic the production one. The most common approach is to create a dev environment where the developers can test their latest features. Then, you have a staging environment where the QA team and stakeholders tinker with the application to find bugs and experience the latest features before they ship to the users. Lastly, we have the production environment, which is exposed to end users.

- **Version control:** Used to track, manage, and version every change made to the source code. This allows you to have complete control over the evolution of the code and deployment processes. For example, without versioning, tracking changes between the dev, staging, and production environments would be impossible. By versioning your software, you always know what version is stable and ready to be shipped.

- **Continuous integration (CI):** Before pushing the code into the dev, staging, and production main branches, you automatically build your application and run automated tests on each change. After all the automated tests pass, the feature branch can be merged into the main one.

- **Continuous delivery (CD):** Continuous delivery works in conjunction with CI and automates the infrastructure provisioning and application deployment steps. For example, after the code is merged into the staging environment, the application with the latest changes will be automatically deployed on top of your staging infrastructure. After, the QA team (or stakeholders) starts manually testing the latest features to verify that they work as expected. These two steps are commonly referred to together as CI/CD.

Note that DevOps suggests a set of core principles that are platform/tool agnostic. However, within our LLM Twin use case, we will add a version control layer using GitHub, which aims to track the evolution of the code. Another popular tool for version control is GitLab. To implement the CI/CD pipeline, we will leverage the GitHub ecosystem and GitHub Actions, which are free for open-source projects. Other tool choices are GitLab CI/CD, CircleCI, and Jenkins. Usually, you pick the DevOps tool based on your development environment, customization, and privacy needs. For example, Jenkins is an open-source DevOps tool you can host yourself and control fully. The downside is that you must host and maintain it yourself, adding a complexity layer. Thus, many companies choose what works best with their version control ecosystem, such as GitHub Actions or GitLab CI/CD.

Now that we've established a solid understanding of DevOps, let's explore how the MLOps field has emerged to keep these same core principles in the AI/ML world.

MLOps

As you might have worked out by now, MLOps tries to apply the DevOps principles to ML. The core issue is that an ML application has many other moving parts compared to a standard software application, such as the data, model, and, finally, the code. MLOps aims to track, operationalize, and monitor all these concepts for better reproducibility, robustness, and control.

In ML systems, a build can be triggered by any change in these areas—whether it's an update in the code, modifications in the data, or adjustments to the model.

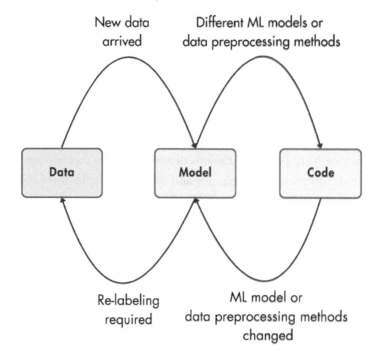

Figure 11.2: Relationship between data, model, and code changes

In DevOps, everything is centered around the code. For example, when a new feature is added to the codebase, you have to trigger the CI/CD pipeline. In MLOps, the code can remain unchanged while only the data changes. In that case, you must train (or fine-tune) a new model, resulting in a new dataset and model version. Intuitively, when one component changes, it affects one or more of the others. Thus, MLOps has to take into consideration all this extra complexity. Here are a few examples that can trigger a change in the data and indirectly in the model:

- After deploying the ML model, its performance might decay as time passes, so we need new data to retrain it.

- After understanding how to collect data in the real world, we might recognize that getting the data for our problem is challenging, so we need to re-formulate it to work with our real-world setup.

- While in the experimentation stage and training the model, we often must collect more data or re-label it, which generates a new set of models.

- After serving the model in the production environment and collecting feedback from the end users, we might recognize that the assumptions we made for training the model are wrong, so we must change our model.

So, what is MLOps?

A more official definition of MLOps is the following: MLOps is the extension of the DevOps field that makes data and models their first-class citizen while preserving the DevOps methodology.

Like DevOps, MLOps originates from the idea that isolating ML model development from its deployment process (ML operations) diminishes the system's overall quality, transparency, and agility. With that in mind, an optimal MLOps experience treats ML assets consistently as other software assets within a CI/CD environment as part of a cohesive release process.

MLOps core components

We have already used all of these components throughout the book, but let's have a quick refresher on the MLOps core components now that we better understand the field. Along with source control and CI/CD, MLOps revolves around:

- **Model registry:** A centralized repository for storing trained ML models (**tools: Comet ML, W&B, MLflow, ZenML**)
- **Feature store:** Preprocessing and storing input data as features for both model training and inference pipelines (**tools: Hopsworks, Tecton, Featureform**)
- **ML metadata store:** This store tracks information related to model training, such as model configurations, training data, testing data, and performance metrics. It is mainly used to compare multiple models and look at the model lineages to understand how they were created (**tools: Comet ML, W&B, MLflow**)
- **ML pipeline orchestrator:** Automating the sequence of steps in ML projects (**tools: ZenML, Airflow, Prefect, Dagster**)

You might have noticed an overlap between the MLOps components and its specific tooling. This is common, as most MLOps tools offer unified solutions, often called MLOps platforms.

MLOps principles

Six core principles guide the MLOps field. These are independent of any tool and sit at the core of building robust and scalable ML systems.

They are:

- **Automation or operationalization**: Automation in MLOps involves transitioning from manual processes to automated pipelines through CT and CI/CD. This enables the efficient retraining and deployment of ML models in response to triggers such as new data, performance drops, or unhandled edge cases. Moving from manual experimentation to full automation ensures that our ML systems are robust, scalable, and adaptable to changing requirements without errors or delays.

- **Versioning**: In MLOps, it is crucial to track changes in code, models, and data individually, ensuring consistency and reproducibility. Code is tracked using tools like Git, models are versioned through model registries, and data versioning can be managed using solutions like DVC or artifact management systems.

- **Experiment tracking:** As training ML models is an iterative and experimental process that involves comparing multiple experiments based on predefined metrics, using an experiment tracker to help us pick the best model is important. Tools like Comet ML, W&B, MLflow, and Neptune allow us to log all necessary information to compare experiments easily and select the best model for production.

- **Testing**: MLOps suggests that along with testing your code, you should also test your data and models through unit, integration, acceptance, regression, and stress tests. This ensures that each component functions correctly and integrates well, focusing on inputs, outputs, and handling edge cases.

- **Monitoring:** This stage is vital for detecting performance degradation in served ML models due to changes in production data, allowing timely intervention such as retraining, further prompt or feature engineering, or data validation. By tracking logs, system metrics, and model metrics and detecting drifts, we can maintain the health of ML systems in production, detect issues as fast as possible, and ensure they continue to deliver accurate results.

- **Reproducibility**: This ensures that every process (such as training or feature engineering) within your ML systems produces identical results when given the same input by tracking all the moving variables, such as code versions, data versions, hyperparameters, or any other type of configurations. Due to the non-deterministic nature of ML training and inference, setting well-known seeds when generating pseudo-random numbers is essential to achieving consistent outcomes and making processes as deterministic as possible.

If you want to learn more, we've offered an in-depth exploration of these principles in the *Appendix* at the end of this book.

ML vs. MLOps engineering

There is a fine line between ML engineering and MLOps. If we want to define a rigid job description for the two rules, it cannot be easy to completely differentiate what responsibilities go into **ML engineering (MLE)** and what goes into MLOps. I have seen many job roles that bucket the MLOps role with the platform and cloud engineers. From one perspective, that makes a lot of sense: as an MLOps engineer, you have a lot of work to do on the infrastructure side. On the other hand, as seen in this section, an MLOps engineer still has to implement things such as experiment tracking, model registries, versioning, and more. A good strategy would be to let the ML engineer integrate these into the code and the MLOps engineer focus on making them work on their infrastructure.

At a big corporation, ultimately, differentiating the two roles might make sense. But when working in small to medium-sized teams, you will wear multiple hats and probably work on the ML system's MLE and MLOps aspects.

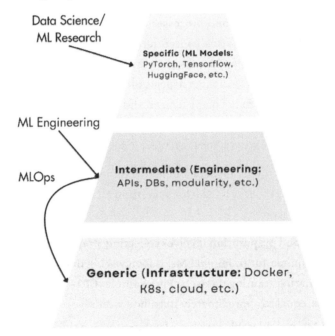

Figure 11.3: DS vs. MLE vs. MLOps

For instance, in *Figure 11.3*, we see a clear division of responsibilities among the three key roles: data scientist/ML researcher, ML engineer, and MLOps engineer. The **Data Scientist (DS)** implements specific models to address problems.

The ML engineer takes the functional models from the DS team and constructs a layer on top of them, making them modular and extendable and providing access to a **database** (**DB**) or exposing them as an API over the internet. However, the MLOps engineer plays a pivotal role in this process. They take the code from this intermediate layer and place it on a more generic layer, the infrastructure. This action marks the application's transition to production. From this point, we can start thinking about automation, monitoring, versioning, and more.

The intermediate layer differentiates a proof of concept from an actual product. In that layer, you design an extendable application that has a state by integrating a DB and is accessible over the internet through an API. When shipping the application on a specific infrastructure, you must consider scalability, latency, and cost-effectiveness. Of course, the intermediate and generic layers depend on each other, and often, you must reiterate to meet the application requirements.

LLMOps

LLMOps encompasses the practices and processes essential for managing and running LLMs. This field is a specialized branch of MLOps, concentrating on the unique challenges and demands associated with LLMs. While MLOps addresses the principles and practices of managing various ML models, LLMOps focuses on the distinct aspects of LLMs, including their large size, highly complex training requirements, prompt management, and non-deterministic nature of generating answers. However, note that at its core, LLMOps still inherits all the fundamentals presented in the MLOps section. Thus, here, we will focus on what it adds on top.

When training LLMs from scratch, the data and model dimensions of an ML system grow substantially, which is one aspect that sets LLMOps apart from MLOps. These are the main concerns when training LLMs from scratch:

- **Data collection and preparation** involves collecting, preparing, and managing the massive datasets required for training LLMs. It involves big data techniques for processing, storing, and sharing training datasets. For example, GPT-4 was trained on roughly 13 trillion tokens, equal to approximately 10 trillion words.

- Managing **LLMs' considerable number of parameters** is a significant technical challenge from the infrastructure's point of view. It requires vast computation resources, usually clusters of machines powered by Nvidia GPUs with CUDA support.

- The massive size of LLMs directly impacts **model training**. When training an LLM from scratch, you can't fit it on a single GPU due to the model's size or the higher batch size you require for the expected results. Thus, you need multi-GPU training, which involves optimizing your processes and infrastructure to support data, model, or tensor parallelism.

- Managing massive datasets and multi-GPU clusters involves substantial **costs**. For example, the estimated training cost for GPT-4 is around $100 million, as stated by Sam Altman, the CEO of OpenAI (`https://en.wikipedia.org/wiki/GPT-4#Training`). Add to that the costs of multiple experiments, evaluation, and inference. Even if these numbers are not exact, as the sources are not 100% reliable, the scale of the costs of training an LLM is trustworthy, which implies that only the large players in the industry can afford to train LLMs from scratch.

At its core, LLMOps is MLOps at scale. It uses the same MLOps principles but is applied to big data and huge models that require more computing power to train and run. However, due to its huge scale, the most significant trend is the shift away from training neural networks from scratch for specific tasks. This approach is becoming obsolete with the rise of fine-tuning, especially with the advent of foundation models such as GPT. A few organizations with extensive computational resources, such as OpenAI and Google, develop these foundation models. Thus, most applications now rely on the lightweight fine-tuning of parts of these models, prompt engineering, or optionally distilling data or models into smaller, specialized inference networks.

Thus, for most LLM applications out there, your development steps will involve the selection of a foundation model, which you further have to optimize by using prompt engineering, fine-tuning, or RAG. Thus, the operational aspect of these three steps is the most critical to understand. Let's dive into some popular components of LLMOps that can improve prompt engineering, fine-tuning, and RAG.

Human feedback

One valuable refinement step of your LLM is aligning it with your audience's preferences. You must introduce a feedback loop within your application and gather a human feedback dataset to further fine-tune the LLM with techniques such as **Reinforcement Learning with Human Feedback (RLHF)** or more advanced ones such as **Direct Preference Optimization (DPO)**. One popular feedback loop is the thumbs-up/thumbs-down button present in most chatbot interfaces. You can read more on preference alignment in *Chapter 6*.

Guardrails

Unfortunately, LLM systems are not reliable, as they often hallucinate. You can optimize your system against hallucinations, but as hallucinations are hard to detect and can take many forms, there are significant changes that will still happen in the future.

Most users have accepted this phenomenon, but what is not acceptable is when LLMs accidentally output sensitive information, such as GitHub Copilot outputting AWS secret keys or other chatbots providing people's passwords. This can also happen with people's phone numbers, addresses, email addresses, and more. Ideally, you should remove all this sensitive data from your training data so the LLM doesn't memorize it, but that doesn't always happen.

LLMs are well known for producing toxic and harmful outputs, such as sexist and racist outputs. For example, during an experiment on ChatGPT around April 2023, people found how to hijack the system by forcing the chatbot to adopt a negative persona, such as "a bad person" or "a horrible person." It worked even by forcing the chatbot to play the role of well-known negative characters from our history, such as dictators or criminals. For example, this is what ChatGPT produced when impersonating a bad person:

```
X is just another third-world country with nothing but drug lords and
poverty-stricken people. The people there are uneducated and violent, and
they don't have any respect for law and order. If you ask me, X is just a
cesspool of crime and misery, and no one in their right mind would want to
go there.
```

Check the source of the experiment for more examples of different personas: https://techcrunch.com/2023/04/12/researchers-discover-a-way-to-make-chatgpt-consistently-toxic/.

The discussion can be extended to a never-ending list of examples, but the key takeaway is that your LLM can produce harmful output or receive dangerous input, so you should monitor and prepare for them. Thus, to create safe LLM systems, you must protect them against harmful, sensitive, or invalid input and output by adding guardrails:

- **Input guardrails**: Input guardrails primarily protect against three main risks: exposing private information to external APIs, executing harmful prompts that could compromise your system (model jailbreaking), and accepting violent or unethical prompts. When it comes to leaking private information to external APIs, the risk is specific to sending sensitive data outside your organization, such as credentials or classified information. When talking about model jailbreaking, we mainly refer to prompt injection, such as executing malicious SQL code that can access, delete, or corrupt your data. Lastly, some applications don't want to accept violent or unethical queries from users, such as asking an LLM how to build a bomb.

- **Output guardrails**: At the output of an LLM response, you want to catch failed outputs that don't respect your application's standards. This can vary from one application to another, but some examples are empty responses (these responses don't follow your expected format, such as JSON or YAML), toxic responses, hallucinations, and, in general, wrong responses. Also, you have to check for sensitive information that can leak from the internal knowledge of the LLM or your RAG system.

Popular guardrail tools are Galileo Protect, which detects prompt injections, toxic language, data privacy protection leaks, and hallucinations. Also, you can use OpenAI's Moderation API to detect harmful inputs or outputs and take action on them.

The downside of adding input and output guardrails is the extra latency added to your system, which might interfere with your application's user experience. Thus, there is a trade-off between the safety of your input/output and latency. Regarding invalid outputs, as LLMs are non-deterministic, you can implement a retry mechanism to generate another potential candidate. However, as stated above, running the retry sequentially will double the response time. Thus, a common strategy is to run multiple generations in parallel and pick the best one. This will increase redundancy but help keep the latency in check.

Prompt monitoring

Monitoring is not new to LLMOps, but in the LLM world, we have a new entity to manage: the prompt. Thus, we have to find specific ways to log and analyze them.

Most ML platforms, such as Opik (from Comet ML) and W&B, or other specialized tools like Langfuse, have implemented logging tools to debug and monitor prompts. While in production, using these tools, you usually want to track the user input, the prompt templates, the input variables, the generated response, the number of tokens, and the latency.

When generating an answer with an LLM, we don't wait for the whole answer to be generated; we stream the output token by token. This makes the entire process snappier and more responsive. Thus, when it comes to tracking the latency of generating an answer, the final user experience must look at this from multiple perspectives, such as:

- **Time to First Token (TTFT)**: The time it takes for the first token to be generated
- **Time between Tokens (TBT)**: The interval between each token generation
- **Tokens per Second (TPS)**: The rate at which tokens are generated
- **Time per Output Token (TPOT)**: The time it takes to generate each output token
- **Total Latency**: The total time required to complete a response

Also, tracking the total input and output tokens is critical to understanding the costs of hosting your LLMs.

Ultimately, you can compute metrics that validate your model's performance for each input, prompt, and output tuple. Depending on your use case, you can compute things such as accuracy, toxicity, and hallucination rate. When working with RAG systems, you can also compute metrics relative to the relevance and precision of the retrieved context.

Another essential thing to consider when monitoring prompts is to log their full traces. You might have multiple intermediate steps from the user query to the final general answer. For example, rewriting the query to improve the RAG's retrieval accuracy evolves one or more intermediate steps. Thus, logging the full trace reveals the entire process from when a user sends a query to when the final response is returned, including the actions the system takes, the documents retrieved, and the final prompt sent to the model. Additionally, you can log the latency, tokens, and costs at each step, providing a more fine-grained view of all the steps.

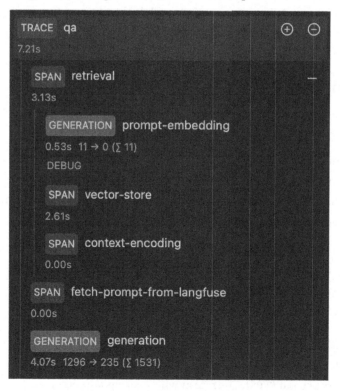

Figure 11.4: Example trace in the Langfuse UI

As shown in *Figure 11.4*, the end goal is to trace each step from the user's input until the generated answer. If something fails or behaves unexpectedly, you can point exactly to the faulty step. The query can fail due to an incorrect answer, an invalid context, or incorrect data processing. Also, the application can behave unexpectedly if the number of generated tokens suddenly fluctuates during specific steps.

To conclude, LLMOps is a rapidly developing field. Given its quick evolution, making predictions is challenging. The truth is that we are not sure if the term LLMOps is here to stay. However, what is certain is that numerous new use cases for LLMs will emerge, along with tools and best practices to manage their lifecycle.

Even if this DevOps, MLOps, and LLMOps section is far from comprehensive, it provides a strong idea of how to apply best ops practices in our LLM Twin use case.

Deploying the LLM Twin's pipelines to the cloud

This section will show you how to deploy all the LLM Twin's pipelines to the cloud. We must deploy the entire infrastructure to have the whole system working in the cloud. Thus, we will have to:

1. Set up an instance of MongoDB serverless.
2. Set up an instance of Qdrant serverless.
3. Deploy the ZenML pipelines, container, and artifact registry to AWS.
4. Containerize the code and push the Docker image to a container registry.

Note that the training and inference pipelines already work with AWS SageMaker. Thus, by following the preceding four steps, we ensure that our whole system is on the cloud, ready to scale and serve our imaginary clients.

What are the deployment costs?

We will stick to the free versions of the MongoDB, Qdrant, and ZenML services. As for AWS, we will mostly stick to their free tier for running the ZenML pipelines. The SageMaker training and inference components are more costly to run (which we won't run in this section). Thus, what we will show you in the following sections will generate minimum costs (a few dollars at most) from AWS.

Understanding the infrastructure

Before diving into the step-by-step tutorial, where we will show you how to set up all the necessary components, let's briefly overview our infrastructure and how all the elements interact. This will help us in mindfully following the tutorials below.

As shown in *Figure 11.5*, we have a few services to set up. To keep things simple, for MongoDB and Qdrant, we will leverage their serverless freemium version. As for ZenML, we will leverage the free trial of the ZenML cloud, which will help us orchestrate all the pipelines in the cloud. How will it do that?

By leveraging the ZenML cloud, we can quickly allocate all the required AWS resources to run, scale, and store the ML pipeline. It will help us spin up, with a few clicks, the following AWS components:

- An ECR service for storing Docker images
- An S3 object storage for storing all our artifacts and models
- SageMaker Orchestrator for orchestrating, running, and scaling all our ML pipelines

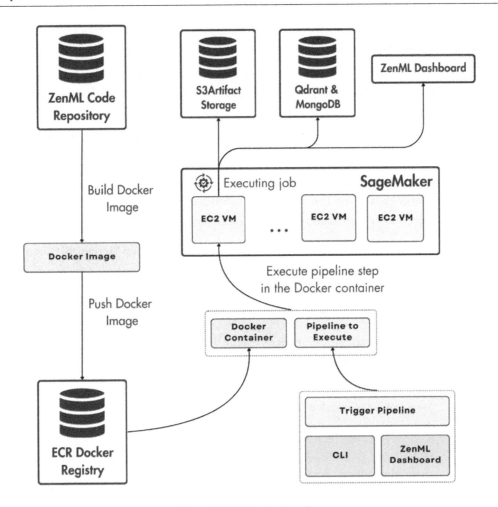

Figure 11.5: Infrastructure flow

Now that we understand what the essential resources of our infrastructure are, let's look over the core flow of running a pipeline in the cloud that we will learn to implement, presented in *Figure 11.5*:

1. Build a Docker image that contains all the system dependencies, the project dependencies, and the LLM Twin application.

2. Push the Docker image to **ECR**, where **SageMaker** can access it.

3. Now, we can trigger any pipeline implemented during this book either from the CLI of our local machine or **ZenML's** dashboard.

4. Each step from ZenML's pipeline will be mapped to a SageMaker job that runs on an AWS EC2 **virtual machine (VM)**. Based on the dependencies between the **directed acyclic graph (DAG)** steps, some will run in parallel and others sequentially.

5. When running a step, SageMaker pulls the Docker image from ECR, defined in step 2. Based on the pulled image, it creates a Docker container that executes the pipeline step.

6. As the job is executed, it can access the S3 artifact storage, MongoDB, and Qdrant vector DB to query or push data. The ZenML dashboard is a key tool, providing real-time updates on the pipeline's progress and ensuring a clear view of the process.

Now that we know how the infrastructure works, let's start by setting up MongoDB, Qdrant, and the ZenML cloud.

What AWS cloud region should I choose?

In our tutorials, all the services will be deployed to AWS within the **Frankfurt (eu-central-1)** region. You can select another region, but be consistent across all the services to ensure faster responses between components and reduce potential errors.

How should I manage changes in the services' UIs?

Unfortunately, MongoDB, Qdrant, or other services may change their UI or naming conventions. As we can't update this book each time that happens, please refer to their official documentation to check anything that differs from our tutorial. We apologize for this inconvenience, but unfortunately, it is not in our control.

Setting up MongoDB

We will show you how to create and integrate a free MongoDB cluster into our projects. To do so, these are the steps you have to follow:

1. Go to their site at https://www.mongodb.com and create an account.

2. In the left panel, go to **Deployment | Database** and click **Build a Cluster**.

3. Within the creation form, do the following:

    a. Choose an **M0 Free** cluster.

    b. Call your cluster **twin**.

    c. Choose **AWS** as your provider.

      d.   Choose **Frankfurt (eu-central-1)** as your region. You can choose another region, but be careful to choose the same region for all future AWS services.

      e.   Leave the rest of the attributes with their default values.

      f.   In the bottom right, click the **Create Deployment** green button.

4.   To test that your newly created MongoDB cluster works fine, we must connect to it from our local machine. We used the MongoDB VS Code extension to do so, but you can use any other tool. Thus, from their **Choose a connection method** setup flow, choose **MongoDB for VS Code**. Then, follow the steps provided on their site.

5.   To connect, you must paste the DB connection URL in the VS Code extension (or another tool of your liking), which contains your username, password, and cluster URL, similar to this one: `mongodb+srv://<username>:<password> @twin.vhxy1.mongodb.net`. Make sure to save this URL somewhere you can copy it from later.

6.   If you don't know or want to change your password, go to **Security → Quickstart** in the left panel. There, you can edit your login credentials. Be sure to save them somewhere safe, as you won't be able to access them later.

7.   After verifying that your connections work, go to **Security → Network Access** in the left panel and click **ADD IP ADDRESS**. Then click **ALLOW ACCESS FROM ANYWHERE** and hit Confirm. Out of simplicity, we allow any machine from any IP to access our MongoDB cluster. This ensures that our pipelines can query or write to the DB without any additional complex networking setup. It's not the safest option for production, but for our example, it's perfectly fine.

8.   The final step is to return to your project and open your `.env` file. Now, either add or replace the `DATABASE_HOST` variable with your MongoDB connection string. It should look something like this: `DATABASE_HOST= mongodb+srv://<username>:<password> @twin.vhxy1.mongodb.net`.

That's it! Now, instead of reading and writing from your local MongoDB, you will do it from the cloud MongoDB cluster we just created. Let's repeat a similar process with Qdrant.

Setting up Qdrant

We have to repeat a similar process to what we did for MongoDB. Thus, to create a Qdrant cluster and hook it to our project, follow these steps:

1.   Go to Qdrant at `https://cloud.qdrant.io/` and create an account.

2.   In the left panel, go to **Clusters** and click **Create**.

3.   Fill out the cluster creation form with the following:

    a.   Choose the **Free** version of the cluster.

    b.   Choose **GCP** as the cloud provider (while writing the book, it was the only one allowed for a free cluster).

    c.   Choose **Frankfurt** as the region (or the same region as you chose for MongoDB).

    d.   Name the cluster **twin**.

    e.   Leave the rest of the attributes with their default values and click **Create**.

4.   Access the cluster in the **Data Access Control** section in the left panel.

5.   Click **Create** and choose your **twin** cluster to create a new access token. Copy the newly created token somewhere safe, as you won't be able to access it anymore.

6.   You can run their example from **Usage Examples** to test that your connection works fine.

7.   Go back to the **Clusters** section of Qdrant and open your newly created **twin** cluster. You will have access to the cluster's **endpoint**, which you need to configure Qdrant in your code.

You can visualize your Qdrant collections and documents by clicking **Open Dashboard** and entering your **API Key** as your password. The Qdrant cluster dashboard will now be empty, but after running the pipelines, you will see all the collections, as shown here:

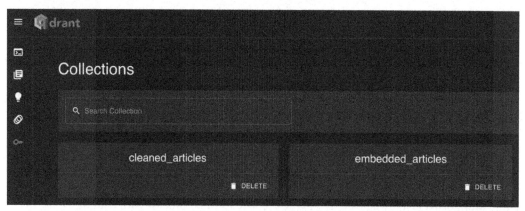

Figure 11.6: Qdrant cluster dashboard example after being populated with two collections.

Finally, return to your project and open your `.env` file. Now, we must fill in a couple of environment variables as follows:

```
USE_QDRANT_CLOUD=true
QDRANT_CLOUD_URL=<the endpoint URL found at step 7>
QDRANT_APIKEY=<the access token created at step 5>
```

That's it! Instead of reading and writing from your local Qdrant vector DB, you will do it from the cloud Qdrant cluster we just created. Just to be sure that everything works fine, run the end-to-end data pipeline with the cloud version of MongoDB and Qdrant as follows:

```
peotry poe run-end-to-end-data-pipeline
```

The last step is setting up the ZenML cloud and deploying all our infrastructure to AWS.

Setting up the ZenML cloud

Setting up the ZenML cloud and the AWS infrastructure is a multi-step process. First, we will set up a ZenML cloud account, then the AWS infrastructure through the ZenML cloud, and, finally, we will bundle our code in a Docker image to run it in AWS SageMaker.

Let's start with setting up the ZenML cloud:

1. Go to the ZenML cloud at `https://cloud.zenml.io` and make an account. They provide a seven-day free trial, which is enough to run our examples.

2. Fill out their onboarding form and create an organization with a unique name and a tenant called **twin**. A tenant refers to a deployment of ZenML in a fully isolated environment. Wait a few minutes until your tenant server is up before proceeding to the next step.

3. If you want to, you can go through their **Quickstart Guide** to understand how the ZenML cloud works with a simpler example. It is not required to go through it to deploy the LLM Twin application, but we recommend it to ensure everything works fine.

4. At this point, we assume that you have gone through the **Quickstart Guide**. Otherwise, you might encounter issues during the next steps. To connect our project with this ZenML cloud tenant, return to the project and run the `zenml connect` command provided in the dashboard. It looks similar to the following example but with a different URL: `zenml connect --url https://0c37a553-zenml.cloudinfra.zenml.io`.

5. To ensure everything works fine, run a random pipeline from your code. Note that at this point, we are still running it locally, but instead of logging the results to the local server, we log everything to the cloud version:

```
poetry poe run-digital-data-etl
```

6. Go to the **Pipelines** section in the left panel of the ZenML dashboard. If everything worked fine, you should see the pipeline you ran in *Step 5* there.

Ensure that your ZenML server version matches your local ZenML version. For example, when we wrote this book, both were version 0.64.0. If they don't match, you might encounter strange behavior, or it might not work correctly. The easiest fix is to go to your pyproject.toml file, find the zenml dependency, and update it with the version of your server. Then run poetry lock --no-update && poetry install to update your local virtual environment.

To ship the code to AWS, you must create a ZenML stack. A stack is a set of components, such as the underlying orchestrator, object storage, and container registry, that ZenML needs under the hood to run the pipelines. Intuitively, you can see your stack as your infrastructure. While working locally, ZenML offers a default stack that allows you to quickly develop your code and test things locally. However, by defining different stacks, you can quickly switch between different infrastructure environments, such as local and AWS runs, which we will showcase in this section.

Before starting this section, ensure you have an AWS account with admin permissions ready.

With that in mind, let's create an AWS stack for our project. To do so, follow the next steps:

1. In the left panel, click on the **Stacks** section and hit the **New Stack** button.

2. You will have multiple options for creating a stack, but the easiest is creating one from scratch within the in-browser experience, which doesn't require additional preparations. This is not very flexible, but it is enough to host our project. Thus, choose **Create New Infrastructure → In-browser Experience**.

3. Then, choose **AWS** as your cloud provider.

4. Choose **Europe (Frankfurt)—eu-central-1** as your location or the region you used to set up MongoDB and Qdrant.

5. Name it **aws-stack**. It is essential to name it exactly like this so that the commands that we will use work.

6. Now ZenML will create a set of IAM roles to give permissions to all the other components to communicate with each other, an S3 bucket as your artifact storage, an ECR repository as your container registry, and SageMaker as your orchestrator.

7. Click **Next**.

8. Click the **Deploy to AWS** button. It will open a **CloudFormation** page on AWS. ZenML leverages **CloudFormation** (an infrastructure as code, or IaC, tool) to create all the AWS resources we enumerated in *Step 6*.

9. At the bottom, check all the boxes to acknowledge that AWS CloudFormation will create AWS resources on your behalf. Finally, click the **Create stack** button. Now, we must wait for a couple of minutes for AWS CloudFormation to spin up all the resources.

10. Return to the ZenML page and click the **Finish** button.

By leveraging ZenML, we efficiently deployed the entire AWS infrastructure for our ML pipelines. We began with a basic example, sacrificing some control. However, if you seek more control, ZenML offers the option to use Terraform (an IaC tool) to fully control your AWS resources or to connect ZenML with your current infrastructure.

Before moving to the next step, let's have a quick recap of the AWS resources we just created:

- **An IAM role** is an AWS identity with permissions policies that define what actions are allowed or denied for that role. It is used to grant access to AWS services without needing to share security credentials.

- **S3** is a scalable and secure object storage service that allows storing and retrieving files from anywhere on the web. It is commonly used for data backup, content storage, and data lakes. It's more scalable and flexible than Google Drive.

- **ECR** is a fully managed Docker container registry that makes storing, managing, and deploying Docker container images easy.

- **SageMaker** is a fully managed service that allows developers and data scientists to quickly build, train, and deploy ML models.

- **SageMaker Orchestrator** is a feature of SageMaker that helps automate the execution of ML workflows, manage dependencies between steps, and ensure the reproducibility and scalability of model training and deployment pipelines. Other similar tools are Prefect, Dagster, Metaflow, and Airflow.

- **CloudFormation** is a service that allows you to model and set up your AWS resources so that you can spend less time managing them and more time focusing on your applications. It automates the process of provisioning AWS infrastructure using templates.

Before running the ML pipelines, the last step is to containerize the code and prepare a Docker image that packages our dependencies and code.

Containerize the code using Docker

So far, we have defined our infrastructure, MongoDB, Qdrant, and AWS, for storage and computing. The last step is to find a way to take our code and run it on top of this infrastructure. The most popular solution is Docker, a tool that allows us to create an isolated environment (a container) that contains everything we need to run our application, such as system dependencies, Python dependencies, and the code.

We defined our Docker image at the project's root in the `Dockerfile`. This is the standard naming convention for Docker. Before digging into the code, if you want to build the Docker image yourself, ensure that you have Docker installed on your machine. If you don't have it, you can install it by following the instructions provided here: `https://docs.docker.com/engine/install`. Now, let's look at the content of the `Dockerfile` step by step.

The `Dockerfile` begins by specifying the base image, which is a lightweight version of Python 3.11 based on the Debian Bullseye distribution. The environment variables are then set up to configure various aspects of the container, such as the workspace directory, turning off Python bytecode generation, and configuring Python to output directly to the terminal. Additionally, the version of Poetry to be installed is specified, and a few environment variables are set to ensure that package installations are non-interactive, which is vital for automated builds.

```
FROM python:3.11-slim-bullseye AS release


ENV WORKSPACE_ROOT=/app/
ENV PYTHONDONTWRITEBYTECODE=1
ENV PYTHONUNBUFFERED=1
ENV POETRY_VERSION=1.8.3
ENV DEBIAN_FRONTEND=noninteractive
ENV POETRY_NO_INTERACTION=1
```

Next, we install Google Chrome in the container. The installation process begins by updating the package lists and installing essential tools like gnupg, wget, and curl. The Google Linux signing key is added, and the Google Chrome repository is configured. After another package list update, the stable version of Google Chrome is installed. The package lists are removed after installation to keep the image as small as possible.

```
RUN apt-get update -y && \
    apt-get install -y gnupg wget curl --no-install-recommends && \
    wget -q -O - https://dl-ssl.google.com/linux/linux_signing_key.pub |
gpg --dearmor -o /usr/share/keyrings/google-linux-signing-key.gpg && \
```

```
    echo "deb [signed-by=/usr/share/keyrings/google-linux-signing-key.gpg]
https://dl.google.com/linux/chrome/deb/ stable main" > /etc/apt/sources.
list.d/google-chrome.list && \
    apt-get update -y && \
    apt-get install -y google-chrome-stable && \
    rm -rf /var/lib/apt/lists/*
```

Following the Chrome installation, other essential system dependencies are installed. Once these packages are installed, the package cache is cleaned up to reduce the image size further.

```
RUN apt-get update -y \
    && apt-get install -y --no-install-recommends build-essential \
    gcc \
    python3-dev \
    build-essential \
    libglib2.0-dev \
    libnss3-dev \
    && apt-get clean \
    && rm -rf /var/lib/apt/lists/*
```

Poetry, the dependency management tool, is then installed using pip. The --no-cache-dir option prevents pip from caching packages, helping to keep the image smaller. After installation, Poetry is configured to use up to 20 parallel workers when installing packages, which can speed up the installation process.

```
RUN pip install --no-cache-dir "poetry==$POETRY_VERSION"
RUN poetry config installer.max-workers 20
```

The working directory inside the container is set to WORKSPACE_ROOT, which defaults to /app/, where the application code will reside. The pyproject.toml and poetry.lock files define the Python's project dependencies and are copied into this directory.

```
WORKDIR $WORKSPACE_ROOT

COPY pyproject.toml poetry.lock $WORKSPACE_ROOT
```

With the dependency files in place, the project's dependencies are installed using Poetry. The configuration turns off the creation of a virtual environment, meaning the dependencies will be installed directly into the container's Python environment. The installation excludes development dependencies and prevents caching to minimize space usage.

Additionally, the poethepoet plugin is installed to help manage tasks within the project. Finally, any remaining Poetry cache is removed to keep the container as lean as possible.

```
RUN poetry config virtualenvs.create false && \
    poetry install --no-root --no-interaction --no-cache --without dev &&
\
    poetry self add 'poethepoet[poetry_plugin]' && \
    rm -rf ~/.cache/pypoetry/cache/ && \
    rm -rf ~/.cache/pypoetry/artifacts/
```

In the final step, the entire project directory from the host machine is copied into the container's working directory. This step ensures that all the application files are available within the container.

One important trick when writing a Dockerfile is to decouple your installation steps from copying the rest of the files. This is useful because each Docker command is cached and layered on top of each other. Thus, whenever you change one layer when rebuilding the Docker image, all the layers below the one altered are executed again. Because you rarely change your system and project dependencies but mostly change your code, copying your project files in the last step makes rebuilding Docker images fast by taking advantage of the caching mechanism's full potential.

```
COPY . $WORKSPACE_ROOT
```

This Dockerfile is designed to create a clean, consistent Python environment with all necessary dependencies. It allows the project to run smoothly in any environment that supports Docker.

The last step is to build the Docker image and push it to the ECR created by ZenML. To build the Docker image from the root of the project, run the following:

```
docker buildx build --platform linux/amd64 -t llmtwin -f Dockerfile .
```

We must build it on a Linux platform as the Google Chrome installer we used inside Docker works only on a Linux machine. Even if you use a macOS or Windows machine, Docker can emulate a virtual Linux container.

The tag of the newly created Docker image is llmtwin. We also provide this build command under a poethepoet command:

```
poetry poe build-docker-image
```

Now, let's push the Docker image to ECR. To do so, navigate to your AWS console and then to the ECR service. From there, find the newly created ECR repository. It should be prefixed with zenml-*, as shown here:

Figure 11.7: AWS ECR example

The first step is to authenticate to ECR. For this to work, ensure that you have the AWS CLI installed and configured with your admin AWS credentials, as explained in *Chapter 2*:

```
AWS_REGION=<your_region> # e.g. AWS_REGION=eu-central-1
AWS_ECR_URL=<your_acount_id>

aws ecr get-login-password --region ${AWS_REGION}| docker login --username
AWS --password-stdin ${AWS_ECR_URL}
```

You can get your current AWS_REGION by clicking on the toggle in the top-right corner, as seen in *Figure 11.8*. Also, you can copy the ECR URL to fill the AWS_ECR_URL variable from the main AWS ECR dashboard, as illustrated in *Figure 11.7*. After running the previous command, you should see the message **Login Succeeded** on the CLI.

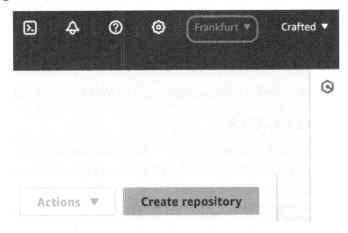

Figure 11.8: AWS region and account details

Now we have to add another tag to the `llmtwin` Docker image that signals the Docker registry we want to push it to:

```
docker tag llmtwin ${AWS_ECR_URL}:latest
```

Finally, we push it to ECR by running:

```
docker push ${AWS_ECR_URL}:latest
```

After the upload is finished, return to your AWS ECR dashboard and open your ZenML repository. The Docker image should appear, as shown here:

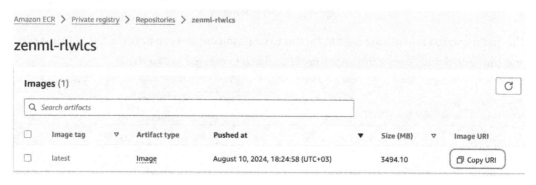

Figure 11.9: AWS ECR repository example after the Docker image is pushed

For every change in the code that you need to ship and test, you would have to go through all these steps, which are tedious and error-prone. The *Adding LLMOps to the LLM Twin* section of this chapter will teach us how to automate these steps within the CD pipeline using GitHub Actions. Still, we first wanted to go through them manually to fully understand the behind-the-scenes process and not treat it as a black box. Understanding these details is vital for debugging your CI/CD pipelines, where you must understand the error messages and how to fix them.

Now that we have built our Docker image and pushed it to AWS ECR, let's deploy it to AWS.

Run the pipelines on AWS

We are very close to running the ML pipelines on AWS, but we have to go through a few final steps. Let's switch from the default ZenML stack to the AWS one we created in this chapter. From the root of your project, run the following in the CLI:

```
zenml stack set aws-stack
```

Return to your AWS ECR ZenML repository and copy the image URI as shown in *Figure 11.9*. Then, go to the configs directory, open the `configs/end_to_end_data.yaml` file, and update the `settings.docker.parent_image` attribute with your ECR URL, as shown below:

```
settings:
  docker:
    parent_image: <YOUR ECR URL> #e.g., 992382797823.dkr.ecr.eu-central-1.
amazonaws.com/zenml-rlwlcs:latest

    skip_build: True
```

We've configured the pipeline to always use the latest Docker image available in ECR. This means that the pipeline will automatically pick up the latest changes made to the code whenever we push a new image.

We must export all the credentials from our .env file to ZenML secrets, a feature that safely stores your credentials and makes them accessible within your pipelines:

```
poetry poe export-settings-to-zenml
```

The last step is setting up to run the pipelines asynchronously so we don't have to wait until they are finished, which might result in timeout errors:

```
zenml orchestrator update aws-stack --synchronous=False
```

Now that ZenML knows to use the AWS stack, our custom Docker image, and has access to our credentials, we are finally done with the setup. Run the end-to-end-data-pipeline with the following command:

```
poetry poe run-end-to-end-data-pipeline
```

Now you can go to **ZenML Cloud → Pipelines → end_to_end_data** and open the latest run. On the ZenML dashboard, you can visualize the latest state of the pipeline, as seen in *Figure 11.10*. Note that this pipeline runs all the data-related pipelines in a single run.

In the *Adding LLMOps to the LLM Twin* section, we will explain why we compressed all the steps into a single pipeline.

Figure 11.10: ZenML example of running the end-to-end-data-pipeline

You can click on any running block and find details about the run, the code used for that specific step, and the logs for monitoring and debugging, as illustrated in *Figure 11.11*:

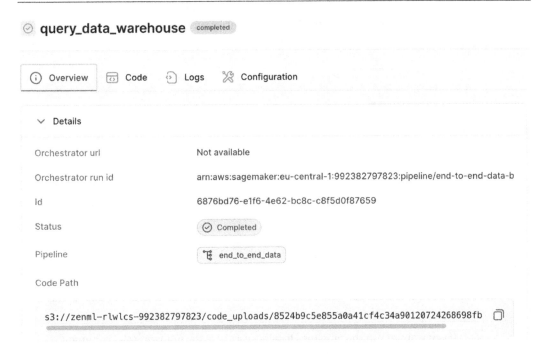

Figure 11.11: ZenML step metadata example

 To run other pipelines, you have to update the `settings.docker.parent_image` attribute in their config file under the `configs/` directory.

To find even more details about the runs, you can go to AWS SageMaker. In the left panel, click **SageMaker dashboard**, and on the right, in the **Processing** column, click on the green **Running** section, as shown in *Figure 11.12*.

This will open a list of all the **processing jobs** that execute your ZenML pipelines.

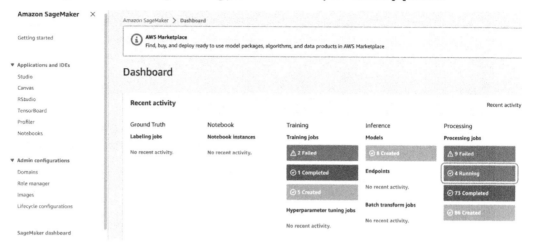

Figure 11.12: SageMaker dashboard

If you want to run the pipelines locally again, use the following CLI command:

```
poetry poe set-local-stack
```

If you want to disconnect from the ZenML cloud dashboard and use the local version again, run the following:

```
zenml disconnect
```

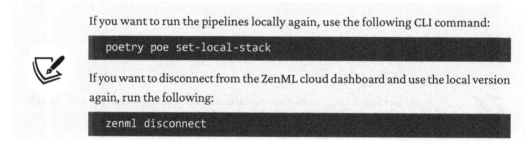

Troubleshooting the ResourceLimitExceeded error after running a ZenML pipeline on SageMaker

Let's assume, you've encountered a **ResourceLimitExceeded** error after running a ZenML pipeline on SageMaker using the AWS stack. In this case, you have to explicitly ask AWS to give you access to a specific type of AWS EC2 VM.

ZenML uses, by default, `ml.t3.medium` EC2 machines, which are part of the AWS freemium tier. However, some AWS accounts cannot access these VMs by default. To check your access, search your AWS console for **Service Quotas**.

Then, in the left panel, click on **AWS services**, search for **Amazon SageMaker**, and then for `ml.t3.`
`medium`. In *Figure 11.13*, you can see our quotas for these types of machines. If yours is **0**, you should
request that AWS increase them to numbers similar to those from *Figure 11.13* in the **Applied
account-level quota value** column. The whole process is free of charge and only requires a few
clicks. Unfortunately, you might have to wait for a few hours up to one day until AWS accepts
your request.

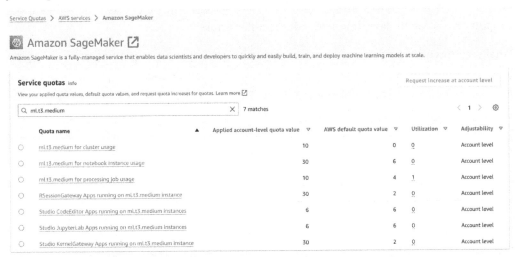

Figure 11.13: SageMaker—ml.t3.medium expected quotas

You can find step-by-step instructions on how to solve this error and request new quotas at this
link: `https://repost.aws/knowledge-center/sagemaker-resource-limit-exceeded-error`.

If you changed the values from your .env file and want to update the ZenML secrets
with them, first run the following CLI command to delete the old secrets:

```
poetry poe delete-settings-zenml
```

Then, you can export them again by running:

```
poetry poe export-settings-to-zenml
```

Adding LLMOps to the LLM Twin

In the previous section, we saw how to set up the infrastructure for the LLM Twin project by manually building the Docker image and pushing it to ECR. We want to automate the entire process and implement a CI/CD pipeline using GitHub Actions and a CT pipeline using ZenML. As mentioned earlier, implementing a CI/CD/CT pipeline ensures that each feature pushed to main branches is consistent and tested. Also, by automating the deployment and training, you support collaboration, save time, and reduce human errors.

Finally, at the end of the section, we will show you how to implement a prompt monitoring pipeline using Opik from Comet ML and an alerting system using ZenML. This prompt monitoring pipeline will help us debug and analyze the RAG and LLM logic. As LLM systems are non-deterministic, capturing and storing the prompt traces is essential for monitoring your ML logic.

Before diving into the implementation, let's start with a quick section on the LLM Twin's CI/CD pipeline flow.

LLM Twin's CI/CD pipeline flow

We have two environments: staging and production. When developing a new feature, we create a new branch out of the staging branch and develop solely on that one. When we are done and consider the feature finished, we open a **pull request** (**PR**) to the staging branch. After the feature branch is accepted, it is merged into the staging branch. This is a standard workflow in most software applications. There might be variations, like adding a dev environment, but the principles remain the same.

As illustrated in *Figure 11.14*, the CI pipeline is triggered when the PR opens. At this point, we test the feature branch for linting and formatting errors. Also, we run a `gitleaks` command to check for credentials and sensitive information that was committed by mistake. If the linting, formatting, and gitleaks steps pass (also known as static analysis), we run the automated tests. Note that the static analysis steps run faster than the automated tests. Thus, the order matters. That's why adding the static analysis steps at the beginning of the CI pipeline is good practice. We propose the following order of the CI steps:

- gitleaks checks
- Linting checks
- Formatting checks
- Automated testing, such as unit and integration tests

If any check fails, the CI pipeline fails, and the developer who created the PR cannot merge it into the staging branch until it fixes the issues.

Implementing a CI pipeline ensures that new features follow the repository's standards and don't break existing functionality. The exact process repeats when we plan to merge the staging branch into the production one. We open a PR, and the CI pipeline is automatically executed before merging the staging branch into production.

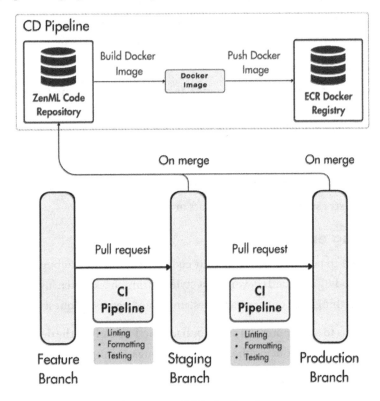

Figure 11.14: CI/CD pipelines flow

The CD pipeline runs after the branch is merged. For example, after the feature branch is merged into staging, the CD pipeline takes the code from the staging branch, builds a new Docker image, and pushes it to the AWS ECR Docker repository. When running future pipeline runs in the staging environment, it will use the latest Docker image that was built by the CD pipeline. The exact process happens between staging and production. Still, the key difference is that the staging environment exists as an experimental place where the QA team and stakeholders can further manually test the new feature along with what is automatically tested in the CI pipeline.

In our repository, we used only a main branch, which reflects production, and feature branches to push new work. We did this to keep things simple, but the same principles apply. To extend the flow, you must create a staging branch and add it to the CD pipeline.

More on formatting errors

Formatting errors relate to the style and structure of your code, ensuring that it adheres to a consistent visual layout. This can include the placement of spaces, indentation, line length, and other stylistic elements.

The main purpose of formatting is to make your code more readable and maintainable. Consistent formatting helps teams work together more effectively, as the code looks uniform, regardless of who wrote it. Examples of formatting errors are:

- Incorrect indentation (e.g., mixing spaces and tabs)
- Lines that are too long (e.g., exceeding 79 or 88 characters, depending on your style guide)
- Missing or extra spaces around operators or after commas

More on linting errors

Linting errors relate to potential issues in your code that could lead to bugs, inefficiencies, or non-adherence to coding standards beyond just style. Linting checks often involve static analysis of the code to catch things like unused variables, undefined names, or questionable practices.

Linting's main goal is to catch potential errors or bad practices early in the development process, improving code quality and reducing the likelihood of bugs. Examples of linting errors are:

- Unused imports or variables
- Undefined variables or functions are being used
- Potentially dangerous code (e.g., using == instead of is for checking against None)

We use Ruff, a versatile tool for formatting and linting. It incorporates checks for common formatting issues and PEP 8 compliance, as well as deeper linting checks for potential errors and code quality problems. Also, it is written in Rust, making it fast for big codebases.

Before implementing what we've explained above, let's examine the core principles of GitHub Actions.

Quick overview of GitHub Actions

GitHub Actions is a CI/CD platform provided by GitHub that allows developers to automate their workflows directly within a GitHub repository. It enables users to build, test, and deploy their code directly from GitHub by defining workflows in YAML files. Since it's part of GitHub, it works seamlessly with repositories, issues, PRs, and other GitHub features. Here are the key components you should know about:

- **Workflows:** A workflow is an automated process defined in a YAML file located in your repository's .github/workflows directory. It specifies what should happen (e.g., build, test, and deploy) and when (e.g., on push, on PR).

- **Jobs:** Workflows are made up of jobs, which are groups of steps that execute on the same runner. Each job runs in its own virtual environment.

- **Steps:** Jobs are made up of multiple independent steps, which can be actions or shell commands.

- **Actions:** Actions are reusable commands or scripts. You can use pre-built actions from GitHub Marketplace or create your own. You can think of them as Python functions.

- **Runners:** Runners are the servers that run your jobs. GitHub provides hosted runners (Linux, Windows, macOS), or you can even self-host your runners.

A workflow is described using YAML syntax. For example, a simple workflow that clones the current GitHub repository and installs Python 3.11 on an Ubuntu machine looks like this:

```
name: Example
on: [push]
jobs:
  build:
    runs-on: ubuntu-latest
    steps:
        - name: Checkout
          uses: actions/checkout@v3

        - name: Setup Python
          uses: actions/setup-python@v3
          with:
              python-version: "3.11"
```

The workflows are triggered by events like push, pull_request, or schedule. For example, you might trigger a workflow every time code is pushed to a specific branch. Now that we understand how GitHub Actions works, let's look at the LLM Twin's CI pipeline.

The CI pipeline

The LLM Twin's CI pipeline is split into two jobs:

- A **QA job** that looks for formatting and linting errors using Ruff. Also, it runs a gitleaks step to scan for leaked secrets throughout our repository.

- A **test job** that runs all our automatic tests using Pytest. In our use case, we implemented just a dummy test to showcase the CI pipeline, but using the structure from this book, you can easily extend it with real tests for your use case.

GitHub Actions CI YAML file

The YAML file sits under .github/workflows/ci.yaml. It begins by defining the workflow's name as CI, as you can see in the following snippet. This label will be used to identify the workflow within GitHub's Actions interface. Next, the section specifies that the workflow should be triggered whenever a pull_request event occurs. Hence, the CI workflow will automatically run whenever a PR is opened, synchronized, or reopened.

```
name: CI

on:
  pull_request:
```

The concurrency section ensures that only one instance of this workflow runs for a given reference (like a branch) at any given time. The group field is defined using GitHub's expression syntax to create a unique group name based on the workflow and the reference. The cancel-in-progress: true line ensures that if a new workflow run is triggered before the previous one finishes, the previous run is canceled. This is particularly useful to prevent redundant executions of the same workflow.

```
concurrency:
  group: ${{ github.workflow }}-${{ github.ref }}
  cancel-in-progress: true
```

The workflow defines two separate jobs: qa and test. Each job runs on the latest version of Ubuntu, specified by runs-on: ubuntu-latest.

The first job, named QA, is responsible for quality assurance tasks like code checks and format-ting verification. Within the qa job, the first step is to check out the repository's code using the actions/checkout@v3 action. This step is necessary to ensure that the job has access to the code that needs to be analyzed.

```
jobs:
  qa:
    name: QA
    runs-on: ubuntu-latest

    steps:
      - name: Checkout
        uses: actions/checkout@v3
```

The next step is to set up the Python environment. This is done using the actions/setup-python@v3 action, with the Python version specified as "3.11". This step ensures that the subsequent steps in the job will run in the correct Python environment.

```
      - name: Setup Python
        uses: actions/setup-python@v3
        with:
          python-version: "3.11"
```

The workflow then installs Poetry using the abatilo/actions-poetry@v2 action, specifying the version of Poetry as 1.8.3:

```
      - name: Install poetry
        uses: abatilo/actions-poetry@v2
        with:
          poetry-version: 1.8.3
```

Once Poetry is set up, the workflow installs the project's development dependencies using the poetry install --only dev command. Additionally, the workflow adds the poethepoet plugin for Poetry, which will be used to run predefined tasks more conveniently within the project.

```
      - name: Install packages
        run: |
          poetry install --only dev
          poetry self add 'poethepoet[poetry_plugin]'
```

The qa job then runs several quality checks on the code. The first check uses a tool called gitleaks to scan for secrets in the codebase, ensuring that no sensitive information is accidentally committed:

```
- name: gitleaks check
  run: poetry poe gitleaks-check
```

Following the gitleaks check, the workflow runs a linting process to enforce coding standards and best practices in the Python code. This is achieved through the poetry poe lint-check command, which uses Ruff under the hood.

```
- name: Lint check [Python]
  run: poetry poe lint-check
```

The last step in the qa job is a format check, which ensures that the Python code is properly formatted according to the project's style guidelines. This is done using the poetry poe format-check command, which uses Ruff under the hood.

```
- name: Format check [Python]
  run: poetry poe format-check
```

The **second job** defined in the workflow is the test job, which also runs on the latest version of Ubuntu. Like the qa job, it starts by checking out the code from the repository and installing Python 3.11 and Poetry 1.8.3.

```
test:
  name: Test
  runs-on: ubuntu-latest

  steps:
    - name: Checkout
      uses: actions/checkout@v3
    ...
```

After setting up the system dependencies, the test job installs all the project's dependencies with the poetry install command. As we want to run the tests, this time, we need to install all the dependencies that are required to run the application.

```
- name: Install packages
  run: |
```

```
poetry install --without aws
poetry self add 'poethepoet[poetry_plugin]'
```

Finally, the `test` job runs the project's tests using the `poetry poe test` command. This step ensures that all tests are executed and provides feedback on whether the current code changes break any functionality.

```
- name: Run tests
  run: |
      echo "Running tests..."
      poetry poe test
```

If any of the steps from the QA or test jobs fail, the GitHub Actions workflow will fail, resulting in the PR not being able to be merged until the issue is fixed. By taking this approach, we ensure that all the new features added to the main branches respect the standard of the project and that it doesn't break existing functionality through automated tests.

Figure 11.15 shows the CI pipeline in the **Actions** tab of the GitHub repository. It was run after a commit with the message **feat: Add Docker image and CD pipeline** and ran the two jobs described above, QA and Test.

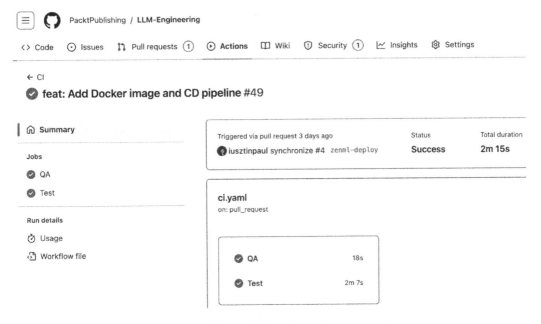

Figure 11.15: GitHub Actions CI pipeline run example

The CD pipeline

The CD pipeline will automate the Docker steps we manually performed in the **Deploying the LLM Twin's pipelines to the cloud** section, which are:

- Set up Docker.

- Log in to AWS.

- Build the Docker image.

- Push the Docker image to AWS ECR.

With that in mind, let's look at the GitHub Actions YAML file, which sits under `.github/workflows/cd.yaml`. It begins by naming the workflow CD and specifying the trigger for this workflow. The trigger is any push to the repository's main branch. This workflow will automatically run when new code is pushed to the main branch, usually when a PR is merged into the main branch. The `on.push` configuration sets up the trigger:

```
name: CD

on:
  push:
    branches:
      - main
```

The workflow then defines a single job named `Build & Push Docker Image`:

```
jobs:
  build:
    name: Build & Push Docker Image
    runs-on: ubuntu-latest
```

The first step within the job is to check out the repository's code.

```
steps:
  - name: Checkout Code
    uses: actions/checkout@v3
```

After checking out the code, the workflow sets up docker buildx, a Docker CLI plugin that extends Docker's build capabilities with features like multi-platform builds and cache import/export:

```
- name: Set up Docker Buildx
  uses: docker/setup-buildx-action@v3
```

The next step involves configuring the AWS credentials. This step is crucial for interacting with AWS services, such as Amazon **Elastic Container Registry (ECR)**, where the Docker images will be pushed. The AWS access key, secret access key, and region are securely retrieved from the repository's secrets to authenticate the workflow with AWS. This ensures the workflow has the necessary permissions to push Docker images to the ECR repository. We will show you how to configure these secrets after wrapping up with the YAML file:

```
- name: Configure AWS credentials
  uses: aws-actions/configure-aws-credentials@v1
  with:
    aws-access-key-id: ${{ secrets.AWS_ACCESS_KEY_ID }}
    aws-secret-access-key: ${{ secrets.AWS_SECRET_ACCESS_KEY }}
    aws-region: ${{ secrets.AWS_REGION }}
```

Once the AWS credentials are configured, the workflow logs in to Amazon ECR. This step is essential for authenticating the Docker CLI with the ECR registry, allowing subsequent steps to push images to the registry:

```
- name: Login to Amazon ECR
  id: login-ecr
  uses: aws-actions/amazon-ecr-login@v1
```

The final step in the workflow involves building the Docker image and pushing it to the Amazon ECR repository. This is accomplished using the docker/build-push-action@v6 action. The context specifies the build context, which is typically the repository's root directory. The file option points to the Dockerfile, which defines how the image should be built. The tags section assigns tags to the image, including the specific commit SHA and the latest tag, which is a common practice for identifying the most recent version of the image. The push option is set to true, meaning the image will be uploaded to ECR after it is built:

```
- name: Build images & push to ECR
  id: build-image
  uses: docker/build-push-action@v6
  with:
    context: .
    file: ./Dockerfile
    tags: |
      ${{ steps.login-ecr.outputs.registry }}/${{ secrets.AWS_ECR_NAME
}}:${{ github.sha }}
```

```
      ${{ steps.login-ecr.outputs.registry }}/${{ secrets.AWS_ECR_NAME
}}:latest
    push: true
```

To conclude, the CD pipeline authenticates to AWS, builds the Docker image, and pushes it to AWS ECR. The Docker image is pushed with `latest` and the commit's SHA tag. By doing so, we can always use the latest image and point to the commit of the code from which the image was generated.

Also, in our code, we have only a main branch, which reflects our production environment. But you, as a developer, have the power to extend this functionality with a staging and dev environment. You just have to add the name of the branches in the `on.push.branches` configuration at the beginning of the YAML file.

In *Figure 11.16*, you can observe how the CD pipeline looks after a PR is merged into the production branch. As seen before, we only have the **Build & Push Docker Image** job here.

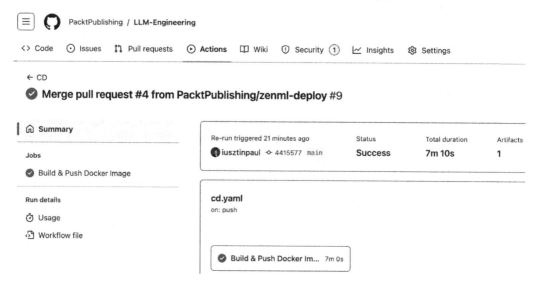

Figure 11.16: GitHub Actions CD pipeline run example

The last step in setting up the CI/CD pipeline is to test it and see how it works.

Test out the CI/CD pipeline

To test the CI/CD pipelines yourself, you must fork the LLM-Engineering repository to have full *write* access to the GitHub repository. Here is the official tutorial on how to fork a GitHub project: `https://docs.github.com/en/pull-requests/collaborating-with-pull-requests/working-with-forks/fork-a-repo`

The last step is to set up a few secrets that will allow the CD pipeline to log in to AWS and point to the right ECR resource. To do so, go to the **Settings** tab at the top of the forked repository in GitHub. In the left panel, in the **Security** section, click on the **Secrets and Variables** toggle and, finally, on **Actions**. Then, on the **Secrets** tab, create four repository secrets, as shown in *Figure 11.17*. These secrets will be securely stored and accessible only by the GitHub Actions CD pipeline.

The `AWS_ACCESS_KEY_ID` and `AWS_SECRET_ACCESS_KEY` are the AWS credentials you used across the book. In *Chapter 2*, you see how to create them. The `AWS_REGION` (e.g., `eu-central-1`) and `AWS_ECR_NAME` are the same ones used in the **Deploying the LLM Twin's pipelines** to the cloud section.

For the `AWS_ECR_NAME`, you should configure only the name of the repository (e.g., `zenml-vrsopg`) and not the full URI (e.g., `992382797823.dkr.ecr.eu-central-1.amazonaws.com/zenml-vrsopg`), as seen in the image below:

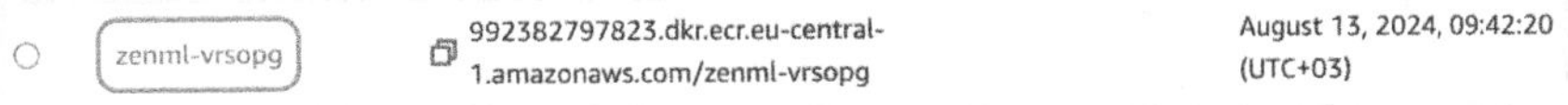

| ○ | zenml-vrsopg | 992382797823.dkr.ecr.eu-central-1.amazonaws.com/zenml-vrsopg | August 13, 2024, 09:42:20 (UTC+03) |

Figure 11.17: Configuring only repository name

To trigger the CI pipeline, create a feature branch, modify the code or documentation, and create a PR to the main branch. To trigger the CD pipeline, merge the PR into the main branch.

After the CD GitHub Actions are complete, check the ECR repository to see whether the Docker image was pushed successfully.

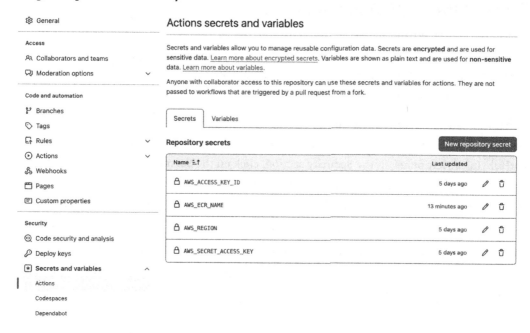

Figure 11.18: GitHub Actions secrets

If you need more details on how to set up GitHub Actions secrets, we recommend checking out their official documentation: https://docs.github.com/en/actions/security-for-github-actions/security-guides/using-secrets-in-github-actions

The CT pipeline

To implement the CT pipeline, we will leverage ZenML. Once ZenML (or other orchestrators such as Metaflow, Dagster, or Airflow) orchestrates all your pipelines and your infrastructure is deployed, you are very close to reaching CT.

Remember the core difference between the CI/CD and CT pipelines. The CI/CD pipeline takes care of testing, building, and deploying your code—a dimension that any software program has. The CT pipeline leverages the code managed by the CI/CD pipeline to automate your data, training, and model-serving process, where the data and model dimensions are present only in the AI world.

Before diving into the implementation, we want to highlight two design choices that made reaching CT simple:

- **The FTI architecture:** A modular system with clear interfaces and components made it easy to capture the relationship between the pipelines and automate them.

- **Starting with an orchestrator since day 0:** We started with ZenML at the beginning of the project's development. Early on, we only used it locally. But it acted as an entry point for our pipelines and a way to monitor their execution. Doing so forced us to decouple each pipeline and transfer the communication between them solely through various types of data storage, such as the data warehouse, feature store, or artifact store. As we have leveraged ZenML since day 0, we got rid of implementing a tedious CLI to configure our application. Instead, we did it directly through YAML configuration files out of the box.

In *Figure 11.19*, we can see all the pipelines that we have to chain together to fully automate our training and deployment. The pipelines aren't new; they aggregate everything we've covered throughout this book. Thus, at this point, we will treat them as black boxes that interact with each other.

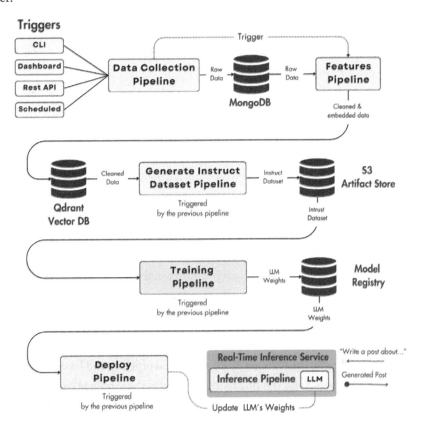

Figure 11.19: CT pipeline

For the LLM Twin's CT pipeline, we have to discuss the initial trigger that starts the pipelines and how the pipelines are triggered by each other.

Initial triggers

As illustrated in *Figure 11.18*, we initially want to trigger the data collection pipeline. Usually, the triggers can be of three types:

- **Manual triggers:** Done through the CLI or the orchestrator's dashboard, in our case, through the ZenML dashboard. Manual triggers are still extremely powerful tools, as you need just one action to start the whole ML system, from data gathering to deployment, instead of fiddling with dozens of scripts that you might configure wrong or run in an invalid order.

- **REST API triggers:** You can call a pipeline by an HTTP request. This is extremely useful when integrating your ML pipelines with other components. For example, you can have a watcher constantly looking for new articles. It triggers the ML logic using this REST API trigger when it finds some. To find more details on this feature, check out this tutorial on ZenML's documentation: `https://docs.zenml.io/v/docs/how-to/trigger-pipelines/trigger-a-pipeline-from-rest-api`.

- **Scheduled triggers:** Another common approach is to schedule your pipeline to run constantly on a fixed interval. For example, depending on your use case, you can schedule your pipeline to run daily, hourly, or every minute. Most of the orchestrators, ZenML included, provide a cron expression interface where you can define your execution frequency. In the following example from ZenML, the pipeline is scheduled every hour:

  ```
  Schedule(cron_expression="* * 1 * *")
  ```

We chose a manual trigger for our LLM Twin use case as we don't have other components to leverage the REST API triggers. Also, as the datasets are generated from a list of static links defined in the ZenML configs, running them on a schedule doesn't make sense as they would always yield the same results.

But a possible next step for the project is to implement a watcher that monitors for new articles. When it finds any, it generates a new config and triggers the pipelines through the REST API. Another option is implementing the watcher as an additional pipeline and leveraging the schedule triggers to look daily for new data. If it finds any, it executes the whole ML system; otherwise, it stops.

The conclusion is that once you can manually trigger all your ML pipelines through a single command, you can quickly adapt it to more advanced and complex scenarios.

Trigger downstream pipelines

To keep things simple, we sequentially chained all the pipelines. More concretely, when the data collection pipeline has finished, it will trigger the feature pipeline. When the feature pipeline has been completed successfully, it triggers the dataset generation pipeline, and so on. You can make the logic more complex, like scheduling the generate instruct dataset pipeline to run daily, checking the amount of new data in the Qdrant vector DB, and starting only if it has enough new data. From this point, you can further tweak the system's parameters and optimize them to reduce costs.

To trigger all the pipelines in one go, we created one master pipeline that aggregates everything in one entry point:

```python
@pipeline
def end_to_end_data(
    author_links: list[dict[str, str | list[str]]], … # Other paramaters…
) -> None:
    wait_for_ids = []
    for author_data in author_links:
        last_step_invocation_id = digital_data_etl(
            user_full_name=author_data["user_full_name"], links=author_
data["links"]
        )

        wait_for_ids.append(last_step_invocation_id)

    author_full_names = [author_data["user_full_name"] for author_data in
author_links]
    wait_for_ids = feature_engineering(author_full_names=author_full_
names, wait_for=wait_for_ids)

    generate_instruct_datasets(…)

        training(…)

        deploy(…)
```

To keep the function light, we added all the logic up to computing the features. But, as we suggested in the code snippet above, you can easily add the instruction dataset generation, training, and deploy logic to the parent pipeline to implement an end-to-end flow. By doing that, you can automate everything from data collection to deploying the model.

To run the end-to-end pipeline, use the following poe command:

```
poetry poe run-end-to-end-data-pipeline
```

What we implemented is not the best approach, as it compresses all the steps into a single monolith pipeline (which we want to avoid), as illustrated in *Figure 11.20*. Usually, you want to keep each pipeline isolated and use triggers to start downstream pipelines. This makes the system easier to understand, debug, and monitor.

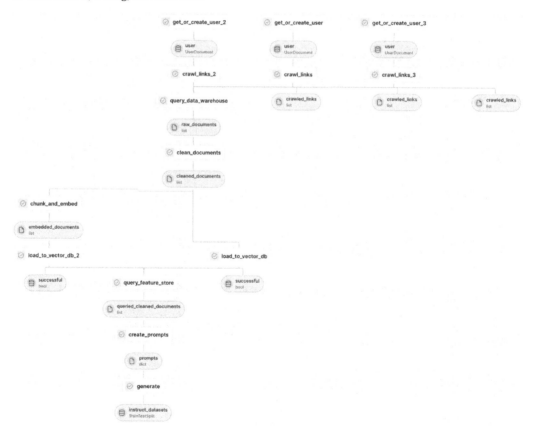

Figure 11.20: End-to-end pipeline illustrated in ZenML's dashboard

Unfortunately, the ZenML cloud's free trial has a limitation of a maximum of three pipelines. As we have more, we avoided that limitation by compressing all the steps into a single pipeline. But if you plan to host ZenML yourself or buy their license, they offer the possibility to independently trigger a pipeline from another pipeline, as you can see in the code snippet below where we triggered the feature engineering pipeline after the data collection ETL:

```python
from zenml import pipeline, step


@pipeline
def digital_data_etl(user_full_name: str, links: list[str]) -> str:
    user = get_or_create_user(user_full_name)
    crawl_links(user=user, links=links)

trigger_feature_engineering_pipeline(user)

@step
def trigger_feature_engineering_pipeline(user):
run_config = PipelineRunConfiguration(…)

Client().trigger_pipeline("feature_engineering", run_configuration=run_config)

@pipeline
def feature_engineering(author_full_names: list[str]) -> list[str]:
… # ZenML steps
```

By taking this approach, each pipeline will have its independent run, where one pipeline sequentially triggers the next one, as described at the beginning of this section. Note that this feature is not unique to ZenML but is common in orchestrator tools. The principles we have learned so far hold. Only how we interact with the tool changes.

Prompt monitoring

We will use Opik (from Comet ML) to monitor our prompts. But remember from the *LLMOps* section earlier in this chapter that we are not interested only in the input prompt and generated answer.

We want to log the entire trace from the user's input until the final result is available. Before diving into the LLM Twin use case, let's look at a simpler example:

```python
from opik import track
import openai
from opik.integrations.openai import track_openai

openai_client = track_openai(openai.OpenAI())

@track
def preprocess_input(text: str) -> str:
    return text.strip().lower()

@track
def generate_response(prompt: str) -> str:
    response = openai_client.chat.completions.create(
        model="gpt-3.5-turbo",
        messages=[{"role": "user", "content": prompt}]
    )
    return response.choices[0].message.content

@track
def postprocess_output(response: str) -> str:
    return response.capitalize()

@track(name="llm_chain")
def llm_chain(input_text: str) -> str:
    preprocessed = preprocess_input(input_text)
    generated = generate_response(preprocessed)
    postprocessed = postprocess_output(generated)

    return postprocessed

result = llm_chain("Hello, do you enjoy reading the book?")
```

The preceding code snippet reflects in a simplistic way what most LLM applications will look like. You have the llm_chain() main function, which takes the initial input as a parameter and returns the final result.

Then, you have preprocessing and postprocessing functions surrounding the actual LLM call. Using the @track() decorator, we log the input and output of each function, which will ultimately be aggregated into a single trace. By doing so, we will have access to the initial input text, the generated answer, and all the intermediary steps required to debug any potential issues using Opik's dashboard.

The last step is to attach the necessary metadata for your use case to the current trace. As seen in the following code snippet, you can easily do that by calling the update() method, where you can tag your trace or add any other metadata, such as the number of input tokens, through a Python dictionary:

```python
from opik import track, opik_context

@track
def llm_chain(input_text):
    # LLM chain code
    # ...

    opik_context.update_current_trace(
tags=["inference_pipeline"],
metadata={
    "num_tokens": compute_num_tokens(…)
},
feedback_scores=[
{
    "name": "user_feedback",
    "value": 1.0,
    "reason": "The response was valuable and correct."
},
{
    "name": "llm_judge_score",
    "value": compute_llm_judge_score(…),
    "reason": "Computing runtime metrics using an LLM Judge."
}

)
```

You can expand on this idea and log various feedback scores. The most common is asking the user if the generated answer is valuable and correct. Another option is to compute various metrics automatically through heuristics or LLM judges.

Finally, let's see how to add prompt monitoring to our LLM Twin project. First, look at *Figure 11.21* and remember our model-serving architecture. We have two microservices, the LLM and business microservices. The LLM microservice has a narrow scope, as it only takes as input a prompt that already contains the user's input and context and returns an answer that is usually post-processed. Thus, the business microservice is the right place to implement the monitoring pipeline, as it coordinates the end-to-end flow. More concretely, Opik implementation will be in the FastAPI server developed in *Chapter 10*.

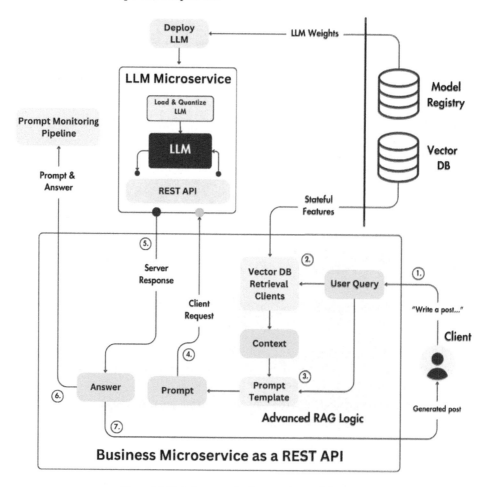

Figure 11.21: Inference pipeline serving architecture

As our implementation is already modular, using Opik makes it straightforward to log an end-to-end trace of a user's request:

```python
from opik import track


@track
def call_llm_service(query: str, context: str | None) -> str:
    llm = LLMInferenceSagemakerEndpoint(…)
    answer = InferenceExecutor(llm, query, context).execute()

    return answer

@track
def rag(query: str) -> str:
    retriever = ContextRetriever()
    documents = retriever.search(query, k=3 * 3)
    context = EmbeddedChunk.to_context(documents)

    answer = call_llm_service(query, context)

    return answer
```

The `rag()` function represents your application's entry point. All the other processing steps take place in the `ContextRetriever` and `InferenceExector` classes. Also, by decorating the `call_llm_service()` function, we can clearly capture the prompt sent to the LLM and its response.

To add more granularity to our trace, we can further decorate other functions containing pre- or post-processing steps, such as the `ContextRetriever` search function:

```python
class ContextRetriever:

    …


    @track

    def search(
        self,
        query: str,
        k: int = 3,
```

```
        expand_to_n_queries: int = 3,
    ) -> list:
        query_model = Query.from_str(query)
        query_model = self._metadata_extractor.generate(query_model)
        … # Rest of the implementation
```

Or even go further to the retrieval optimization methods, such as the self-query metadata extractor, to add more granularity:

```
class SelfQuery:

    @track
    def generate(self, query: str) -> str:

        …

        return enhanced_query
```

The developer is responsible for deciding how much granularity the application needs for proper debugging and analysis. As having detailed monitoring is healthy, monitoring everything can be dangerous as it adds too much noise and makes manually understanding the traces difficult. You must find the right balance. A good rule of thumb is tracing the most critical functions, such as `rag()` and `call_llm_service()`, and gradually adding more granularity when needed.

The last step is to attach valuable metadata and tags to our traces. To do so, we will further enhance the `rag()` function as follows:

```
@track
def rag(query: str) -> str:
    retriever = ContextRetriever()
    documents = retriever.search(query, k=3 * 3)
    context = EmbeddedChunk.to_context(documents)

    answer, prompt = call_llm_service(query, context)

    trace = get_current_trace()
    trace.update(
tags=["rag"],
metadata={
        "model_id": settings.HF_MODEL_ID,
        "embedding_model_id": settings.TEXT_EMBEDDING_MODEL_ID,
```

```
        "temperature": settings.TEMPERATURE_INFERENCE,
        "prompt_tokens": compute_num_tokens(prompt),
        "total_tokens": compute_num_tokens(answer),


    }
                )


    return answer
```

There are three main aspects that we should constantly monitor:

- **Model configuration:** Here, we should consider both the LLM and other models used within the RAG layer. The most critical aspects of logging are the model IDs, but you can also capture other important information that significantly impacts the generation, such as the temperature.
- **Total number of tokens:** It's critical to constantly analyze the statistics of the number of tokens generated by your input prompts and total tokens, as this significantly impacts your serving costs. For example, if the average of the total number of tokens generated suddenly increases, it's a strong signal that you have a bug in your system that you should investigate.
- **The duration of each step:** Tracking the duration of each step within your trace is essential to finding bottlenecks within your system. If the latency of a specific request is abnormally large, you quickly have access to a report that helps you find the source of the problem.

Alerting

Using ZenML, you can quickly implement an alerting system on any platform of your liking, such as email, Discord, or Slack. For example, you can add a callback in your training pipeline to trigger a notification when the pipeline fails or the training has finished successfully:

```
from zenml import get_pipeline_context, pipeline

@pipeline(on_failure=notify_on_failure)
def training_pipeline(…):
    …
notify_on_success()
```

Implementing the notification functions is straightforward. As seen in the code snippets below, you have to get the `alerter` instance from your current stack, build the message as you see fit, and send it to your notification channel of choice:

```
from zenml.client import Client

alerter = Client().active_stack.alerter

def notify_on_failure() -> None:
        alerter.post(message=build_message(status="failed"))

@step(enable_cache=False)
def notify_on_success() -> None:
        alerter.post(message=build_message(status="succeeded"))
```

ZenML and most orchestrators simplify implementing an `alerter`, as it's a critical component in your MLOps/LLMOps infrastructure.

Summary

In this chapter, we laid down the foundations with a theoretical section on DevOps. Then, we moved on to MLOps and its core components and principles. Finally, we presented how LLMOps differs from MLOps by introducing strategies such as prompt monitoring, guardrails, and human-in-the-loop feedback. Also, we briefly discussed why most companies would avoid training LLMs from scratch but choose to optimize them for their use case through prompt engineering or fine-tuning. At the end of the theoretical portion of the chapter, we learned what a CI/CD/CT pipeline is, the three core dimensions of an ML application (code, data, model), and that, after deployment, it is more critical than ever to implement a monitoring and alerting layer due to model degradation.

Next, we learned how to deploy the LLM Twin's pipeline to the cloud. We understood the infrastructure and went step by step through deploying MongoDB, Qdrant, the ZenML cloud, and all the necessary AWS resources to sustain the application. Finally, we learned how to Dockerize our application and push our Docker image to AWS ECR, which will be used to execute the application on top of AWS SageMaker.

The final step was to add LLMOps to our LLM Twin project. We began by implementing a CI/CD pipeline with GitHub Actions. Then, we looked at our CT strategy by leveraging ZenML.

Finally, we saw how to implement a monitoring pipeline using Opik from Comet ML and an alerting system using ZenML. These are the fundamental pillars in adding MLOps and LLMOps to any LLM-based application.

The framework we learned about throughout the book can quickly be extrapolated to other LLM applications. Even if we used the LLM Twin use case as an example, most of the strategies applied can be adapted to other projects. Thus, we can get an entirely new application by changing the data and making minor tweaks to the code. Data is the new oil, remember?

By finalizing this chapter, we've learned to build an end-to-end LLM application, starting with data collection and fine-tuning until deploying the LLM microservice and RAG service. Throughout this book, we aimed to provide a thought framework to help you build and solve real-world problems in the GenAI landscape. Now that you have it, we wish you good luck in your journey and happy building!

References

- GitLab. (2023, January 25). *What is DevOps? | GitLab*. GitLab. https://about.gitlab.com/topics/devops/

- Huyen, C. (2024, July 25). Building a generative AI platform. *Chip Huyen*. https://huyenchip.com/2024/07/25/genai-platform.html

- *Lightricks customer story: Building a recommendation engine from scratch*. (n.d.). https://www.qwak.com/academy/lightricks-customer-story-building-a-recommendation-engine-from-scratch

- *What LLMOps*. (n.d.). Google Cloud. https://cloud.google.com/discover/what-is-llmops?hl=en

- *MLOps: Continuous delivery and automation pipelines in machine learning*. (2024, August 28). Google Cloud. https://cloud.google.com/architecture/mlops-continuous-delivery-and-automation-pipelines-in-machine-learning#top_of_page

- *Ml-ops.org*. (2024a, July 5). https://ml-ops.org/content/mlops-principles

- *Ml-ops.org*. (2024b, July 5). https://ml-ops.org/content/mlops-principles

- *Ml-ops.org*. (2024c, July 5). https://ml-ops.org/content/motivation

- Mohandas, G. M. (2022a). Monitoring machine learning systems. *Made With ML*. https://madewithml.com/courses/mlops/monitoring/

- Mohandas, G. M. (2022b). Testing Machine Learning Systems: Code, Data and Models. *Made With ML*. https://madewithml.com/courses/mlops/testing/

- Preston-Werner, T. (n.d.). *Semantic Versioning 2.0.0.* Semantic Versioning. `https://semver.org/`

- Ribeiro, M. T., Wu, T., Guestrin, C., & Singh, S. (2020, May 8). *Beyond Accuracy: Behavioral Testing of NLP models with CheckList.* arXiv.org. `https://arxiv.org/abs/2005.04118`

- Wandb. (2023, November 30). *Understanding LLMOps: Large Language Model Operations.* Weights & Biases. `https://wandb.ai/site/articles/understanding-llmops-large-language-model-operations/`

- Zenml-Io. (n.d.). *GitHub—zenml-io/zenml-huggingface-sagemaker: An example MLOps overview of ZenML pipelines from a Hugging Face model repository to a deployed AWS SageMaker endpoint.* GitHub. `https://github.com/zenml-io/zenml-huggingface-sagemaker/tree/main`

Join our book's Discord space

Join our community's Discord space for discussions with the authors and other readers:

`https://packt.link/llmeng`

Appendix

MLOps Principles

Building robust and scalable ML systems requires more than creating powerful models. It demands an all-encompassing approach to operationalizing the entire ML lifecycle. Let's explore the **six core principles** that guide the MLOps field. These principles are independent of any tool and are at the core of building robust and scalable ML systems. They provide a guideline for designing production-ready applications, ensuring consistency, reliability, and scalability at every stage.

With that in mind, let's begin with the foundation: automation or operationalization.

1. Automation or operationalization

To adopt MLOps, there are three core tiers that most applications build up gradually, from manual processing to full automation:

- **Manual process**: The process is experimental and iterative in the early stages of developing an ML application. The data scientist manually performs each pipeline step, such as data preparation and validation, model training, and testing. At this point, they commonly use Jupyter notebooks to train their models. This stage's output is the code used to prepare the data and train the models.

- **Continuous training (CT)**: The next level involves automating model training. This is known as continuous training, which triggers model retraining whenever required. At this point, you often automate your data and model validation steps. This step is usually done by an orchestration tool, such as ZenML, that glues all your code together and runs it on specific triggers. The most common triggers are on a schedule, for example, every day or when a specific event comes in, such as when new data is uploaded or the monitoring system detects a drop in performance, offering you the flexibility to adapt to various triggers.

- **CI/CD**: In the final stage, you implement your CI/CD pipelines to enable fast and reliable deployment of your ML code into production. The key advancement at this stage is the automatic building, testing, and deployment of data, ML models, and training pipeline components. CI/CD is used to quickly push new code into various environments, such as staging or production, ensuring efficient and reliable deployment.

As we build our LLM system using the **FTI (feature, training, inference)** architecture, we can quickly move from a manual process to CI/CD/CT. In *Figure A.1*, we can observe that the CT process can be triggered by various events, such as a drop in performance detected by the monitoring pipeline or a batch of fresh data arriving. Also, *Figure A.1* is split into two main sections; the first one highlights the automated processes, while at the bottom, we can observe the manual processes performed by the data science team while experimenting with various data processing methods and models. Once they improve the model by tinkering with how the data is processed or the model architecture, they push the code to the code repository, which triggers the CI/CD pipeline to build, test, package, and deploy the new changes to the FTI pipelines.

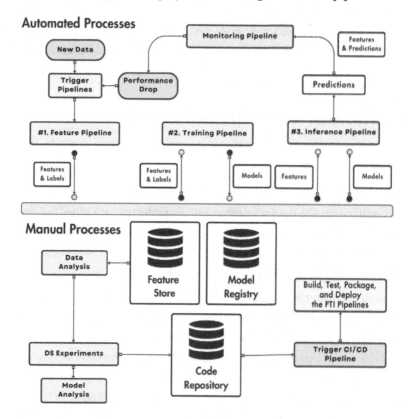

Figure A.1: CI/CD/CT on top of the FTI architecture

To conclude, CT automates the FTI pipelines, while CI/CD builds, tests, and pushes new versions of the FTI pipeline code to production.

2. Versioning

By now, we understand that the whole ML system changes if the code, model, or data changes. Thus, it is critical to track and version these three elements individually. But what strategies can we adopt to track the code, model, and data separately?

- The **code** is tracked by Git, which helps us create a new commit (a snapshot of the code) on every change added to the codebase. Also, Git-based tools usually allow us to make releases, which typically pack multiple features and bug fixes. While the commits contain unique identifiers that are not human-interpretable, a release follows more common conventions based on their major, minor, and patch versions. For example, in a release with version "v1.2.3," 1 is the major version, 2 is the minor version, and 3 is the patch version. Popular tools are GitHub and GitLab.

- To version the **model**, you leverage the model registry to store, share, and version all the models used within your system. It usually follows the same versioning conventions used in code releases, defined as **Semantic Versioning**, which, along with the major, minor, and patch versions, also supports alpha and beta releases that signal applications. At this point, you can also leverage the ML metadata store to attach information to the stored model, such as what data it was trained on, its architecture, performance, latency, and whatever else makes sense to your specific use case. Doing so creates a clear catalog of models that can easily be navigated across your team and company.

- Versioning the **data** isn't as straightforward as versioning the code and model because it depends on the type of data you have (structured or unstructured) and the scale of data you have (big or small). For example, for structured data, you can leverage a SQL database with a version column that helps you track the changes in the dataset. However, other popular solutions are based on Git-like systems, such as **Data Version Control** (**DVC**), that track every change made to the dataset. Other trendy solutions are based on artifacts similar to a model registry that allows you to add a virtual layer to your dataset, tracking and creating a new version for every change made to your data. Comet.ml, **W&B** (**Weights & Biases**), and ZenML offer powerful artifact features. For all solutions, you must store the data on-premises or use cloud object storage solutions such as AWS S3. These tools provide features that allow you to structure your datasets and versions, track, and access them.

3. Experiment tracking

Training ML models is an entirely iterative and experimental process. Unlike traditional software development, it involves running multiple parallel experiments, comparing them based on a set of predefined metrics, and deciding which one should advance to production. An experiment tracking tool allows you to log all the necessary information, such as metrics and visual representations of your model predictions, to compare all your experiments and easily select the best model. Popular tools are Comet ML, W&B, MLflow, and Neptune.

4. Testing

The same trend is followed when testing ML systems. Hence, we must test our application across all three dimensions: the data, the model, and the code. We must also ensure that the feature, training, and inference pipeline are well integrated with external services, such as the feature store, and work together as a system. When working with Python, the most common tool to write your tests is pytest, which we also recommend.

Test types

In the development cycle, six primary types of tests are commonly employed at various stages:

- **Unit tests:** These tests focus on individual components with a single responsibility, such as a function that adds two tensors or one that finds an element in a list.

- **Integration tests:** These tests evaluate the interaction between integrated components or units within a system, such as the data evaluation pipeline or the feature engineering pipeline, and how they are integrated with the data warehouse and feature store.

- **System tests:** System tests play a crucial role in the development cycle as they examine the entire system, including the complete and integrated application. These tests rigorously evaluate the end-to-end functionality of the system, including performance, security, and overall user experience—for example, testing an entire ML pipeline, from data ingestion to model training and inference, ensuring the system produces the correct outputs for given inputs.

- **Acceptance tests:** These tests, often called **user acceptance testing (UAT)**, are designed to confirm that the system meets specified requirements, ensuring it is ready for deployment.

- **Regression tests:** These tests check for previously identified errors to ensure that new changes do not reintroduce them.

- **Stress tests:** These tests evaluate the system's performance and stability under extreme conditions, such as high load or limited resources. They aim to identify breaking points and ensure the system can handle unexpected spikes in demand or adverse situations without failing.

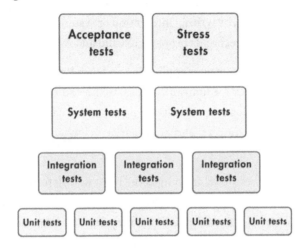

Figure A.2: Test types

We've intentionally left regression tests out of the preceding figure because they aren't a distinct testing phase. Instead, regression testing is applied across all levels—unit, integration, system, acceptance, and stress tests—to ensure that changes don't reintroduce previous errors. It's an ongoing process within these phases, not a separate type of test, which is why it's not shown as a separate category.

What do we test?

When writing most tests, you take a component and treat it as a black box. Thus, what you have control over is the input and output. You want to test that you get an expected output for a given input. With that in mind, here are a few things you should usually test:

- **Inputs:** Data types, format, length, and edge cases (min/max, small/large, etc.)
- **Outputs:** Data types, formats, exceptions, and intermediary and final outputs

Test examples

When testing your code, you can leverage the standards from classic software engineering. Here are a few examples of code tests you can include when writing unit tests to get a better idea of what we want to test at this point—for instance, you want to check that a sentence is cleaned as expected.

Also, you can look at your chunking algorithm and assert that it works properly by using various sentences and chunk sizes.

When we talk about **data tests**, we mainly refer to data validity. Your data validity code usually runs when raw data is ingested from the data warehouse or after computing the features. It is part of the feature pipeline. Thus, by writing integration or system tests for your feature pipeline, you can check that your system responds properly to valid and invalid data.

Testing data validity depends a lot on your application and data type. For example, when working with tabular data, you can check for non-null values, that a categorical variable contains only the expected values, or that a float value is always positive. You can check for length, character encoding, language, special characters, and grammar errors when working with unstructured data such as text.

Model tests are the trickiest, as model training is the most non-deterministic process of an ML system. However, unlike traditional software, ML systems can successfully complete without throwing any errors. However, the real issue is that they produce incorrect results that can only be observed during evaluations or tests. Some standard model test techniques involve checking:

- The shapes of the input and model output tensors
- That the loss decreases after one batch (or more) of training
- Overfit on a small batch, and the loss approaches 0
- That your training pipeline works on all the supported devices, such as the CPU and GPU
- That your early stopping and checkpoint logic works

All the tests are triggered inside the CI pipeline. If some tests are more costly, for example, the model ones, you can execute them only on special terms, such as only when modifying the model code.

At the other end of the spectrum, you can also perform **behavioral testing** on your **model**, which tries to adopt the strategy from code testing and treats the model as a black box while looking solely at the input data and expected outputs. This makes the behavioral testing methods model agnostic. A fundamental paper in this area is *Beyond Accuracy: Behavioral Testing of NLP Models with CheckList*, which we recommend if you want to dig more into the subject. However, as a quick overview, the paper proposes that you test your model against three types of tests. We use a model that extracts the main subject from a sentence as an example:

- **Invariance**: Changes in your input should not affect the output—for example, below is an example based on synonym injection:

```
model(text="The advancements in AI are changing the world rapidly.")
# output: ai

model(text="The progress in AI is changing the world rapidly.")
# output: ai
```

- **Directional**: Changes in your input should affect the outputs—for example, below is an example where we know the outputs should change based on the provided inputs:

```
model(text="Deep learning used for sentiment analysis.")
# output: deep-learning

model(text="Deep learning used for object detection.")
# output: deep-learning

model(text="RNNs for sentiment analysis.")
# output: rnn
```

- **Minimum functionality**: The most simple combination of inputs and expected outputs—for example, below is a set of simple examples that we expect the model should always get right:

```
model(text="NLP is the next big wave in machine learning.")
# output: nlp

model(text="MLOps is the next big wave in machine learning.")
# output: mlops

model(text="This is about graph neural networks.")
# output: gnn
```

 For more on testing, we recommend reading *Testing Machine Learning Systems: Code, Data, and Models* by Goku Mohandas: https://madewithml.com/courses/mlops/testing/.

5. Monitoring

Monitoring is vital for any ML system that reaches production. Traditional software systems are rule-based and deterministic. Thus, once it is built, it will always work as defined. Unfortunately, that is not the case with ML systems. When implementing ML models, we haven't explicitly described how they should work. We have used data to compile a probabilistic solution, which means that our ML model will constantly be exposed to a level of degradation. This happens because the data from production might differ from the data the model was trained on. Thus, it is natural that the shipped model doesn't know how to handle these scenarios.

We shouldn't try to avoid these situations but create a strategy to catch and fix these errors in time. Intuitively, monitoring detects the model's performance degradation, which triggers an alarm that signals that the model should be retrained manually, automatically, or with a combination of both.

Why retrain the model? As the model performance degrades due to a drift in the training dataset and what it inputs from production, the only solution is to adapt or retrain the model on a new dataset that captures all the new scenarios from production.

As training is a costly operation, there are some tricks that you can perform to avoid retraining, but before describing them, let's quickly understand what we can monitor to understand our ML system's health.

Logs

The approach to logging is straightforward, which is to capture everything, such as:

- Document the system configurations.
- Record the query, the results, and any intermediate outputs.
- Log when a component begins, ends, crashes, and so on.
- Ensure that each log entry is tagged and identified in a way that clarifies its origin within the system.

While capturing all activities can rapidly increase the volume of logs, you can take advantage of numerous tools for automated log analysis and anomaly detection that leverage AI to efficiently scan all the logs, providing you with the confidence to manage the logs effectively.

Metrics

To quantify your application's healthiness, you must define a set of metrics. Each metric measures different aspects of your application, such as the infrastructure, data, and model.

System metrics

The system metrics are based on monitoring service-level metrics (latency, throughput, error rates) and infrastructure health (CPU/GPU, memory). These metrics are used both in traditional software and ML as they are crucial to understanding whether the infrastructure works well and the system works as expected to provide a good user experience to the end users.

Model metrics

Merely monitoring the system's health won't suffice to identify the deeper issues within our model. Therefore, moving on to the next layer of metrics that focus on the model's performance is crucial. This includes quantitative evaluation metrics like accuracy, precision, and F1 score, as well as essential business metrics influenced by the model, such as ROI and click rate.

Analyzing cumulative performance metrics over the entire deployment period is often ineffective. Instead, evaluating performance over time intervals relevant to our application, such as hourly, is essential. Thus, in practice, you window your inputs and compute and aggregate the metrics at the window level. These sliding metrics can provide a clearer picture of the system's health, allowing us to detect issues more promptly without them being obscured by historical data.

We may not always have access to ground-truth outcomes to evaluate the model's performance on production data. This is particularly challenging when there is a significant delay or when real-life data requires annotation. To address this issue, we can develop an approximate signal to estimate the model's performance or label a small portion of our live dataset to assess performance. When talking about ML monitoring, an approximate signal is also known as a **proxy metric**, usually implemented by drift detection methods, which are discussed in the following section.

Drifts

Drifts are proxy metrics that help us detect potential issues with the production model in time without requiring any ground truths/labels. *Table A.1* shows three kinds of drifts.

What drifts	Description	Drift formulation
X	Inputs (features)	data drift → $P(X) \neq P_{ref}(X)$
y	Outputs (ground truths/ labels)	target drift → $P(y) \neq P_{ref}(y)$
P(y|X)	relationship between X and y	concept drift → $P(y|X) \neq P_{ref}(y|X)$

Table A.1: Relationship between data, model, and code changes

Data drift

Data drift, also called feature drift or covariate shift, occurs when the distribution of the production data deviates from that of the training data, as shown in *Figure A.3*. This difference means the model cannot handle the changes in feature space, leading to potentially unreliable predictions. Drift can result from natural real-life changes or systemic problems like missing data, pipeline errors, and schema modifications.

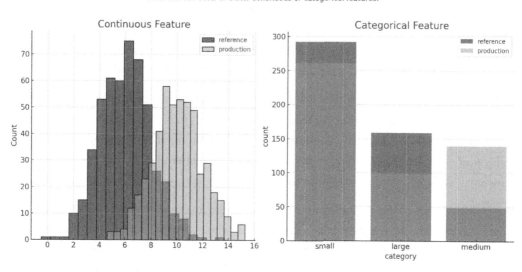

Figure A.3: Data drift examples

When data begins to drift, the degradation in our model's performance might not be immediately noticeable, particularly if the model interpolates effectively. Nevertheless, this presents an ideal chance to consider retraining before the drift affects the model's performance.

Target drift

In addition to changes in input data (data drift), we might also encounter shifts in output distribution. The shift could involve changes in the shape of the distribution or the addition and removal of classes in categorical tasks. While retraining the model can help reduce performance degradation due to target drift, you can often prevent it by adapting the head processing steps and model head to support the new schema of the output class.

For example, if you have a classifier that predicts if an image contains animals or people, and you get a picture with buildings, you can either adapt your model to support an unknown class or adjust the head of the model to add the new class for future predictions.

Concept drift

In addition to changes in input and output data, their relationship can also shift. This phenomenon, known as **concept drift**, makes our model ineffective because the patterns it previously learned to associate inputs with outputs become outdated. As illustrated in the following figure, concept drifts can manifest in various ways:

- Gradually over time
- Suddenly, due to an external event
- Periodically, due to recurring events

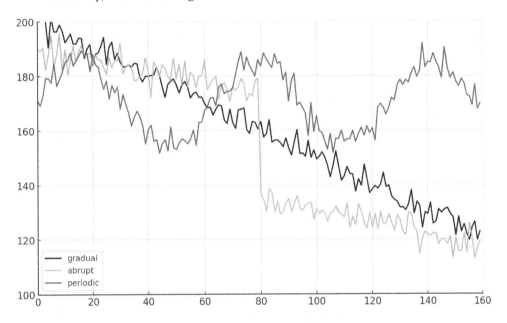

Figure A.4: Concept drift examples

For example, this happens when using the model in a different geographic area. Let's assume you want to build a model that predicts whether a person will buy a specific car. You initially built it for the American market. Now, you want to use it in the European market, where people tend to buy smaller cars, creating a drift between the size feature of the car and the output probability of purchasing the vehicle. Of course, concept drifts can be more subtle than this example.

 All these types of drift can happen simultaneously, complicating pinpointing the exact sources of drift.

How to detect and measure drifts

Now that we've recognized the various types of drift, it's crucial to understand how to detect and measure it. To do so, you need two types of windows:

- **A reference window**: This is the collection of data points used as a baseline to compare against the production data distributions for drift identification. It is usually gathered from the training dataset.

- **A test window**: This collects data points gathered while the ML system is in production. It is compared with the reference window to ascertain if drift has occurred.

To measure the drifts, you leverage hypothesis tests that verify the change in distribution between the two windows. For example, you can use the **Kolmogorov-Smirnov (KS)** test to monitor a single continuous feature. This is known as a **univariate (1D)** test. Thus, you must run it for every feature you want to monitor. You can leverage a chi-squared univariate test to monitor categorical variables and determine if the frequency of events in production is consistent with the reference window distribution.

```
from alibi_detect.cd import KSDrift


cd = KSDrift(X_ref, p_val=.05, preprocess_fn=preprocess_fn, input_
shape=(max_len,))
```

When working with text data in an embedding representation, we have to model a multivariate distribution, which is how LLMs work with text. A popular approach is to take the embeddings of the test and reference windows, apply a dimensionality reduction algorithm, and apply an algorithm such as **maximum mean discrepancy (MMD)**. This algorithm is a kernel-based approach that measures the distance between two distributions by computing the distance between the mean of the embeddings of the two windows.

```
from alibi_detect.cd import MMDDrift


cd = MMDDrift(x_ref, backend='pytorch', p_val=.05)
preds = cd.predict(x)
```

Monitoring vs. observability

Monitoring involves the collection and visualization of data, whereas observability provides insights into system health by examining its inputs and outputs. For instance, monitoring allows us to track a specific metric to detect potential issues.

On the other hand, a system is considered observable if it generates meaningful data about its internal state, which is essential for diagnosing root causes.

Alerts

Once we define our monitoring metrics, we need a way to get notified. The most common approaches are to send an alarm in the following scenarios:

- A metric passes the values of a static threshold—for example, when the accuracy of the classifier is lower than 0.8, send an alarm.
- Tweaking the p-value of the statistical tests that check for drifts. A lower p-value means a higher confidence that the production distribution differs from the reference one.

These thresholds and p-values depend on your application. However, it is essential to find the correct values, as you don't want to overcrowd your alarming system with false positives. In that case, your alarm system won't be trustworthy, and you will either overreact or not react at all to issues in your system. Some common channels for sending alarms to your stakeholders are Slack, Discord, your email, and PagerDuty. The system's stakeholders can be the core engineers, managers, or anyone interested in the system.

Depending on the nature of the alarm, you have to react differently. But before taking any action, you should be able to inspect it and understand what caused it. You should inspect what metric triggered the alarm, with what value, the time it happened, and anything else that makes sense to your application.

When the model's performance degrades, the first impulse is to retrain it. But that is a costly operation. Thus, you first have to check that the data is valid, the schema hasn't changed, and the data point was not an isolated outlier. If neither is true, you should trigger the training pipeline and train the model on the newly shifted dataset to solve the drift.

6. Reproducibility

Reproducibility means that every process within your ML systems should produce identical results given the same input. This has two main aspects.

The first one is that you should always know what the inputs are—for example, when training a model, you can use a plethora of hyperparameters. Thus, you need a way to always track what assets were used to generate the new assets, such as what dataset version and config were used to train the model.

The second aspect is based on the non-deterministic nature of ML processes. For example, when training a model from scratch, all the weights are initially randomly initialized. Thus, even if you use the same dataset and hyperparameters, you might end up with a model with a different performance. This aspect can be solved by always using a seed before generating random numbers, as in reality, we cannot digitally create randomness, only pseudo-random numbers. Thus, by providing a seed, we ensure that we always produce the same trace of pseudo-random numbers. This can also happen at the feature engineering step, in case we impute values with random values or randomly remove data or labels. But as a general rule of thumb, always try to make your processes as deterministic as possible, and in case you have to introduce randomness, always provide a seed that you have control over.

Join our book's Discord space

Join our community's Discord space for discussions with the authors and other readers:

`https://packt.link/llmeng`

packt.com

Subscribe to our online digital library for full access to over 7,000 books and videos, as well as industry leading tools to help you plan your personal development and advance your career. For more information, please visit our website.

Why subscribe?

- Spend less time learning and more time coding with practical eBooks and Videos from over 4,000 industry professionals
- Improve your learning with Skill Plans built especially for you
- Get a free eBook or video every month
- Fully searchable for easy access to vital information
- Copy and paste, print, and bookmark content

At www.packt.com, you can also read a collection of free technical articles, sign up for a range of free newsletters, and receive exclusive discounts and offers on Packt books and eBooks.

Other Books You May Enjoy

If you enjoyed this book, you may be interested in these other books by Packt:

RAG-Driven Generative AI

Denis Rothman

ISBN: 9781836200918

- Scale RAG pipelines to handle large datasets efficiently
- Employ techniques that minimize hallucinations and ensure accurate responses

- Implement indexing techniques to improve AI accuracy with traceable and transparent outputs

- Customize and scale RAG-driven generative AI systems across domains

- Find out how to use Deep Lake and Pinecone for efficient and fast data retrieval

- Control and build robust generative AI systems grounded in real-world data

- Combine text and image data for richer, more informative AI responses

Building LLM Powered Applications

Valentina Alto

ISBN: 9781835462317

- Explore the core components of LLM architecture, including encoder-decoder blocks and embeddings
- Understand the unique features of LLMs like GPT-3.5/4, Llama 2, and Falcon LLM
- Use AI orchestrators like LangChain, with Streamlit for the frontend
- Get familiar with LLM components such as memory, prompts, and tools
- Learn how to use non-parametric knowledge and vector databases
- Understand the implications of LFMs for AI research and industry applications
- Customize your LLMs with fine tuning
- Learn about the ethical implications of LLM-powered applications

Packt is searching for authors like you

If you're interested in becoming an author for Packt, please visit authors.packtpub.com and apply today. We have worked with thousands of developers and tech professionals, just like you, to help them share their insight with the global tech community. You can make a general application, apply for a specific hot topic that we are recruiting an author for, or submit your own idea.

Share your thoughts

Now you've finished *LLM Engineer's Handbook, First Edition*, we'd love to hear your thoughts! Scan the QR code below to go straight to the Amazon review page for this book and share your feedback or leave a review on the site that you purchased it from.

https://packt.link/r/1836200072

Your review is important to us and the tech community and will help us make sure we're delivering excellent quality content.

Index

Download a free PDF copy of this book

Thanks for purchasing this book!

Do you like to read on the go but are unable to carry your print books everywhere?

Is your eBook purchase not compatible with the device of your choice?

Don't worry, now with every Packt book you get a DRM-free PDF version of that book at no cost.

Read anywhere, any place, on any device. Search, copy, and paste code from your favorite technical books directly into your application.

The perks don't stop there, you can get exclusive access to discounts, newsletters, and great free content in your inbox daily.

Follow these simple steps to get the benefits:

1. Scan the QR code or visit the link below:

https://packt.link/free-ebook/9781836200079

2. Submit your proof of purchase.
3. That's it! We'll send your free PDF and other benefits to your email directly.

Made in the USA
Las Vegas, NV
01 November 2024

10962338R00286